HOUGHTON MIFFLIN ENGLISH

Shirley Haley-James   John Warren Stewig

Kenneth William Bierly
Jacqueline L. Chaparro
Helen Felsenthal
Norman A. Felsenthal
Michael C. Flanigan

Mary Mercer Krogness
Harry D. Laub
Nancy C. Millett
Paula J. Parris
Judy Griswold Parsons

Joy Harris Schlagal
Robert C. Schlagal
June Grant Shane
Helen J. Throckmorton

HOUGHTON MIFFLIN COMPANY • BOSTON
Atlanta • Dallas • Geneva, Illinois • Lawrenceville, New Jersey • Palo Alto • Toronto

Acknowledgments

Abridged Readers' Guide to Periodical Literature, entries. Copyright © 1981 by The H. W. Wilson Company. Material reproduced by permission of the publisher.

"Carlos Charles" (excerpt), from *Carlos Charles,* by Patrick J. Murphy and Shirley Rousseau Murphy. Copyright © 1971 by Patrick J. Murphy and Shirley Rousseau Murphy.

"Charles" (excerpt), from *The Lottery* by Shirley Jackson. Copyright 1948, 1949 by Shirley Jackson, copyright renewed 1976 by Laurence Hyman, Barry Hyman, Mrs. Sarah Webster, and Mrs. Jerome Schnurer. Reprinted by permission of Farrar, Straus & Giroux, Inc., and Brandt & Brandt.

Dictionary entries reprinted by permission from *Students' Dictionary.* © 1981 Houghton Mifflin Company.

Five Days of Living with the Land (excerpt), by Sarah Brown. Copyright © 1971 by Sarah Brown. Used by permission of Addison-Wesley Publishing Company, Reading, MA.

"Green Fingers" (excerpt), by Arthur C. Clarke. Copyright © 1956, 1957 by Fantasy House. Reprinted by permission of the author and the author's agents, Scott Meredith Literary Agency, Inc., 845 Third Avenue, New York, N. Y. 10022.

"Henry Martindale, Great Dane" (excerpt), by Miriam Allen deFord.

"If I Forget Thee, O Earth" (excerpt), by Arthur C. Clarke. Reprinted by permission of the author and the author's agents, Scott Meredith Literary Agency, Inc., 845 Third Avenue, New York, N. Y. 10022.

"Jug of Silver" (two excerpts), from *A Tree of Night and Other Stories,* by Truman Capote. Copyright 1945 and renewed 1973 by Truman Capote. Reprinted by permission of Random House, Inc.

"Lather and Nothing Else" (excerpt), by Hernando Téllez. Reprinted from *Américas,* monthly magazine published by the General Secretariat of the Organization of American States in English, Spanish, and Portuguese.

"Metaphor," from *It Doesn't Always Have to Rhyme,* by Eve Merriam. Copyright © 1964 by Eve Merriam. Reprinted by permission of the author.

"Mrs. Bertha Flowers" (excerpt), from *I Know Why the Caged Bird Sings,* by Maya Angelou. Copyright © 1969 by Maya Angelou. Reprinted by permission of Random House, Inc.

"Of Oyster Stew and Things" (adapted), by Esther S. Buckwalter. Reprinted by permission from the *Warwick River Tide.*

"One Candle Power," from *Once the Hodja,* by Alice Geer Kelsey. David McKay Company, 1945. Reprinted by permission of the author.

"Onomatopoeia," from *It Doesn't Always Have to Rhyme,* by Eve Merriam. Copyright © 1964 by Eve Merriam. Reprinted by permission of the author.

"Primer Lesson," from *Slabs of the Sunburnt West,* by Carl Sandburg. Copyright 1922 by Harcourt Brace Jovanovich, Inc.; renewed 1950 by Carl Sandburg. Reprinted by permission of the publisher.

Acknowledgments continued on page 511

1985 Impression

ISBN: 0–395–31915–3

Contents

The Sentence

1 | Four Kinds of Sentences

When you want to say something in writing, you must say it very clearly. In conversation, you can use gestures, tone of voice, and facial expressions to help make your meaning clear. In writing, you have only words and the way you put them together.

To write clearly, you arrange your words in sentences. A **sentence** is an arrangement of words that expresses a complete thought. It begins with a capital letter and ends with a punctuation mark.

There are four kinds of sentences—declarative, interrogative, imperative, exclamatory. The sentences are named for what they do.

Declarative sentences make statements. Notice how they end.

Ice is frozen water.   Ben will not be singing tonight.

Most of the sentences that you read and write are declarative sentences like these. A declarative sentence ends with a period.

Interrogative sentences ask questions. An interrogative sentence ends with a question mark.

Isn't ice frozen water?   Who rescued the kitten?

Imperative sentences command or request things. An imperative sentence ends with a period.

Come in, please.   Eat your broccoli.

Exclamatory sentences express strong feeling. The strength of an exclamatory statement is indicated by an exclamation mark.

What an easy test that was!   These disruptions must end!

You can make any type of sentence exclamatory if you want it to be expressed with special force. Compare the sentence in each pair below. Notice the different degrees of feeling they express.

My guitar string broke.   My guitar string broke!
Leave immediately.   Leave immediately!
What has Kim done now?   What has Kim done now!

The exclamation mark in writing corresponds to a very strong tone of voice in speaking. Save that forcefulness for the few sentences that really need it. Too many exclamation marks will make your writing seem to shout.

Try It Out

A. How does each sentence end? What kind of sentence is it?

1. Is that our bus?
2. We're five minutes late.
3. That bus is never coming!
4. Please stay calm, Arnold.
5. Couldn't we walk?
6. Wait another minute or two.

B. How should each sentence end? What kind of sentence is it?

7. Will Ida win the slalom
8. She waits nervously
9. Stay low on the turns
10. The snow is blinding her
11. Is that a gate pole
12. Watch out for that pole

- ▸ A **sentence** is a group of words that expresses a complete thought.
- ▸ A **declarative sentence** makes a statement. It ends with a period.
- ▸ An **interrogative sentence** asks a question. It ends with a question mark.
- ▸ An **imperative sentence** gives a command or makes a request. It ends with a period.
- ▸ An **exclamatory sentence** expresses strong feeling. It ends with an exclamation mark.

Written Practice

Copy each sentence, adding end punctuation. Then write *declarative,* *interrogative, imperative,* or *exclamatory* after it.

1. Are you eating your spinach
2. Please finish it
3. Why are you grimacing
4. How awful this spinach is
5. Don't judge spinach by this
6. Fresh spinach is delicious
7. It is crisp and bittersweet
8. Try to grow some spinach
9. What a terrible idea
10. You'll change your mind

- **Writing Sentences**   Use each word group in a sentence. Write the kind of sentences shown.

11. what a day (exclamatory)
12. keep the cat (interrogative)
13. frozen flounder (declarative)
14. in a minute (interrogative)

2 | Subjects and Predicates

You know that a sentence is a group of words that expresses a complete thought. In order to express a complete thought, a sentence must have two parts. One part states what the sentence is about. That part is called the **subject**. The other part tells something about the subject. That part is called the **predicate**.

Subject / Predicate

Potatoes / do not grow on trees.

An important-looking letter / arrived.

The end of the play / should have been more cheerful.

Each of these sentences has been divided into the **complete subject** and the **complete predicate**. The complete subject always contains a key word that names what is talked about in the sentence. This word is underlined in the sentences below.

<u>Potatoes</u> / do not grow on trees.

An important-looking <u>letter</u> / arrived.

The <u>end</u> of the play / should have been more cheerful.

The key word in the complete subject is the **simple subject**. The simple subject is usually a noun or pronoun.

Sometimes the complete subject is one word, like *potatoes*. Then the complete subject and the simple subject are identical.

The complete predicate also contains a key word or words. The key word tells what the subject is, has, does, or feels. In the sentences below, the key word or words are underlined.

Potatoes / <u>do</u> not <u>grow</u> on trees.

An important-looking letter / <u>arrived</u>.

The end of the play / <u>should have been</u> more cheerful.

The key word in the predicate is the **simple predicate**. The simple predicate is always a verb. All of the words that form the verb make up the simple predicate. The parts of the verb may be interrupted by other words: *do (not) grow.*

Sometimes the complete and simple predicates are the same: *arrived.*

You can use the simple predicate to find the simple subject. Ask yourself *who* or *what* about the predicate. "What arrived?" "A letter arrived." The simple subject is *letter.*

Try It Out

Divide each sentence into its complete subject and complete predicate. Then find the simple subject and simple predicate.

1. The fair at school will definitely be held tomorrow.
2. Students in every class are now preparing projects.
3. *Harvey* is being performed by two English classes.
4. Flags of many nations have been collected by some students.
5. An impressive miniature house has been constructed.
6. One class baked cookies in the shape of geometric symbols.

Every sentence has a **subject** and a **predicate**.
▸ The **complete subject** tells what the sentence is about.
▸ The **simple subject** is the key word in the subject. It is usually a noun or a pronoun.
▸ The **complete predicate** tells something about the subject.
▸ The **simple predicate** is the key word or words in the predicate. It is always a verb.

Written Practice

Copy each sentence. Use a slash mark (/) to divide the complete subject and the complete predicate. Then underline the simple subject once and the simple predicate twice.

1. The storm began at night.
2. The pounding rain had become a downpour by dawn.
3. People worried about flooding.
4. The region's rivers had already risen by early afternoon.
5. Worried announcers on the radio warned of high waters.
6. People in low-lying areas fled.
7. Officers of the civil defense prepared for possible evacuation.
8. The heavy rain was suddenly transformed into a light mist.
9. The beaming sun could be seen through a break in the clouds.
10. The danger was over.

● **Writing Sentences**   Write five sentences about a storm or some other dramatic event you remember. Underline the simple subjects once and the simple predicates twice.

3 | Finding the Subject

In all the examples you have seen so far, the subject has come before the predicate. Most sentences are written in this order, called **natural order**. Sometimes, however, the order of subject and predicate is reversed, or inverted. Then all or part of the predicate appears before the subject. Such a sentence is said to be in **inverted order**. These sentences are in inverted order.

On the right are the winners.   Lying under the tree was a nest.

Each of these sentences begins with a part of the complete predicate. Where is the subject?

Interrogative sentences are usually in inverted order. Where are the subjects in these interrogative sentences?

Is Brian late again?   When will he arrive?

To find the subject of a sentence in inverted order, it is often helpful to put the words in their normal order. The subject and the predicate then become obvious.

The winners / are on the right.   Brian / is late again.
A nest / lay under the tree.   He / will arrive (when).

Sometimes the rearrangement will produce a sentence that you would not really use, as in the last example. Nevertheless, this technique can help you locate the subjects of many inverted sentences.

Sentences that begin with the introductory word *there* or *here* are also in inverted order. Locate the subjects of these sentences.

There is a caterpillar on my toe.   Here are your shoes.

Such sentences cannot always be rearranged in normal order. To find the subject, locate the verb and ask yourself *who* or *what* about it. "What is?" "A caterpillar is."

Imperative sentences are in natural order. Still, the subject may seem hard to find since it does not appear in the sentence. Imperative sentences are addressed to "you." The subject *you* is said to be "understood." The subject remains *you* even when the name of a person is used. In the sentences below, the *you* is in parentheses.

(You) Get the mail, please.   Maria, (you) walk the dog.

Try It Out

What is the simple subject of each sentence?

1. Did Hiram Harmon really ride a camel in Egypt?
2. Away from the castle flew the bats.
3. Picture a bicycle painted magenta and chartreuse.
4. Please do not wear a red tie.
5. What do birds do in the rain?
6. There was a gaggle of geese in the garden.
7. Behind the sofa crouched a whimpering wallabee.
8. Here is the answer to all your problems.

In most sentences the subject comes before the predicate. In sentences in **inverted order**, all or part of the predicate comes before the subject.

To find the subject, arrange the subject and predicate in their natural order, or ask *who* or *what* about the predicate.

The subject of imperative sentences is understood to be *you*.

Written Practice

Write the simple subject of each sentence.

1. There is my mother's copy of *Alice in Wonderland* by Lewis Carroll.
2. On the second page is a picture of the author.
3. Do you know his real name?
4. Inez, tell me his name.
5. Is it Charles Lutwidge Dodgson?
6. Please lend me the book.
7. When will you return it?
8. Here is my written promise to return it next week.
9. There is no name on the paper.
10. On the reverse side of the page appears my signature.

- **Writing Sentences** Write eight sentences about some books that you like. Two of the sentences should use the introductory words *here* and *there*, two should be interrogative, two should end with the subject, and two should be imperative. Underline the simple subject of each sentence.

4 | Compound Subjects and Predicates

A sentence need not talk about one thing only. As sentences become more complicated, they can include two or more simple subjects, two or more simple predicates, or both.

How many simple subjects and predicates are there in each of the following sentences? The simple subjects are underlined once, and the simple predicates are underlined twice. A slash mark divides the complete subject and the complete predicate.

COMPOUND SUBJECT: Pancho or Erin / is playing baseball.

COMPOUND PREDICATE: A student / built the sets but did not design them.

COMPOUND SUBJECT AND PREDICATE: The puppy, the kitten, and the cub / ran, leaped, and fell.

Two or more simple subjects with the same predicate form a **compound subject**. Two or more simple predicates with the same subject form a **compound predicate.** The parts of a compound are usually joined by *and, but,* or *or.*

Sentences in inverted order also may have compound subjects and predicates. What is the compound in this example?

Defeated in the golf match were Oxbow, Woodridge, and Chun.

Try It Out

A. Find each simple subject and each simple predicate. Which sentences have compound subjects? Which sentences have compound predicates? Which sentences have both?

1. The teacher has graded and returned all the papers.
2. Alissa and Ed opened the door but did not call the dog.
3. Are the runners, the gymnasts, or the jumpers competing now?
4. Martha cannot study or work on her report tonight.
5. There has been no snow, sleet, or rain today.

B. Expand each sentence. Add one or more subjects or predicates to create the compound indicated. Use *and,* *but,* or *or.*

6. Jill left the house quite early today. (compound subject)
7. Here are the new suitcases for the trip. (compound subject)
8. The bear grew tired of its audience. (compound predicate)
9. Many children have been swimming in the pool. (compound subject, compound predicate)

> ▸ A **compound subject** is made up of two or more simple subjects with the same predicate.
> ▸ A **compound predicate** is made up of two or more simple predicates with the same subject.

Written Practice

A. Copy each sentence. Underline each simple subject once and each simple predicate twice. Then describe the subject and predicate by writing *compound subject,* *compound predicate,* or both.

1. The exhausted runner fell across the finish line and collapsed.
2. Will Horace, Karen, Donald, or Elsa be the next president?
3. Here are my cousin and her Airedale.
4. Kelly designed, constructed, and finished the house alone.
5. Watching and shouting from the sidelines were my parents and my cousin.

B. Rewrite each sentence. Add one or more simple subjects or predicates to create the compound indicated.

6. The train gathered speed. (compound predicate)
7. Four bands were part of the parade. (compound subject)
8. Old lace can be found in the flea market. (compound subject)
9. Bennett MacIntyre opened the front door quietly. (compound predicate)
10. David visited the new high school. (compound subject, compound predicate)

● **Writing Sentences** Write five sentences about animals of different kinds. Two sentences should have a compound subject, two should have a compound predicate, and one should have both.

5 | Compound Sentences

You know that a subject or predicate can be simple or it can be compound. A sentence, too, can be simple or compound. A **simple sentence** has just one complete subject and one complete predicate. A **compound sentence** contains two or more simple sentences.

SIMPLE SENTENCES: The door was locked. The house looked dark.

COMPOUND SENTENCE: The door was locked, <u>and</u> the house looked dark.

The parts of a compound sentence, like the parts of a compound subject or predicate, are joined by a word like *and*, *but*, or *or*. In a compound sentence, a comma is used before the joining word. If the joined sentences are very short, the comma may be omitted.

People shouted and horns blew.

Remember that a simple sentence may have a compound subject, a compound predicate, or both. Be careful not to confuse compound predicates with compound sentences.

SIMPLE SENTENCE: The **shelf** <u>creaked</u> but <u>did</u> not <u>fall</u>.

COMPOUND SENTENCE: The **shelf** <u>creaked</u>, but **it** <u>did</u> not <u>fall</u>.

The simple sentence has a compound predicate but only one subject-predicate pair—*shelf / creaked, did fall*. The compound sentence has two subject-predicate pairs—*shelf / creaked* and *it / did fall*.

To decide whether a sentence is compound, ask yourself whether it divides into separate sentences when the joining word is omitted. If it does, the sentence is compound.

Try It Out

Which sentences are simple sentences? Which are compound sentences? Where should commas be added?

1. The car developed a flat tire and came to a stop.
2. The driver and the passenger got out, saw the flat tire, and groaned.
3. The driver opened the trunk lid, and the passenger took out the spare tire.

(continued)

4. One placed the jack and the other loosened the bolts.
5. The passenger locked the emergency brake and jacked up the car.
6. The driver set out the warning reflector and watched for cars.
7. The passenger removed the lug nuts and the tire and then she rolled the tire to the trunk.
8. The driver placed the spare tire on the bolts and tightened them and this time the passenger watched the traffic.
9. The driver tightened the lug nuts and lowered the jack.
10. The passenger and the driver put the equipment in the trunk and they returned to the car and drove away.

Conjunctions

The parts of a compound sentence can be joined by *and, but, or, nor, yet, for,* or *so.*

Jill will sing, Ron will juggle, <u>or</u> Hy will tell jokes.

Words like *and, but,* and *or* are called **coordinating conjunctions**. Coordinating conjunctions are used to connect words or word groups used in the same way—nouns used as subjects, for example.

The words or groups of words joined by conjunctions must be related in some way. Different conjunctions can be used to show different relationships.

and = addition: Carol will go <u>and</u> Brian will stay.
but = contrast: Carol will go <u>but</u> Brian will stay.
or = choice: Carol will go <u>or</u> Brian will stay.

Paired conjunctions like *either . . . or, neither . . . nor, both . . . and* are called **correlative conjunctions**. Like coordinating conjunctions, correlative conjunctions join words or groups of words used the same way.

<u>Either</u> the car will start, <u>or</u> it will not.

Try It Out

Combine each group of sentences to form a compound sentence. Use an appropriate conjunction. What relationship does it express?

1. Gil must earn some money. He will not be able to ski.
2. The sky had turned dark gray. The air felt heavy.

3. Will Bill be at the party tonight? Will he not?
4. Under the fence went the skunk. No one saw him.
5. Sumner is writing about Thoreau. Judy has chosen Emerson.

> ▸ A **simple sentence** is made up of one complete subject and one complete predicate. Either or both may be compound.
> ▸ A **compound sentence** is made up of two or more related simple sentences. The sentences are usually joined by a comma and a **coordinating conjunction**.

Written Practice

Rewrite each group of sentences as one compound sentence. Use the conjunction in parentheses, and add commas where necessary.

1. Edith Hamilton was born in Germany. Her parents were from the United States. (but)
2. She loved to study. Many people in the late 1800's did not consider that appropriate for a woman. (but)
3. Evidently her father was not one of those people. He introduced her to the study of the classics. (for)
4. At the age of seven she was already studying Latin. She learned Greek soon afterward. (and)
5. At the University of Munich she had to sit apart from the male students. She could not attend classes. (or)
6. Her interest in the classical world lasted all her life. She devoted herself to teaching and writing about it. (and)
7. She did not start writing until after her retirement. She produced many popular books about ancient Greece and Rome. (yet)
8. Many honors were bestowed on her. In her ninetieth year she was made an honorary citizen of Athens, Greece. (and)

● **Writing Sentences**   Add one or more simple sentences to each sentence, forming a compound sentence. Use an appropriate conjunction.

9. Justin felt weak.
10. The storm would end soon.
11. There was an ant on my toe.
12. Trudy could not see the lion.
13. Down the path came Mr. Wu.
14. Do you have a spare pencil?

6 | Complex Sentences

A sentence, as you know, contains a subject and a predicate and expresses a complete thought. When a simple sentence becomes part of another sentence, it is called an **independent clause**. Compound sentences are made up of independent clauses.

> The game ended. We had lunch.
> The game ended, and we had lunch.

What is different about the following clause?

> After the game ended.

This clause has a subject and a predicate, but it does not express a complete thought. We keep waiting to know what happened when the game ended. An added independent clause can tell us.

> After the game ended, we had lunch.

Together the two clauses express a complete thought. Since the clause *after the game ended* "depends" on another clause to complete its meaning, it is called a **dependent clause**. When one or more dependent clauses join with an independent clause, the sentence they form is called a **complex sentence**.

> DEPENDENT CLAUSE: After the game ended
> INDEPENDENT CLAUSE: we had lunch
> COMPLEX SENTENCE: After the game ended, we had lunch.

Dependent clauses can occur in different places in a sentence. Where are the dependent clauses in these complex sentences?

> Although Winona arrived early, she did not get a seat.
> Give Bernie the keys when you see him.

Notice that you always use a comma after a dependent clause at the beginning of a sentence.

Many dependent clauses begin with words like *although, when,* and *after*. These words are conjunctions because they join things, just as coordinating and correlative conjunctions do. Words like *although, when,* and *after* that join dependent clauses to independent clauses are called **subordinating conjunctions**.

Here are some of the most common subordinating conjunctions. They will help you to recognize many dependent clauses.

after	because	since	until	where
although	before	though	when	wherever
as	if	unless	whenever	while

You can use subordinating conjunctions, like coordinating conjunctions, to join related ideas.

> We eat chicken. The raccoon visits our garbage.
> <u>Whenever we eat chicken</u>, the raccoon visits our garbage.

Whenever shows exactly how these ideas are related. Different conjunctions express different relationships.

> <u>After</u> I caught the ball, Charles whistled.
> <u>Whenever</u> I caught the ball, Charles whistled.
> <u>Unless</u> I caught the ball, Charles whistled.
> <u>Until</u> I caught the ball, Charles whistled.

Try It Out

A. What is the subordinating conjunction and the dependent clause in each of these complex sentences. Where should commas be added?

1. If Caleb's diagnosis is correct the lawnmower needs a new sparkplug.
2. After you wash the car we can wax it.
3. The dog came in after he had slept in the sun for an hour.
4. The little boy dragged the string while the kitten chased it.
5. Although the sun had set Dorian still worked on the sand castle.
6. We cannot leave until you find the keys.
7. Whenever Ms. Beasley goes into town she buys birdseed.
8. The research paper is due before we leave for Toronto.

B. Which clauses are independent clauses? Which are dependent?

9. when the storm ended
10. although the ants were busy
11. the trees shone after the rain
12. if Jonathan knows the song
13. I cannot go until Friday
14. when is Irwin leaving

> ▸ An **independent clause** has a subject and a predicate and can stand alone.
> ▸ A **dependent clause** has a subject and a predicate but cannot stand alone. Many dependent clauses begin with **subordinating conjunctions**.
> ▸ A sentence with one or more dependent clauses and an independent clause is a **complex sentence**.

Written Practice

A. Write each complex sentence. Underline the dependent clause or clauses. Draw a circle around each subordinating conjunction. Add commas where needed.

1. When early spring comes so does maple syrup.
2. Because a sugary sap rises in certain maples they give us syrup.
3. The sap rises whenever the temperature is below freezing at night and above freezing during the day.
4. Holes are drilled in trees when the weather becomes milder.
5. After the holes have been drilled collecting pipes are inserted.
6. When the sap rises it flows through the pipes and drips into a bucket.
7. The sap is taken to a sap house where it is strained and boiled until a thick syrup remains.
8. Since almost forty gallons of sap make only one gallon of syrup a great deal of sap must be collected.

B. If the clause is an independent clause, write *independent clause*. If it is a dependent clause, add an independent clause of your own to form a complex sentence.

9. because the phone rang
10. behind the door hid Martin
11. while the orchestra played
12. before we leave
13. when did the lumber arrive
14. whenever it snows hard

● **Writing Sentences**   Write a complex sentence of your own for each of these clauses. Use commas correctly.

15. after we get home
16. unless you disagree
17. we were waiting
18. because it is late

7 | Avoiding Fragments and Run-ons

The capital letter and closing punctuation of a sentence show where a thought begins and ends. You confuse your reader if you use sentence punctuation for an incomplete thought or for more than one thought.

Sentence Fragments

Any word group that does not contain a subject and a predicate and express a complete thought is not a sentence; it is a **sentence fragment**. What sentence parts are missing from these fragments?

Going to the game.   Hector and Alice at the store.
At the store.   When you finish.

If you are uncertain whether or not a word group is a sentence, try reading it aloud. Your ear is sometimes better than your eye at judging sentences.

Try It Out

Is each word group a sentence fragment or a sentence?

1. Since Carrie has time.
2. Go tomorrow instead.
3. In the tree sits Donald.
4. Diving into the pool and splashing noisily each time.
5. When the car broke down and had to be towed.
6. When are they leaving?
7. Has Kay seen the movie?
8. Hasn't seen it yet.

Run-on Sentences

Sentences that are improperly joined are called **run-on sentences**, for they run on in an uncontrolled way. Like sentence fragments, run-on sentences are unclear because the beginning and end of the thought are not correctly marked. Why are these sentences confusing?

Dean searched the room, the book and the pen were not there.
Abe owns the red car the blue car belongs to his cousin.
The balloon was descending and up the hill sped the car.

You can usually correct a run-on sentence by (1) dividing it into separate sentences, (2) punctuating it as a compound sentence, or (3) rewriting it as a complex sentence. The three run-ons on the preceding page might then be corrected as follows.

Dean had searched the room. The book and pen weren't there.
Abe owns the red car, and the blue car belongs to his cousin.
Up the hill sped the car as the balloon was descending.

Try It Out

Which word groups are run-on sentences? How would you correct them?

1. In the desk you can find the papers and the pen is on the floor.
2. Lori prepared a report for the school board and Tom assisted her.
3. Dino entered the room and sneezed, everyone stared at him.
4. As the librarian tried to explain, Tony tried to understand.
5. The boat and camper show is next week, are you going?

▸ A **sentence fragment** is a word group that lacks a subject or a predicate or does not express a complete thought.
▸ A **run-on sentence** is a series of two or more sentences that are run together with commas or with no punctuation.
To correct a run-on, rewrite it as a separate sentence, as a compound sentence, or as a complex sentence.

Written Practice

Rewrite the passage, correcting all fragments and run-ons.

Canoeing can be a challenging sport. Especially when the water is fast and scattered with obstacles. Many of the rivers in Canada near Hudson Bay are excellent for canoeing, there are also certain rivers where the sport would be quite dangerous. For the rapids are long and swift. Feeding into the Moose River, for example, there is a small river with rapids they called Dead Man's Rapids. Because they are so violent.

● **Writing a Paragraph**   Write a paragraph about a trip you have taken or would like to take. Check carefully for fragments and run-ons.

8 | Writing Good Sentences

Good writing means good sentences. Good sentences are correct, clear, direct, and interesting.

A. A good sentence is correct. Spelling, punctuation, and capitalization must be correct. Errors distract and confuse the reader.

INCORRECT: Did the baby's rattle fall.
CORRECT: Did the baby's rattle fall?

B. A good sentence is clear. The meaning is obvious to the reader.

UNCLEAR: The gardeners worked hard, but rabbits ate them.
CLEAR: The gardeners worked hard, but rabbits ate the beans.

C. A good sentence is direct. Every word has a reason for being.

NOT DIRECT: At this point in time Wanda's worry is in reference to an exam that will take place tomorrow.
DIRECT: Now Wanda is worried about tomorrow's exam.

D. A good sentence is interesting. It works well with the other sentences to avoid monotony and keep the reader reading.

MONOTONOUS: Len saw the dog. I saw the dog. We ran.
INTERESTING: When Len and I saw the dog, we ran.

Using Subordinating Conjunctions

You can often make your sentences clearer by using subordinating conjunctions to connect ideas. Which sentence is clearest?

SEPARATE SENTENCES: The truck roared away. Melville barked.
COMPOUND SENTENCE: The truck roared away, and Melville barked.
COMPLEX SENTENCE: As the truck roared away, Melville barked.

Exactly how are the roar and the bark related? The two separate sentences tell you little. Combining the sentences with *and* tells a bit more, but not much. Combining them with the subordinating conjunction *as* answers the question clearly.

As you write and rewrite, look for places where subordinating conjunctions can be used to combine sentences and make them clearer.

Try It Out

Combine each pair of sentences to form a complex sentence. Use the subordinating conjunction given in parentheses to show how the clauses are related.

1. The senators continued their discussion. They ate lunch. (while)
2. The lawn looks overgrown. The mower is being repaired. (because)
3. The band plays "Again." I will ask Dino to dance. (when)
4. Skunks look sweet and harmless. I would not recommend petting one. (although)
5. Sasha walks down the path. She finds a four-leaf clover. (whenever)

Compound Subjects and Predicates

Compare the sets of sentences below. Which sentence in each group seems the most direct?

SEPARATE SENTENCES: Ty signed the yearbook. I did, too.
COMPOUND SENTENCE: Ty signed the yearbook, and I did, too.
COMPOUND SUBJECT: Ty and I signed the yearbook.

SEPARATE SENTENCES: Jane looked for Bill. She did not find him.
COMPOUND SENTENCE: Jane looked for Bill, but she did not find him.
COMPOUND PREDICATE: Jane looked for Bill but did not find him.

You can sometimes make your writing more direct by using compound subjects and predicates to combine sentences.

Try It Out

Combine each pair of sentences. Use a compound subject or predicate. Do not make compound sentences.

1. The jade plant has grown too big. It has to be repotted.
2. Mr. Ault bought the posters and the streamers. He forgot the big red balloons.
3. The carrot tops were peeking through the soil. The bean plants had also just broken through the soil.
4. The mare jumped the fence. She disappeared into the woods.
5. A broken bookcase remained in the deserted apartment. There was a soiled rug, too.

Sentences with Varied Structure

Repeated sentences of the same form can become monotonous. The following passage is clear, but it is also dull.

> Winslow Homer was born in Massachusetts in 1836. He died in Maine in 1910. He spent his early years as a magazine illustrator. He eventually became a renowned painter of seascapes.

All of the sentences are simple sentences with simple subjects and simple predicates. What happens when the passage is revised to use a variety of sentence structures?

> Winslow Homer was born in Massachusetts in 1836 and died in Maine in 1910. Although he spent his early years as a magazine illustrator, he eventually became a renowned painter of seascapes.

You have learned to identify compound subjects, compound predicates, compound sentences, and complex sentences. Now think about using them to make your writing more interesting and more mature.

Try It Out

Using the conjunctions given in parentheses, combine each set of sentences into two sentences. Some simple sentences will remain. The first set has been done for you.

1. You may think of climate simply as cold or hot weather. Other factors are involved. Temperature is important. Precipitation, humidity, sunshine, and wind must also be considered. (although, but)
   Although you may think of climate simply as cold or hot weather, other factors are involved. Temperature is important, but precipitation, humidity, sunshine, and wind must also be considered.

2. Do not confuse weather with climate. Weather is the condition of the atmosphere over a brief period. Climate is the average weather over a long period. (while)

3. One day may be sunny and clear. The next day may be overcast and wet. The weather of a region may change from day to day. Weather must be distinguished from climate. (and, since)

4. Scientists want to determine the climate of an area. They must study its daily weather for many years. Otherwise they may miss important features of the climate. (if)

Written Practice

Rewrite the following passage. Correct punctuation and eliminate fragments and eliminate frag-ments and run-ons. Combine sentences to give variety.

Places on opposite sides of the world may have similar climates. Neighboring areas may have different climates. Do you know what determines climate? Latitude controls the climate of a region. So does nearness to a body of water. Surface land features and other factors, too. These are different in different areas, and climates are different as well.

Check Your Writing

Check the passage you wrote by asking yourself the following questions about your sentences. Then make appropriate changes.

A. Are my sentences correct?

1. Does each sentence begin with a capital letter and end with the correct punctuation mark?
2. Does each sentence have a subject and predicate and express a complete thought?
3. Have I used a comma to separate the parts of a compound sentence?
4. Have I used a comma after a dependent clause?

B. Are my sentences clear?

1. Do the conjunctions mean what I want them to mean?
2. Can I make sentences clearer by combining them with a coordinating conjunction or a subordinating conjunction?

C. Are my sentences direct?

Can I shorten or combine sentences by using a compound subject or predicate?

D. Are my sentences interesting?

Have I used complex and compound sentences as well as simple sentences?

- **Writing a Paragraph**   Write a paragraph of at least six sentences about the weather in your area. Then ask yourself each of the questions above. Make any needed changes, and rewrite your paragraph if necessary.

9 Using Words Correctly

Some words can be confused with each other because they look or sound alike. *Uninterested* and *disinterested* are two words that seem alike. Look them up in the dictionary. If you were a trial lawyer, would it be important to you whether a jury was uninterested or disinterested?

lie, lay

Lie and *lay* may seem alike, but they are different verbs. *Lie* means "to recline or remain." *Lay* means "to put or place." You can substitute *put* or *place* for the verb *lay* but never for the verb *lie*.

Tony lies on the beach all day.   He lays his towel on the sand.

Notice that you always put or place *something*. Therefore, a noun or pronoun usually follows the verb *lay*. Above, the noun is *towel*.

Verbs have different forms. The important forms, or principal parts, for *lie* and *lay* are these.

lie (*present*)	(is) lying	lay (*past*)	(have) lain
lay (*present*)	(is) laying	laid (*past*)	(have) laid

One reason these verbs are confused with each other is that the past tense form of *lie* is the same as the present tense form of *lay*. Can you tell which is which in these sentences? (Remember that you can substitute *put* or *place* for *lay* but not for *lie*.)

Yesterday Cara lay on the sofa.   Lay the papers on the desk.

Practice

Is the underlined verb correct or incorrect? If it is incorrect, supply the correct form.

1. Spot likes to <u>lay</u> in the sun.
2. The pen was <u>laying</u> there.
3. It had <u>lain</u> there all day.
4. Pat has <u>lain</u> bricks before.
5. Yesterday Homero <u>lay</u> in bed.
6. Where has he <u>laid</u> the nails?
7. Where shall I <u>lay</u> the ruler?
8. Paloma <u>laid</u> there, thinking.
9. <u>Lie</u> down and rest, please.
10. I am <u>lying</u> down.

rise, raise,

The verb *rise* means "to get up or move upward." The verb *raise* means "to lift or cause to rise." Both words involve upward motion, but *rising* occurs by itself, while *raising* is done by someone or something to something else.

Rachel <u>rises</u> at 6 A.M.   She <u>raises</u> the window.

In a sentence using *raise*, there is normally something that is raised. In the sentence above, it is the window. Therefore, *raise* is almost always followed by a noun or pronoun.

The principal parts of the two verbs are given below.

rise (*present*)   (is) rising   rose (*past*)   (have) risen
raise (*present*)   (is) raising   raised (*past*)   (have) raised

Practice

Which verb form or forms correctly complete each sentence?

1. Are Edward's neighbors (rising, raising) corn again this year?
2. The sun will (rise, raise) at 5:47 tomorrow morning.
3. Please see whether the bread dough has (risen, raised) yet.
4. (Rise, Raise) your arm slowly.
5. The treasurer (rose, raised) an interesting question.
6. As the Sawyers rushed into the theater, the curtain was (rising, raising).
7. The smoke (rose, raised) lazily up the chimney.
8. Doris (risen, raised) the window in order to see whether the moon had (risen, raised) yet.

let, leave

The verb *let* means "to allow, to permit." The verb *leave* means "to go away, to exit."

Ann <u>lets</u> Art drive sometimes.   Kirsten <u>leaves</u> the car.

Here are the principal parts of *let* and *leave*.

let (*present*)   (is) letting   let (*past*)   (have) let
leave (*present*)   (is) leaving   left (*past*)   (have) left

Practice

Choose the correct verb from the pair in parentheses.

1. Why don't you (let, leave) him go?
2. Please (let, leave) the cat alone.
3. Brendan had been (let, left) alone in the house.
4. (Let, Leave) me go to the party, and I will come home early.
5. Shelly (let, left) go of the rope too soon.
6. Do not (let, leave) the fire unattended, please.

> *Lie* means "to recline or remain"; *lay* means "to put or place."
> *Rise* means "to get up or move upward"; *raise* means "to lift."
> *Let* means "to allow or permit"; *leave* means "to go away."

Practice

Write the verb form that correctly completes each sentence.

1. I think I will (lie, lay) down for a few minutes.
2. Ted felt better after having (lain, laid) in bed all day.
3. If we (rise, raise) early, we can avoid the traffic.
4. The sun had already (risen, raised) when the rain started.
5. Please (let, leave) Johnny finish his work.
6. (Let, Leave) go of the handle immediately!
7. Ms. Garcia (rose, raised) the curtain for the first set.
8. The mouse had (let, left) the room in a great hurry.
9. The cat (lay, laid) in wait for the mouse.
10. Have you (lain, laid) the damp towel on the chair again?

- **Writing Sentences** Use each of the following verb forms in a sentence of your own.

| 11. leave | 13. laid | 15. will let | 17. has lain |
| 12. rose | 14. has raised | 16. lying | 18. lay (past) |

10 Building Vocabulary

Writing Definitions

What do the words you use really mean? If you have ever had to define a word for someone, you know that it is not an easy thing to do.

Definitions are important. You need to know the exact meaning of words you use. Otherwise, you may end up saying something different from what you want to say. The more precisely you can use words the clearer and better your writing will be.

A good definition has two main parts:

(1) the general class of things to which the word belongs, and
(2) the specific features that set it apart from others in its class.

Here are some examples of two important parts of a definition.

Word	General Class	Special Features
surgeon	doctor	performs operations
uniform	distinctive clothing	identifies wearer as a member of a profession or group
unicorn	mythical animal	horselike, with a single horn on its forehead

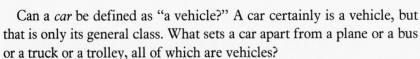

Can a *car* be defined as "a vehicle?" A car certainly is a vehicle, but that is only its general class. What sets a car apart from a plane or a bus or a truck or a trolley, all of which are vehicles?

First, a car moves on land. That distinguishes it from a plane. Then, a car is a passenger vehicle. That eliminates a truck. A car also has four wheels and seats for two to six people. The bus is now eliminated. Finally, a car, although driven by someone, is not pushed or pulled. That and the seating distinguish it from a trolley.

A car, then, can be defined in the following way.

> *car:* a 4-wheeled, self-propelled land vehicle that seats a driver and from one to five passengers

There are additional points which you should remember when you create definitions.

1. A definition should not include any form of the word being defined. Do not say, for example, that a *circle* is "something circular."
2. A definition should not be expressed in language that will send the reader to other definitions. Do not, for instance, define *football* as "oblate spheroid."
3. A definition should be like an equation. The definition should be equal to the word defined. "Doctor" does not define *surgeon* because "doctor" includes other things, like pediatrician and eye doctor. "Unicorn," on the other hand, does not define *mythical animal* because "unicorn" excludes other things, like dragons.

A good definition states (1) the general class to which a word belongs, and (2) the features that distinguish it from others in the class.

Practice

Define each word. Include both its general class and its special characteristics in the definition. You may use the dictionary to help you, but phrase the definition in your own words.

1. furnace	**6.** scissors	**11.** photograph	**16.** bachelor
2. tuxedo	**7.** encyclopedia	**12.** magazine	**17.** cup
3. desk	**8.** ribbon	**13.** lemon	**18.** dictionary
4. rake	**9.** reindeer	**14.** microscope	**19.** roller skate
5. spoon	**10.** pencil	**15.** hammer	**20.** conversation

• **Writing Sentences** Use six words from exercise B in a sentence of your own. Try to write sentences that show the exact meaning of each word.

Review

- **Kinds of Sentences** *(pp. 9–10)* Write each sentence, adding the correct end punctuation. After the sentence, write *declarative, interrogative, imperative,* or *exclamatory* to tell what kind of sentence it is.

    1. Did Howard and Carol find you after the game
    2. Mr. Irving will meet Beth and show her around the school
    3. Kathleen, set the table for dinner
    4. What a silly program that is
    5. Will Howard be here this afternoon

- **Subjects and Predicates** *(pp. 11–12)* Copy each sentence. Draw a slash mark (/) between the complete subject and the complete predicate. Underline the simple subject once and the simple predicate twice.

    6. The first nature walk will be held next Saturday.
    7. Both experienced and inexperienced hikers are invited.
    8. Everyone should bring a pair of binoculars.
    9. Flat, comfortable shoes are necessary.
    10. The trails through the woods can be steep and rocky.

- **Finding the Subject** *(pp. 13–14)* Write each simple subject.

    11. Can you climb over those rocks without falling?
    12. Please be careful, Annette.
    13. There is a male cardinal in that tree.
    14. Where did I put my binoculars?
    15. On the same branch is the cardinal's mate.

- **Compound Subjects and Predicates** *(pp. 15–16)* Copy each sentence. Underline each simple subject once and each simple predicate twice. Write *CS* for a compound subject, *CP* for a compound predicate, *CS-CP* for both.

    16. Kathy and some other hikers made alternative plans.
    17. They went to the library and rented a videotape on birds.
    18. The group and some others gathered and viewed the tape.
    19. Characteristics and habits of many birds were thoroughly covered.

- **Compound Sentences** *(pp. 17–19)* Write *simple* or *compound* to describe each sentence. For compound sentences, write the coordinating conjunction.

  20. The hikers gathered early, but a sudden storm came up.
  21. The hikers peered glumly out the windows and watched the storm.
  22. The rain would end in an hour, or they would cancel the hike.

- **Complex Sentences** *(pp. 20–22)* Combine each pair of sentences into one complex sentence, using the subordinating conjunction given. Add a comma if needed. Underline the dependent clause.

  23. It did not rain. The nature walk was held this week. (since)
  24. The participants received maps of the area. They left. (before)

- **Fragments and Run-ons** *(pp. 23–24)* Rewrite the passage, correcting all fragments and run-ons.

  25–30. The trail was overgrown. With vines and branches. The hikers cleared the way as they walked. Wallace spotted a colorful bird, it flew away. The hikers remained very quiet and lifted their binoculars slowly, they were delighted when they saw an orange oriole.

- **Writing Good Sentences** *(pp. 25–28)* Rewrite the following paragraph. Use one complex sentence, one sentence with a compound predicate, and one with a compound subject.

  31–33. We knew summer was finally over. We knew this because of a coolness in the mornings. The leaves were turning yellow. They were showering down in every slight wind. Our summer clothes suddenly seemed outdated. So did our summer activities.

- **Using Words Correctly** *(pp. 29–31)* If the underlined verb is correct, write *correct*. If it is incorrect, write the correct verb.

  34. Ty has <u>laid</u> in the sun all day.
  35. Where <u>did</u> she <u>lay</u> the pliers?
  36. We must <u>raise</u> early tomorrow.
  37. The smoke <u>rose</u> quickly.
  38. Please <u>let</u> the dog alone.
  39. <u>Leave</u> him go with you.

- **Building Vocabulary** *(pp. 32–33)* Complete the following definitions. You may use a dictionary.

  40. cradle: a bed that is small and low
  41. embroidery: the act of decorative sewing

Listening and Speaking

1 | Hearing or Listening?

You live in a world filled with sound. Listen for a moment. What do you hear? A classmate whispers an assignment. Fabric rustles against your leg. A clock whirs softly. Your heart pounds. Sounds tell you that the world is alive, but often you are not aware of what you hear.

Think of all the ways in which people say, "I wasn't listening." "Huh?" "What did you say?" "I tuned out for a minute." "I wasn't paying attention." "It went in one ear and out the other." "I missed what you said." "I didn't hear you." You hear, but do you listen?

Listening is probably the single most important *skill* for getting information. How much time do you spend listening in every class? Reading, writing, and speaking take up only a fraction of the time that goes to listening. In fact, most people spend at least half of their day listening.

How carefully do you listen when your teacher is explaining something?

1. Do you tune out if the material is difficult or not especially interesting to you? *Ask questions when you do not understand something.*
2. Do you let your mind wander to other subjects or to sounds around you? *Concentrate.*
3. Do you focus on details and tune in and out of discussions? *Follow the main points of a discussion.*

If you tune out of discussions when the material is uninteresting, if your mind wanders to other subjects, or if you often miss the main point, then you are like most other people. Listening carefully takes practice. It does not come naturally. Listening, like reading, is a skill that you must develop.

Here are three facts about listening that will help you to understand why training helps you to listen more effectively.

1. People shut out things they do not want to hear. Training helps you to get more involved in everything you listen to.
2. People's minds wander after about thirty seconds. You can learn techniques that will help you to keep listening.
3. People listen six to ten times faster than they speak. That means they grow impatient while they listen. Training helps you use that extra listening time to think about and evaluate what you hear.

Learn the following rules for good listening skills. Think of the word *TRACK,* and you will not forget them. Then keep TRACK of what you hear.

T reminds you to **think.**

Examine the speaker's ideas and evidence. Do you understand the point? If not, ask questions.

R reminds you to **review.**

Think back over the speaker's important points. Did you understand them all? Have you forgotten anything? Make sure you fill in any information you have forgotten or do not understand.

A reminds you to pay **attention.**

Do you have anything to add to the speaker's ideas? Do you have any questions? Participate.

C reminds you to **concentrate.**

Do not let your mind wander to other subjects or to other sounds. Think about the topic of discussion. Focus on the speaker's words.

K reminds you to **keep up.**

Do not get lost. Are you following the speaker's points? Accept the challenge, and keep pace with the speaker.

Practice

A. How much time do you spend listening compared to reading, writing, and speaking? Keep an hour-by-hour chart of your day. Write down how much time you listen, write, read, or speak. At the end of a day, see how much of your learning comes from listening.

B. Form a group of five or six students. Discuss ideas for an adventure story about one of the following topics or choose one of your own.

a time machine that travels to the year 1776
traveling to the planet Lissen
a world under the sea

Decide what the plot of your story will be, but do not decide each and every detail. Each person in the group will tell one part of the story to the rest of the class. Each person continues the story from where the previous person left off. After you finish telling the story, call upon members of the class to repeat incidents from the story. See how well the class listened.

2 | Listening Clues

Words alone do not always convey your complete message. Facial expressions and intonation, how words are said, also give clues to the meaning of your words.

Have you ever been in a playground or in a bus *watching* people talk, but not hearing any of their words? You see two people laughing and smiling. One is talking, waving her arms in wide circles, a humorous look on her face. She smiles. The other person laughs, starts to say something, then laughs again. Could these people be in the middle of an argument? Probably not. Come a little closer, and listen in on their conversation. The words in parentheses tell you about their facial expressions and intonation.

BETTY: (*Laughs and shakes her head*) A kid walks into a restaurant and asks the waitress, "Do *you* have frogs' legs?" "Yes," says the waitress. "Good," says the kid. (*Pauses and grins; her voice rises slightly*) "Then hop into the kitchen and get me a glass of milk."

DAVE: (*Laughing*) That's pretty good. Do you know this one? (*He grins*) A kid walks into a restaurant and asks the waiter, "Do you serve crabs?" "Sure," says the waiter. (*Pauses*) "We serve anybody."

Intonation, how you say things, has three parts—*stress, pitch,* and *juncture.* Each can change the meaning of what you are saying.

Stress

Stress is the emphasis you put on each word as you speak. When you stress one word more than another, your listeners get a clue to your meaning. Stress can change a sentence from a statement into a question. See how stress changes the meaning of the sentences below.

Leah is in the chorus this year.	(a declarative statement)
Leah is in the chorus this year?	(a question: Leah, not someone else)
Leah is in the *chorus* this year?	(a question: the chorus, not something else)
Leah is in the chorus *this* year?	(a question: this year, not some other)

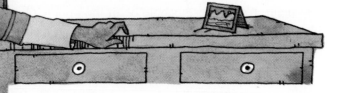

Practice

Pair up with another student. Say these sentences stressing a different word each time. Take turns. How many different meanings did you think of?

1. Leon is going to Maine on Wednesday.
2. Yesterday, the president spoke to our class.
3. Harry bought a present for Eileen.
4. Melissa won first prize in the dance competition.
5. The hawk hovered over the nest.

Pitch

Pitch is the rising and falling of your voice. Pitch tells you whether a statement is declarative, interrogative, exclamatory, or imperative. If you were going to the movies, and your friend asked you the time, you might say, "It's time to go" in an even voice. That would be a declarative statement. If you were amazed that it was so late, you might exclaim, "It's time to go!" Your voice would rise gradually to show your excitement and surprise. If your friend was not ready to leave yet, he or she might ask, "Really? It's time to go?" Your friend's voice would rise suddenly. Perhaps, instead, his or her voice would dip with disappointment, "It's time to go."

Practice

Read each of the following sentences first as a declarative statement, next as an interrogative one, and then as an exclamation. Can any of these statements express disappointment?

1. Fred says he saw a spaceship.
2. Those are Priscilla's glasses.
3. The horse cleared the fence by an inch.
4. Linda won the spelling bee.
5. The fish got away.

Juncture

Just as you punctuate sentences to break up phrases, lists, or complete ideas, you pause with your voice to make your meaning clear. These pauses are called **juncture.** When you speak, you pause between thoughts and between items in a list. Sometimes you may pause for emphasis.

How is the meaning of each of the following sentences changed by juncture?

1. We bought cinnamon bread, vanilla yogurt, and beansprouts.
   We bought cinnamon, bread, vanilla yogurt, and beansprouts.
   We bought cinnamon, bread, vanilla, yogurt, and beansprouts.
2. Do you know Boston baked beans are their specialty?
   Do you know Boston? Baked beans are their specialty.

Practice

A. Practice saying each sentence below in two or three different ways by changing juncture.

1. Lisa bought tuna fish, cream cheese, and bread at the market.
2. Did Ed see Tracy and Peggy run to the baseball field to get them?
3. Rachel let the dog out.
4. Jon Thomas and I are taking skating lessons.

B. Practice saying one of the jokes on page 39. When should you pause, or use juncture, to bring out the humor? When should you speed up your rhythm?

3 | Listening Skills for Learning

Using Context Clues

Much of your knowledge about the world comes from listening. Children learn how to speak by listening to people and by imitating the words they hear. Children learn what words mean by noticing how the words are used. Eventually they learn to use the words correctly.

An effective way to develop your vocabulary is by **using the context.** You do this when you read, and you can do this when you listen. When you hear a word that you do not know, think about what it means. (Remember the *T* in TRACK) Notice how the word is used. Then try to substitute a word in place of the unknown word; that may help you to find a synonym for the word.

People often give clues to the meanings of difficult words they use. They may do this without even thinking about it. Look for these types of context clues.

1. a definition within the sentence or following it

Pitch, or the highs and lows of your voice, affects your meaning.

2. a synonym near the difficult word

Stress, or emphasis, may change the meaning of your statement.

3. a comparison that helps to explain the word through similarity or contrast

When you use juncture, it is like punctuating your speech.

4. a summary in which the meaning of the difficult word is clarified

You know that intonation is composed of pitch, stress, and juncture.

Using the context works, and it is a natural way to help develop your vocabulary.

Practice

A. On a blank piece of paper, write each of the four words your teacher writes on the chalkboard. Listen while your teacher reads some sentences using each of the words. Draw a sketch illustrating the meaning of one of the difficult words.

B. Copy the words your teacher has written on the chalkboard. Leave room on your paper to write definitions of the words.

1. Listen carefully to the passage your teacher reads to you. Try to figure out the meaning of the words by using the context clues.
2. Write down a synonym for each word or a short definition.
3. Compare answers with the rest of the class. Check your definitions in the dictionary. How close did you come?

Listening for Main Ideas

Look at the picture on this page. Focus on the whole image, and you see what the picture is about. Next, look at all the details, and notice how the artist developed the design. If you look at the dots and details first, you will likely miss the major image. Similarly, when you listen, your first task is to understand what the speaker is talking about. Then you fit in the details.

If you have started to use the TRACK rules for listening, you probably listen for the main idea of what you hear. The **main idea** is the most important point the speaker is making. Keeping TRACK of the speaker's point will help you to concentrate. Following the main idea will also help you to understand and remember what you hear.

When the speaker is done talking, mentally review the main points. (Remember the *R* in TRACK.) Jot them down if you have time. You will be surprised how many details will come back automatically, because they are connected in your memory to the main point.

Imagine that you are listening to someone discuss Granville Woods, the inventor.

Granville Woods's many inventions in the field of electricity helped modernize transportation. In 1884, when Granville Woods was twenty-eight years old, he patented his first invention. It was an improved steam boiler furnace. In the years that followed, the man who became known as "the black Edison" patented over sixty inventions, most of them in the field of electricity. One of his most important contributions was railway telegraphy. This invention enabled messages to be sent between moving trains and railway stations or other moving trains. Railway telegraphy has prevented many serious accidents.

What is the main idea of the discussion? If you said, "Granville Woods patented sixty inventions" or "Granville Woods is known as 'the black Edison,' " you chose details. The main idea is the speaker's most important point. The main idea of this paragraph is the topic sentence: *Granville Woods's many inventions in the field of electricity helped modernize transportation.*

Practice

A. Listen carefully while your teacher reads you two paragraphs. Write down the main idea of each paragraph in your own words. Compare answers with your classmates. Did you select details?

B. Bring in a short article from a newspaper. Write down its main idea.

1. Form a group of four or five students.
2. Read the article to the group. Give group members a minute or two to review mentally what you read. Then each member should write down the main idea in his or her own words.
3. After everyone has read an article, review the main ideas. Discuss answers which were too specific. Reread the article, if necessary.

Listening for Details

How does a speaker use details to support the main point? Follow the details closely, and you will understand how the speaker arrives at the main point. (Remember the *K* in TRACK.) You will see why the speaker has chosen certain illustrations, examples, facts, descriptions, comparisons, or contrasts. You will also be able to weigh the evidence and to evaluate how strong the speaker's arguments really are.

Imagine that you are listening to someone discuss techniques for watching wildlife.

If you are an untrained naturalist but enjoy watching wildlife, a few techniques will help you. The secret is to remain unseen and unheard. After all, animals have keen senses. First, use camouflage. Dress in clothing that cannot be seen easily against the background where you will be observing. Second, learn to walk silently. This means choosing your footwear thoughtfully, moving slowly, and placing your feet down carefully. Finally, be sure you know exactly where you are going. Notice landmarks, study maps, and keep a compass. Follow these techniques to ensure happy wildlife watching.

The speaker's point is that if you enjoy watching wildlife, you should practice a few techniques for remaining unseen and unheard. What details does the speaker use to make this point?

Signal words can help you to follow the details. (Remember the *K* in TRACK.) Listen for words such as *first, second, third,* or *first, next,* and *last* that show you when the speaker begins and ends a list of related details. Other signal words show the relationship between ideas. Notice these words: *however, furthermore, on the other hand, also, therefore.* What signal words did the speaker use in the paragraph above?

Practice

1. Choose one of these main ideas to develop into a paragraph.

   Watching too much television can be harmful to your grades.
   Embarrassing situations can result from not listening carefully.

2. List three or four details that help support the main idea. Then, write your paragraph using the main idea you chose and the details you listed. Try using signal words in your paragraph.
3. Pair up with another student. Read your paragraphs to each other, and try to recall the details and the main idea.

Listening to Remember

Often students complain that they cannot remember what they learned in class a day or a week before. When you read and forget, at least you can go back and reread. Listening to remember requires special care, because often you do not have a second chance to hear a speech, talk, or discussion. The following techniques, based on research about memory, can help you to remember what you have learned.

1. Be sure that you *understand what you hear.* Understanding is necessary if you expect to remember, so ask questions if something is unclear.
2. *Review.* The best way to review is in intervals, over a period of time. At the end of a discussion, try to recall the main points and important details mentally, or review your notes. Repeat this procedure about an hour later and again after a week and after a month.
3. People tend to remember what they hear from the beginning and end of a situation. Make a special effort to *concentrate in the middle* of a discussion or speech. That is when your mind wanders naturally.
4. *Form a strong mental image* of the topic as you listen. The more absurd, lively, and colorful your mental picture is, the better. People remember things which are unusual.

Practice using these techniques regularly. You will find that you can also apply them to reading and other materials you study.

Practice

Your teacher read you a paragraph at the beginning of your lesson today. How much do you remember of it now? Write down the main idea and the important details.

Listening to Directions

Lisa had been waiting for her father in front of Grayson's Drug Store for almost an hour. Her hands and toes were getting numb from the cold. Then she heard her father's voice, "Where have you been?" he asked. "I told you to meet me at the cafeteria across the street from Grayson's."

Perhaps Lisa's situation sounds familiar. Most people at one time or another have caused themselves trouble and inconvenience by not listening carefully to directions. Use these guidelines to help you remember directions.

1. Be sure you understand each step. Ask questions if you do not.
2. Think about the reasons for the order and for each step.
3. Keep TRACK of the number of steps.
4. Form a mental image of each step. If you cannot, ask to hear them again.
5. Mentally review the directions.
6. Write down the directions if they are too complicated to remember.

Practice

Make up directions for an activity that can be done on paper without reference books. Here are some examples.

1. Put words in alphabetical order, backwards.
2. Draw the figure that I will describe.
3. Add two numbers, subtract 10, multiply by 12, divide by 2. What is the number?

Form a group with four or five students, and take turns reading your directions to the group. Each group member should try to follow your directions. Be clear and imaginative.

4 | You as a Speaker

The skills you acquire to become a good listener will also help you to be an effective speaker. Translate what you know about listening into guidelines for good speaking skills.

1. Clearly presented ideas are easy to follow. Try to organize your ideas for a speech or a discussion into main ideas, and develop each main idea with details. If your thoughts are organized, you are less likely to fill your speech with stallers such as *um, uh,* and *er.*
2. Signal words such as *first, then, the following,* or *finally,* help a listener follow the important ideas and details of a discussion. Use signal words to help your audience.
3. People have trouble concentrating if they do not understand what they hear. Try to present your ideas as clearly as possible. Use visual aids such as charts or illustrations if they will make your talk clearer. From time to time, ask if your audience has questions.
4. Difficult words are easier to understand if they are defined within the context. Be sure to explain vocabulary your audience may not understand.
5. People remember better when they review. Review your important points in a summary at the end of your talk, speech, or discussion.
6. Distractions make concentration difficult. Unless movement is part of your talk, do not move around or wave your hands. That would distract your audience. Instead, be as natural as possible. Your body language should indicate that what you are saying is important. Keep eye contact by looking at specific people, stand straight without being rigid, and smile.
7. Intonation, how you use your voice, gives listeners clues about your meaning. Use intonation to your advantage. Make sure your pitch is under control—not too high or too low. Stress the correct words to make your points, and use juncture to break your sentences into phrases for meaning. Also project your voice so it is not too loud or too soft.

Remember that practice helps. The more often you speak with other people or in front of a group, the easier it becomes. You can start out by asking appropriate questions. Then, try adding brief comments or telling a personal anecdote. Work up to a longer discussion of your own ideas or a talk.

Practice

A. Develop a checklist of speaking skills with your classmates. Include these topics: body language, voice, content. What is important to remember about each? Evaluate your own speaking skills.

B. Write down (1) the title of a favorite book, (2) something you did over the summer, and (3) a subject you know something about.

1. Pair up with another student, and give that student your paper.
2. Think of several questions to ask about your partner's favorite book, summer vacation, or subject.
3. Begin a conversation by asking your partner a question about his or her book, vacation, or subject. You should continue the conversation by asking a new question based on your partner's answer or by asking another question.
4. Your partner should then ask you about your book, vacation, or subject.
5. Evaluate your speaking by using the checklist from Practice A.

C. Stallers are the "um's," "uh's," and "er's" that some speakers use when they forget a word or idea or when they are thinking about what to say next.

1. Pair up with another classmate.
2. Begin telling a familiar story such as "The Three Little Pigs."
3. Your partner will clap each time you use a staller.
4. When you have finished, your partner will begin telling some other well-known story, perhaps "Jack and the Beanstalk," and you will clap when he or she uses a staller.

D. Practice saying this sentence to a partner.

Quality of voice affects quality of listening.

Each of you say the sentence in the ways listed below.

1. a high-pitched whiny voice
2. a harsh, gravelly voice
3. a mumbling voice, without moving your tongue
4. a nasal voice, talking through your nose
5. a clear, pleasant voice

Then discuss with your partner what it was like listening to each kind of voice.

5 | Everyday Speaking

Think of all the situations in which you have to speak. All day people exchange news and experiences, carry on casual conversations, discuss ideas, answer questions, ask questions, and give directions.

The need to communicate is constant. Being able to speak effectively helps make our lives easier. In certain situations clear communication is particularly important.

Consider this situation. The water in Jill's neighborhood was turned off for street repairs. The repair crew left in the afternoon without turning the water back on. Jill called City Hall about the problem, and an answering machine answered the phone. This is the message Jill left.

> Hello, this is Jill Bailey. I live at 45 Wilson Road. The repair crew left our neighborhood without turning the water back on. Please call me right away to let me know what can be done. My number is 621-2345.

Did Jill forget any important information? The reason for her call was clear enough, but she forgot to tell when she made the call. Answering machines can record many messages, and whoever listened to Jill's message would not know when the call was made. This person might assume that the problem was cleared up by the time he or she heard Jill's message.

Whenever you *leave a message,* include the following information.

1. your name
2. the date and time of your call
3. a telephone number where you can be reached
4. the reason for your call
5. whether your call should be returned quickly

When you *take a message,* include the following information.

1. the name of the person who called
2. the time and date of the call
3. the message
4. the caller's number and when to call, if appropriate
5. the name of the message taker

Do not worry if someone does not want to leave a message. If it is important, the person will call back.

Some speaking situations can be embarrassing if you do not know the correct procedures. When you make introductions, do you know who to introduce first? How formal should you be? What if you are introducing someone to a group? Follow the formulas below.

1. When you introduce a younger person to an adult, say the older person's name first.
   "Hello, Dad, this is Barry Greene. Barry, meet my father, Mr. Sulla."
2. Add something pleasant and informative about the person you introduce.
   "Barry is the president of the Glee Club. He's a fine alto."
3. Do not be too formal or short with your introductions.
   AWKWARD: "Hello, Marilyn Maynard, I am very pleased to be able to introduce you to my neighbor, Jeff MacFarland."
   AWKWARD: "Hello, Jeff, Marilyn. Marilyn, Jeff."
   BETTER: "Hi, Marilyn, I'd like you to meet my neighbor, Jeff MacFarland."
4. When you introduce someone to a group, mention the group first.
   "Hi, everybody. This is Rita Thomas. She'd like to join the Glee Club. She's a great soprano."

Practice

A. Pair up with another student. Then practice leaving messages to the following people about these situations.

1. the dentist, about a toothache you have
2. a friend, about a date you have to break
3. an adult, about a babysitting job you want

B. Pair up with another student. Take turns being the caller who leaves a message for someone and the person who takes the message. Practice several times as the following people: a pharmacist, a teacher, an out-of-town friend, a newspaper carrier.
C. Form a group with two other students. Take turns making the following introductions.

1. introduce a friend from camp to your uncle
2. introduce a parent to your French teacher
3. the president of the Chess Club introduces a student who wants to join the club to the rest of the club

6 | Giving a Talk

Talking in front of an audience can be a pleasant experience. However, getting on a stage or in front of a classroom is only a small part of the experience. The most difficult part of giving a talk comes long before you face your audience. It is important, therefore, to remember the five P's—*Prepare, Plan,* and *Practice, Practice, Practice.*

Prepare

1. Choose a topic that interests you.
2. Make sure that you select a topic that you know about or can research effectively.
3. Include interesting details and anecdotes.

Plan

1. Write all of your notes on cards that you can refer to during your speech. These notes should contain only key words to remind you of your main ideas and details. Number your note cards for easy reference.
2. Make sure that any charts or illustrations you use are large enough for the audience to see.
3. Ask family and friends to set aside time to listen to your speech.
4. Give yourself time to do some relaxation exercises before your speech. (See the *relaxation exercises* on the following page.)

Practice

1. First, read over your notes several times until you have them at least partially memorized.
2. Next, practice in front of a mirror. Check to see that you do the following things.
   a. Stand in a natural position with your weight evenly balanced on both feet.
   b. Do not move around or wave your hands unnecessarily.
   c. Hold your notes comfortably or place them on a table in front of you so you can refer to them.
   d. Emphasize important ideas using stress, pitch, and juncture.
   e. Vary your tone of voice to show your feelings about what you are discussing.
3. Finally, practice in front of friends or family. Time yourself to be sure you are within your time limit. You may have to speed up

slightly or slow down. If you are very far from your limit, you may have to alter the length of your talk. After you give your talk, ask your listeners to comment on your strong points as well as any problems they noticed with your delivery. Do not forget to practice with any illustrations you are using.

The more relaxed you feel, the better speaker you will be. Try these *relaxation exercises.*

Sit quietly and concentrate on tightening, then relaxing your muscles. Start with your feet, then your legs. Tighten and relax all the muscles of your body. Rotate your head slowly, so your chin touches your chest. Then, move your head to one side, to your back, to the other side, and down to your chest again. To relieve tension in your jaw, open your mouth as wide as you can. Then close your mouth. Breathe deeply. Repeat.

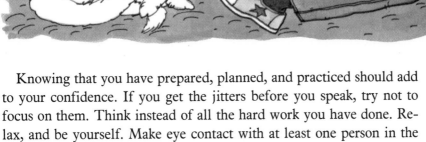

Knowing that you have prepared, planned, and practiced should add to your confidence. If you get the jitters before you speak, try not to focus on them. Think instead of all the hard work you have done. Relax, and be yourself. Make eye contact with at least one person in the audience, and pretend that you are talking with that person. Do not be distracted by interruptions. They are annoying, but nothing to take seriously. Enjoy yourself.

Practice

Write notes or an outline for a five-minute talk on one of the following topics, or choose one of your own.

> my favorite book or movie
> the person in history I admire most
> the best day I ever had

Deliver the talk to your class. Remember the five P's.

7 | Taking Part in Committee and Panel Discussions

You may have worked on a committee as a member of a club or in a student group to organize an event or discuss a topic. Committees meet for a definite purpose usually to develop a plan or an action. Committee members may research a topic to share with the committee, and a chairperson is usually appointed to run the meeting.

A panel discussion is a more formal kind of discussion. Three to ten people are selected to research a particular subject. If the panel were discussing endangered species, for example, each member might research a particular animal. Later, the panel sits before an audience, and each panelist presents his or her information or point of view, usually within a previously decided time limit. Unlike a committee discussion, a panel is not expected to reach a decision or take an action. The purpose of a panel discussion is to inform an audience and exchange ideas.

The chairperson remains impartial throughout and helps move the discussion along. At the beginning of the discussion, the chairperson explains the topic and introduces members of the panel. The chairperson calls on each member to speak, and when they are through often calls on members of the audience to join the discussion.

Leading a Discussion	Participating in a Discussion
1. have ready information you might need	1. understand the purpose or topic of the discussion
2. state the topic or purpose of the discussion	2. contribute facts, ideas, or suggestions
3. introduce participants to the audience (panel)	3. listen to other participants
4. handle disagreements well	4. treat participants politely; do not interrupt when others are speaking
5. choose the order of the speakers	5. ask thoughtful questions
6. keep to the topic	6. cooperate with the leader or chairperson
7. encourage participants to contribute (committee)	7. help the group reach a decision (committee)
8. summarize ideas and opinions (committee)	

Read the following discussion among members of a bowling club.

DANNY: As chairperson, I thought we should discuss paying dues for our bowling club.

MARCI: Well, I think that's a terrible idea.

LEE: Hold it, Marci. Let's hear why Danny wants to collect dues.

DANNY: Thanks, Lee. At the end of the year, we could buy trophies for the best bowler or the most improved bowler with our dues money.

JOHN: That's a good idea. We could also buy tee shirts with our club name on them. How much money are you talking about?

DANNY: We'd have to decide what we could afford and vote on it.

FELICIA: I suggest that we do some research into the cost of tee shirts, trophies, and anything else we want. Then we will know how much money we would need.

CATHY: That's a good idea, Felicia. What about having a party?

STAN: How much would the dues be?

DANNY: Stan, you weren't listening. First, we will find out how much things will cost.

MARCI: What about . . .

LEE: Let's first decide how many things we want to do with our dues.

DANNY: Does anyone have other suggestions besides trophies, tee shirts, and a party? No, then who will find out how much these things cost?

CATHY: I'll find out about the tee shirts with someone else.

STAN: I'll help Cathy.

JOHN: I know a store that sells trophies. Will someone go with me?

LEE: I will.

DANNY: Good. At our next meeting, Cathy and Stan will report on the cost of tee shirts. John and Lee will report on trophies. Let's bowl.

Look back at the guidelines for leading and participating in discussions. In the discussion above, which rules did the participants follow? Which did they not follow?

Practice

With five or six classmates, take part in a committee discussion on a topic of your choice or choose one of these.

> how to raise money for a class trip
> how to improve your school grounds

8 | Holding Meetings

If you have ever been to a club or school meeting where everyone talked at the same time, then you know what a disorderly meeting is like. Little business gets accomplished. Groups can avoid disorderly meetings by following a set of rules called **parliamentary procedure.** All officers and members of a club should know parliamentary procedure and follow it.

Order of business	Explanation
1. Calling the meeting to order	The president or acting chairperson starts the meeting.
2. Reading the minutes	The secretary reads the minutes—a record of motions, reports, decisions, and other business.
3. Treasurer's report	The treasurer reports on incoming and outgoing money.
4. Unfinished business	Committee reports; discussions not completed at prior meetings
5. New business	Topic not previously discussed
6. Program (if any)	Guest speakers, movies, etc.
7. Adjournment	Ending of meeting

Terminology	Explanation
1. Making motions	A motion is a suggestion for doing something. To make a motion, rise and address the chair. After being recognized, say, "I move . . . ."
2. Seconding motions	A second is a support of the motion. If a motion is not seconded, it is dropped. A motion can be discussed after it is seconded.
3. Voting on motions	Motions must be voted on. In the case of a tie, the chairperson votes.

Ann followed parliamentary procedure when she presided at this meeting of the Photography Club.

ANNE: The meeting will please come to order. The secretary will read the minutes of the last meeting. (*The minutes are read.*) Are there any corrections or additions to the minutes?

TOBY: (*Rising*) Anne?

ANNE: Toby.

TOBY: Jamie, not Luis, was appointed chairperson of the Program Committee.

ANNE: Thank you. The secretary will please make the correction. If there are no further corrections, the minutes are approved as corrected. Is there a treasurer's report?

PHIL: (*Rising*) The balance at our last meeting was $7.58. We collected $3.50 from dues. We spent $2.75 for refreshments and $.89 for a new secretary's notebook, leaving a balance of $7.44 in the treasury.

ANNE: Is there any unfinished business?

ELENA: The Program Committee reports that arrangements have been made to show the movie *Photography People* at our next meeting.

ANNE: Is there other unfinished business? (*Pause*) Is there any new business? (*Pause*) We will now turn the meeting over to our program chairperson, Jamie Rivera.

JAMIE: For our program today, Bobby Jo will show some slides that she took on a trip to the Grand Canyon last summer. (*The program follows.*)

ANNE: Thanks very much for a good program.

JEAN: (*Rising*) Anne?

ANNE: Jean.

JEAN: I move that we adjourn for refreshments.

KIM: I second the motion.

ANNE: All in favor say "Aye." (*Many "Ayes"*) All opposed, "No." (*Silence*) The meeting is adjourned.

Practice

Form a group with five or six other students to conduct a club meeting. Decide who will be chairperson, secretary, treasurer, and committee chairperson. Following the order of business and using the correct terminology, conduct a ten-minute meeting of one of the following clubs: Hiking Club, Spanish Club, Chess Club. For help, refer to the order of business and terminology and the model meeting above.

9 | Electing Officers

Organized groups such as clubs often elect officers who have different titles and responsibilities. The charts below show the four most important officers and their duties and how to elect officers.

Officer	Duties
1. President	Presides at all meetings, may call special meetings, appoints committees, votes only in case of a tie
2. Vice President	Acts for the president only when he or she is absent; assists the president
3. Secretary	Handles correspondence; keeps a record, *minutes,* of each meeting; reads minutes of last meeting and files them
4. Treasurer	Collects dues and other money, keeps a record of expenses; reports at meetings

---

How to Elect Officers

1. Choose someone to act as chairperson until the president is elected
2. Rise and address the chair for these procedures
  a. For permission to speak
  b. To make a nomination
  c. To make a motion
3. Do not rise to second a motion
4. Do not second nominations
5. Vote for officers by secret ballots or a show of hands

The sample meeting that follows shows the correct way to elect club or class officers. Until the president is elected, a temporary chairperson is asked to preside. In the following meeting, Kate is the temporary chairperson (the *chair*) of the Drama Club. She conducts the meeting correctly. Notice the procedure that was followed.

KATE: The meeting will please come to order. The purpose of this meeting is to elect officers for the Drama Club. Nominations for president are now open.

JOSH: (*Rising to address the chair and request the floor*) Kate?

KATE: Josh, you have the floor. (Gives permission to speak)

JOSH: I nominate Vera Chan for president of the club.

JULIE: (*Rising*) Kate?

KATE: Julie.

JULIE: I nominate Alex Levin.

WES: (*Rising*) Kate?

KATE: Wes.

WES: I nominate Oliver Watson.

KATE: Are there any other nominations?

ERIC: (*Rising*) I move that the nominations be closed.

KERI: (*Remaining seated*) I second the motion.

KATE: It is moved and seconded that nominations are closed. All in favor say "Aye." (*Many "Ayes"*) Those opposed say "No." (*Silence*) The motion is carried. We'll move on to the voting now. The three candidates are Vera Chan, Alex Levin, and Oliver Watson. Please write your choice for president on the slip of paper that will be your ballot. I appoint Alma Mendoza and Joe Parsegian to collect and count the ballots.

(*Alma and Joe do as instructed and hand their ballot tally to the chair. Vera Chan received the most votes. She comes forward and conducts the rest of the meeting. The election continues until the remaining officers are elected.*)

Practice

A. Explain the meaning of each of these expressions and actions.

1. The meeting came to order.
2. Kate was the temporary chair.
3. Josh had the floor.
4. Julie made a nomination.
5. Eric moved the nominations be closed.
6. Keri seconded the motion.
7. The motion was carried.
8. Vera took the chair.

B. As a class, elect officers in the correct manner for a club of your own choice or choose one of these: the Drama Club, the Photography Club, the Spanish Club. Refer to the rules on page 58 and to the sample meeting above.

Nouns

1 | Identifying Nouns

When you go to your favorite restaurant and order a sandwich, salad, and milk, you are using nouns. Nouns are the names of anything and everything. The name can be as ordinary as *toothbrush* or as exotic as *chalaza* (the little white stringy tissue at each end of an egg yolk).

A **noun** is the name of a person, place, thing, quality, act, or feeling.

PERSON: Fred, man, Alice, mother
PLACE: city, Utah, crossroad
THING: pencil, furnace, curtain
QUALITY: truth, beauty
ACT: leap, dance, sigh
FEELING: homesickness, love

Try It Out

Which words are used as nouns in the following sentences?

1. Cathy took a trip to Ireland.
2. The loud cry was a surprise.
3. My parents bought a boat.
4. The dance was a success.
5. Is the owner of the store in?
6. No explanation can be found.

> ▶ A **noun** names a person, place, thing, quality, act, or feeling.

Written Practice

Write the noun or nouns in each sentence.

1. The show had begun.
2. There were many riders.
3. Do horses feel the tension?
4. One pony waited quietly.
5. Its name was Gremlin.
6. Lynn held the reins.
7. Was her nervousness obvious?
8. Gremlin was in fine form.
9. Their performance was good.
10. Would the pair win a ribbon?

● **Writing Sentences**   Use each word as a noun in a sentence of your own.

11. uncle   12. town   13. pin   14. truth   15. jump   16. joy

2 | Kinds of Nouns

Common and Proper Nouns

Nouns are names. Since there are different kinds of things to be named, there are different kinds of nouns.

A **proper noun** names a particular person, place, thing, or idea. Detroit is a particular city. *Detroit* is a proper noun. The word *city* does not name any particular city. It refers to a general class of things, namely, cities. *City* is a **common noun**. Any noun that is not a proper noun is a common noun.

Compare these pairs of common and proper nouns. Notice that a proper noun is always capitalized, even when it is more than one word.

Common	Proper	Common	Proper
house	White House	language	Hungarian
people	Mexicans	dog	Snoopy
lake	Lake Erie	holiday	Thanksgiving
friend	Steve Lobell	school	Carter High School

Try It Out

Find each noun and tell whether it is a proper noun or a common noun. Which nouns should be capitalized?

Richard berg lives in dallas, texas. On thursday, he and his family will take a trip to the city of washington, d.c. There they will stay in a hotel for a week. The bergs will visit such famous places as the lincoln memorial and the smithsonian museum.

Concrete and Abstract Nouns

Concrete nouns name things you can touch or see, like concrete, the material used in sidewalks. You can also see or touch the things named by *pen, water, Aunt Karen*. These are all concrete nouns.

Joy, belief, job, and *truth* are not like *concrete*. They name things that cannot be touched or seen. Nouns that name acts, qualities, feelings, and ideas are **abstract nouns**.

Try It Out

Which nouns are concrete, and which are abstract?

1. worry   **2.** trunk   **3.** ski   **4.** greeting   **5.** love   **6.** duck

Compound Nouns

Some nouns are made up of more than one word: *White House, high school.* A noun of two or more words is a **compound noun**.

Some compound nouns are written as one word (*bookcase*), some are written as two words (*book review*), and some are written with hyphens (*father-in-law*). Check your dictionary to be sure.

Notice that a noun may be classified in several ways.

Boston Celtics: proper, concrete, compound
theory: abstract, common

Try It Out

Classify each noun as common or proper, concrete or abstract, compound.

1. airplane   **2.** Chicago   **3.** opinion   **4.** salmon   **5.** make-believe

---

▸ A **proper noun** names a particular thing and is capitalized.
▸ A **common noun** is any noun that is not a proper noun.
▸ A **concrete noun** names a thing that can be touched and seen.
▸ An **abstract noun** names a thing that cannot be touched or seen.
▸ A **compound noun** is made up of more than one word.

Written Practice

Copy each noun and tell whether it is common or proper, concrete or abstract, compound.

1. playground   **2.** teacher   **3.** love   **4.** justice   **5.** White Sox

● **Writing Sentences**   Write a sentence for each noun you copied.

3 | Singular and Plural Nouns

In math classes you have all kinds of numbers—positive and negative, real and imaginary, and integers from zero to infinity. In language there are only two numbers: one, or **singular**, and more than one, or **plural**. Nouns change form to show a change from singular to plural.

1. Most nouns form their plurals by adding *-s* to the singular form.

   day–days globe–globes Michael–Michaels

2. If a noun ends in *-s*, *-x*, *-z*, *-sh*, or *-ch*, the plural is formed with *-es*.

   boss–bosses box–boxes buzz–buzzes dash–dashes beach–beaches

3. If a noun ends in *o* preceded by a vowel, *-s* is added.

   radio–radios stereo–stereos

   Certain words ending in *o* from other languages also take *s*.

   piano–pianos alto–altos

   Otherwise, nouns ending in *o* usually take *-es*.

   echo–echoes hero–heroes tomato–tomatoes

4. If a noun ends in *-y* preceded by a vowel, add *-s*. If *y* is preceded by a consonant, change *y* to *i* and add *-es*.

   donkey–donkeys valley–valleys boy–boys
   beauty–beauties fly–flies lady–ladies

   Proper nouns ending in *-y* always take *-s*: *Malloys, Bradys.*

5. If a noun ends in *-f* or *-fe*, sometimes only *-s* is added, and sometimes the *f* is changed to *v* and then *-es* is added. Memorize the most common words and consult the dictionary for the rest.

belief–beliefs	hoof–hoofs	handkerchief–handkerchiefs
chef–chefs	proof–proofs	roof–roofs
chief–chiefs	reef–reefs	safe–safes
calf–calves	leaf–leaves	shelf–shelves
half–halves	life–lives	thief–thieves
knife–knives	self–selves	wife–wives

6. Some plurals are formed by a change in spelling. They are called **irregular plurals** because there is no rule for their formation.

child–children   man–men   tooth–teeth
foot–feet   mouse–mice   woman–women

7. Some nouns show no change from the singular to the plural form.

a deer–many deer   a fish–many fish   a sheep–many sheep

8. Other nouns are used only in the plural form.

clothes   odds   pliers   scissors   slacks   pants

9. Some nouns appear to end in plural *s* but have a singular meaning.

acoustics   economics   mathematics   measles   mumps   series

10. Some foreign nouns form their plurals as in the original language.

analysis–analyses   bacterium–bacteria   alumnus–alumni

Other foreign words may use *s* or *es*: *stadiums*. Check the dictionary to make sure.

11. The plural of compound nouns is usually formed by adding *-s* to the word that names the person or thing being talked about.

commander*s* in chief   brother*s*-in-law   passer*s*-by

Exceptions include (**a**) words ending in *ful—cupfuls, teaspoonfuls*, and (**b**) compound expressions without nouns—*mixups*.

12. Letters, numbers, symbols, and words used as words add an apostrophe and an *-s*.

You omitted two *s*'s.   There are five 6's on that bill.
Do not write &'s.   The sentence has four *but*'s.

Try It Out

Give the plural form. Use your dictionary if you need it.

1. safe
2. ox
3. foot
4. mouse
5. basis
6. index
7. *
8. 3
9. life
10. stimulus
11. series
12. patch
13. story
14. soprano
15. monkey
16. sister-in-law
17. veto
18. maid of honor
19. Harry
20. tablespoonful

> ▸ A **singular noun** names one person, place, thing, quality, act or feeling.
> ▸ A **plural noun** names more than one.
> To form the plural of most nouns, add -s.
> For nouns ending in -s, -x, -z, -sh, or -ch, add -es.
> For nouns ending in -o, add -s or -es.
> For nouns ending with a vowel and -y, add -s. For nouns ending with a consonant and -y, change y to i and add -es.
> For some nouns ending in -f or -fe, add -s. For others, change f to v and add -es. Check your dictionary.
> For most compound nouns, add -s to the most important word.
> For letters, numbers, symbols, and words that are used as words, add -'s.

Written Practice

A. If the word is singular, write its plural form. If it is plural, write its singular form. Use your dictionary if you need it.

1. echoes	**6.** attorney general	**11.** trophies	**16.** leaves
2. bucketful	**7.** church	**12.** crash	**17.** oxen
3. turkeys	**8.** forget-me-not	**13.** potato	**18.** species
4. 20	**9.** grandchild	**14.** deer	**19.** hoaxes
5. +	**10.** cousin	**15.** torpedoes	**20.** crises

B. Change any incorrect singular or plural noun to the correct form.

Red-wing blackbirds spend their lifes in marshs and fields. They have many opportunities to sing while they sit in treeses or on fence postes and spread their wings and tailes. For food they eat insects and seedes but not fishes or mouses. Male blackbirds have red and yellow patchs on their shoulders. Females look like large dark sparrows with sharp bills. They are heavily striped on the underside with light stripes over their eyes. From the eggs laid by each female every year hatch four to five babys.

● **Writing Sentences**   Choose five words from exercise A of Written Practice, and write a sentence using the plural form of each word.

4 | Possessive Nouns

A noun is made possessive to show ownership or possession: *Delia's scissors*. A possessive noun can also show a connection or relationship: *Pasteur's discovery*. Where you can use an *of* construction or the verb *have*, you can usually use a possessive noun.

the contents of the book   the book's contents
the demands of the worker   the worker's demands
Mike has a new address.   Mike's new address

The possessive form of a noun always has an apostrophe. To make a singular noun possessive, add an apostrophe and an *-s*.

book–book's   bass–bass's   Boris–Boris's

Biblical and ancient names ending in *-s* take an apostrophe alone.

Moses–Moses'   Achilles–Achilles'   Hercules–Hercules'

To form the possessive of a plural noun, add only an apostrophe if the plural ends in *-s*. If the plural ends in something other than *-s*, add both an apostrophe and an *-s*.

Singular	Possessive	Plural	Possessive
girl	girl's	girls	girls'
baby	baby's	babies	babies'
foot	foot's	feet	feet's
Jones	Jones's	Joneses	Joneses'
		pliers	pliers'

The *-'s* is added at the *end* of a compound: *sister-in-law's*.

If two or more people own a single thing, the apostrophe is placed after the last name. If Doug and Scott own a basketball jointly, it is *Doug and Scott's* basketball. If each has a basketball, the two basketballs are *Doug's and Scott's* basketballs.

Sometimes you will see names of businesses written without an apostrophe: *Lerma Groceries*. Write the name as the business does.

Try It Out

Change each word group into a phrase with a possessive noun.

1. the footprints of the dog
2. Ted and Nick each has a bike.
3. the antics of a monkey
4. the color of the towels
5. Lewis and Doris have a cat.
6. the windows of the houses
7. The Johnsons have a dog.
8. the labors of Hercules
9. the glances of the passers-by
10. Her son-in-law has cars.

> ▶ A **possessive noun** shows ownership or possession.
> To form the possessive of a singular noun, add an apostrophe and -s.
> To form the possessive of a plural noun that ends in -s, add an apostrophe only. To form the possessive of a plural noun that does not end in -s, add an apostrophe and an -s.

Written Practice

Copy the following list and headings. Then complete the last three columns. The first item has been done for you.

Singular	Possessive	Plural	Possessive
1. letter	letter's	letters	letters'
2. photograph			
3. marble			
4. glass			
5. box			
6. fly			
7. foot			
8. crane			
9. shelf			
10. Carlos			
11. maid of honor			
12. briefcase			

- **Writing Sentences**   Write a sentence using the possessive form of each of these nouns.

13. **Joneses**   14. cocker spaniel   15. mens   16. deer   17. chiefs

5 | Appositives

An appositive is a noun that appears next to another noun or a pronoun and identifies, describes, or renames it. An appositive may be a noun alone or a noun with accompanying words.

> Vermont, <u>the Green Mountain State</u>, has lovely old inns.
> Graham Hill, <u>a British race car driver</u>, was world champion twice.
> The writer <u>Edgar Allan Poe</u> is famous for his gothic short stories.

Most appositives are set off with commas. If the appositive is needed to identify the noun it accompanies, then the appositive is not set off with commas.

Look at the last example above. If the words *Edgar Allan Poe* were left out of the sentence, you would not know which writer was being talked about. Because the appositive is needed to identify the writer, no commas are used with it.

In the first example, *the Green Mountain State* does not identify Vermont; it merely describes it. If the appositive were left out, the sentence would still say basically the same thing. Therefore, commas are used.

You can think of the commas as handles by which you can lift the appositive out of the sentence if you wish. When there are no such "handles," or no commas, the appositive cannot be lifted out.

Commas can change the meaning of a sentence with an appositive.

> My sister Molly plays the clarinet. (*There is more than one sister. The name* Molly *identifies which* sister.)
> My sister, Molly, plays the clarinet. (*There is only one sister. Molly, incidentally, is her name.*)

Try It Out

A. Which sentences have appositives? Identify each appositive.

1. Willa Cather is the author of *My Ántonia*.
2. The French Impressionist painters Manet and Monet are often mistaken for each other.
3. The brook trout, a wily fish, is a hard fish to catch.
4. Neil Armstrong was the first person on the moon.

B. Identify each appositive. Should it be set off with commas?

5. Mozart the classical composer was a child prodigy.
6. Both he and his only sister Maria Anna were musical geniuses.
7. Mozart began to compose when he was five a remarkable age.
8. One of Mozart's operas *The Magic Flute* has two characters with wonderful names Papageno and Papagena.
9. His opera *Don Giovanni* sets to music the story of Don Juan an old Spanish legend.

▶ An **appositive** is a noun, with or without accompanying words, that identifies or explains another noun.

An appositive is set off with commas unless it is needed to identify the other noun.

Written Practice

Write the sentences. Underline each appositive. Add commas if needed.

1. The poet and essayist, Emma Lazarus was born in 1849.
2. Lazarus, a precocious child, began writing poetry at an early age.
3. Ralph Waldo Emerson, a famous writer, liked these poems.
4. The novel *Alide* impressed another well-known writer the Russian author Turgenev.
5. Lazarus is best known for the sonnet "The New Colossus."
6. Its words are inscribed on the pedestal of the Statue of Liberty the gate to the port of New York.
7. In the last decade of her life the 1880's she grew concerned with the plight of persecuted Jews.
8. Her book *Songs of a Semite* was written on their behalf in 1802.
9. Lazarus died in 1887 in New York City the city of her birth.
10. *Poems* a collection of her verse was published two years later.

● **Writing Sentences** Write five sentences about well-known people. Use appositives with commas in three sentences and without commas in the other two.

6 | Writing Well with Nouns

Using Appositives

In the unit on sentences, you learned that you could join sentences to make your writing clearer, more direct, and more interesting. There you used independent and dependent clauses to combine sentences. You can use appositives in a similar way.

SEPARATE SENTENCES: The pocket calculator is a recent invention. It allows people to avoid arithmetic errors.

APPOSITIVE: The pocket calculator, a recent invention, allows people to avoid arithmetic errors.

An appositive and the noun it refers to can sometimes be interchanged. Then the emphasis changes. Compare this sentence about the pocket calculator with the one just above.

APPOSITIVE: A recent invention, the pocket calculator, allows people to avoid arithmetic errors.

Using appositives is one way to add variety to your sentences. Appositives can help you to make your sentences (1) clearer, by identifying a noun in the sentence, (2) more direct, by using fewer words to identify that noun, and (3) more interesting, by allowing you to vary sentence structure.

Try It Out

Use an appositive to combine each pair of sentences.

1. Abraham Lincoln was the sixteenth president of the United States. He was the "great emancipator."
2. Basil is used a great deal in Italian cooking. Basil is an herb with broad green leaves.
3. The marathon is more than twenty-six miles long. It is the longest race in the Olympics.
4. The Bugatti Royales were built by Ettore Bugatti. They are the largest passenger cars ever made.
5. Stein was a reliable relief pitcher. She approached the mound with confidence.

Using Precise Nouns

Which sentence gives you a clearer picture of what is happening?

> The dog hid under the furniture.
> The Great Dane hid under the grand piano.

While all nouns name things, some name them more precisely than others. Precise nouns will usually give your reader a clearer, more vivid picture of what you are saying. Here are some examples of general versus precise nouns.

General	Precise	General	Precise
bird	robin	person	woman
emotion	love	metal	iron
doctor	surgeon	language	Spanish

Try It Out

Substitute a more precise noun for each underlined noun.

1. I walked to the store with a book tucked under my arm.
2. A relative is staying with us for a time.
3. A person saw an animal in the building.
4. The scientist's feeling made her pursue the experiment.
5. The foreigner learned the language quickly.

Written Practice

Rewrite the passage, using correct plural and possessive forms and correct capitalization. There is one place where you should replace a general noun with a more precise one. There are three sets of sentences that should be combined to form appositives.

Amy Lowell was a famous poet and critic. She was born in massachusetts in 1874. Her first volume of poetry was published in 1912. It was called *A Dome of Many-Colored Glass*. The woman became a leader of the Imagist poets, whose poemes put great value on images. Many of her workes utilize polyphonic prose. This is writing in paragraph form that uses the devices of poetry. Amy Lowell's position as one of the outstanding poets of her time was strengthened by her activitys as an editor and lecturer.

Check Your Writing

Review your passage on Amy Lowell, asking yourself these questions. Make appropriate changes.

A. Are my sentences correct?

   1. Have I capitalized all proper nouns?
   2. Have I used the correct plural forms of nouns?
   3. Have I used the correct possessive forms of nouns?
   4. Have I written compound nouns correctly?
   5. Have I used commas with appositives where necessary?

B. Are my sentences clear?

   1. Can I use appositives to identify any nouns?
   2. Have I used precise nouns?

C. Are my sentences direct?

   Have I used appositives to combine sentences and to avoid repetition?

D. Are my sentences interesting?

   Have I used appositives to vary the sentence structure?

● **Writing a Paragraph** Write a paragraph of at least six sentences about a visit to a zoo or museum. Include some noun plurals and possessives, some compound nouns, and some proper nouns in your sentences. Also use some appositives. Then review the paragraph, asking yourself the questions above. Make appropriate changes in your paragraph, and rewrite it if necessary.

Writing Well with Nouns   **73**

7 Using Words Correctly

affect, effect

The words *affect* and *effect* are often confused.
Affect, a verb, means "to influence, have an effect on."

The hot weather <u>affected</u> the singer's performance.

Effect as a verb means "to accomplish, cause to happen."

A cool breeze can <u>effect</u> a noticeable improvement in her singing.

Effect as a noun means "the result of action."

Does hot weather have a bad <u>effect</u> on you?

Practice

Which is the correct word to use in each sentence?

1. The rain (affected, effected) the outcome of the game.
2. The long-range (affects, effects) of the pesticide are not known.
3. Careful planning allowed Alice to (affect, effect) her plan.
4. What was the (affect, effect) of the heavy rain on your garden?
5. Six changes were (affected, effected) by the new city council.

accept, except

Another pair of words that may be confused are *accept* and *except*.
Accept is a verb and means "to receive willingly."

Howard <u>accepted</u> his promotion graciously.

Except is usually used as a preposition (see p. 325). The preposition means "excluding, other than."

Everything Tom planted came up <u>except</u> the corn.

Except can also be used as a verb meaning "to leave out, exclude."

Mark asked Ms. Wang to <u>except</u> his lowest quiz grade.

Practice

Choose the correct word to complete each sentence.

1. I (accepted, excepted) the invitation to Myra's party.
2. Eunice had difficulty (accepting, excepting) the fact that she did not make the honor roll.
3. The old car ran well (accept, except) for the transmission.
4. Tad (accepted, excepted) the bad news well.
5. (Accept, Except) for Melissa, everyone is ready to go.
6. The final score is figured by (accepting, excepting) the high and low scores and averaging the remaining scores.

> Do not confuse the verb *affect* ("to influence") with the verb *effect* ("to cause to happen") or the noun *effect* ("result").
> Do not confuse the verb *accept* ("to receive") with the preposition *except* ("excluding") or the verb *except* ("to exclude").

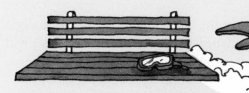

Written Practice

Write the word that correctly completes the sentence.

1. Will the general (accept, except) the terms of the surrender?
2. Acid rain is one (affect, effect) of air pollution.
3. Martina remembered everything (accept, except) her goggles.
4. (Accept, Except) for a brief drizzle, the day has been perfect.
5. Were Mr. Mackey's trees (affected, effected) by the storm?
6. Sean had three bad scores, but he asked the committee to (accept, except) them from his final score.
7. The heat seems to (affect, effect) Karl more than the others.
8. Natalie could not decide whether to (accept, except) the gift.

- **Writing Sentences**   Write a sentence using each word correctly.

9. affect
10. accept
11. effect (noun)
12. except (verb)
13. effect (verb)
14. except (preposition)

Building Vocabulary

Synonyms

If you were writing about a house, you would not want to repeat the word *house* every time you referred to it. You could use the word *it* sometimes, but that could become monotonous, too. To avoid repetition, you can substitute words that mean very much the same thing as *house*, such as *home, residence,* or *dwelling.*

Words with similar meanings are called **synonyms**. Think about the meaning of these synonyms for *house.*

house: home, residence, abode, dwelling, domicile

House refers to the structure in which someone lives, while *home, residence, abode,* and *dwelling* refer more to the place. *Domicile* is a legal residence.

Synonyms rarely mean exactly the same thing. Sometimes a slight difference in meaning will not matter. Other times that difference will be important. You may want to emphasize the structure, the place, or the legality of a home, for example.

Since synonyms usually have slightly different meanings, you should choose among them carefully so that you will get the meaning you want.

Use your dictionary to help you work with synonyms.

Practice

A. Choose the synonym that best completes each sentence. You may use the dictionary to help you.

1. Sara's (unhappiness, melancholy) about her grade lasted for six seconds.
2. The hikers accidentally discovered the (source, root) of the river).
3. The broad, tree-lined (lane, boulevard) was magnificent.
4. It took all of Kip's (strength, force) to move the piano.
5. The six-lane (road, street) was heavily patrolled during rush hour.

B. Write each noun; then write two synonyms. Use the dictionary.

    6. event   **7.** result   **8.** relaxation   **9.** respect   **10.** leader

• **Writing Sentences**   Choose three pairs of synonyms from exercise B. Use them in sentences.

Antonyms

Antonyms are words that have opposite meanings, like *heat* and *cold*. You can make good use of antonyms to contrast one thing with another.

> Was the defendant telling the <u>truth</u>, or was it all a <u>lie</u>?
> The <u>sadness</u> of leaving old friends can be relieved by the <u>happiness</u> of meeting new ones.

Noun antonyms are sometimes formed by adding a negative prefix like *dis-*, *un-*, or *in-* to another noun: *dis-honesty*, *in-justice*, *un-truth*.

Notice that all of these nouns are abstract. Concrete nouns, like *tree* or *table*, rarely have antonyms.

▸ **Synonyms** are words with similar meanings. Use them carefully to vary your writing.
▸ **Antonyms** are words that have opposite meanings.

Practice

A. Complete the sentence with an antonym of the underlined noun.

    1. The cheery <u>light</u> of midday turned into a dreary ____.
    2. The <u>appearance</u> of the clouds meant the ____ of the sun.
    3. Fortunately Lisa's <u>tolerance</u> was greater than Roy's ____.
    4. The jury had to judge the <u>likelihood</u> or ____ of the story.
    5. The <u>ugliness</u> of the house's <u>exterior</u> does not prepare you for the ____ of its ____.

B. Write each noun and then write an antonym.

    6. honesty   **7.** poverty   **8.** victory   **9.** tension   **10.** beauty

• **Writing Sentences**   Choose three pairs of antonyms from exercise B. Use all of the words in sentences.

Review

- **Kinds of Nouns** *(pp. 62–63)*   List every noun. Next to it, write whether it is a compound, common or proper, abstract or concrete.

  1–47. Automobiles moved slowly up the driveway. Trunks, suitcases, and laundry bags were unloaded under the blazing sun. The excitement and commotion increased as more people arrived. It was the start of a new season at Camp Wachanaga on the shore of Lake Melrose.

  With a brief introduction, Gene greeted his bunkmates Charles and Manuel. Would they become real friends? Only time would tell. Together, the three campers took the path to the dining hall.

- **Singular and Plural Nouns** *(pp. 64–66)*   Write the plural form of each noun.

  48. monkey   **52.** son-in-law   **56.** hero   **60.** crisis
  49. shelf   **53.** deer   **57.** lady   **61.** *A*
  50. buzz   **54.** life   **58.** capful   **62.** goose
  51. fly   **55.** calf   **59.** tooth   **63.** veto

- **Possessive Nouns** *(pp. 67–68)*   Write the singular possessive form for each noun. Then write the plural possessive form.

  64. Iris   **68.** father-in-law   **72.** gentleman   **76.** library
  65. chief   **69.** German shepherd   **73.** cello   **77.** business
  66. foot   **70.** zucchini   **74.** sheep   **78.** attaché case
  67. baby   **71.** worker   **75.** house   **79.** runner

- **Appositives** *(pp. 69–70)*   Copy the appositive from each sentence. Insert commas if needed.

  80. The camp a large one offered something for everyone.
  81. Charlie's bunkmate Gene excelled in swimming.
  82. That activity did not interest Charlie a poor swimmer.
  83. He devoted his time to dramatics his main interest.
  84. All three boys liked two things music and food.
  85. For Roberto an outdoors person the long hikes were best.
  86. The hike around the lake, a six-mile walk, was Roberto's favorite.

- **Writing Well with Nouns** *(pp. 71–73)* Rewrite each sentence. Substitute a more precise noun for each underlined noun.

  87. Chris loaded the dirty dishes into the machine.
  88. The window coverings were a faded color.
  89. The bird built a nest in the tree in our front yard.
  90. Ellen left the sports field with muddy clothing.
  91. As the man entered the building, his emotion increased.
  92. We saw a person walking alone on the beach.
  93. My favorite furniture is made of wood.
  94. That room made Linda feel optimistic about the future.
  95. The sculptures on display were made of metal.

- **Using Words Correctly** *(pp. 74–75)* If the underlined verb is correct, write *correct*. If it is incorrect, write the correct form.

  96. Will Mr. Haupt accept the invitation to be our adviser?
  97. Everyone voted for him except Tammy, who did not vote at all.
  98. If we except Tammy, the vote for Mr. Haupt will be unanimous.
  99. A unanimous vote usually has a positive effect on people.
  100. Do you think it will effect Mr. Haupt's decision?
  101. If he becomes our advisor, Mr. Haupt will effect his plans.

- **Building Vocabulary** *(pp. 76–77)* Write a suitable synonym for each noun in parentheses.

  102. The (completion) of the game came very fast.
  103. A (male) walked quickly out of the (home).
  104. The (brightness) of the jewel impressed its new (possessor).
  105. Marigold dug a (cavity) in the (earth) to hide her bone.
  106. Jeannette's (response) was certainly not a (falsehood).
  107. Ted's feeling of (unhappiness) lasted throughout the foggy day.
  108. The fire trucks raced through the narrow (streets).
  109. For five summers, no one had stayed at the (house) that over-looked the lake.

  Write a suitable antonym for each noun in parentheses.

  110. The stranger's (honesty) was immediately obvious.
  111. The diamond had a slight (perfection).
  112. My father complained about the razor's (sharpness).
  113. The (appearance) of the weapon puzzled the detective.
  114. The children's carelessness caused (pleasure).

Maintain

- **Sentences/Subjects and Predicates** *(pp. 9–14)* Write *declarative, interrogative, imperative,* or *exclamatory* to describe each sentence. Then write the simple subject and the simple predicate.

  1. Is Matthew going to the fair today?
  2. Please come, too.
  3. There are more than forty cows in that barn!
  4. Did Timothy raise that sheep by himself?
  5. Here is Mr. Scott with his handmade quilt.
  6. On the other side of the barn are the fresh breads.

- **Compound Subjects and Predicates/Compound and Complex Sentences** *(pp. 15–22)* Describe each sentence by writing *simple sentence, compound sentence,* or *complex sentence.* If the sentence is a simple sentence, also write *compound subject, compound predicate,* or *compound subject and predicate* to describe it.

  7. The owners watch nervously as their animals are judged.
  8. A blue ribbon or a red ribbon is received with a smile.
  9. Timothy's sheep wins a red ribbon, but Arlene's chickens receive no prize at all.
  10. Although Arlene is disappointed, she will try again next year.
  11. Ivan Hoyte baked zucchini bread and is slicing it carefully.
  12. Annabella likes the zucchini bread but prefers cranberry bread.

- **Writing Good Sentences** *(pp. 23–27)* Combine each pair of sentences. Use the conjunction in parentheses to create one simple sentence, one compound sentence, or one complex sentence.

  13. Charlotte is arranging carnations and marigolds. Earl sets up his vegetable display. (while)
  14. Some cows, pigs, and goats seem unhappy. They are expressing their complaints in a loud chorus. (and)
  15. Shall we visit the crafts area next? Shall we watch the horse competition? (or)
  16. We must leave now. We shall certainly return. (although)

- **Kinds of Nouns** *(pp. 62-63)* List each noun. Label it *compound, common,* or *proper,* and *abstract* or *concrete.*

17–48. The Brewster County Fair opened this weekend. The large fairgrounds and the bright tents made it very inviting. A walk through the sheds revealed a variety of barnyard animals. Their proud owners stood beside their sheep, pigs, cows, and chickens. The animals came from farms with names like Huckleberry Hill and Mount Concord.

- **Singular and Plural Nouns / Possessives** *(pp. 64-68)* Examine each underlined noun. If it is written correctly, write *correct.* If it is not written correctly, write the correct singular, plural, or possessive form.

The **(49)** sheep were the first **(50)** animals to be judged. The Jones family had entered one **(51)** sheep in this **(52)** years' contest. The **(53)** sheep's name was Mavis. **(54)** Mavis's coat was protected by Leon **(55)** Joneses' old **(56)** sheets. One of **(57)** Susans' **(58)** scarves was tied around its head. **(59)** Mavises **(60)** eyes and the **(61)** hooves at the end of its **(62)** feet were the only **(63)** parts of Mavis that showed. **(64)** Passer-bys gave Mavis strange **(65)** glancs. Oh, no. The **(66)** scarve's **(67)** knots could not be untied. Who had the **(68)** scissor? The **(69)** Joneses' equipment was in their **(70)** carry-alls next to the **(71)** ponys' stalls. Two of the **(72)** childrens were the **(73)** morning's **(74)** heros. They found the **(75)** scissors' and removed **(76)** Mavis's **(77)** scarf.

- **Appositives / Writing Well with Nouns** *(pp. 71-73)* Rewrite each pair of sentences. Turn one sentence into an appositive.

78. Moe was the prize-winning pig. He wore his ribbon with dignity.
79. First prize for bread went to Ivan. He is a wonderful baker.

- **Using Words Correctly** *(pp. 29-31, 74-75)* Correct each sentence.

80. Please except Anthony's apology.
81. Music has a calming affect on my dog.
82. The bus driver did not leave the passengers enter.
83. Can anyone rise this stubborn window?
84. If I lay down now, I'll fall asleep.

- **Building Vocabulary** *(pp. 76-77)* Write a synonym and an antonym for each of the following words.

85. difficulty   **86.** delight   **87.** shininess   **88.** height

1 | Main Idea of a Paragraph

You have already learned how to write effective sentences that express a complete thought or combine related thoughts. What if one or two sentences are not enough to express your ideas? You can organize your writing into paragraphs. Most of the printed materials you read every day are made up of paragraphs. A paragraph is a group of sentences that relate to one main idea.

Read the following paragraph. Do all the sentences in this paragraph relate to one main idea?

Almost anyone can tell you whose picture appears on a one-dollar bill. Can anyone you know name the artist who painted the original portrait of that familiar face? Probably not many people know that Gilbert Stuart, a famous American artist in the late 1700's, painted the portrait of George Washington that appears on our currency. Stuart, who was born in Rhode Island in 1755 and later studied painting in London, painted three portraits of Washington between 1794 and 1796. Of these three, none is more famous or familiar than the unfinished portrait—the "Athenaeum"—that is on the dollar.

The paragraph above has unity. All the sentences relate to the main idea: *Gilbert Stuart is the artist who painted the portrait of George Washington that is on the dollar bill.* Is the paragraph indented?

Now read the paragraph below and decide whether it is unified.

When you think of famous New York City skyscrapers, which one pops into your mind? Is it the Empire State Building? the Chrysler Building? Two other tall buildings rise dramatically over the edge of lower Manhattan—the twin hundred-story towers of the World Trade Center. These skyscrapers were planned in 1965 by Minoru Yamasaki. Another architect who has designed many modern buildings is I.M. Pei. One of these is the John Hancock Tower in Boston, a skyscraper which seems like a needle of glass. Modern architectural design has recently fallen on slow times because of budget cuts by cities, businesses, and universities.

- Does this paragraph have unity? Explain why or why not.
- Which of the sentences relate to skyscrapers in New York City?
- Which sentences do not relate specifically to buildings in New York City?

When you write a paragraph, try to develop only one main idea. When the main idea changes, start a new paragraph. Read the following group of sentences. They should be divided into two paragraphs. Decide where the second paragraph should begin.

Painting is one of my favorite hobbies. Ever since I was very small, I've been drawing and painting pictures of what I see or from my imagination. At first, my parents encouraged me to use crayons, which are much less messy than paints. Then when they realized what a great six-year-old talent they had on their hands, they gave me a set of watercolors. Now I work in watercolor, including tempera, and in oils as well. An artist I admire, and whose style I sometimes try to copy, is Andrew Wyeth. He is one of America's most famous modern painters. I like the sharp detail that makes his paintings look so real.

- What main idea does the paragraph begin to tell about?
- What main idea does it switch to?
- Where should you begin a second paragraph? Why?

Practice

A. In the following group of sentences there are two main ideas. What are they? Which sentence or sentences do not keep to either of these main ideas? Decide where a second paragraph should begin.

I always enjoy my annual October slumber party. The same six girls have been getting together since sixth grade. Everyone brings sleeping bags, pillows, and records. Ellie had a barbecue at her house. Once we had a contest to see who could stay awake the longest. Of all my friends, Judy is the one I've had the best times with and known the longest. If I want to share some exciting news, she's the person I call. If I need a confidante, I can tell her my innermost dreams and secrets. Even if I feel like crabbing about getting a terrible grade on a test or unexpectedly having to baby-sit my younger brother, I can count on her to listen. I'm lucky to have a friend like Judy, and she's pretty lucky to have one like me.

B. Using the sentences above, write two paragraphs. Be sure to indent each one. Omit any sentences that do not relate to either of the main ideas.

2 | Topic Sentences and Supporting Details

The best way to signal the main idea of your paragraph is to write a topic sentence. A **topic sentence** gives a clear, general statement of the main idea. Other sentences in the paragraph develop the main idea and give **supporting details.** The topic sentence is not always first.

Read the paragraphs below. Notice each underlined topic sentence.

1. The area I chose for my "survival week" was the Town Forest and land belonging to Dan DeWolf in Holliston, Massachusetts. This totaled about two hundred acres of virtually uninhabited land. The woods were logged in the mid-1930's, so the trees are relatively young. They are mainly red and white oak, and hickory. There are also swamps, with maple trees dominant, and some deserted overgrown farmlands, where sassafras, cedar, birch, and white pine have grown up. –*Sarah Brown*

2. *Survivor* is an apt word to describe gulls, for not only do they have the ability to eat almost anything, alive or dead, but they can also walk, fly, and swim extremely well, a combination of assets most birds do not have. Survival is a constant concern in gull life. Even after the immature bird learns to fly well, it must obey territorial regulations. If, while flying, it lands on claimed ground, it is immediately attacked and driven away. –*Jack Denton Scott*

- What main idea is stated in each of these topic sentences?
- Where is each topic sentence located?
- What supporting details do the other sentences give?

How do the sentences in the following paragraph lead up to the topic sentence? What supporting details do they provide?

The ostrich, largest of all the world's birds, can weigh as much as 300 pounds. However, the ostrich does not appear heavy or bulky. It has a long, thin neck and long, thin, stiltlike legs coming from its feathered body. These legs are powerful and can carry the ostrich to incredible speeds. But could nature have played a trick on the ostrich? Even though they can run like the wind, ostriches cannot fly! The ostrich is unique not only for its size, appearance, and speed, but also for this peculiar lack of ability.

Once you decide on a topic for a paragraph and know what details you will include, how do you go about writing a good topic sentence? Suppose for a minute that you are writing a paragraph of instructions for making your favorite sandwich. Which of these four topic sentences would you use and why?

1. I know how to make a delicious triple-decker sandwich.
2. If you try my triple-decker specialty, you'll discover that it's not just a meal, it's a banquet!
3. Try making this big sandwich, which is my specialty.
4. This sandwich has a lot of things in it, but it's easy to make and you'll probably like it.

A topic sentence should not only give a clear statement of the main idea, it should express that idea in lively, exact language. Which sentence above uses the most exact and interesting words? Which sentences use dull, flat words?

Practice

A. The following paragraph needs a topic sentence. Read the paragraph and decide what the main idea is. Write three possible topic sentences. Read your sentences to a classmate and discuss them. Decide which sentence makes a clear statement in the most interesting way.

One day last week the phone rang. I ran to answer it, but I didn't quite make it. As I jumped down the only two steps in our entire house, I tripped. I took off like a rocket and then landed with one leg under me. Of course, I broke a bone. Now my leg is in a cast, and I have to use crutches. Getting around isn't easy. Someone else has to run for the phone! Apart from the inconvenience, though, I've enjoyed collecting autographs on my cast.

B. Make up a topic sentence that makes a clear statement about one of these ideas, or use your own idea. Use lively, exact words.

1. the best way to take care of a dog (or cat, horse, bike, fishing rod)
2. why you enjoy canoeing (or chess, soccer, needlepoint, other hobby)
3. your recent visit to ___ (a city, the dentist, a friend's house)

3 | Order in Paragraphs

When you write about a procedure that includes steps or about events that involve a time sequence, it is important to explain things in order from first to last. This order for steps or sequence is called **chronological order.** To clarify instructions or explanations, use order words, such as *first, next, now, then, for example, afterwards,* and *finally.* Not every sentence, however, needs an order word.

As you read the following paragraph, notice the order words.

> Every spring my dad gets his vegetable garden ready, with my expert assistance. It's fun. We start by clearing out all the winter debris. Then we plow the soil, tilling it in neat rows. We choose the kinds of seeds, such as peas, radishes, spinach, beets, and lettuce, for early planting. Next, as I sow the seeds, Dad marks each row to identify the kind of vegetable. Then we pat each row with the hoe. Finally, to keep out hungry rabbits, we put up a wire fence.

- What order words did the writer use? Does every sentence have an order word?
- How do the order words help clarify this explanation about getting the garden ready?

Practice

A. Read this paragraph. Are the steps in chronological order? Should any steps be rearranged? Where would order words help?

> Some of the toothbrushers in my family are really sloppy! I should probably tape these rules above our bathroom sink. Put the cap back on the toothpaste when you've finished brushing your teeth. Rinse out the sink so that the next person can make a clean start! Squeeze the tube from the *bottom.* Use just enough toothpaste to cover the top of your brush—that way you don't waste it or drip blobs all over the sink bowl. Instead of leaving your toothbrush next to the faucet, rinse it and hang it up.

B. Rewrite the paragraph, putting the steps in order. Add appropriate order words to some sentences, but not to every sentence.

4 | Getting Started

From the time you get up until the time you go to bed, your days are filled with directions and instructions. People say to you, "Clean your room"; "Read the next three chapters"; "Do twenty situps." You say, "Catch Bus 44 at Central and First. Ask the driver to let you off at Arnold Street. Our house is the third one on the right."

Many of the instructions you use are written. Written instructions are usually essential for tasks like cutting out shirt pieces from a pattern, putting together the parts of a model plane, or doing anything that involves a number of steps. Every day you make, do, use, or look for many things. Knowing how to give and follow instructions is one of the most important skills you can develop. Try the exercise below to test your instruction-giving skill.

Practice

A. Take turns with three or four others giving instructions on how to brush teeth, braid hair, juggle tennis balls, whistle, smile, or whatever else you know how to explain. Tell your listeners exactly what they should do and what order they should follow. Use words only—no gestures, no demonstrations, no props.

When you are the listener, listen carefully. Follow each step in your imagination. Do the instructions work? Were the steps in order? Was the wording precise? Was anything left out?

B. Discuss which directions were easiest to follow. What made them clear or interesting? How could some of the other directions have been improved?

Steps for Writing Instructions   Here are the steps for writing a paragraph of instructions. You will follow these steps to write your own paragraph.

Step One	Choose a topic.
Step Two	Write your instructions.
Step Three	Revise your instructions.
Step Four	Proofread your instructions.
Step Five	Make a final copy to share.

5 | Step One
Choose a Topic

Written directions or instructions are sometimes easier to give than spoken ones. When you write, you always have a second chance. You can change your mind about wording and make it clearer; you can re-arrange steps; you can cross out and start again. You can make your written instructions interesting or even funny.

Think about some things you could write instructions for. What do you know how to do that others do not? Is there something you want to learn how to do? What simple, everyday procedure could you explain in an original way?

Steve thought about some of the things he liked doing. He jotted down a list of possible topics for instructions. This is Steve's list.

stamp collecting   how to make a kite
playing backgammon   soap carving
my special recipe   my best card trick

Steve thought about his first topic and decided that since this was a new hobby, he should have more experience before writing about his stamp collection. He decided that playing backgammon involved too many detailed steps, instructions for making a kite would need dia-grams, and soap carving should be demonstrated. The two topics he liked best were his card trick and his special recipe, so he made notes on these. As Steve read over his notes, he decided that instructions for his famous card trick would give it away! He thought that his special hamburger concoction would be fun and interesting to explain. He circled *my special recipe*.

Assignment
- **Make a List**
- **Make Notes**
- **Choose a Topic**

A. Make a list of five or more topics for written instructions.

B. Choose the two topics that appeal to you most and make notes on them. List the steps in order. Then check your notes. Is each step included? Are the steps in chronological order? Which topic would you most like to write about?

C. Choose your topic, and circle it on your list.

6 | Step Two
Write Your Instructions

When you practiced giving instructions for the exercise on page 88, you probably found out that what seems clear to the person speaking does not always seem clear to the person listening. Writers face the same problem with their readers.

As Steve wrote his first draft, he tried to keep his reader in mind. He used his notes as a guide in getting his steps on paper. Before you begin writing your own instructions, read Steve's first draft, and imagine yourself following these steps to make hamburgers.

Steve's first draft

Hamberger Special

My mom showed me how to do this, but I changed a bunch of stuff so it's really my idea. It makes three really big ones or four ~~pretty good~~ regular size ones. What you do is you mix up a pound of hamberger with an egg and a half cup of crumbs. Beat the egg up first, of course. Add a fourth cup of chopped ~~up~~ onion, then put in a fourth cup of catchup and a teaspoon of W. sauce. You can add a teaspoon of mustard if you want to, or a tablespoon of horseradish (which I like). Mix it all up, but don't mess around with it too much. ~~It's nice~~ You can use a fork, but hands are best I think. It can get pretty squishy if you don't have enough crumbs. Make it into hambergers and mash flat. Get a pan real hot but don't add any greace. The meat has fat in it already and too much fat ~~will be~~ isn't good for you. If the hamberger looks too gooey or feels really squishy, sprinkle some more crumbs on it. This ~~mixture of my~~ hamberger receipe is good because it is cheap and it tastes good.

- Do Steve's directions keep to one main idea? Why, or why not?
- Does Steve's paragraph have a topic sentence? If so, what is it? Do you think it could be improved? How?
- Are Steve's directions clear? What steps do you find difficult to understand?
- How would you change the order of any of these steps?

Assignment   • **Write Your First Draft**

Write the first draft of your instructions. Concentrate on getting your ideas down on paper. You can revise your instructions later. Keep these questions in mind.

1. Am I keeping to the main idea?
2. Are my instructions clear and complete?
3. Are the steps in order and easy to follow?

As you write, use your notes as a guide. Remember, the important thing is to put the steps down on paper as clearly as possible. You can look for problems in spelling and punctuation later. You may want to skip a line as you write so that you have space to make changes later on.

7 | Step Three
Revise Your Instructions

When you revise, you have a chance to improve your writing. You can add or cross out words and change the order of sentences.

Steve looked over his first draft to see whether his directions were clear. He tried to put himself in the place of a reader, and he pretended that he had never used this recipe. This approach worked. He could see where he needed to make some revisions.

Steve decided that he did not need to mention that this recipe had been his mother's. He crossed out the first sentence. He thought the last sentence would be the best topic sentence and made some changes to improve it. He also thought that this sentence would be a good introduction to his recipe, so he wrote a paragraph symbol (¶) before it and he drew an arrow to the beginning of his instructions. Then Steve realized that some steps were in the wrong order; he drew arrows to show the new arrangement.

Next, Steve wanted to get another opinion on his paper. He explained to his classmate Michael that his directions were for making his favorite kind of hamburgers. Then he read Michael his paper. When Steve finished, Michael said, "The hamburgers sound great. I'd like to try them. How long do they take to cook?"

"I forgot to mention that, didn't I!" said Steve. He decided to add that information before he forgot. He used a caret (∧) to show where the words belonged. Then he asked, "Do you think you'd have any trouble following my instructions?"

"I think I could follow them," said Michael, "but when I make something, I like to get all the stuff I'll need together in one place at the beginning. Then I don't find out halfway through that something important isn't around. It might help if you first listed all the things that go into the hamburger and then told what to do with them."

"It might," said Steve, "but wouldn't it sound just like a regular cookbook recipe?"

"It wouldn't have to," said Michael. "You can still make it interesting when you tell how to do it."

"OK," said Steve, "I'm going to think about it some more."

Steve decided to use Michael's suggestion. He made a few other changes as well. Then he rewrote his paper. Look at Steve's revision on the next page.

Steve's revision

Steve's Hamberger Special

Here is a receipe for hambergers that makes more, costs less, and tastes really good! It makes three really big hambergers or four regular size ones and these are the things you need:

1 pound hamberger

1 egg

½ cup of ~~crumbs~~ bread or cracker crumbs

¼ cup chopped onion

¼ cup catchup

1 teaspoon ~~W. sauce~~ Wostershire sauce or 1 teaspoon mustard or 1 tablespoon horseradish

(Be sure to try the horseradish sometime)

First, beat the egg with a fork. Mix in the crumbs. Crumble in the hamberger then add everything else. Next, mix it all up with a fork or with your hands, but dont mix it too much. If the hamberger looks too gooey or feels too squishy, sprinkle some more crumbs on it. Stop ~~adding~~ mixing when the meat is soft but doesn't look wet. Finally make the hambergers. Fry them in a hot frying pan for five or six minutes on each side, but don't use any extra greace. The meat has fat in it already if you like your hambergers well done cook them a little longer.

- How did Steve improve his topic sentence?
- What order words did he add?
- What information did Steve add about the cooking time?

Assignment

- **Revise Your Instructions**
- **Discuss Your Instructions**

A. Read over your own paper again. Pretend that you are reading your instructions for the first time, so that you can look at them with a more critical eye. Change any words or sentences to make your instructions clearer and easier to follow. Use these questions to guide your revision.

1. Are my directions clear? Add details or change wording to make a step easier to understand or follow.
2. Are my steps in the right order? Rearrange the order if any steps are misplaced. Draw an arrow from the step to the place where it should be inserted in the instructions. Add any appropriate order words.
3. Do I repeat myself or say more than I need to say? Cross out any sentences that do not keep to the topic or that are unnecessary.

B. Tell a classmate what your instructions are about. Then read them out loud. Ask your listener to keep the following questions in mind as you read.

1. Is there anything I don't understand?
2. Are the steps in the best order?
3. Could I follow these instructions easily?
4. Is there anything that should be left out?
5. Is there any information that should be added?

C. Discuss your paper with your listener. Then make your final revision. Use any of your listener's suggestions that will improve your instructions. If other ideas for improving your paper occurred to you during the discussion, make those changes as well.

8 | Step Four
Proofread Your Instructions

Now that you have made your instructions as clear and complete as you can, it is time to shift your attention to mechanical details. This step is called proofreading.

When you proofread, you check for mistakes in spelling, capitalization, and punctuation. Look up the words you are unsure of in a dictionary. If your paper is hard to read, make a clean copy before proofreading it.

This is how the first part of Steve's paper looked when he had finished proofreading it.

Part of Steve's paper after proofreading

Steve's Hambúrger Special

Here is a recéipe for hambúrgers that makes more, costs less, and tastes really good! It makes three really big hambúrgers or four regular size ones and these are the things you need:

1 pound hambúrger

1 egg

½ cup of ~~crumbs~~ bread or cracker crumbs

¼ cup chopped onion

¼ cup catchup

1 teaspoon ~~W. sauce~~ *Worcestershire* Wostershire sauce or 1 teaspoon mustard or 1 tablespoon horseradish

(Be sure to try the horseradish sometime)

First, beat the egg with a fork. Mix in the crumbs. Crumble in the hambúrger then add everything else.

Look back at Steve's proofreading corrections.

- What misspelled words did Steve correct?
- What punctuation marks did he add or change, and why?
- How did he correct a long, stringy sentence and a run-on sentence?

Practice

Proofread the last part of Steve's paper for other mistakes. Copy these sentences and make the necessary corrections. Use a dictionary to check spellings. You should find nine proofreading errors.

Next, mix it all up with a fork or with your hands, but dont mix it too much. If the hamberger looks too gooey or feels too squishy, sprinkle some more crumbs on it. Stop ~~adding~~ mixing when the meat is soft but doesn't look wet. Finally make the hambergers. Fry them in a hot frying pan for five or six minutes on each side, but don't use any extra greace. The meat has fat in it already if you like your hambergers well done cook them a little longer.

Assignment • **Proofread Your Instructions**

Proofread your paper, using these questions as a guide.

1. Have I made appropriate paragraph breaks?
2. Have I spelled all the words correctly, checking the dictionary?

— Grammar skills checklist —

3. Have I capitalized and punctuated my sentences correctly?
4. Have I corrected any run-on sentences or sentence fragments?
5. Have I used commas correctly with compound sentences and dependent clauses?
6. Have I written noun plurals and possessives correctly?
7. Have I used commas correctly with appositives?

9 | Step Five
Make a Final Copy

Steve copied his instructions over on a clean sheet of paper as neatly as possible, and then he checked to make sure he had not made any new errors. Before he shared his paper with his class, he wanted to add an original touch.

First, he drew pictures of the various ingredients in the space around the list: a ketchup bottle, a package of hamburger, a box of crumbs, a bottle of Worcestershire sauce, a bottle of horseradish, an onion, an egg, a set of measuring spoons and cups, a fry pan, and a spatula. Then, at the bottom of the paper he attached a snapshot of himself with a chef's cap on and a spatula in his hand, frying hamburgers at a family cookout. His teacher made machine copies of his paper so that he could pass out his recipe and instructions to each of his classmates.

Assignment
- **Make a Final Copy**
- **Share Your Instructions**

A. Copy your instructions neatly on a clean sheet of paper.
B. Check your paper carefully to make sure that you made no copying mistakes.
C. Think of a way to share your instructions.

- Make a poster with photographs or drawings to illustrate your instructions. Illustrate each step, or illustrate the things that are needed in order to follow the instructions, as Steve did.
- Make an instruction booklet, or make copies of your instructions, so that someone else can use them.
- Tape record your instructions, read them aloud, or give a demonstration, as Steve did.

Verbs

1 | Kinds of Verbs

Action and Being

Every sentence has a verb. The **verb** is the word or words that make a statement about the subject. The verb is the most important part of the predicate.

Ed and Iris <u>run</u> every day.   They <u>are</u> long-distance runners.

Verbs express **action** (*run*) or **being** (*are*).

It is easy to see that *run* is an action verb. Verbs like *run, throw, sew, write, boil*, all refer to obvious physical action. Verbs like *think, worry, consider*, are also action verbs. They refer to mental action.

Verbs that express a state of being do not refer to any action at all, physical or mental. Instead, they tell what the subject is.

Iris <u>is</u> a runner.   Her time <u>was</u> good today.

Is and *was* are forms of *be*, along with *am, are, were, been, being*. Some other verbs that can express being are listed below.

appear	feel	look	seem	sound	taste
become	grow	remain	smell	stay	

Some of these verbs can also be used as action verbs.

Being   **Action**

Ms. Wiles <u>grew</u> old.   Ms. Wiles <u>grew</u> tomatoes.

The beans <u>tasted</u> salty.   The cook <u>tasted</u> the beans.

If you can substitute a form of *be* for the verb, it is probably a verb of being.

The beans <u>tasted</u> salty. = The beans <u>are</u> salty.

Try It Out

Find each verb. Does it express being or action?

1. Ann chopped the wood.
2. Was Roscoe late again?
3. The turtle won the race.
4. I preferred the blue tie.
5. Al and Rose are the losers.
6. The milk smells spoiled.
7. I believed the forecast.
8. Does he appear lonely?

Main Verbs and Helping Verbs

A verb like *run, think,* or *taste* is called a **main verb**. Main verbs carry the main meaning of the predicate. Without them, you would not be able to say much about what the subject does or is. Sometimes, though, a main verb needs help from other verbs to complete its meaning. A verb that helps the main verb is called a **helping** or **auxiliary verb**. A main verb and its helping verb or verbs form a **verb phrase**.

> Iris is running well today.
> Soon she will have been running for an hour.

Running is the main verb in both of the underlined verb phrases above. What are the helping verbs?

The most common helping verbs are listed below.

be, am, are, is,	have, has, had	can, could	will, would
was, were, been	do, does, did	shall, should	may, might

Be, have, and *do* can be used as both main verbs and helping verbs. The uses are quite different. (See also pp. 110-111.)

> MAIN: Iris is not tired. She has an athlete's endurance.
> HELPING: She is still running. She has run eight miles.

Sometimes a helping verb is hidden in a contraction. The helping verbs are underscored in the following sentences.

> She's running well today.   Soon she'll be ready for the race.

Certain words can interrupt a verb phrase.

> Do you see any signs?   I can't find the map.
> I cannot learn this route.   I shall never learn it.

The subject of an interrogative sentence, the contraction *n't*, and words like *not, never, always, still,* and *really* are never considered part of the verb phrase.

Try It Out

Find the verb phrase in each sentence. Then locate the main verb and the helping verb or verbs.

1. Pietro has been swimming since nine o'clock this morning.
2. The heat has certainly been oppressive for the last week.

3. We may not have thunderstorms this afternoon after all.
4. A swim in a cold mountain stream will always refresh us.
5. Where did you find that elegant velvet dress?
6. Ervin should have arrived an hour ago.
7. He couldn't have mistaken the date of the meeting.
8. Does Alice know anything about hermit crabs?
9. The meal cannot be served until seven o'clock.
10. By Friday Joni will have been working at the garage for a week.

▶ A **verb** expresses action, either physical or mental, or it expresses a state of being.
▶ A **verb phrase** includes a main verb and one or more helping or auxiliary verbs.
▶ The **main verb** expresses the action or being.
▶ The **helping** or **auxiliary verb** or verbs help complete the meaning of the main verb.

Written Practice

Copy every verb phrase, underlining the main verb. After the verb phrase, write *action* or *being* to tell what it expresses.

1. Sanford's party is planned for this afternoon.
2. How many people has he invited?
3. There will not be more than ten people there.
4. Sanford hasn't invited everyone from the softball team.
5. He couldn't possibly have asked all of his teammates.
6. He might hurt someone's feelings, but he has invited only three of them.
7. The weather has really remained cooperative.
8. Sanford will probably receive several miniature cars as gifts.
9. Doesn't he have dozens of miniature cars in his collection?
10. By December he will have been collecting them for four years.
11. A few of the models may become very valuable.
12. A cake in the shape of a car should have been ordered for him.

● **Writing Sentences**   Write a passage of five to six sentences describing a special event—a party, a game, a visit to or from someone, for example. Underline every verb and verb phrase.

2 | Tenses

Verbs tell not only what action is taking place, but also *when* the action takes place. This time-telling feature of verbs is called **tense**. Verbs use different tenses to express different times.

Previously we <u>rehearsed</u> all day. (*past*)
Now we <u>rehearse</u> in the afternoon. (*present*)
Tomorrow we <u>will rehearse</u> in the morning. (*future*)

Principal Parts

To construct their tenses, verbs use forms called **principal parts**.

Verb	Present Participle	Past	Past Participle
jump	(is) jumping	jumped	(have) jumped
chop	(is) chopping	chopped	(have) chopped
type	(is) typing	typed	(have) typed
cry	(is) crying	cried	(have) cried

There are four principal parts. The first is the verb itself: *jump*. The second principal part is the **present participle**. It is formed by adding *-ing* to the verb: *jumping*. The present participle is used with the helping verb *be*: *is jumping*.

The other two principal parts are the **past** and the **past participle**. In regular verbs, they are formed by adding *-ed* or *-d* to the verb: *jumped*. The past participle is used with the helping verb *have*: *have jumped*.

Look at the list of principal parts above. A few spelling changes regularly take place.

1. A one-syllable verb that ends in a single consonant usually doubles the consonant before *-ing* or *-ed*: *chopping*.
2. Verbs ending in *-e* drop the *e* before *-ing*: *typing*.
3. Verbs ending in a consonant + *-y* change the *y* to *i* before *-ed*: *cried*.

Try It Out

Give the principal parts of each verb. Are there any spelling changes?

1. wish **2.** open **3.** try **4.** expect **5.** compare **6.** plan

Simple and Perfect Tenses

The three simple tenses are the **present tense**, the **past tense**, and the **future tense**.

PRESENT: They <u>walk</u> home on Broadway almost every day.
PAST: Yesterday they <u>walked</u> home a different way.
FUTURE: Tomorrow they <u>will walk</u> on Broadway again.

The present tense is used for situations that exist now or for repeated situations, like walking home the same way every day. The past tense is used for situations that occurred in the past. The future tense is used for situations that will occur in the future.

The present tense is formed from the first principal part. When it is used with *she, he, it,* or a singular noun, *-s* is added to the verb.

The ostrich <u>hides</u> its head.   It <u>feels</u> frightened.

The past tense is the third principal part. It is formed by adding *-d* or *-ed* to the basic verb form: *bothered, liked.*

The future tense is formed with the helping verb *will* (or sometimes *shall*) and the first principal part: *will bother, will like.*

In addition to these three simple tenses, all verbs use three **perfect tenses** to express time. There is a perfect tense for every simple tense: the **present perfect**, the **past perfect**, and the **future perfect**. All three perfect tenses are formed with *have* and the past participle.

PRESENT PERFECT: I <u>have finished</u> my essay.
PAST PERFECT: I <u>had finished</u> before the bell rang.
FUTURE PERFECT: I <u>shall have finished</u> by the time the bell rings.

The present perfect is used to talk about something that took place at some time in the past and may still be going on: *I have studied all day* (and am still studying). The past perfect is used to tell about something that took place before something else in the past: *When she came, I had already left.* The future perfect is used to tell about something that will take place before something else in the future: *I will have turned thirteen by next Sunday.* (The uses of the tenses are discussed further on pages 108-109.)

The helping verb *have* shows the tense. The **present perfect** is formed with the present tense of *have* plus the past participle. The **past perfect** is formed with the past tense of *have* plus the past participle. The **future perfect** is formed with the future tense of *have* plus the past participle.

Try It Out

Give the three simple tenses and the three perfect tenses of each verb. First use *she* as the subject; then use *they*.

1. open   **2.** mix   **3.** turn   **4.** step   **5.** survive

---

▸ Every verb has four **principal parts**: the verb, the present participle, the past, and the past participle.

The principal parts of a verb are used to show different time, or tense. Verbs have six tenses, three simple and three perfect.

The **present tense** is formed from the basic verb form. The letters *-s* and *-es* are added with *he, she, it,* or a singular noun.

The **past tense** is formed with the verb plus *-d* or *-ed*.

The **future tense** is formed with the verb plus *will* or *shall*.

The three perfect tenses—**present perfect**, **past perfect**, and **future perfect**—are formed with *have* and the past participle.

Written Practice

A. Write all six tenses for each verb. Use *he* as the subject.

    1. start   **2.** play   **3.** skip   **4.** deny   **5.** finish   **6.** tickle

B. Write the verb form indicated.

    7. Elena ＿＿ our club for three years. (represent, *present perfect*)
    8. The team ＿＿ the heat and the opponent. (conquer, *past*)
    9. By the time we get there, they ＿＿ dinner. (start, *future perfect*)
    10. Congress has promised that it ＿＿ that proposal. (consider, *future*)
    11. Before he was asked, Tim ＿＿ the canteens. (fill, *past perfect*)
    12. When Rufus receives a letter, he ＿＿. (reply, *present*)
    13. If he attends the next game, he ＿＿ every one. (attend, *future perfect*)
    14. Ted ＿＿ the ball repeatedly. (fumble, *present perfect*)

• **Writing Sentences**   Use each of the perfect tenses in a sentence of your own.

3 | Irregular Verbs

A **regular verb** forms the past and past participle by adding -d or -ed. An **irregular verb** forms the past and past participle differently. The principal parts of each irregular verb have to be learned. As you are learning them, it may help you to use the verb forms in short sentences such as these.

Today I speak.　　　　　　　Yesterday I spoke.
Now I am speaking.　　　　　Often I have spoken.

Always use *have* when you are learning the past participle. It will help you to distinguish the participle form from the past form.

Here are the principal parts of some common irregular verbs. Use the dictionary to check the principal parts of other verbs.

Verb	Present Participle	Past	Past Participle
begin	beginning	began	begun
break	breaking	broke	broken
bring	bringing	brought	brought
catch	catching	caught	caught
choose	choosing	chose	chosen
cost	costing	cost	cost
do	doing	did	done
fly	flying	flew	flown
go	going	went	gone
grow	growing	grew	grown
have	having	had	had
know	knowing	knew	known
lose	losing	lost	lost
put	putting	put	put
ride	riding	rode	ridden
sing	singing	sang	sung
sit	sitting	sat	sat
speak	speaking	spoke	spoken
swim	swimming	swam	swum
take	taking	took	taken
think	thinking	thought	thought
throw	throwing	threw	thrown
wear	wearing	wore	worn

Try It Out

Give the four principal parts of each of these irregular verbs.

1. begin	**3.** choose	**5.** fly	**7.** have	**9.** sit
2. bring	**4.** do	**6.** go	**8.** know	**10.** take

> ▸ **Irregular verbs** do not add -*d* or -*ed* to form the past and past participle.
>
> The principal parts of each irregular verb must be learned.

Written Practice

A. Write the principal parts of each verb. Use your dictionary.

1. blow	**6.** give
2. come	**7.** run
3. drive	**8.** see
4. fall	**9.** teach
5. find	**10.** write

B. Write the past or past participle form of the verb in parentheses.

(**11**) Our science class (go) on a nature hike last week. (**12**) Our teacher, Mr. Elias, had (drive) to the area several times and (know) the trails. (**13**) He had (give) us careful instructions. (**14**) Everyone (bring) a lunch and (wear) sturdy shoes. (**15**) Amazingly, no one (lose) lunches or anything else.

(**16**) When the group (come) upon some footprints, Mr. Elias (speak) to us about the wildlife in the area. (**17**) Several days earlier, a thunderstorm had (blow) down several trees and had (break) many large limbs. (**18**) Someone found a squirrel's nest that had (fall) out of a tree. (**19**) Beautiful flowers (grow) wild, bright birds (fly) by, and small animals (run) past.

(**20**) After many other discoveries, Mr. Elias (think) it was time to leave. (**21**) We (sing) on the bus going back. (**22**) Then we (write) reports describing what we had (see). (**23**) We (find) that the trip had (teach) us a great deal.

● **Writing Sentences** Choose four irregular past tense forms and four irregular past participles. Write a sentence for each form.

4 | Using Tenses Correctly

Shifts in Tense

The sentences that follow describe certain events. Can you tell when these events took place?

IMPROPER SHIFT: When I came home, I sit down and study.

IMPROPER SHIFT: The car comes to a stop, and three men got out.

The first event begins in the past and then shifts suddenly to the present. The second event begins in the present and then leaps backward to the past. Tense expresses time. The tense should not change unless the time changes.

PRESENT: When I come home, I sit down and study.

PAST: The car came to a stop, and three men got out.

Needless shifts in tenses are confusing wherever they occur—within a sentence, between sentences, within a paragraph, or within a story.

IMPROPER SHIFTS: Brenda knew she was right. The lion tamer is guilty. Now, how could she prove what she knows? She had to think of a plan before the next performance begins.

PRESENT: Brenda knows she is right. The lion tamer is guilty. Now, how can she prove what she knows? She has to think of a plan before the next performance begins.

PAST: Brenda knew she was right. The lion tamer was guilty. Now, how could she prove what she knew? She had to think of a plan before the next performance began.

You do not always have to express yourself in the same tense. Time changes, and so do tenses.

PROPER SHIFT: Brenda is certain that she will solve the problem.

PROPER SHIFT: Yesterday the bus was early, but today it is late.

PROPER SHIFT: "Where is my coach?" wondered Cinderella.

Not all changes in tense are incorrect; only needless changes are. Pay attention to tense when you write.

Try It Out

Correct any needless shifts in tense.

(1) After Leopold and Sara returned from the concert, they want to hear more music. **(2)** Sara chooses four albums and placed them by the record player. **(3)** After she started the first record, she goes to the kitchen and made some sandwiches. **(4)** When she came back, Leopold announces that he really wanted to hear a different record. **(5)** Patiently, but with a sigh, Sara put down her sandwich, removes the record, and searched for Leopold's song.

Perfect Tenses

As you have seen, there are times when you must shift tenses. What tenses are used in this sentence?

After Joe <u>had seen</u> the movie, he <u>read</u> the book.

Which action came first? When you are writing about two related actions, use the past perfect for the one that came first. The past perfect *had seen* tells you that the seeing came before the reading. What do the tenses in this sentence tell you?

FAULTY: Halfway home, Joe remembered that he forgot his keys.

This sentence implies that Joe remembered and forgot at the same time. The past perfect makes clear which action came first.

IMPROVED: Halfway home, Joe <u>remembered</u> that he <u>had forgotten</u> his keys.

Just as the past and past perfect are used together, so are the present and the future perfect. The future perfect expresses the action that will take place first.

By the time Joe <u>walks</u> back to school, everyone <u>will have left</u>.

The present perfect expresses an action that occurred at an unspecified time in the past. The action may or may not still be going on.

FAULTY: I have seen Todd last week.
CORRECT: I <u>saw</u> Todd last week. *(past tense: occurred in the past, at a definite time)*
CORRECT: I <u>have seen</u> Todd only once this week. *(present perfect: occurred at some indefinite time in the past)*

Try It Out

Identify the tense of each underlined verb.

1. Victor <u>had revealed</u> the secret before he <u>realized</u> it.
2. Even after Iris <u>had chosen</u> the dress, she still <u>wasn't</u> sure about it.
3. Natalie <u>has attended</u> a different school every year.
4. By the time we <u>get</u> home, our guests <u>will have arrived</u>.
5. He <u>had turned</u> off the lights before he <u>left</u> the house.
6. Although Bettina <u>had studied</u>, she <u>found</u> the test rather difficult.
7. I <u>have</u> never <u>seen</u> a more exciting play.
8. By the time we <u>arrive</u>, she <u>will have hidden</u> the gift.
9. Detective Casey <u>has known</u> the truth for a long time.
10. Before we <u>reach</u> the halfway mark, Sybil <u>will have finished</u>.

Do not shift from one tense to another unnecessarily.

Use the past perfect to discuss the earlier of two related past actions and the past tense to express the later action.

Use the future perfect to express the earlier of two related future actions and the present to express the later action.

Use the present perfect to express an action that occurred at an unspecified time in the past.

Written Practice

Rewrite each sentence. Correct all needless shifts in tense.

(**1**) The television special had been on for only ten minutes when Maureen rose from her chair. (**2**) The program was boring, and she does not want to watch it. (**3**) Her brother, however, would not watch anything else. (**4**) Maureen searches for a particular book, but she could not find it. (**5**) Then she settled for a mystery that seems interesting. (**6**) Several pages into the book, she realizes that she will have read it already. (**7**) Impatiently, she tossed it aside. (**8**) Next she picks up a magazine and starts to read an article. (**9**) She realized that the article is about the boring television program she had started to watch earlier. (**10**) Finally, she gave up and goes to bed. (**11**) Fortunately, her dreams were pleasant. (**12**) She woke up cheerful.

• **Writing Paragraphs**   Write about an adventure. Use tenses correctly.

5 | Forms of *be, have, do*

Be, have, and *do* can be used as both main and helping verbs.

Main Verbs	**Helping Verbs**
Whales are not fish.	We are going to the new museum.
Whales have flippers.	We have gone to the new museum.
Whales do what they like.	Do you like the museum?

Be as a main verb expresses a state of being. As a helping verb, *be* is used with the present participle in verb phrases.

Have as a main verb usually means "own, possess." As a helping verb, it is used with the past participle to form the perfect tenses.

Do as a main verb generally means "to carry out, create, put into action." As a helping verb, *do* forms questions and negatives.

Do you like the museum?   We do not like that exhibit.

Do can also be used to create the emphatic form. The emphatic form is used to emphasize the main verb.

I do like the museum.   Alvin really did see a whale.

All three verbs can form contractions with *not: isn't, hasn't, don't.*
Be, have, and *do* are all irregular. Be sure that you know their forms.

Be

	Present	**Past**	**Future**
I	am	was	shall be
she, he, it	is	was	will be
we, you, they	are	were	will be

	Present Perfect	**Past Perfect**	**Future Perfect**
I	have been	had been	shall have been
she, he, it	has been	had been	will have been
we, you, they	have been	had been	will have been

Have

	Present	**Past**	**Future**
I, we, you, they	have	had	will (shall) have
she, he, it	has	had	will have

	Present Perfect	Past Perfect	Future Perfect
I, we, you, they	have had	had had	will (shall) have had
she, he, it	has had	had had	will have had

Do

	Present	Past	Future
I, we, you, they	do	did	will (shall) do
she, he, it	does	did	will do

	Present Perfect	Past Perfect	Future Perfect
I, we, you, they	have done	had done	will (shall) have done
she, he, it	has done	had done	will have done

Try It Out

Choose the correct form.

(**1**) The Dunns (be, is, are) good farmers, but the weather (been, has been, have been) very dry this year. (**2**) They (doesn't, don't) know what they will do if it (doesn't, don't) rain. (**3**) The crops (hasn't done, haven't done) well at all, and the animals (has had, have had) their problems, too. (**4**) They (does, do) hope it rains soon.

> *Be,* *have,* and *do* can be used both as main verbs and as helping verbs. They are irregular in form.

Written Practice

Write the correct form.

(**1**) The crops (has had, have had) no rain for weeks. (**2**) They (been, has been, have been) wilting. (**3**) We (done, has done, have done) everything we can. (**4**) (Does, Do) the sky look dark, or (am, is) I imagining it? (**5**) I (does, do) believe it (be, am, is) raining!

● **Writing Sentences** Write two sentences with *be* as a helping verb and two with *be* as a main verb. Do the same using *have* and *do.*

6 | Progressive Forms

You know that verbs can express action in six different tenses. Sometimes, even these six forms are not enough to express all kinds of time. How does the action in these sentences differ?

Tillie flies a kite.   Tillie is flying a kite.

The sentence on the left makes a statement about something that Tillie does. The right-hand sentence says that she is doing it right now.

Forms like *is flying* are called **progressive forms** because they refer to actions *in progress*. The progressive is not another tense. Each of the six tenses has a progressive form to express continuing action. The progressive is formed by combining the helping verb *be* with the present participle of the main verb.

PRESENT PROGRESSIVE:	Sid is resting now.
PAST PROGRESSIVE:	Sid was resting.
FUTURE PROGRESSIVE:	Sid will be resting all day.
PRESENT PERFECT PROGRESSIVE:	Sid has been resting all day.
PAST PERFECT PROGRESSIVE:	Sid had been resting for an hour when we arrived.
FUTURE PERFECT PROGRESSIVE:	Sid will have been resting for an hour by the time we arrive.

The helping verb shows the tense. In the present progressive, *be* is in the present tense; in the future progressive, *be* is in the future tense; in the past perfect progressive, *be* is in the past perfect tense; and so on.

The progressive form can create some complicated-sounding verb phrases: *will have been resting*. Still, there will be times when you need the progressive to say exactly what you want to say. Imagine you want to tell someone how hard your friend has been working. The future perfect progressive is the way to say it.

By noon, he will have been working for three hours straight.

Progressive Forms of *Live*

	Present	**Past**	**Future**
I	am living	was living	shall be living
she, he, it	is living	was living	will be living
you, we, they	are living	were living	will be living

	Present Perfect	**Past Perfect**	**Future Perfect**
I	have been living	had been living	shall have been living
she, he, it	has been living	had been living	will have been living
you, we, they	have been living	had been living	will have been living

Try It Out

First determine the tense of the verbs in parentheses. Then change each verb to the corresponding progressive form.

1. Emilio (has worked) since nine, and at five he (will go) home.
2. The squirrel (stands) very still and (watches) the cat suspiciously.
3. By next week, Hazel (will have read) *War and Peace* for a month.
4. The artist (had painted) landscapes, but he (switched) to seascapes.

> Each tense has a progressive form to express continuing action.
> The progressive is formed with *be* and the present participle.

Written Practice

Change each underlined verb to the corresponding progressive form.

1. Lil had washed the car all morning but finally finished the job.
2. I shall sell seashells by the seashore this afternoon.
3. The reliable zinnias have bloomed magnificently for weeks.
4. The relief pitcher walks to the mound with a determined stride.
5. In five minutes we shall have stood in this line for two hours.

• **Writing Sentences** Use each verb form in two different sentences.

6. were repairing 7. will have been walking 8. has been cooking

7 | Linking Verbs

Verbs, you will recall, can express action or being. A verb that expresses being is called a **linking verb** because it links the subject with a word in the predicate.

Mahalia Jackson was a singer.   Those yellow roses are beautiful.

The word in the predicate can be a noun (or pronoun) like *singer*, or it can be an adjective like *beautiful* (see pp. 152–153). Whether it is a noun or an adjective, the word always refers to the subject. In many cases the linking verb acts like an equals sign in that the predicate and the subject refer to the same person or thing.

Mahalia Jackson = singer

If you substitute an action verb for the linking verb, the predicate and the subject no longer refer to the same person or thing.

Mahalia Jackson listened to a singer.

The verb *be* is the most common linking verb, but it is not the only one. Other verbs that can be used as linking verbs include these.

appear	feel	look	seem	smell	taste
become	grow	remain	stay	sound	

All forms of these verbs are used as linking verbs.

The apple might have been too green.

A seed can remain dormant for years.

Remember that some of these verbs can be used as action verbs, too.

Linking	**Action**
The panda looked happy.	The panda looked around him.
Ruth feels content.	Ruth feels the wind on her face.
The kumquat tasted good.	I tasted the kumquat.

In most cases, if you can substitute a form of *be* for the verb, then it is a linking verb.

The panda looked happy. The panda was happy.
The kumquat tasted good. The kumquat was good.

Try It Out

Which verbs are linking verbs?

1. Raymond grew thoughtful.
2. He looked at the mobile by Alexander Calder.
3. The term *mobile* was invented by the artist Marcel Duchamp.
4. The bell sounded muffled.
5. Had it been covered with a thick cloth?
6. Joyce immediately sounded the alarm.
7. Under other conditions, Franklin might have been a success.
8. The garlic in the sauce smelled strong but good.
9. The deer had smelled the dogs and run away.
10. The city could become a very different world at night.
11. The actual events would remain a mystery forever.
12. Donna will be a fearless test pilot.

> ▶ A **linking verb** expresses being. It links the subject with a word in the predicate that refers to the subject.

Written Practice

List each verb and write *action* or *linking* beside it.

1. Beth felt a cold rush of air and grew anxious.
2. The welcoming committee should be arriving at the airport now.
3. Jeanine looked everywhere for her lost earring.
4. The mosquito larvae were wiggling in the puddle.
5. The blue cheese smelled strong and tasted delicious.
6. The trumpets sounded brassy in the last selection.
7. The forest looks peaceful and green after yesterday's rain.
8. Ari should have remained a musician.
9. Should she become a doctor, or is law a better field for her?
10. Do you feel well today?
11. The fussy cat smelled the food in her dish and looked unhappy.
12. To everyone's surprise, the dinner bell was sounding.

- **Writing Sentences**   Write eight to ten sentences about a person you admire. Try to give details about the person's activities, likes and dislikes, appearance, voice, personality. Use linking verbs.

8 | Transitive and Intransitive Verbs

Most verbs express action. Often that action is "sent" to another word in the predicate. To what or to whom is the action sent in each of these sentences?

The pitcher threw the ball.   The crowd watched the batter.

The pitcher threw something. The crowd watched someone. In each case, something or someone receives the action of the verb. A verb that sends action to something or someone named in the predicate is called **a transitive verb**. *Threw* and *watched* in these sentences are transitive verbs.

The noun (or pronoun) that receives the action of a transitive verb is called an **object**. *Ball* and *batter* in the sentences above are objects. A transitive verb always has one or more objects.

Are the verbs in these sentences transitive?

Mr. Kiley disappeared again.   The crowd watched silently.

Did Mr. Kiley disappear something? Did the crowd watch someone? No nouns receive the action of the verbs in these sentences. A verb that does not have an object is called an **intransitive verb**. *Disappeared* and *watched* are intransitive verbs in the sentences above.

Look again at the sentences with *watched*.

TRANSITIVE VERB: The crowd watched the batter.
INTRANSITIVE VERB: The crowd watched silently.

Watch, like many verbs, can be used as either a transitive or an intransitive verb. Which sentence below contains a transitive verb?

Joy draws fine caricatures.   Joy draws with a felt-tip pen.

To determine how a verb is used, ask "What?" or "Whom?" after the verb. If there is an answer, then the verb is transitive. Draws what? Draws caricatures. The sentence on the left has a transitive verb.

The sentence on the right also has words following the verb. *With a felt-tip pen*, however, does not answer the question "Draws what or whom?" The verb in this sentence is intransitive.

Linking verbs are always intransitive. They do not express action.

Try It Out

Identify the verbs in these sentences as transitive or intransitive.

1. Kyle very carefully hung the picture on the wall.
2. First he put some tape on the wall.
3. The tape would protect the plaster.
4. He placed a nail in the center of the tape and hammered gently.
5. Fortunately, the plaster did not crack under the tape.
6. The picture felt heavy to Lyle.
7. He attached strong wire to the back of the picture frame.
8. Finally, he lowered the picture over the nail.
9. Kyle stepped back from the picture.
10. It looked a little crooked to him.

> ▸ A **transitive verb** expresses action that is sent to a noun or pronoun in the predicate.
> ▸ The word that receives the action is the **object** of the verb.
> ▸ An **intransitive verb** does not have an object.
> Linking verbs are always intransitive.

Written Practice

List each verb. Label it *transitive* or *intransitive*.

(1) The heavy rains had destroyed part of the road. (2) After a few weeks, a road crew arrived at the spot. (3) First, trucks dumped several loads of dirt and rocks in a pile. (4) The workers shoveled dirt into the uneven places. (5) At lunchtime, they sat on some rocks and ate their sandwiches. (6) Several hours of work remained for the workers. (7) Next the road grader came to the site. (8) It pushed piles of dirt into the washed-out area. (9) The grader moved back and forth several times. (10) The roller compacted the dirt. (11) The workers left the area in the afternoon. (12) Lightly at first, the rain began again.

- **Writing Sentences** Have you ever watched anything being repaired—a road, a bicycle, a watch, a loose button, a torn hem? Write five to ten sentences about it. When you have finished, write *transitive* or *intransitive* above each main verb.

9 | Active and Passive Voices

Look at these sentences.

Roger throws the discus.   The discus is thrown by Roger.
Mia teaches guitar lessons.   Guitar lessons are taught by Mia.

In the first sentence on the left, *Roger* is the subject. Roger does the throwing—the subject performs the action. In the first sentence on the right, *discus* is the subject, but the discus does not do the throwing. The subject is the *receiver* of the action rather than the doer. What is the subject of the second sentence on the left? Does it perform the action or receive it? How about the subject of the second sentence on the right?

When the subject *performs* the action, as it does in most sentences, the verb is said to be in the **active voice.** When the subject *receives* the action, the verb is said to be in the **passive voice**.

Notice how this pair of sentences is related.

Laurie dug the hole. *(active)*   The hole was dug by Laurie. *(passive)*

1. The object in the active sentence becomes the subject in the passive.
2. The subject of the active sentence moves to the predicate of the passive.
3. The verb in the active voice becomes a past participle in the passive voice.

The performer of the action need not appear in a passive sentence.

The hole was dug. (*by someone*)

Can you turn this sentence into a passive sentence?

Mr. Sato travels to Tokyo frequently.

Only transitive verbs can be made passive. If there is no object, then there is nothing to become the subject of a passive verb.

Try It Out

A. Which verbs are in the active voice? Which are in the passive?

1. *Pride and Prejudice* was written by Jane Austen.
2. Austen also wrote *Emma*.

3. The paintings had been hung by the artist herself.
4. Brian discovered a hidden cave by the stream.
5. The clock was repaired at last.

B. Change each active sentence to passive and each passive sentence to active.

6. The tasks were assigned by Mr. Hennessey.
7. Page completed the assignment.
8. Sid spotted the mountain peak.
9. Raoul's broken leg was set by the doctor.
10. The missing pages were found by Donna.

▸ A verb is in the **active voice** if the subject performs the action.
▸ A verb is in the **passive voice** if the subject receives the action.

Written Practice

A. List each verb and label it *active* or *passive*.

(**1**) The train had rolled into the station by five o'clock. (**2**) Higgins's luggage was taken by the porter, and he was led to his compartment. (**3**) After a few miles, he was lulled to sleep by the motion of the train. (**4**) He was moaning in his sleep. (**5**) Suddenly, he was awakened by the conductor's voice. (**6**) The conductor stood by his side. (**7**) Higgins had slept through the whole trip.

B. Rewrite each active sentence in the passive voice. Rewrite each passive sentence in the active voice.

8. The long downfield pass was dropped by Bennett.
9. The hikers spotted some animal tracks.
10. Peter Piper picked a peck of pickled peppers.
11. The beams were weakened by the hungry termites.

● **Writing Sentences**   Use each verb in two sentences. First use the verb in the active voice and then in the passive voice.

12. see   **13.** frighten   **14.** construct   **15.** follow   **16.** drop

10 | Subject-Verb Agreement

Singular and Plural Subjects

A verb must agree with its subject in number. A singular subject must have a singular verb, and a plural subject must have a plural verb.

	Singular	**Plural**
PRESENT:	The kitten <u>plays</u>. He <u>runs</u>.	The kittens <u>play</u>. They <u>run</u>.

In the present tense, the verb form changes. It adds *-s* to agree with a singular noun or with *he*, *she*, or *it*: *play–plays*, *run–runs*. In the past, the form stays the same for both singular and plural subjects: *played*, *ran*. Recall that the verb *be* is an exception to this rule (see p. 110).

Keep in mind that nouns add *-s* to become plural forms, while present tense verbs add *-s* to become singular forms.

Try It Out

Choose the verb form in parentheses that agrees with the subject.

1. The bottles (is, are) on the table.
2. The avalanche (begins, begin) slowly.
3. The telephone (does, do) not ring loudly enough.
4. The strutting peacocks (spreads, spread) their tails proudly.

Compound Subjects

Compound subjects can require either a singular or a plural verb, depending upon how the compounds are joined.

1. When two or more subjects are joined by *and*, the verb is plural.

   The **telephone and** the **doorbell** <u>are ringing</u>.
   The **knight and** the **dragon** <u>are eyeing</u> each other warily.

2. When two or more subjects are joined by *or* or *nor* (or *either . . . or*, *neither . . . nor*), the verb agrees with the noun nearest to it.

   Michele, Jan, or Everett <u>is</u> likely to win the race.
   Neither the **players nor** the **coach** <u>seems</u> nervous.
   The **senator or** her **aides** <u>are</u> responding to all inquiries.

Try It Out

Select the correct verb form from the pair in parentheses.

1. Cy or Ty (plays, play) basketball while the other one plays hockey.
2. The Wexler children and Rachel (gets, get) along well together.
3. Neither the insects nor the spider (frightens, frighten) me.
4. *Moby Dick* and *Billy Budd* (was, were) written by Herman Melville.
5. The teacher or the students (has, have) the wrong answer.
6. Carrots, peas, or a potato (accompanies, accompany) the chicken.

Titles and Names

A title or a name may look plural because it ends in *-s* or because it includes nouns joined by *and*. However, if the thing named is considered to be a single thing, it takes a singular verb.

> **Anthony and Cleopatra** was written by Shakespeare.
> **The United States** is over two hundred years old.
> **Styx, Baer and Fuller** sells quality clothing in St. Louis.

Certain nouns ending in *-s* are always regarded as singular.

> **Mumps** is no longer a common childhood ailment.
> The **news** was encouraging today.

Other nouns ending in *-s* are regarded as plural even though they refer to a single thing.

> The **scissors** have been misplaced again.
> Those **pants** are in the washing machine.

Try It Out

Choose the correct verb form from the pair in parentheses.

1. Farrar, Straus and Giroux (has, have) hired a new editor.
2. The United Nations (is, are) housed in New York City.
3. The scissors (does, do) not cut anything at all.
4. (Is, Are) mathematics required in eighth grade?
5. "The Waltons" (was, were) a popular television program.
6. *Little Women* (was, were) written by Louisa May Alcott.
7. *People* (tells, tell) about the lives of celebrities.
8. The news (is, are) broadcast three times daily on that station.

Collective Nouns

A collective noun names a group that is thought of as a unit—*team, herd, flock, orchestra*, for example. Usually a collective noun is regarded as singular and takes a singular verb. When the sentence refers to the individuals in the group, however, the collective noun is regarded as plural and takes a plural verb.

SINGULAR: The **team** is playing well tonight.
PLURAL: The **team** are playing against one another.

When a team plays well, it is usually working as a unit and can be thought of as singular. If the team members are not playing together but are trying to make individual plays, they can be thought of as individuals. Here are similar examples with *family*, another collective noun.

SINGULAR: The **family** is going to the seashore for the summer.
PLURAL: The **family** are all going to different places this summer.

Terms that refer to amounts, such as money, time, weight, measurements, or fractions, are usually considered singular when thought of as a single unit and plural when thought of as separate units.

SINGULAR: **Ten dollars** is too much for that silly hat.
PLURAL: **Ten quarters** are in each cup.
SINGULAR: **Twelve years** seems like a long time.
PLURAL: Those **twelve years** are important ones.

Try It Out

Choose the correct verb forms from the pairs in parentheses.

1. Three quarters of an hour (has, have) passed already.
2. The jury (has, have) disagreed on every issue.
3. The flock (is, are) flying in formation.
4. Ten pounds (is, are) enough for now.

122

> A subject and verb must agree in number.
> A compound subject with *and* takes a plural verb. A compound subject with *or* takes a verb that agrees with the nearer noun.
> A title or name of a single thing takes a singular verb.
> A collective noun takes a singular verb unless the group's members are referred to.
> A noun referring to an amount usually takes a singular verb unless the individual units are referred to.

Written Practice

If the underlined verb form is correct, write *correct*. If it is not correct, write the correct form.

1. *The Brothers Karamazov* is a famous Russian novel.
2. Fifteen gallons of punch were prepared for the prom.
3. The budget committee have never agreed on anything.
4. Ducks Unlimited is dedicated to the preservation of wild fowl.
5. When Felicia and Ramon arrives, the whole family will be here.
6. Neither the dictionary nor the thesaurus are on the shelf.
7. Bananas, raisins, or applesauce goes well with the cereal.
8. The flock slink slowly to the sea.
9. The forceps seems to have disappeared.
10. A sand dollar live in the ocean, not in a bank.
11. Either the shutter speed or the lens openings were set wrong.
12. Chiang, Marvin, and Yvonne is going to medical school.
13. *The Globe and Mail* is published in Canada.
14. Physics are taught four times a week.

● **Writing Sentences**   Write sentences with present tense verbs, using these subjects.

15. General Motors
16. Jack and Jill
17. ten minutes
18. *Better Homes and Gardens*
19. some leaves or a branch
20. neither rain nor snow
21. *Star Wars*
22. chorus
23. jeans

11 | Inverted and Interrupted Order

Inverted Order

You know from your study of sentences that the subject is not always found at the beginning of a sentence. No matter where the subject appears, the basic rule of agreement still holds: the subject and verb must always agree.

A sentence that begins with the subject is in **natural order**. A sentence that begins with all or part of the predicate is in **inverted order**. Which order describes these interrogative sentences?

Where <u>is</u> the **car** with the dents?   Have **Brad** and **Sam** <u>called</u> you?

In most interrogative sentences, the subject is found after the helping verb. Subject and verb still must agree: *car is; Brad, Sam, have called.*

In sentences that begin with *there* or *here*, the subject again follows the verb. Do subject and verb still agree?

There <u>are</u> two **roads** to the zoo.   Here <u>is</u> the **book** on bees.

In some inverted sentences, the subjects move to the very end. Even here, the verb must agree with the subject.

By the pond <u>live</u> four **ducks**.   Among the trees <u>walks</u> a **deer**.

In deciding whether a verb should be singular or plural, your first step should be to find the subject. Then make the verb agree with it.

Try It Out

Find the subject and then select the verb form that agrees with it.

1. (Has, Have) Angus and Martha turned in the report?
2. There (is, are) two correct answers to the problem.
3. Down the window (crawls, crawl) a spider and an ant.
4. What (does, do) the experts recommend for the old building?
5. Here (is, are) the missing photographs under the tablecloth.
6. Next to the road (struts, strut) an irritable goose.
7. (Has, Have) you ever seen a stranger-looking house?
8. Here (is, are) my schedule for the next two weeks.

Interrupted Order

Do not automatically make the verb agree with the nearest noun, for it may not be the subject. Another noun may appear between the subject and the verb. Find the subject and make the verb agree with that.

The **plants** in the kitchen <u>are growing</u> too fast.
The **clocks** on the wall all <u>tell</u> the same time.
Kiri, one of the marchers, <u>is</u> in my music class.

Try It Out

1. Fred, together with his nieces, (is, are) going to the soccer match.
2. The composer of the songs (seems, seem) imaginative.
3. The stones in his collection (is, are) semi-precious.
4. The book on top of the shelves (has, have) not been catalogued.

Subject and verb must always agree, no matter where the subject is.
First find the subject. Then make the verb agree with it.

Written Practice

If the underlined verb form is correct, write *correct*. If it is incorrect, write the correct form.

1. The photographs on that page <u>are</u> out of focus.
2. There <u>is</u> three kinds of trout in the Battenkill River.
3. When <u>is</u> Peter and Mimi leaving for the party?
4. Here <u>are</u> the list of senators and their committees.
5. <u>Does</u> the French and Laughlin Company repair chimneys?
6. The bouquet of yellow roses <u>light</u> up the room.
7. Near the corner <u>stand</u> Minnie and her husband Mickey.
8. The earthquakes in Italy <u>were</u> severe that year.
9. Why <u>don't</u> Manuel check the horses?
10. Cora, one of the scouts, <u>have dropped</u> her flashlight.

- **Writing Sentences**   Write five or ten sentences describing your classroom. Use some sentences with inverted order and some with interrupted order.

12 | Writing Well with Verbs

Using the Active and Passive

Writing well with verbs involves more than just making sure that the subject and verb agree. For example, the choice between using the active or the passive voice is usually up to you, the writer. Does it make a difference which voice you use? The answer very often is yes.

The passive voice, in general, is weaker and more awkward than the active voice.

PASSIVE: Too much money was paid by Ogden for his new wallet.
ACTIVE: Ogden paid too much money for his new wallet.

The awkwardness increases with the increased use of the passive.

PASSIVE: A perfect deep pool was found by Lucia. A fly was tied on the line by her, and it was cast on the water. In a short time, a trout was smoothly pulled by her from the pool.

Use the active voice rather than the passive when you want direct, forceful sentences.

ACTIVE: Lucia found a perfect deep pool. She tied a fly on the line and cast it into the water. In a short time, she smoothly pulled a trout from the pool.

While the active voice emphasizes the *doer* of the action, the passive voice emphasizes the *receiver* of the action. Use the passive when the doer of the action is not important or is not known.

The flag was unfurled.
A truckload of old newspapers was collected by the group.

You have learned to avoid needless shifting from one tense to another. You should also avoid needless shifting from one voice to another. Unnecessary changes in voice make your sentences harder to understand.

NEEDLESS SHIFT: Harvey remembered that the letter had not yet been mailed by him.
IMPROVED: Harvey remembered that he had not yet mailed the letter.

Try It Out

A. Change the voice from passive to active, where appropriate.

1. Her wallet was forgotten by Carolla.
2. The tickets to the game had been left on the couch.
3. The laces on Jeremy's skates were tightened by the coach.
4. The special assembly was finished by eleven.
5. His binoculars were left by Mr. Boynton by the brook.

B. Change the voice from passive to active, where appropriate.

(6) Machines were used by Clement and his father to harvest hay. (7) The special tractor was driven over the hayfield by Clement. (8) Then the hay was raked by a machine called a tedder. (9) For two days, the hay was left in the field to dry. (10) After two more rakings, the hay was baled by Clement.

Using Inverted Order

A long series of declarative sentences all starting with the subject can become monotonous. Often you can vary your sentences by inverting the order of subject and predicate. A few sentences in inverted order can help to make your writing more interesting.

MONOTONOUS: Clem scooped the hay. A large wagon was behind the baler. The hay went into the wagon. Clem drove the wagon to the barn afterward.

IMPROVED: Clem scooped the hay. There was a large wagon behind the baler. Into the wagon went the hay. Afterward, Clem drove the wagon to the barn.

Try It Out

Invert the order of subject and predicate in each sentence. Begin the sentence with all or part of the predicate, use the introductory word *there* or *here*, or make the sentence interrogative.

1. A hungry squirrel was in the birdhouse. *(use* there*)*
2. The floats came down the boulevard. *(use part of the predicate)*
3. The table hasn't been set. *(interrogative)*
4. The list of refreshments is here. *(use* here*)*

Written Practice

Rewrite the passage to improve the sentences. Change the passive to the active where appropriate. Put some of the sentences in inverted order: use *here* or *there*, put part of the predicate first, or make a sentence interrogative.

Interesting sounds of music and speech-making come from the gym. Their class play is being rehearsed by the seniors. Great excitement is in the air, for the players for the lead parts have been chosen. The leads will be played by Marguerita and Arnold, perhaps. They are both extremely talented. Marguerita and Arnold are here now. We shall ask them.

Check Your Writing

Review the passage you wrote about the senior play. Ask yourself these questions and make any needed changes.

A. Are my sentences correct?

    1. Do the subjects and verbs agree?

    2. Have I used the correct forms of regular and irregular verbs?

B. Are my sentences clear?

    1. Have I used the tense that best expresses my meaning?

    2. Have I shifted from one tense to another only when necessary?

    3. Have I shifted from one voice to another only when necessary?

C. Are my sentences direct?

Have I used the passive voice only when it is appropriate?

D. Are my sentences interesting?

Have I occasionally used sentences in inverted order?

- **Writing Sentences** Write a passage of five to ten sentences about an interesting item in the news. Review the sentences, asking yourself the questions listed above. Make appropriate changes in the passage, rewriting it if necessary.

shall, will

In very careful or formal usage, a distinction may be made between *shall* and *will*. To form the future, *shall* is used with *I* and *we*, and *will* is used with all other subjects.

I <u>shall</u> leave at eight o'clock.   The **train** <u>will</u> leave at nine.

To express determination, exactly the opposite is done. *Will* is used with *I* and *we*, and *shall* with all other subjects.

I <u>will</u> not wait any longer.   Our **efforts** <u>shall</u> not be in vain.

The differences between *shall* and *will* are no longer observed by many writers. *Will* has come to be acceptable in just about all cases. Still, it is helpful to be aware of the distinctions so that you can understand them, and, if appropriate, use them.

Try It Out

Choose the correct form for formal usage.

1. I (shall, will) not be ready to leave before it gets dark.
2. (Shall, Will) the bags be packed by five o'clock?
3. A determined effort (shall, will) be made.
4. We (shall, will) have to leave tomorrow instead.

Avoiding Expressions such as *could of, had ought*

You have learned about the helping verb *have*. *Have* can be used with *could, should, would,* and *must* to form verb phrases. These verb phrases are often used as contractions, especially when they are spoken: *could've, should've, would've, must've.* Because the spoken *-ve* sounds like *of*, the forms are sometimes written incorrectly as *could of, should of, would of, must of.* There are no such forms. Writing these phrases with *of* rather than *have* is incorrect.

Frank <u>could have</u> *(not* could of*)* been on the team.
He <u>should have</u> *(not* should of*)* trained harder.

The expression *had ought (*or *hadn't ought)* is not accepted as standard usage. Use *ought (not)* or *should (not)* instead.

You <u>ought</u> *(not* had ought*)* to be in class now.
Pam <u>should not</u> *(not* hadn't ought to*)* leave early again today.

Try It Out

Substitute the correct form for any incorrect form.

1. Hannah must of left her notebook in the auditorium.
2. You hadn't ought to be here.
3. You ought not to miss the French quiz.
4. I should of studied last night.

> *Shall* is used with *I* and *we* in very careful usage.
> Use *have,* not *of,* with *could, should, would, must.*
> Use *ought* or *should,* not *had ought.*

Written Practice

A. Write the appropriate form for very careful or formal usage.

1. I (shall, will) go to the supermarket later this afternoon.
2. We (shall, will) be needing lots of groceries.
3. The store (shall, will) be open until nine tonight.
4. (Will, Shall) you be going before then?
5. I (will, shall) certainly try to get there early.

B. Rewrite correctly any incorrect forms.

(**6**) Lydia could have done a better job if she had mowed the lawn a few days ago. (**7**) The grass would not of been so tall then. (**8**) She had ought to mow the tall grass twice. (**9**) Furthermore, she should have had the mower blade sharpened. (**10**) One ought not to mow with a dull blade. (**11**) The grass must of looked better last week.

- **Writing Sentences** Write two sentences each for *could have, should have, would have, must have, ought,* and *ought not.*

14 Building Vocabulary

Verb Synonyms

The action or state of being that is expressed by one verb can usually be expressed by other verbs also. You can use verb synonyms, like noun synonyms (see page 76), to avoid repetition in your writing. You can also use verb synonyms, like noun synonyms, to make your writing precise. Even synonyms have slightly different meanings.

Consider the verb *walk* and some of its synonyms.

Bartholomew (walked, ambled, strode, stepped) down the path.

The synonyms do not name exactly the same activity, however. *Walk* refers to the general action of walking. *Amble* means leisurely walking, *stride* means energetic walking, *step* means walking only a short distance, and so on for the other synonyms. Exactly how did Bartholomew move? If you choose a precise verb, your reader will know.

To make your writing more interesting and more precise, look for the verb that says exactly what you mean. Use the dictionary and the thesaurus to help you find the right verb.

> Use verb synonyms for more interesting and precise writing.

Practice

Replace each underlined verb with a more precise synonym.

1. Keven <u>told</u> the secret to Audrey at last.
2. The cat <u>moved</u> away from the snake.
3. Julian was <u>writing</u> illegible notes all over the margins.
4. We <u>looked</u> at the beautiful scene for a long time.
5. I saw Will <u>look</u> at Bernice and then look away.

- **Writing Sentences**   Find a more precise synonym for each verb. Then use both verbs in sentences.

  6. talk   **7.** jump   **8.** eat   **9.** walk   **10.** see   **11.** shine

Review

- **Kinds of Verbs** *(pp. 99–101)*   Copy each verb or verb phrase and underline the main verb. Then label the verb *action* or *being*.

  1. Have you seen the newspaper?   **3.** It feels heavy, too.
  2. It does look big today.   **4.** There certainly is a lot of news.

- **Tenses** *(pp. 102–104)*   Copy each verb and name its tense.

  5. If the bus comes now, we shall have waited only ten minutes.
  6. When I arrived at the stop, a bus had just left.
  7. If I have missed the last bus, I shall go back home.

- **Irregular Verbs** *(pp. 105–106)*   Write each verb's principal parts.

  8. begin   **9.** break   **10.** lose   **11.** know   **12.** swim

- **Using Tenses Correctly** *(pp. 107–109)*   Rewrite the paragraph, avoiding needless shifts in tense and adding necessary shifts.

  13–16. I looked through the photographs and feel very proud. Although I still have lots to learn about photography, I did quite well. The lighting was good, and the subjects are interesting.

- ***be, have, do*** *(pp. 110–111)*   Write the correct verb form.

  17. Peggy (done, did) her math homework yesterday.
  18. I (be, am, is) going to finish my homework now.

- **Progressive Forms** *(pp. 112–113)*   Write the progressive forms.

  19. Julio <u>has rehearsed</u> for hours, but he <u>will stop</u> soon.
  20. The rehearsal <u>had gone</u> well, but Julio <u>became</u> tired.
  21. By tomorrow, Julio <u>will have stayed</u> with us for a month.

- **Linking Verbs** *(pp. 114–115)*   Copy only the linking verbs.

  22. The artist looked at the paint, for the color did not seem right.
  23. He had mixed the colors, but they still didn't look right.

- **Transitive and Intransitive Verbs** *(pp. 116–117)* List each verb and write *transitive* or *intransitive* to describe it.

  24. Tennessee remains thirty-fourth in size among the states.
  25. Many country and western stars record their songs in Nashville.

- **Active and Passive Voices** *(pp. 118–119)* Rewrite each active sentence in the passive voice and each passive sentence in the active voice.

  26. A gifted guitarist accompanied the singer.
  27. The hit song had been written by the guitarist.
  28. The audience applauded both performers.

- **Agreement** *(pp. 120–123)* Write the present tense of each verb.

  29. When Ty or my parents _____, they _____ to music. (relax, listen)
  30. Neither *Annie* nor *The King and I* _____ my favorite show. (be)

- **Inverted and Interrupted Order** *(pp. 124–125)* Write the present tense.

  31. Here _____ the album of Beethoven piano sonatas. (be)
  32. Near the bookcase _____ my other records. (lie)

- **Writing Well with Verbs** *(pp. 126–127)* Rewrite the sentences that would be more appropriate in the active voice.

  33. A trip to Africa by ship will be taken by the Reeses.
  34. The tickets were received by them today.
  35. The tickets were mailed by the agent.

  Rewrite the following paragraph, using inverted order for variety.

  36–38. We can see the Blue Hills in the distance. We had never visited them. We plan to go next weekend. It will be strange to be there after so many years of seeing their outlines against the sky.

- **Using Words Correctly** *(pp. 129–130)* Correct the sentences.

  39. You should of seen the race. **41.** He hadn't ought to have come.
  40. Hal must of been there. **42.** She had ought to be there now.

- **Building Vocabulary** *(p. 131)* Write a synonym for each verb.

  43. try **44.** throw **45.** remember **46.** help **47.** change **48.** move

Writing a Descriptive Paragraph

1 | Observing Details

You automatically recognize thousands of things—objects, people, and places—every day. You reach for the bowl you eat cereal out of in the morning; you meet your Aunt Sue at the bus station; you turn down your own street or your own driveway—all without thinking. However, if you want someone else to get your cereal bowl, meet your aunt, or find your driveway, you need to think about the details that you have absorbed automatically. You need to ask yourself what makes one dish, one person, one driveway, different from all the others.

Your memory alone will give you some details about the bowl, your aunt, and your driveway. However, the best way to gather accurate, complete details is to observe them. Pick up your cereal bowl. How heavy is it? Turn it upside down. What distinguishing marks does it have?

Instead of just trying to recall what color eyes your Aunt Sue has, visit with her. Observe her. Are her eyes blue-gray or bright blue? Instead of guessing what the surface of your driveway feels like, observe it up close. Touch it. Is it hot? bumpy? smooth? oily?

You recognize all these things through your senses. When you need to describe something to someone else, you will find yourself using sensory details. Sensory details come from the information provided by your five senses—sight, sound, taste, touch, and smell.

How well do you use your senses? Try these exercises in coming up with details about an object, a person and a place.

Practice

A. Look at your own shoe or at a shoe that one of your classmates is wearing. Write a list of words or phrases that describe the shoe. Include as many details as you can to give a sharp picture of this shoe. Then compare lists with your classmates.

B. Now imagine that someone else is going to meet one of your friends or family members at the bus station. Make a list of details that would help a stranger pick this person out of a crowd.

C. Now test your memory. List at least ten details about your school cafeteria. What color are the floors? the walls? Describe the chairs and the tables. Then compare lists with at least one other person. Did you disagree on any details?

2 | Choosing Details

When you described the shoe, you tried to give a complete picture. Suppose, however, that you want someone to see the shoe as funny or as worn out or as the perfect shoe. Probably you would use different details to make each of these points. If the shoe were lost and you were writing a description for the bulletin board, you would use still different details.

Usually, when you describe something, you choose details that suit your purpose. Look at the difference in these two descriptions of a building.

The skyscraper is sixty stories high and faced with panels of mirror-like glass. Each of the 10,344 windows is one-half inch thick, tinted gray, and framed with black aluminum. The top floor is an observatory with a view of the whole city.

The building is like a sliver of glass. Because it seems to be made out of mirrors, it changes color with the sky and the weather. In the morning it can be a clear blue, and in the evening, when the inside lights are still on, it looks like a building made out of light.

- Which description simply gives factual information about the building?
- How would you guess the writer of the second description feels about this building?

Suppose that instead of giving only a physical description of the person being met at the bus station, you wanted to show something about that person—that he or she was lively, had a sense of humor, was often sad. You would choose details that would make these points.

Often just a few details can give you a sharp picture of someone.

Uncle Wash was a tall man with a hard leathery face, dark discolored teeth and blue eyes that had a faraway look in them. *–Jesse Stuart*

. . . her printed voile dresses and flowered hats were as right for her as denim overalls for a farmer. . . . I don't think I ever saw Mrs. Flowers laugh, but she smiled often. A slow widening of her thin black lips to show even, small white teeth, then the slow effortless closing. *–Maya Angelou*

- What four physical characteristics of Uncle Wash has the writer mentioned in this single sentence?
- What is one conclusion that you could draw about Uncle Wash from this description?
- Notice that in the second description the writer shows Mrs. Flowers doing something—smiling. What is one conclusion that you could draw about the kind of person Mrs. Flowers is from the way she smiles?
- Writers often use comparisons to make their descriptions clear. What is the skin on Uncle Wash's face compared to? What comparison is used to describe the way Mrs. Flowers dresses?

Many of the opinions you have about people come from simply observing them. If you want to show something about a person's personality, you can try to think how *you* came to this conclusion. Probably it is through some action that you observed. Suppose that you want to say that your piano teacher seems to care a lot about how he looks, but that he gets carried away by the music and forgets about his appearance. You could think about how you came to realize this, and then show your reader.

Before Mr. Schultz starts a lesson he pulls a comb out of his pocket and runs it carefully through his thick, wavy hair. By the time I leave an hour later, it is flying all over from the fast pieces he has played to show me how they should sound.

If you are going to describe a place, it is important to choose what impression you want to give before you begin. Otherwise you could be almost overwhelmed by all the details. Suppose you were going to describe your room at home. You could describe the floor, the ceiling, the walls, the windows, the door, the bed, the dresser, the lamp, your desk. You could tell what color and size and shape all these things are. You would take up a great deal of space in this way without really letting your readers know how it feels to walk into your room or what overall impression it gives.

You could take a point of view toward your room, however, and decide *how* you want someone to see it. Then you would automatically begin to weed out many of the things you see and choose only the ones that fit your purpose. If you decided, for example, that your room has more objects per square foot than most rooms, that would be your point of view. Then you would choose only the details that show how crowded your room is.

What is this writer's point of view about Dominic's Deli?

When you open the door to Dominic's Deli, the smell rushes out and flows around you. It is a mixture of vinegary pickles, peppery pastrami, grilling hamburgers, and garlic. It's like all my favorite food smells mixed together. With people eating elbow to elbow at jam-packed tables, wriggling into coats, and piling up at the cash register, it's too noisy to talk or read, so you just concentrate on the food. You'd want to concentrate on the food anyway. No wonder the sign in Dominic's window brags, "This isn't a good place to eat. It's the best!"

- Does the writer describe every detail about Dominic's Deli?
- What impression does the description give?
- Do all the details support that point of view?

Now try these exercises in choosing details about an object, a person, and a place.

Practice

A. Go back to the list of details you made about the shoe, or choose some other object. Decide how you want someone to see this object, and then choose details that make your point. List at least five or six details.

B. Choose a person you know, and list several details that would help someone see what this person is like. You may want to use details about an action.

C. Imagine that you know the place shown in the photograph on page 134 and that you love to spend time there. Choose five descriptive details that show how you feel about it without your actually saying so. Now take the point of view that this is a place that makes you feel uneasy or unhappy. Write down five descriptive details that convey this. Try to choose words that show the feeling you are expressing about the place.

3 | Using Exact Words

The right word makes the difference between a dull or vague description and a lively and accurate one. Compare these descriptions.

The sole of the shoe was thick.	The shoe had a spongy, half-inch thick, tan sole.
Her hair is wavy.	Her hair waves in even ripples.
The lawn was dry.	The grass was parched brown.

Using comparisons can help make your word pictures vivid.

His car was dented and needed a paint job.	His car looked like a tin can that had been kicked from Boston to San Francisco.
Jody had a lot of freckles.	Jody had as many freckles as the sky has stars.
From the plane window you could see the outlines of thousands of waves.	From the plane window the ocean looked like a giant wrinkled cloth.

The words you use can show your attitudes and feelings. Look at the differences in these pairs of descriptions of the same thing.

The coat was a loud shade of red with great brassy buttons.	The coat was a brilliant scarlet with gleaming brass buttons.
She was frail, with a washed-out complexion and pale blue eyes.	She was delicate and fair-skinned with light blue eyes.
The severely trimmed bushes were laid out in rigid patterns.	The bushes were neatly trimmed and arranged in a formal pattern.

Practice

Rewrite each of these descriptions. Use exact and vivid words. Try to show your point of view. Use at least two comparisons.

1. Ben always looks careless. His clothes and hair are a mess.
2. The jacket looked as though it had been around for a long time.
3. The vacant lot looked really neat and pleasant.

4 | Getting Started

You have had some practice in making lists of descriptive details. You have practiced using words that convey exact and vivid pictures. It is time to begin thinking about the description you will write.

If you write your description about an object, you might choose anything from a baseball glove to a motorcycle. You could try to describe it completely, or you could try to get your reader to see it in a certain way. You could even choose a group of objects to write about, such as the contents of your desk or locker.

If you describe a person, you should think about how your details give an idea of what the person is like and how you feel about the person. You could use some of the things the person does, or the way he or she does them, to help you convey the picture you want.

If you describe a place, you could concentrate on what the place looks like at a certain time of the day or in a certain kind of weather. You could show your reader the mood of the place—the way it makes you feel—by the details you choose and the words you use. If the place is public, like a subway station, classroom, or gym, you could pick a time when it is full of people and describe it as a scene in motion.

Practice

Spend a few minutes thinking about something you might like to describe: an object, a person, or a place. Make a choice and then pair up with a classmate. Describe whatever you chose to your classmate. Did your classmate get a clear and vivid picture? Discuss how you might make your description even better.

Steps for Writing a Description Here are the steps for writing a description. You will follow these steps to write your own description.

Step One   Choose a topic.
Step Two   Write your description.
Step Three Revise your description.
Step Four   Proofread your description.
Step Five   Make a final copy to share.

5 | Step One
Choose a Topic

The first and perhaps the most important step in writing a description is choosing a topic (1) that interests you and (2) that you can write about well.

Julie made a list of possible topics for her description.

Aunt Lillian's new car   *Dad's plumbing shop*
my soccer ball   *Mrs. Quinn, my neighbor*
Aunt Pat's farm   *my little brother*

Julie looked at her list. When she thought about describing the new car, she realized how much there was to say. She couldn't decide which details she would choose. Describing a soccer ball might be fun, especially if she didn't say what it was until the very end. Aunt Pat's farm was small—would she describe the pastures and the building and the animals? Julie was afraid there was too much on even a small farm to choose from. The more she thought about the plumbing shop, the better she liked that idea. It was a place she had a special feeling about. She also thought she might like to write about Mrs. Quinn because she was unusual-looking, but very nice, or her little brother because she knew him so well. Julie decided that the plumbing shop and Mrs. Quinn were her best possibilities. She made a list of details about them both. After looking at her list, she decided on the plumbing shop as the thing she felt most excited about describing.

Assignment

- **Make a List**
- **Make Notes**
- **Choose a Topic**

A. Make a list of people, places, and objects that you would like to describe. List at least two of each.
B. Look over your list carefully. Select two topics.
C. For each of the two topics, write a list of details. Try to make your list while you are observing your subject.
D. Compare your two lists. Which did you feel the most excited about as you wrote? Which do you think you could make into the better description? Circle your choice on your list.

6 | Step Two
Write Your Description

Before she began to write, Julie visited the plumbing shop again to refresh her memory. Then she wrote this description. She knew she had made some mistakes in it, but there would be time to correct them later.

Julie's first draft

> When I was little, I used to play in the back of Dad's plumbing shop. It seemed dark and mysterious ~~to be~~ because it was so full of strange things and so quiet. My favrite thing was a big bench covered with oil and grease. There were a lot of tools on it and racks over it. ~~I~~ There were rows and rows of bins on the wall clear up to the cieling. If Dad was looking for something and turned on the light everything would suddenly look ordnary and dirty. Then he would turn it off, my room would be dark and mysterius again.

- How do you think Julie decided which details to include?
- What overall impression is Julie trying to give? How could she do a better job at giving it?
- Where could Julie have used more exact words and details?
- What sensory details did she use?

Assignment • **Write Your First Draft**

Write the first draft of your description. Before you begin, decide what overall impression you want to give. Then look back at your list of details. Should you add some details? Should you leave some out? Then just write. Let your words flow onto the paper. You will have a chance later to make changes and correct mistakes.

7 | Step Three
Revise Your Description

The next day, Julie read her description again. She was surprised at what she saw. The middle part seemed more like a list of the things in the shop than a picture of them. She was afraid she hadn't given the feeling about the shop that she had wanted to give. She decided that the way the shop smelled was an important part of her feeling about it. She added a sentence about that. She added some details about the bench. Then she remembered the most interesting thing about the bins, and she added that, too.

Julie decided to read her description to Portia. She asked Portia to try to form an exact mental picture of the place she was going to describe. She also asked her to see what overall feeling she got from the description. Then she read her description out loud.

When she had finished, Portia said, "It sounds like a great place to have played in. You were really lucky. I like the ending especially. You did give the feeling of a dark and mysterious place by showing the difference when the lights were turned on."

"Is there anything I could change to make it better?" asked Julie.

"I thought you said *there were* a lot when you were reading it," said Portia. "Maybe you could do something about that."

"I noticed the same thing," said Julie. "I'll see if I can start some of those sentences in a different way."

Julie thanked Portia for her comments. Then she went back to her desk to make the changes right away, before she forgot the discussion.

Julie's revision

When I was little, I used to play in the back of Dad's plumbing shop. It seemed dark and mysterious ~~to be~~ because it was so full of strange things and so quiet. My
long wooden
favrite thing was a ~~big~~ bench covered with oil and
Wrenches and vices were attached to it the held metal
grease. ~~There were a lot of tools on it and~~ racks over it,
pipes and rods.   Rows   wooden   were bolted
~~I There were rows~~ and rows of bins on the wall clear up to the cieling. If Dad was looking for something and
overhead
turned on the light everything would suddenly look ordnary and dirty. Then he would turn it off,
and
my room would be dark and mysterius again.

It smelled mysterius, too — dry and dusty with a background smell of heavy oil.

Whenever you opened a bin full of brass fittings, it was like finding gold in a dark cave.

- What words did Julie use instead of *big* to describe the bench?
- How did she change the two sentences that began with *There were*?
- What comparison does Julie use in her revision?

Assignment
- **Revise Your Description**
- **Discuss Your Description**

A. Read over your first draft, keeping these questions in mind.

1. Have I used details to back up the impression I want to give?
2. Have I used exact and precise words?

B. Revise your draft. Add new words or details; cross out vague words.
C. Read your description out loud to a classmate. Discuss it, using the same questions you asked yourself. If you get new ideas from the discussion or from reading it aloud, make more changes.

8 | Step Four
Proofread Your Description

Julie was now ready to proofread her description. Because she had made so many changes, she first copied it over onto a fresh sheet of paper. Then she checked for mistakes in spelling, capitalization, punctuation, and word usage. Whenever she came to a word she was unsure of, she looked it up in a dictionary. At this point, Julie finally thought of a good title for her description. She wrote it at the top of her paragraph, capitalizing each word.

Julie's description after proofreading

Pipe Dreams

When I was little, I used to play in the back of Dad's plumbing shop. It seemed dark and mysterious because it was so full of strange things and so quiet. It smelled mysterious, too—dry and dusty with a background smell of heavy oil. My favorite thing was a long wooden bench covered with oil and grease. Wrenches and vices were attached to it, and the racks over it held metal pipes and rods. Rows and rows of wooden bins were bolted on the wall clear up to the ceiling. Whenever you opened a bin full of brass fittings, it was like finding gold in a dark cave. If Dad was looking for something and turned on the overhead light, everything would suddenly look ordinary and dirty. Then he would turn it off, and my room would be dark and mysterious again.

- Which words did Julie correct for spelling? What is the correct spelling for each of them?
- Where did she add punctuation? Why?
- How did Julie correct a run-on sentence? What other way could she have chosen to correct it?

Practice

Proofread this paragraph, checking for errors in pu͟ ͟ ͟ation, capitalization, word usage, subject-verb agreement, and spelling. You should find twelve errors. Look up in a dictionary the words you are unsure of. Write the paragraph correctly.

Old Sturbridge Village in Massachusetts is one of my favrite places. Visiting Sturbridge is like stepping back in History. The village is a replica of a typical New England town in the ninteenth century. A large white meetinghouse overlook the town common where a flock of sheep often graze. You can sit on the old benches in the schoolhouse and write on a small piece of slate. You can watch the pottery maker or shoemaker visit the farm, or drop by the genral store. You can watch a printing press at work, people spinning yarn or weaving. There is ever a bank at Sturbridge village. All of the guides are dressed in ninteenth-century costumes. Stirbridge Village is a great place to visit.

Assignment • **Proofread Your Description**

Proofread your own description now. Ask yourself these questions.

1. Have I indented my paragraph or paragraphs?
2. Are all the words spelled correctly?
3. Have I looked up any word I am unsure about?

Grammar skills checklist

4. Have I corrected any run-on sentences and sentence fragments?
5. Have I used commas correctly with compound sentences and dependent clauses?
6. Have I written noun plurals and possessives correctly?
7. Does the subject of each sentence agree with its verb?

9 | Step Five
Make a Final Copy

Julie copied her description in her best handwriting onto a new piece of paper. Then she checked over her work to be sure she had not made any copying mistakes. Julie was satisfied with her description, but she wanted to add some artwork to make it look even better.

She decided to draw a sketch of the back room of the plumbing shop. First, Julie mounted her description onto a sturdy piece of cardboard. Then she chose a gray piece of construction paper because it suggested a dark and dusty place. Along the left side of the paper, Julie sketched in charcoal a row of bins attached to the wall. On the right side, she drew the bench at the bottom of her paper. She filled the bench with work tools—wrenches, vises, etc. Above the bench, she drew racks for rods and pipes of all different lengths. Finally, Julie drew one more bin, but this one was special. She used a gold-colored marker to draw brass fittings inside it. The gold sparkled amid the otherwise gray and charcoal picture. When she finished, Julie put her sketch on display with her description so that her classmates could enjoy them both.

Assignment
- **Make a Final Copy**
- **Share Your Description**

A. Copy your description in your best handwriting.

B. Check it over once more to make sure that you did not leave out or repeat words or introduce any new mistakes.

C. Think of a special way to share your description.

1. You can make a separate sketch as Julie did.
2. You can assemble a collage.
3. You can draw a portrait or put together a photo composition.
4. You can read your description to the class.

Completing the Predicate

1 | Direct and Indirect Objects

Direct Objects

You have learned that the verb is the key word in the predicate. Sometimes, in fact, it is the only word in the predicate.

> The car **swerved.**
> The storm **approached.**

More often, the predicate needs additional words to complete its meaning.

> Arlene **hit** the ball.
> The storm **caused** extensive damage.

Most action verbs, like *hit* or *caused*, send their action to another word in the sentence. The word that "receives" the action, like *ball* or *damage*, is called the **direct object**. If you can ask *whom?* or *what?* after the verb and get an answer, the answer will be the direct object. It is usually a noun or a pronoun.

> Carmen **gave** the record to me. *(Gave what? The record.)*
> The squirrel **noticed** Aldo by the tree. *(Noticed whom? Aldo.)*

Can you find any direct objects in these sentences?

> The car swerved suddenly.
> We will leave this evening.

Suddenly and *this evening* do not receive the action of the verbs; rather, they describe the action. If you ask "Swerved what?" or "Leave what?" there is no answer. *Swerved* and *leave* have no objects in these sentences.

Just as subjects and predicates of a sentence may be compound, so may direct objects.

> Theresa **attended** the wedding ceremony and the reception.
> The bride **had invited** Theresa but not Emile.
> The photographer **asked** the bride or groom for a smile.

Verbs that have direct objects are called transitive verbs, while verbs that do not have direct objects are called intransitive verbs (see pages 116–117).

Try It Out

Which nouns are direct objects?

(**1**) Ezra's clean car had very dirty tires. (**2**) He had not washed the dust, dirt, and grime from them in a long time. (**3**) The tires ruined the appearance of the car. (**4**) Plain soap and water did not remove the dirt. (**5**) Finally Ezra tried a commercial cleaner. (**6**) The local garage owner had recommended the product highly. (**7**) Ezra used the cleaner, and it worked instantly. (**8**) He just sprayed the solution on the tires, and the dirt came off. (**9**) Ezra wrote a letter to the manufacturer. (**10**) Could he do a commercial about the cleaner and his dazzling tires?

Indirect Objects

Sometimes a sentence has more than one object.

The librarian gave <u>Seymour</u> the <u>book</u>.

Gave what? The book. *Book* is the direct object. *Seymour* is the indirect object. The **indirect object** precedes the direct object and tells to or for whom or what the action of the verb is done. To whom did the librarian give the book? To Seymour.

When *to* or *for* is used with a noun, the noun is not an indirect object. Only one of these sentences has an indirect object. Which one is it?

We bought Walter a ticket.   We bought a ticket for Walter.

Like a direct object, an indirect object may be compound.

Mr. Fisk assigned <u>Isaac</u> and <u>Jenny</u> the same topic.

Assigned what? The same topic. *Topic* is the direct object. Assigned to whom? Isaac and Jenny. *Isaac* and *Jenny* are the indirect objects.

There can be no indirect object without a direct object. The indirect object will appear between the verb and the direct object.

Try It Out

Identify the direct objects and indirect objects. Not all the sentences have indirect objects.

1. Morris tied a square knot with the rope.
2. We attended both the practice and the game.

3. Mountain climbing always gave Lillian a feeling of freedom.
4. My brother gave the lawnmower an oil change.
5. I made Bianca some warm milk for her cold.
6. The single plant produced three bushels of zucchini.
7. The singer sang his new hit song for the cheering audience.
8. The mail brought Mr. Buttrick two magazines and five bills.
9. Ms. Heiple allowed Hans extra time for his science project.
10. The committee awarded scholarships to three students.

> ▸ The **direct object** is a noun or pronoun in the predicate that receives the action of the verb.
> ▸ The **indirect object** is a noun or pronoun in the predicate that tells to or for whom or what the action is done. It comes between the verb and the direct object.

Written Practice

Write each direct and indirect object. Label it *DO* or *IO*.

1. Sanford searched the ground for his lost dime.
2. He found not only the dime but a four-leaf clover.
3. The principal mailed the teachers the schedule for next term.
4. Did the mail carrier leave a package or a letter for me?
5. Mr. Kiparsky gave his English class a vocabulary quiz.
6. I made Emily a glass of lemonade.
7. The babysitter read Tonio and Ella a silly bedtime story.
8. Ms. Jackson showed a safety film to her driver education class.
9. The snowstorm caused long delays for most drivers.
10. Have you showed Stella the new red rug for your room?
11. Beth told her mother and her sister some startling news.
12. The travel agent sold the Ortizes airplane tickets to Brazil.
13. Can you show me that parka in red?
14. Ben sent a copy of his paper to the *Daily Times.*
15. This boat ride is giving me a problem.

● **Writing Sentences**   Write a passage of eight to ten sentences about things you do around the house—for example, wash dishes, baby-sit, wash the car, mow the lawn. Use direct and indirect objects in your sentences.

2 | Predicate Nouns and Adjectives

Some verbs do not express action. As you know, linking verbs express a state of being (see pages 114–115). With action verbs, there is movement from the subject to the predicate. With linking verbs, there is a connection, a link, between subject and predicate.

ACTION VERB: The class **elected** a new president.

LINKING VERB: Kate **is** the new president.

Class and *president*, which are connected by the action verb *elected*, refer to different people. *Kate* and *president*, which are linked by the linking verb *is*, refer to the same person. A noun that follows a linking verb and refers back to the subject is a **predicate noun**. Predicate nouns identify or rename the subject.

The enormous animal was a young hippopotamus.

Dudley remained a loyal friend.

Although *be* is the most common linking verb, other verbs are also used this way. *Remained* in the sentence above is one example. *Appear, become, feel, grow, remain, sound, stay,* and *taste* are others. (See also pages 114–115.)

Linking verbs can be followed by adjectives as well as by nouns. An adjective that follows a linking verb and refers back to the subject is a **predicate adjective**. Predicate adjectives describe the subject.

Kate's campaign was successful.

The tree grew tall.

Do not confuse the linking verb *be* with the helping verb *be*. The use of the verbs is quite different.

HELPING VERB: Daniel **is throwing** darts. *(direct object)*

LINKING VERB: Daniel **is** interesting. *(predicate adjective)*

Like other parts of a sentence, predicate nouns and adjectives may be compound.

Oscar McNeil is the quarterback and the captain of the team.

From the hill, the stars seem brighter, clearer, and nearer.

Try It Out

Find the subject and the linking verb in each sentence, and tell whether the underlined word is a predicate noun or a predicate adjective.

1. Cheese has long been an important <u>part</u> of the human diet.
2. Cow's milk is the <u>base</u> for most of our cheese.
3. Cheese from the milk of goats is also <u>common</u> and <u>available</u>.
4. In parts of Asia, buffalo milk remains the major <u>ingredient</u> of some cheese.
5. Cheese made from reindeer's milk seems <u>similar</u> to Swiss cheese.
6. Camel's milk cheese is <u>popular</u> in certain portions of middle Asia.

> ▸ A **predicate noun** identifies or renames the subject.
> ▸ A **predicate adjective** describes the subject.
> Predicate nouns and predicate adjectives follow linking verbs.

Written Practice

List the predicate nouns and predicate adjectives. Label each *PN* or *PA*.

1. About 400 kinds of cheese are available in the world.
2. The manufacturing processes are similar for all cheese.
3. The curd is the solid part of the milk.
4. The liquid part is the whey.
5. Separation of the curd from the whey is necessary to make cheese.
6. Rennet is a substance in the lining of a calf's fourth stomach.
7. Rennet and certain bacteria work on the milk, and it becomes curdled and more solid.
8. The curdled, semisolid mass eventually becomes cheese.
9. Cheesemakers drain off the whey, while the curd stays semisolid.
10. The curd is pressed together and it becomes more solid.
11. Finally, the curd goes to curing rooms, and it becomes drier and stronger over a period of months.
12. To most people, the result of this procedure tastes delicious.

● **Writing Sentences**   Write eight to ten sentences describing a place you know—the classroom, someone's home, a park. Use predicate nouns and adjectives.

3 | Writing Well with Objects

You can sometimes use indirect objects to make your sentences clearer, and smoother. Compare these sentences.

I mailed the directions to my house to Jody.
I mailed Jody the directions to my house.

Try It Out

Revise each sentence to include an indirect object.

1. Ms. Hillman taught algebra to the class for two months.
2. Did you give an answer to that startling question to Daren?
3. My father sang a special song to my mother for their anniversary.
4. Will you give the tickets to the concert to me?

Written Practice

Improve the passage by using indirect objects where appropriate.

Rolf lent his record of the Goldies to Flora yesterday. She had given a different record of the same group to Rolf a week ago. I saw the program for the Goldies' concert in the newspaper today. Did Rolf buy tickets for the concert for Flora?

Check Your Writing

Reread the passage you wrote, asking yourself this question.

Have I used indirect objects to help make my sentences clear and direct?

- **Writing a Paragraph** Write a passage of eight to ten sentences relating the story of a special book, movie, or television program. Include some of these verbs: *give, buy, offer, send, grant, bring, show, lend, tell, award, offer, write.* Then ask yourself the question above. If necessary, revise your sentences so that you use indirect objects.

4 Using Words Correctly

anywhere, somewhere, a way; besides, beside

You may occasionally hear the forms *anywheres, somewheres, a ways*. While these forms may be understandable, they are not acceptable as standard usage. An unnecessary *-s* is added to the end of each word. Avoid the *-s* and use the standard forms *anywhere, somewhere, a way*.

> <u>Anywhere</u> we go, we seem to see Frank. *(not* anywheres*)*
> My cousin lives <u>somewhere</u> on this street. *(not* somewheres*)*
> We may still have a long <u>way</u> to go. *(not* ways*)*

The words *beside* and *besides* are used in different ways. *Besides* means "in addition to." *Beside* is a different word which means "next to."

> <u>Besides</u> an essay, Fritz has a research paper due today.
> Fritz sits <u>beside</u> me in the science lab.

> Use *anywhere, somewhere, a way*. Avoid adding an *-s*.
> *Besides* means "in addition to." *Beside* means "next to."

Practice

Rewrite each sentence correctly. Write *C* if it is correct.

1. I left the screwdriver somewheres around here.
2. Are you planning to go anywhere in particular this morning?
3. Uncle Rafael has to drive a long ways to get to work.
4. The accident occurred somewhere on the north side of town.
5. Whom should we invite beside Celia and Arthur?
6. The light switch is besides the mirror.
7. We can go anywheres you would like.

- **Writing Sentences** Write a sentence for each of the following forms: *anywhere, somewhere, a way, besides, beside*.

Roots, Prefixes, Suffixes

Certain words can be divided into parts that will help you understand what the words mean. These word parts have generally come into English from other languages, primarily Latin and Greek.

The main part of a word is called the **root**. A part added to the beginning of the root is a **prefix**. A part added to the end is a **suffix**.

Consider the word *contraction*. It can be divided into three parts: *con-tract-ion*. The prefix *con-* means "together"; the root *-tract-* means "pull, draw"; the suffix *-ion* means "act of." *Contraction*, then, means "the act of drawing together." That definition can apply to what a muscle does and to what a form like *isn't* does.

There are hundreds of prefixes, suffixes, and roots, and you cannot be expected to learn them all. The more you do learn, however, the better you will be able to understand and use words.

Prefix	Usual Meaning	Example
a-, ab-	without, not	atypical
co-, com-	together, with	co-author
de-	away, from, away from	depart
dis-	not, lack of	disapprove
ex-	away from, out	expel
in-, il-	in, not	incapable
mis-	wrong, opposite	misspell
pre-	before	predate
re-	back, again	return
semi-	half	semicircle
un-	not	unbend

Suffix	Usual Meaning	Example
-able, -ible	capable, able, worthy of	fixable
-ance, -ence	act of, condition	confidence
-er, -or	one who does	sailor
-ious, -ous	characterized by, having	joyous
-ist	one who does	scientist
-ment	act or state of	enjoyment

Root	Usual Meaning	Example
-capit-	head	capital
-cred-	belief, truth	credit
-dic-	speak, say	dictate
-jur-	swear, law, just	juror
-son-	sound	consonant
-spec-	look, see	spectator
-spir-	breathe	inspire
-tract-	pull, draw	extract
-vert-, -vers-	turn	reverse

Practice

Try to determine the meaning of the word from its parts. Then look up the word in the dictionary and compare the meanings.

1. incredible   3. detract   5. extract   7. injury
2. decapitate   4. expire   6. jurist   8. discredit

> Use prefixes, suffixes, and roots to help you understand new words.

Practice

A. Write the root of each of the following words. Then make two new words from each root by adding a new prefix, suffix, or both. Make your new words as different as possible. The first one has been done for you.

1. intractable **tract**   3. dissonance
   retract   4. capitalism
   distraction   5. inspiration
2. inspection   6. reversible

B. Using the list of word parts, create six more words of your own and supply definitions for them.

- **Writing Sentences**   Write ten sentences, using ten of the words you have written for exercises A and B.

Review

- **Direct and Indirect Objects** *(pp. 149–151)* List the direct and indirect objects. Label the direct objects *DO* and the indirect objects *IO*. Not every verb has an object. Write *no object* for these sentences.

   1. Harry Claussen held the hook in his hand.
   2. The tool had a crochet-like hook and a wooden handle.
   3. Ms. Loeb had given him the hook and other materials.
   4. Ms. Loeb was teaching Harry the craft of rug-hooking.
   5. He was making his mother a rug for Mother's Day.
   6. Many craft stores offer their customers rug-hooking kits.
   7. Harry was not using a kit, a prepared pattern, or precut yarn.
   8. Harry worked slowly and carefully.
   9. He was making the rug with strips of woolen cloth.
   10. He was hooking the strips through burlap.
   11. He had stretched the burlap over a wooden frame.
   12. He had shown Ms. Loeb his design for the rug.
   13. Now the design stood in front of him.
   14. Would he ever finish the rug?

- **Predicate Nouns and Adjectives** *(pp. 152–153)* List the predicate nouns and predicate adjectives. Label predicate nouns *PN* and predicate adjectives *PA*.

   15. Harry Claussen is a student of rug-hooking.
   16. His teacher had become an expert in the art many years ago.
   17. The work seems slow to Harry, but he enjoys it.
   18. Traditional rug-hooking is an old craft.
   19. In fact, for a long time it was necessary.
   20. Cottages were drafty and chilly.
   21. Uncovered floors felt cold and looked bare.
   22. There were few rug stores handy in times gone by.
   23. Later, printed patterns became popular.
   24. Farm animals became standard designs in Pennsylvania.
   25. In coastal areas, seafaring scenes were common.
   26. Popular patterns in other areas were floral and geometric designs.
   27. Today, traditional rug-hooking may grow popular once again.

- **Writing Well with Objects** *(pp. 154–155)*   Rewrite the sentences, where possible, to include an indirect object. If there can be no indirect object in the sentence, write *none*.

28. Elizabeth had bought shoelaces with rainbows on them for her older sister.
29. Her sister had given rainbow-colored barrettes to Elizabeth for her long hair.
30. Have you given your lasagna recipe to Buddy for his home economics class?
31. The pilot sent her route to Prince Edward Island to the control tower.
32. The mayor ceremoniously presented the key to the city to the visiting diplomat.
33. Mackenzie found the solution to the math problem with his customary ease.
34. Can you lend your calculator to my sister for her math assignment that is due tomorrow?
35. Has everyone heard the plans for our trip to San Francisco?
36. Mr. Contreras mailed the package for us.
37. I offered my front-row tickets to the concert to Lindsay.

- **Using Words Correctly** *(p. 155)*   Rewrite correctly the sentences in which words are used incorrectly. If the sentence is already correct, write *correct*.

38. I am too tired to go anywheres else today.
39. Have you seen my watch anywheres?
40. I saw it beside the sink a little while ago.
41. Have you misplaced anything beside your watch today?
42. I have left my running shoes somewhere, and I must find them.
43. I had been running and had only a short ways left to go.
44. Exhausted, I sat down under a tree somewheres to rest.
45. I took off my shoes and laid them beside me.

- **Building Vocabulary** *(pp. 156–157)*   Copy the underlined words. Circle the prefixes and suffixes.

46. There was an <u>inscription</u> on the base of the statue.
47. The wheel completed two <u>revolutions</u> before the tire went flat.
48. Isn't her face <u>inscrutable</u> just now!
49. Charlotte refused to <u>involve</u> herself in the discussion.

Maintain

- **Kinds of Verb Tenses** *(pp. 99–104, 112–113)* List the verbs and write *action* or *being* to describe each one. Then write its tense and form—for example, *past perfect* or *future perfect progressive.*

  1. Country stores are becoming popular once again.
  2. They have changed a good deal, however.
  3. You will not go into a country store for bread, onions, or kerosene.
  4. The original country stores had just about disappeared before the new kind appeared.
  5. The typical new country store will be selling only gift items.
  6. One store has been having success with reproductions of old toys.

- **Irregular Verbs** *(pp. 105–106)* Write the principal parts of each verb.

  7. fly   **8.** know   **9.** ring   **10.** steal   **11.** throw   **12.** wear

- **Using Tenses Correctly** *(pp. 107–109)* Write the correct form.

  13. If I remain any longer, I (will be, will have been) here an hour.
  14. We almost (had driven, drove) by before we noticed the store.
  15. After I had seen the old toys, I (felt, had felt) delighted.

- **Transitive and Intransitive Verbs** *(pp. 116–117)* List each verb and label it *transitive* or *intransitive.*

  16. The atmosphere in the store seemed cosy and old-fashioned.
  17. We had entered reluctantly, but the store looked delightful.
  18. Dark wooden shelves lined the walls.
  19. Hundreds of interesting and attractive items filled the shelves.

- **Active and Passive Voice** *(pp. 118–119)* Rewrite the active sentences in the passive voice and the passive sentences in the active voice.

  20. The quilt had been sewn by the store's owner.
  21. Her father had owned the toy tractor by the door.
  22. A miniature sofa and table were purchased by my friend Alisha.
  23. A brass music box fascinated my other friend.

- **Agreement / Inverted and Interrupted Order** *(pp. 120-125)*
Write the correct verb.

24. There (has, have) been toys as long as there (has, have) been a child to play with them.
25. A pull toy, a toy animal, or a ball (was, were) the delight of a child in ancient Egypt.
26. Children in ancient China (was, were) probably flying kites.
27. A puppet and a hobby horse (represents, represent) toys of long ago.
28. Neither electronic games nor a talking doll (is, are) very old.
29. Kelly and Liu Toys (sells, sell) a variety of electronic games.
30. My family (finds, find) the store fascinating.
31. (Is, Are) there ever any special sales in that store?

- **Direct and Indirect Objects / Predicate Nouns and Adjectives** *(pp. 149-153)* Copy each verb and each noun or adjective that completes the predicate. Label the noun or adjective *DO* (direct object), *IO* (indirect object), *PN* (predicate noun), or *PA* (predicate adjective).

32. Until this century, people made dolls by hand.
33. European doll makers were fine artists and craftspersons.
34. Fine German dolls became elaborate and fancy.
35. Dolls in North America remained simple and homemade.
36. Dried apples, cornhusks, acorns, and rags provided the material.
37. Parents would make their sons and daughters hand-carved dolls.
38. In this century, manufacturers produce dolls in large numbers.
39. Some manufactured dolls have become quite famous.
40. The "teddy" (for *Theodore*) bear remains a beloved toy.

- **Using Words Correctly** *(pp. 129-130, 155)* Correct each item.

41. Beside Annette, who is working on the project?
42. I lost my pen somewheres at school.
43. Did you see it besides my books?
44. I could of gone, but Sam had ought to go.

- **Building Vocabulary** *(pp. 156-157)* Divide each underlined word into root, prefix, and/or suffix. Give the meaning of each part and of the whole word.

45. The juror retracted her statement.
46. The incredulous inspector rubbed his eyes.

Writing About Yourself

1 | Writing a Good Beginning

There are many ways to begin every story. A good beginning catches the attention of the readers and makes them want to read the next sentence, and then the next.

You might want to start a story with dialogue, or conversation. A beginning like, "Stop! I don't want to hear another word!" can arouse your readers' curiosity and get them into the action right away.

If the setting of your story is unusual, or if it is crucial to the action, you might begin with some details about where the action takes place.

The wind was howling through the tall pines outside our tent.

You could also show some action taking place in the setting.

I woke some time before dawn to hear the rain pounding on the metal skin of the plane, and I thought I was in the boat shop with rain beating on the roof. Then I felt a terrible thirst and I remembered where I was. I jumped up shouting, *"Ajo, it is raining!"*
 –Patrick J. Murphy and Shirley Rousseau Murphy

You could begin with details about yourself, or about someone else in your story.

My kid sister, Cheryl, and I always bragged about our Sioux grandpa, Joe Iron Shell. Our friends, who had always lived in the city and only knew about Indians from movies and TV, were impressed by our stories.   *–Virginia Driving Hawk Sneve*

Another way you might begin your story is to start in the middle of the action. If you choose this technique, you eventually may have to provide background information about how the situation began.

As I stood in the pet shop cuddling the velvety brown and white bunny to my chin, I melted. The idea of having a pet rabbit was all mine. Convincing my parents, though, hadn't been all that easy.

Some writers begin stories by simply making introductory statements. If you do this, be careful to use lively, exact words to arouse your readers' interest and to keep your beginning from being dull.

People elbowed their way closer to the exhibit. I had to stand on tiptoe and crane my neck to see the huge coiled snake.

Whatever technique you decide to use to begin a story, you should write a beginning that quickly and effectively captures your readers' attention.

Practice

A. Read the following plot description and consider how you might begin the story.

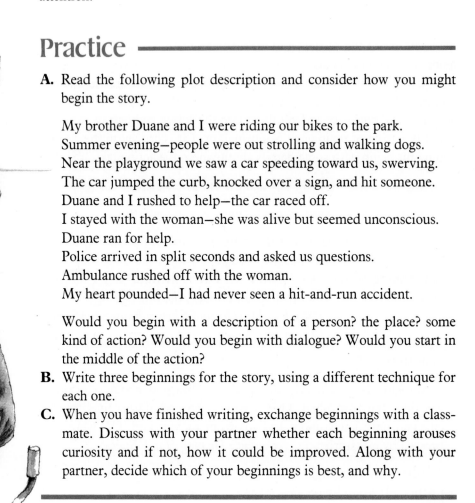

My brother Duane and I were riding our bikes to the park.
Summer evening—people were out strolling and walking dogs.
Near the playground we saw a car speeding toward us, swerving.
The car jumped the curb, knocked over a sign, and hit someone.
Duane and I rushed to help—the car raced off.
I stayed with the woman—she was alive but seemed unconscious.
Duane ran for help.
Police arrived in split seconds and asked us questions.
Ambulance rushed off with the woman.
My heart pounded—I had never seen a hit-and-run accident.

Would you begin with a description of a person? the place? some kind of action? Would you begin with dialogue? Would you start in the middle of the action?

B. Write three beginnings for the story, using a different technique for each one.

C. When you have finished writing, exchange beginnings with a classmate. Discuss with your partner whether each beginning arouses curiosity and if not, how it could be improved. Along with your partner, decide which of your beginnings is best, and why.

2 | Writing a Good Ending

Often writing an ending is more challenging than writing a beginning. When you have told your story, do you simply stop? Do you try to sum it up? What makes a good ending? The end of your story should leave your readers feeling that they have been told just enough—not too much and not too little. Usually the best way to end a story is to show, not tell, the outcome. Which of these endings is better, and why?

1.   Finally, we got Annabelle inside her shed. Joey and I agreed that life with a goat could be a real struggle. This one had been so stubborn that we wondered whether the job was worth it.

2.   I can't remember when I laughed so hard. With my outstretched arms guiding, and Joey's hands nudging from behind, we finally got Annabelle down off the shed roof. As we left her, cozy and secure in her bed of straw, I said, "Well, Joey—I wonder if we could start our own TV series called *Adventures with Annabelle?*"

How you end your story—whether on a humorous, hopeful, surprising, or even sad note—depends on the feeling, or tone, of the story itself. The feeling you leave with your readers should be right for the story.

Practice

A. Read the plot outline on page 164 again. Then use these questions to help you plan a good ending for the story.

   1. Did the car look familiar? Did you see the driver?
   2. Was the woman a stranger? a friend?
   3. Did you and Duane feel frightened? calm? angry? curious? sad? important? How did you express your feelings?
   4. In your role as witness, were you nervous? helpful? shy?
   5. Could you give information about the car? the driver?
   6. Afterwards, did you feel like going to the park? back home?

B. Write two different endings for the story. You might want to use dialogue, description, action, or all three. Whatever technique you use, show rather than summarize the completion of the story. Then tell which ending you like better and why.

3 | Writing Dialogue

One way to make your story come alive is to use conversation. Conversation in a story is called **dialogue.** Through dialogue, people become real. As they speak, their "voices" reveal their thoughts, feelings, reactions, and personalities. In this way, dialogue is often more interesting and lively than what the narrator tells *about* the characters and the action.

Read the following paragraphs. Where could dialogue be used to liven up the action and bring the characters to life?

> On Thursday when Betsy came by the cafeteria for me, she was all groans. She begged me to go to the library and help her with an oral report on Ben Jonson that she had to do for her English class. I told her I couldn't go, and then I asked her why Mr. Moray had assigned Ben Jonson again since that was the assignment for last month.
>
> Betsy looked at me. She was obviously embarrassed. She confessed that it was still the same assignment but that she hadn't done it yet. Then I asked her when it was due, and she told me it was due on Monday.
>
> I was surprised that Betsy hadn't started on it yet. I'd have to keep after her. I reminded her that the girl who makes all the *A*'s in her class had probably started on it last month. Betsy didn't like being compared with someone she didn't even like.

- What would Betsy have said when she asked the narrator to go to the library and help her with her oral report?
- How would Betsy have sounded when she confessed that this was still the same assignment? What would she have said?
- When the narrator was surprised that Betsy hadn't started on the assignment yet, what would she have said? What would her tone of voice express?

Now read the following excerpt. Notice how the dialogue shows attitudes, feelings, and personalities.

> On Thursday when Betsy came by the cafeteria for me, she was all groans.
>
> "Azure, you've got to come to the library and help me. I have to do this oral report on Ben Jonson for my English class. It's a matter of life or death."

"I can't go, Betsy, but how come Mr. Moray assigned you Ben Jonson again? You had that assignment last month," I said.

Betsy looked at me. "Uh . . . no . . . it's not exactly like that, Azure. It's the same one, and I haven't done it yet."

"Good grief, when is it due?"

"Monday," she said, making a horrible face.

"You mean you're starting *now*?" I couldn't believe it. I had to keep after that girl. I said, "You know that girl who makes all the *A*'s in your class? I'll bet she started on it last month."

"Sure. That's the reason she makes all *A*'s. I can't stand her. What that girl needs is a personality transplant. But, you know, she made Mr. Moray smile once, and we all had to pay her a dime."

–Mary Alexander Walker

- What feelings did Betsy show by saying *It's a matter of life or death*?
- What feelings did Azure show when she asked, "You mean you're starting on it *now*?"
- How does the last paragraph of dialogue reveal Betsy's attitude toward the girl who gets all the *A*'s? What does her comment reveal about Mr. Moray?
- How, in general, does the use of dialogue change this story?

Practice

Dialogue would enliven the following story. Rewrite the story. Create as much dialogue as you can by having the narrator and others speak. Try to have the characters' words show the tones of their voices and their feelings.

The day of the school concert had arrived, but my cough had gotten worse, not better. Mom told me that she wouldn't dream of letting me participate because nothing was more important than my health. But I had practiced so hard on my trumpet solo—how could I not be there? I begged and argued, but no amount of persuasion seemed to work. Then my sister made things worse by insisting that I only wanted the limelight. I told her she was a big help!

Finally, I promised my mother that I'd rest all day and go to bed really early for the next two weeks if I could just go for my part of the concert. Luckily, she agreed. Some bargains have high prices!

4 | Improving Your Sentences

A good writer often spends as much time and effort on a story's style as on its content. Would you keep on reading a story if it were written entirely in sentences like these?

> The boy came toward me slowly. He was smiling. I didn't recognize him. Somehow he looked familiar. Then I realized what was different. It was Kevin! He wasn't using a wheelchair anymore!

Using too many short, choppy sentences can weaken or ruin your story. Neither should you use too many long, stringy sentences.

> The boy came toward me slowly and he was smiling but I didn't recognize him, although somehow he looked familiar and then I realized what was different. It was Kevin and he wasn't using a wheelchair anymore.

How would you change the style of the sentences above? To achieve a strong, appealing style, you should vary the length of your sentences. Some should be long and some short.

> The boy coming slowly toward me was smiling. I didn't recognize him, but somehow he looked familiar. Then I realized what was different. It was Kevin! He wasn't using a wheelchair anymore!

Practice

Rewrite each paragraph. Vary the length of the sentences.

1. It was vacation week and Paul and I went to see an old Zorro movie which is one of my favorites, so I didn't mind seeing it again. Besides, Paul said he'd pay my way with his paper-route money but then just at the most exciting part Paul whispered, "I have to leave this minute because I forgot to deliver the *Star*!"

2. My project was due. It was for history. It wasn't quite finished. It needed some cannons. Dad suggested black paper. It seemed too weak. I found a dowel. I sawed it into thirty pieces. I painted them black. Then I got some metal washers for wheels. My tiny cannons looked perfect. Fort Ticonderoga was ready for action.

5 | Getting Started

Think of all the experiences you have enjoyed sharing with other people. Probably you could not wait to tell about some things as soon as they happened. Other stories you may enjoy telling over and over to many different people. Some of these stories are funny, others sad, and still others, suspenseful—such as the first time you caught a fish, or the day your dog died, or your first try at diving off the high board.

Your life is rich with material to write about. You have had experiences that surprised and excited you, made you sad, made you happy, changed you in some way, and made you see something differently. Some of these experiences may not have left you feeling as if you wanted to talk about them. Sometimes, though, these are the very experiences you can write about best.

When you write a personal story, you should try to include as much of yourself—your feelings, your thoughts—as possible. Think of something you did recently, or something that happened to you, that made a difference in your life.

What did you do?

What did you say?

How did you feel?

How did you show your reactions and feelings?

Your story does not have to be about something that happened to you recently, however. Think about experiences from your early childhood that made a strong impression on you. You can use your memory and even your imagination to write about things that happened to you a long time ago.

Practice

A. Make a list of at least one time each of these experiences has happened to you.

1. finding or losing something
2. seeing or doing something that was unexpected or exciting
3. learning how to do something for the first time
4. moving to a new neighborhood or going to a new school
5. doing something by yourself for the first time
6. changing your mind about a person or idea

B. Choose one incident from the list that you think would make a good story. (This will not necessarily be the same incident you will write about.) Explore the incident by making notes on each of these questions. Be as exact as possible.

1. Who was involved? List two details about each person.
2. Where did it take place? What was the place like at this time? List at least five background sounds and sights.
3. What was said? Write two or three statements as exactly as you can.
4. Where would you start in telling this story? Where would you stop?

C. Tell your story to a classmate. Then discuss whether you told enough about yourself—your thoughts, feelings, reactions—and about other people. Did you tell too much? too little? Did your details about the event make it seem real to your listener? Should you expand your story or limit it? Did your listener have a clear picture of what happened and how it felt to be there at the time?

Steps for Writing About Yourself   Here are the steps for writing a story about yourself. You will follow these steps to write your own story.

Step One	Choose a topic.
Step Two	Explore your topic.
Step Three	Write your story.
Step Four	Revise your story.
Step Five	Proofread your story.
Step Six	Make a final copy to share.

6 | Choose a Topic

Which of your experiences should you write about? Your choice is important because you want to please yourself as well as your audience. Suppose you wrote that the happiest event of your life was a certain summer or a vacation trip or a year on the track team. It would be difficult to make a whole summer or a whole trip or a whole year's experience come alive for a reader in just a few pages. Thinking back over those times, you could pick the most exciting or important or amusing part to write about. If you think you would like to write about moving or going to a new school, you could focus on one part of the experience, one day, or even one hour of that day.

Look back at the list of experiences you wrote for the practice exercise on page 170. Then consider them in terms of these questions.

1. Which experience can you recall most clearly? Can you make this experience real for your readers? Can you remember significant details that will carry the story along and bring the event and your feelings to life?
2. Which experience was the most memorable for you? What made it so unforgettable? Did a change take place in your life, or inside you, as a result of this experience?
3. Can you narrow the scope of this experience and highlight a particular incident or brief period of time?

You can ask yourself those basic questions, no matter what kind of experience you plan to write about. You could write about a really exciting game, or a time when you were very sick, or an achievement that made you feel proud and happy, and still use those questions to help you remember and write effectively.

As Marcia thought about experiences that were important and memorable to her, she jotted down ideas for possible topics. This is Marcia's list.

sliding on ice mountains at Lake Erie
the day my cat Coco died
my first time flying
my pizza party

Marcia read over her list. She knew that sliding on the ice on Lake Erie would be fun to write about because it had been different from anything she had ever experienced. Her classmates might be surprised to see how adventurous and brave she could be! She remembered vividly how sad she had felt when her cat was run over, but she decided that the memory was still too painful to explore in detail. She had written her feelings about losing Coco in her diary, but she did not want to write about them again, not yet.

Although her first airplane ride had been exciting, Marcia decided that nothing unusual had happened to make it particularly interesting for someone else to read about. Her pizza party had been fun. Thinking back on it now, though, she realized that her memory of the details had faded. Marcia looked over some notes she had made, and she decided that sliding at Lake Erie was her favorite topic to write about. She circled that choice.

Assignment
- **Make a List**
- **Choose a Topic**

A. Make a list of at least four possible topics. Use the list under practice exercise A on page 170 to help you think of topics that may not have occurred to you before. If your discussion partner gave you other ideas, add them to your list. Then use the questions on page 171 to help you consider and compare your topics.

B. Decide which topic you would most like to write about, and circle your choice.

7 | Step Two
Explore Your Topic

How can you make your experience come alive for your readers? Details are the key, just as they are when you are writing a description. Writing a narrative is simply describing an experience. If you want your reader to feel what it was like to be there and to feel what you felt, you need to imagine yourself back in that situation. What were the sights and sounds and smells and tastes? What were your feelings?

Jog your memory so that you can *show* your readers what really happened, rather than merely explaining or making observations.

Read these paragraphs. Which one is more descriptive?

1.   Our family was all ready to start off on our trip to the Badlands, except for one thing. I suddenly remembered that I hadn't packed my camera. Everyone was impatient when I went back inside the house.

2.   Excitement ran high on that bright, sunny day as we got in the car. Then suddenly I yelled, "Wait a minute! My camera!" I raced for the house, followed by a chorus of groans. I searched drawers and shelves—where could it be?

Which paragraph makes statements? Which one shows you what it was like to have the experience? Which details make the scene real?

Use the following questions to help you recall details about your experience.

1. Where was I? Was I indoors or outdoors? How did the place look? sound? smell? Did the place make me feel comfortable or uneasy?
2. What time of year was it—spring, summer, fall, or winter?
3. What time of day was it? What was the weather like?
4. Who else was involved? What were these people like?
5. What did I and others say? What tones of voice did we use?

Assignment   • **Make Notes on Your Topic**

A. Using the questions above as a guide, make notes on your topic. List as many details as you can. You can choose which details to include or omit later on.

B. Write a sentence about where you want your story to begin and another about where you intend the story to end.

8 | Step Three
Write Your Story

Now you are ready to let words flow from your memory and imagination onto your paper. As Marcia wrote the first draft of her story, she consulted her notes. She did not worry about mistakes in spelling and grammar at this point.

Marcia's first draft

Last year we went to visit my Grandpa and Grandma. They live in New York State on lake Erie and I had never been there before in the winter, so I didn't know what to expect. I had a big surprise waiting for me. The shore of the lake was practically ~~full~~ lined with ice mountains. Everyone in the world seemed to be ~~there~~ sliding on them. I had never slid on this kind of ice before. ~~Anyway,~~ I couldn't wait to go. I borrowed my cousin Sams red parka and Mom and Dad got all buttonned ~~and boots~~ up and off we went. I had a sled called starship and Sam had the Flying Saucer, which he was acting very superier about. ~~The~~ It was ~~like a big~~ a plastic saucer big enough to sit in, and it had two handles to hang onto and I was really scared at first because the mountains were pretty steep, but they were full of people with red noses and cheeks who were having a great time. They were using everything imaginable to slide on. After a little while, I got used to it. Then I wanted to try sliding down my own ice mountain, so I went farther out. ~~Then~~ The sky got gray and cloudy snowflakes began falling. Sam yelled, "We should go back! But there in front of me was the highest slope yet.

"Oh, great! Come on Sam," I called. I started up the slope, but I got a wierd feeling. Sam wasn't with me. I jumped onto the saucer to slide back down. I fell off and rolled. When I got up thick snow swirrled around me. I was definitely lost ~~Then when I~~ Just then I heard Moms voice calling me. I was saved! That was the end of one of the most frightening experiences of my life.

- Does Marcia's beginning catch your attention? Why, or why not?
- What details did Marcia give to make her story come to life?
- Where could she add more details to give you a clearer picture?
- Marcia's story needs paragraph breaks. Where should she make them?
- Does Marcia's ending show or just tell the outcome of her experience? What feeling, if any, does it leave you with?
- Where, if at all, did Marcia write long, stringy sentences? short, choppy sentences?

Assignment • **Write Your First Draft**

Write the first draft of your story. You may want to skip a line as you write in order to make changes later. Consult your list of details and include the best ones. Remember to include dialogue wherever it seems appropriate. Do not worry about mistakes in spelling, punctuation and capitalization at this point. Just get down what you want to say, and then you can revise later on.

9 | Step Four
Revise Your Story

Writers often feel relieved after they finish writing a first draft. Even though they know they will find a lot of things to change later, they know they have made a good start.

When Marcia read over her story, she decided that her beginning would not catch anyone's attention. Marcia wrote a new one. Then she thought of a better idea. Here are the new beginnings.

> The most frightening thing that ever happened to me was the time I got lost on a frozen lake. We were at my Grandpa and Grandma's house, and my dad said, "Let's go sliding on the lake."
>
> Lake Erie started to freeze early in December last year, but then some warmer days broke the ice into giant slabs floting in thick slush when the wind blew hard it drove the slabs up over each other and splashed them with slush. After a couple of days, the shore was lined with ice mountains.

Marcia looked over her beginnings and immediately crossed out the first one; it gave her story away. She liked the second one because she thought it would make someone wonder what had happened there. She noted where to insert it and made some changes to go with it.

Next, Marcia reread her whole story and marked places where she wanted to add details. She also fixed some long, stringy sentences and marked for paragraph breaks. Finally, she crossed out her last two sentences. They were a letdown after such an exciting story. She wrote a new ending.

Then Marcia read her story to Ann. When she finished, Ann said, "I could really see this huge, strange place and I got the feeling it might be dangerous. I really felt as if I was there. But why were you on the flying saucer at the end? Wasn't it Sam's?"

"Yes," said Marcia, "and I should put it in that he let me borrow it. Thanks for the idea. Reading my story to you gave me some other new ideas." Marcia did more work on her paper.

Part of Marcia's revision

^ (insert my new beginning)

My grandparents had just moved to

~~Last year we went to visit my Grandpa and~~ a place.

~~Grandma. They live in New York State~~ on lake Erie

this was the first time we had

and ~~I had never been there before in the winter, so I~~ visited them there.

~~didn't know what to expect.~~ I had a big surprise wait-

ing for me. The shore of the lake was ~~practically full~~

~~lined with~~ ice mountains. Everyone in the world

the ice mountains

seemed to be ~~there~~ sliding on ^them. I had never slid on

this kind of ice before. ~~Anyway,~~ I couldn't wait to go. I

shiney

borrowed my cousin Sam's ^red parka and Mom and

Dad got all buttonned ~~and boots~~ up and off we went. ¶ I

^

had a sled called starship and Sam had the Flying Sau-

cer, which he was acting very superier about. ~~The~~ It

red

was ~~like a big~~ ^a plastic saucer big enough to sit in, and

it had two handles to hang onto ~~and~~ I was really

quite

scared at first because the mountains were ^pretty

steep, but they were full of people with red noses and

cheeks who were having a great time. They were us-

there were sleds, saucers, mats, and trash can lids.

ing everything imaginable to slide on. ^After a little

while, I got used to it. Then I wanted to try sliding

down my own ice mountain, so I went farther out. Sam

was impressed with my sliding and let me

use his saucer.

Look again at Marcia's revisions on the previous page as you answer these questions.

- How did Marcia change her old beginning to go with the new one that she will insert?
- What details did she add? How do they improve her story?
- Where did she indicate new paragraphs? What mark did she use?
- Which long, stringy sentence did Marcia fix?

Marcia's new ending

> I don't know how long I stumbled around those ice mountains, hoping to see someone. It got darker and colder. Suddenly I heard a voice, and I shouted for help.
>
> "Stay where you are and keep yelling, Marcia!" the voice called. It was Mom! I was saved!

- Is Marcia's new ending better than her original one? Why?
- How does the new ending show action? feelings?
- What feeling does the new ending leave you with?

Assignment
- **Revise Your Story**
- **Discuss Your Story**

A. Read your first draft. Have you included enough details to create a true picture of what happened? Have you shown how you felt at the time?

B. Check both your beginning and your ending. Is the beginning interesting? Write two or three new beginnings and use the best one. Does your ending effectively finish the story? Write a new ending and use the best.

C. Read your story to a classmate. Discuss its strong points. Discuss ways to improve it. If your listener has suggestions you like, use them. Make any other changes you think would improve your story.

10 | Step Five
Proofread Your Story

Now it is time to proofread your story for mistakes in spelling, punctuation, and capitalization. If you used dialogue, look on page 466 in the handbook at the back of this book to review punctuation for direct quotations. If necessary, check a dictionary for spellings.

When Marcia had finished making her changes, she copied her paper over. She added a title. Then she proofread her story.

Part of Marcia's story after proofreading

> Lost on the Lake
>
> Lake Erie started to freeze early in December last year, but then some warmer days broke the ice into giant slabs floating in thick slush. when the wind blew hard, it drove the slabs up over each other and splashed them with slush. After a couple of days, the shore was lined with ice mountains.
>
> My grandparents had just moved to a place on lake Erie, and this was the first time we had visited them there. Everyone in the world seemed to be sliding on the ice mountains. I had never slid on this kind of ice before. I couldn't wait to go! I borrowed my cousin Sam's shiney red parka, and Mom and Dad got all buttonned up, and off we went.
>
> I had a sled called Starship and Sam had the Flying Saucer, which he was acting very superier about.

- What misspelled words did Marcia correct?
- Where did she add or change punctuation, and why?
- What other changes did she make?

Practice

Proofread this part of Marcia's story. Try to spot the ten errors. Use a dictionary to check the spellings of any words you are unsure about. Copy the three paragraphs, making the necessary corrections.

After a little while, I got used to it. Then I wanted to try sliding down my own ice mountain, so I went farther out. Sam was impresed with my sliding and let me use his saucer.

The sky got gray and cloudy snowflakes began falling. Sam yelled, "We should go back! But there in front of me was the highest slope yet.

"Oh, great! Come on Sam," I called. I started up the slope, but I got a wierd feeling. Sam wasn't with me. I jumped onto the saucer to slide back down. I fell off and rolled. When I got up thick snow swirrled around me. I was definitely lost

Assignment • Proofread Your Story

Proofread your story, using these questions as a guide.

1. Have I made appropriate paragraph breaks?
2. Are all the words spelled correctly? Have I looked up any word I am unsure of?
3. Have I written dialogue correctly?

Grammar skills checklist

4. Have I punctuated sentences correctly and corrected any run-ons?
5. Have I used commas correctly with compound sentences, dependent clauses, and appositives?
6. Have I used apostrophes with contractions and possessive nouns?
7. Do the subject and verb agree in each sentence?

11 | Step Six
Make a Final Copy

Because Marcia had spent a lot of time and effort polishing her story, she now wanted to share it in a special way. First, she copied it neatly and checked it once more for copying errors. Then she made a display.

Marcia taped her story to the center of a large piece of blue poster paper. Then, around the story, she carefully arranged some snapshots that her family had taken of her sliding on the ice mountains. In addition, she had some pictures that she had cut from a nature magazine that showed the huge slabs of ice along the shore of Lake Erie. When she had finished arranging the pictures and snapshots, she taped them to the poster. Finally, Marcia displayed her poster in the classroom.

Assignment
- **Make a Final Copy**
- **Share Your Story**

A. Write a final, neat copy of your story. When you have finished, check it carefully to be sure you did not omit anything and that you have corrected all your mistakes.

B. Think of a way to share your story with your class.
- Read it aloud, or have someone else read it as you dramatize it.
- Make a poster or a display, as Marcia did, which shows pictures of the story's action, setting, or characters.
- Make a booklet, using drawings, snapshots, or cartoons to illustrate your story.

Pronouns

1 | Personal Pronouns

You would not be likely to say or write something like this.

> Donna and Donna's brother Philip like tennis. Donna and Philip play whenever Donna's and Philip's schedules leave Donna and Philip some time.

That is not how people ordinarily talk or write. It would be much more natural to express the sentences in this way.

> Donna and <u>her</u> brother Philip like tennis. <u>They</u> play whenever <u>their</u> schedules leave <u>them</u> some time.

Her, they, their, and *them* are pronouns. A **pronoun** takes the place of a noun. Pronouns can be used wherever nouns are used in sentences.

The pronouns that took the place of *Donna* and *Philip* in the sentences above are **personal pronouns**. The personal pronouns are listed on the next page.

The form of a personal pronoun is determined by its (1) **person**, (2) **number**, and sometimes (3) **gender**.

A pronoun in the **first person** refers to the person or persons speaking: *I, me, my, mine, we, us, our, ours.* A pronoun in the **second person** refers to the person or persons spoken to: *you, your, yours.* A pronoun in the **third person** refers to the person or persons spoken about: *she, her, hers, he, him, his, it, its, they, them, their, theirs.*

> 1ST PERSON: <u>I</u> reserved three seats for <u>us</u>.
> 2ND PERSON: Have <u>you</u> returned <u>your</u> books to the library?
> 3RD PERSON: <u>She</u> spoke to <u>him</u> about <u>their</u> assignment.

Pronouns show number. Like nouns, they have singular and plural forms.

> SINGULAR: <u>He</u> and <u>I</u> walked the horse to <u>its</u> stall.
> PLURAL: <u>We</u> walked the horses to <u>their</u> stalls.

Third person singular pronouns also show gender. They can be **feminine** (*she*), **masculine** (*he*), or **neuter** (*it*).

> FEMININE: Lottie finally found <u>her</u> suede gloves.
> MASCULINE: Mr. Lenz may be eccentric, but <u>he</u> is very imaginative.
> NEUTER: The fish has a glowing white stripe on <u>its</u> back.

Here is a list of the personal pronouns.

	Singular	**Plural**
1st person	I, me, my, mine	we, us, our, ours
2nd person	you, your, yours	you, your, yours
3rd person	*Masculine:* he, him, his	they, them, their, theirs
	Feminine: she, her, hers	
	Neuter: it, its	

Try It Out

Give the person (1st, 2nd, 3rd) and number (singular, plural) of each underlined pronoun. For a third person singular pronoun, also give the gender (masculine, feminine, neuter).

1. <u>She</u> has spent a lot of <u>her</u> time working on <u>it</u>.
2. Will one of <u>you</u> drive <u>him</u> to <u>my</u> house?
3. <u>They</u> have told <u>us</u> wonderful stories about <u>their</u> childhood.

▸ A **pronoun** is a word that takes the place of a noun.
Personal pronouns have different forms depending on their person (1st, 2nd, 3rd) and number (singular, plural).
Third person singular pronouns have different forms depending on their gender (masculine, feminine, neuter).

Written Practice

Copy each underlined pronoun. Next to it, write its person *(1st, 2nd,* or *3rd)* and number *(singular* or *plural).* If it is a third person singular pronoun, also write its gender *(masculine, feminine,* or *neuter).*

1. <u>He</u> has a part-time job that gives <u>him</u> much satisfaction.
2. <u>She</u> and <u>he</u> pick up used paper, while <u>I</u> drive the truck for <u>them</u>.
3. The three of <u>us</u> work hard, for <u>we</u> know <u>our</u> job is important.
4. Does one of <u>you</u> not know that paper is a valuable product?
5. When <u>it</u> is recycled, energy and trees are conserved for other uses.

● **Writing Sentences**   Write five sentences with various personal pronouns.

2 | Antecedents of Pronouns

A pronoun has little meaning of its own. For its meaning, a pronoun depends on the noun it replaces.

> The catcher's **mitt** is worn, but it is comfortable.
> **Lucas** has painted his bicycle blue.
> The **sneakers** should be under the chair. Are they there?

Mitt, *Lucas*, and *sneakers* name the things to which the pronouns *it*, *his*, and *they* refer. The noun to which a pronoun refers is called its **antecedent**. The prefix *ante-* means "before." The antecedent usually goes before the pronoun that refers to it. The antecedent and pronoun do not have to be in the same sentence, however, as you can see from the last example.

Sometimes the antecedent actually comes after the pronoun rather than before it.

> Although she was late, **Hannah** walked slowly.
> When the hot water touched it, the **glass** cracked.

The antecedent of a pronoun is occasionally another pronoun.

> By seven o'clock, **I** had finished my assignment.

No matter where or what the antecedent is, the pronoun must agree with it. Pronouns must agree with their antecedents in number. If they are third person singular pronouns, they must also agree in gender.

> **Evelyn** finished her work. *(singular, feminine)*
> **Keith** finished his work. *(singular, masculine)*
> The **report** is in its folder. *(singular, neuter)*
> The **students** finished their work. *(plural)*

When the antecedent is made up of two or more nouns joined by *and*, the pronoun is a plural form.

> **Marissa** and **Julia** will give their report next. *(plural)*

When the antecedent is made up of two or more nouns joined by *or*, the pronoun agrees in number with the nearest noun.

> Did **Leon** or **Roy** forget his jacket? *(singular)*
> Will the **lead** or the supporting **players** read their parts? *(plural)*

Try It Out

Complete each sentence with the correct pronoun.

1. During rehearsals, actors sometimes forget (his, their) lines.
2. Neither the papers nor the book was in (their, its) right place.
3. Gauguin painted (his, their) most famous works in the South Pacific.
4. The wolf and its baby rested in (its, their) den.

> ▸ The noun or nouns to which a pronoun refers are known as its **antecedent**.
>
> Pronouns agree with their antecedents in number and gender.

Written Practice

Write the correct personal pronoun. Next to it, write its antecedent.

1. Some authors create (their, his) own illustrations.
2. Neither the characters nor the plot fulfills (their, its) promise.
3. Cora told (its, her) story in the form of a poem.
4. The story has (its, his) beginning in the Revolutionary War.
5. Before (they, she) can appreciate the story, the students must know something about that period in history.
6. I shall review (my, its) notes this afternoon.
7. Have you met Ms. Ellis? (He, She) spoke to our English class today.
8. While (they, it) can be long, her talks are never dull.

● **Writing Sentences**   Think of an appropriate antecedent for each pronoun. Then use the pronoun and antecedent in a sentence.

9. he   10. her   11. it   12. they   13. them

3 | Subject and Object Pronouns

Pronouns take the place of nouns. Therefore, they can be used in sentences in the same ways that nouns are used.

SUBJECT: <u>Claude Monet</u> painted a pond at different times.
<u>He</u> painted a pond at different times.

DIRECT OBJECT: Admirers of Impressionist paintings respect <u>Monet</u>.
Admirers of Impressionist paintings respect <u>him</u>.

INDIRECT OBJECT: Art lovers have given <u>Monet</u> great recognition.
Art lovers have given <u>him</u> great recognition.

Pronouns have different **case** forms. Pronouns used as subjects, like *he*, are in the **nominative case**. Pronouns used as objects, like *him*, are in the **objective case**.

NOMINATIVE CASE: <u>We</u> admired Cara's rock collection.
OBJECTIVE CASE: Cara called <u>us</u>.
OBJECTIVE CASE: She showed <u>us</u> her collection.

Pronouns in the nominative case are called **subject pronouns**. Pronouns in the objective case are called **object pronouns**. Notice in the examples above that object pronouns are used as both direct and indirect objects.

	Subject Pronouns	**Object Pronouns**
1st person	I, we	me, us
2nd person	you	you
3rd person	he, she, it, they	him, her, it, them

A noun used after a linking verb is called a predicate noun. A pronoun used in the same way is called a **predicate pronoun**. A predicate pronoun, like a predicate noun, renames the subject. The subject pronoun form is used.

The man with the easel is <u>he</u>.   The directors are <u>they</u>.

In informal speech, you may hear object pronouns used: *It's me. Is that her?* While object pronouns may be acceptable in casual speech, in your writing use subject pronouns after linking verbs.

Try It Out

Tell how each underlined noun is used—as a subject, predicate noun, direct object, indirect object. Then tell what pronoun can replace the noun.

1. <u>Money</u> can be any agreed-upon medium of exchange.
2. People have used <u>beads, teeth, shells, and cattle</u>.
3. <u>Emily Post</u> wrote books about etiquette.
4. Was it really <u>Emily Post</u>?
5. One of the most loyal servants in literature is <u>Sancho Panza</u>.
6. Sancho Panza, Don Quixote's faithful squire, served <u>Quixote</u> well.
7. Quixote often gave <u>Sancho Panza</u> impossible missions.

▸ Pronouns that are used differently have different **case** forms.
▸ A pronoun used as a subject is in the **nominative case**. It is called a **subject pronoun**.
▸ A pronoun used as an object is in the **objective case**. It is called an **object pronoun**.
Use subject pronoun forms after linking verbs.

Written Practice

Write the correct pronoun form. Then write *subject* or *object* to describe the form.

1. The woman in the gray flannel suit is (she, her).
2. Their employer paid (they, them) a full week's wages.
3. It was (he, him) behind the Halloween mask.
4. Although (he, him) sounded convincing, (they, them) did not fully believe (he, him).
5. Who has sent (I, me) this article about broom making?
6. The elephant did not remember (we, us).
7. (She, Her) had last seen (they, them) on Broadway.
8. The cadets at the end of the line are (they, them).
9. (We, Us) informed (she, her) of our plans to work in the hospital.
10. Please tell (I, me) the story, but don't tell (he, him).

• **Writing Sentences** Use each pronoun in a sentence of your own.

11. I   12. her   13. he   14. them   15. us

4 | Compound Subjects and Objects

Compound subjects can include pronouns as well as nouns, as this series of sentences shows.

> Norman and Beatrice write scripts for radio and television.
> Norman and <u>she</u> write scripts for radio and television.
> <u>He</u> and <u>she</u> write scripts for radio and television.

Like pronouns in simple subjects, pronouns in compound subjects are always in the nominative case.

> <u>He</u> *(not* him*)* and Beatrice are writers.
> Norman and <u>she</u> *(not* her*)* are writers.

If you have any doubt about which pronoun form to use, say the sentence with the pronoun alone. The choice will then become clearer.

> Mr. Toomey and (I? me?) spent the day working.
> <u>I</u> spent the day working.
> Mr. Toomey and <u>I</u> spent the day working.

If the compound includes several pronouns, say each pronoun separately with the rest of the sentence.

> (He? Him?) and (she? her?) spent the day working.
> <u>He</u> spent the day working.
> <u>She</u> spent the day working.
> <u>He</u> and <u>she</u> spent the day working.

Pronouns used as objects are always in the objective case, no matter how many objects there are.

> The skunk did not notice Valentino, Erica, or <u>me</u> *(not* I*)*.
> Our aunt in India sent Peggy and <u>me</u> *(not* Peggy and I*)* a gift.
> Send <u>her</u> and Anne *(not* she and Anne*)* a postcard.

Once again, if you say the sentence with the pronoun alone, it will be easier to decide which form to use.

> Please ask Dr. Torchin and (she? her?) that question.
> Please ask <u>her</u> that question.
> Please ask Dr. Torchin and <u>her</u> that question.

Try It Out

Choose the correct pronoun to complete each sentence.

1. Sandy, Maureen, and (I, me) are good friends.
2. The tiny dog followed Fritz and (I, me) home.
3. Clark may not tell his sister or (we, us) about the results.
4. The only ones here are Lydia, (he, him), and (I, me).
5. Our parents gave Mike and (I, me) a badminton set for the yard.
6. The last visitors were Jake and (she, her).
7. (He, Him) and (I, me) are going shopping.
8. Will they choose Fred or (she, her) to be the representative?

> Use subject pronouns in compound subjects and in compounds
>   following linking verbs.
> Use object pronouns in compound objects.

Written Practice

Write the correct pronoun to complete each sentence.

1. Her cousin and (she, her) shared a room.
2. Has anyone called Lana or (he, him) tonight?
3. (He, Him), Jane, and (we, us) are expected for dinner.
4. Don't give Carol or (I, me) any more, please.
5. Have you seen Ms. Tillinghast or (he, him)?
6. (He, Him) and (I, me) plan to leave immediately after school.
7. Ask the police officer or (he, him) for advice.
8. You cannot convince the committee or (they, them) easily.
9. Will you sell my uncle, my aunt, and (I, me) those records?
10. The librarian asked Kevin, Tony, and (she, her) for assistance.
11. The best candidates for that office are (he, him) and Kurt.
12. (They, Them) and (we, us) are going to the mountains together.
13. (She, Her), Dan, and (I, me) walked slowly in the warm sunshine.
14. It was definitely Denise and (he, him) at the carnival.

- **Writing Sentences**   Use each compound as indicated in a sentence.

15. my friend and I *(subject)*
16. Sal, Ann, and I *(predicate nouns and pronoun)*
17. the puppy and me *(object)*
18. Mr. Nolan and him *(object)*

5 | Possessive Pronouns

Compare the underlined nouns and pronouns in these sentences.

The <u>mayor's aide</u> is here.   The <u>mayors'</u> aides are here.
<u>His</u> aide is here.   <u>Their</u> aides are here.

The underlined words in the top sentences are possessive nouns. The underlined words in the sentences below them are pronouns that can replace possessive nouns. A pronoun that replaces a possessive noun is called a **possessive pronoun**.

As you have learned, pronouns used as subjects are in the nominative case, and pronouns used as objects are in the objective case. Pronouns used to show possession are in the **possessive case**.

POSSESSIVE CASE: <u>Her</u> desk is always covered with papers.

While possessive nouns use apostrophes to show possession, possessive pronouns use special forms.

	Singular	**Plural**
1st person	my, mine	our, ours
2nd person	your, yours	your, yours
3rd person	his, her, hers, its	their, theirs

Notice that most possessive pronouns have two forms for each person: *my, mine*. The different forms have different uses.

That was <u>her</u> decision.   The decision was <u>hers</u>.

One form—*my, your, his, her, its, our, their*—is used before nouns. The other form—*mine, yours, hers, ours, theirs*—is used by itself. *His* can be used in either position.

Remember, possessive nouns always use apostrophes, but possessive pronouns never do. A pronoun used with an apostrophe is a **contraction**, not a possessive form. Certain possessive pronouns and contractions sound alike. Do not confuse them in your writing.

Possessive Pronouns	**Contractions**
your	you're (you are)
its	it's (it is)
their	they're (they are)
theirs	there's (there is)

Try It Out

A. Complete each sentence pair with a possessive pronoun.

1. She and he bought the chess set. It is ____ chess set.
2. She and he bought the chess set. It is ____.
3. That poem is by Edna St. Vincent Millay. It is ____ poem.
4. That poem is by Edna St. Vincent Millay. The poem is ____.

B. Choose the correct form.

5. (They're, Their) letters are filled with details.
6. Can this possibly be (you're, your) little brother?
7. The goat seems to have hurt (it's, its) leg.

> ▸ A **possessive pronoun** can replace a possessive noun.
> Possessive pronouns are in the possessive case.
> Possessive pronouns never use apostrophes.

Written Practice

A. Write the possessive pronoun that correctly completes each sentence.

1. *Silent Spring*, written by Rachel Carson, was ____ book.
2. The book was written by her. The book is ____.
3. The Tanejas have a large dog. The large dog is ____.
4. The Tanejas' dog is large. Have you seen ____ dog?
5. This pin belongs to me. It is ____ pin.
6. This pin belongs to me. It is ____.
7. The discovery was made by him. It was ____ discovery.

B. Write the correct form.

8. A pelican's beak does not hold more than (it's, its) stomach.
9. The gold medal should have been (there's, theirs).
10. You should have put (you're, your) things with ours.
11. (They're, Their) coats have all been hung in the hall closet.

● **Writing Sentences**   Use each form in two sentences.

12. your   13. its   14. their   15. yours

6 | Interrogative Pronouns

Subject, object, and possessive pronouns are all personal pronouns. While personal pronouns are probably the pronouns you use most, there are other kinds of pronouns as well. For example, many of the words you use to ask questions are pronouns, like *who*, *which*, and *what*.

Who said that?   What did he say?   Which do you mean?

A pronoun that is used to form a question is an **interrogative pronoun**. Do you know where the antecedents of these pronouns are? They can be found in the answers to the questions.

Who said that?   I said that.
What did he say?   He said nothing.
Which do you mean?   I mean the dictionary.

The words *which* and *what* can be used before nouns: *which* letter? *what* question? When they are used in this way, they replace adjectives rather than nouns. Therefore they are not considered to be pronouns.

Pronoun Usage	**Adjective Usage**
Which of these pictures do you like?	Which picture do you like?
What is your plan?	What plan will you follow?

The interrogative pronoun *who* changes form according to how it is used in the sentence. *Who* is used as a subject pronoun, *whom* is used as an object pronoun, and *whose* is used as a possessive pronoun.

SUBJECT: He knows the story.   Who knows the story?
OBJECT: I have told him.   Whom have you told?
POSSESSIVE: The car is his.   Whose is the car?

To help you decide whether to use *who* or *whom*, turn the question into a statement.

(Who, Whom) shall we choose?   We shall choose (who, whom).

Whom, the object form, is correct.

Do not confuse *whose* and *who's*, which sound alike. *Whose* is a possessive interrogative pronoun; *who's* is a contraction of *who is*.

Whose are these glasses? *(possessive pronoun)*
Who's at the door? *(contraction of* who is*)*

Try It Out

Choose the correct pronoun or contraction to complete each sentence.

1. (Who's, Whose) are these suitcases?
2. (Who, Whom) did you send for the food?
3. (Who's, Whose) is the car parked on the corner?
4. (Who, Whom) was responsible for the decorations in the corridor?
5. (Who, Whom) should we ask for a ride?
6. (Who, Whom) did Ricardo believe?
7. (Who, Whom) can solve the mystery of the missing glove?
8. (Who's, Whose) going on the picnic to Crane's Beach?

> ▸ **Interrogative pronouns** like *who, which, what, whom,* and *whose* introduce questions.
>
> *Who* is used as a subject, *whom* as an object, and *whose* as a possessive.
>
> Do not confuse *whose* with the contraction *who's*.

Written Practice

Write the correct form to complete each sentence.

1. (Who's, Whose) is the horse that Blake has been riding?
2. (Who, Whom) have you asked to the dance?
3. (Who, Whom) will groom the pony?
4. (Who, Whom) did you meet in Seattle?
5. (Who's, Whose) trying out for the marching band?
6. (Who, Whom) recommended you for this job?
7. (Who, Whom) have you nominated for secretary?
8. (Who, Whom) will you choose to be treasurer?
9. (Who's, Whose) are the posters outside the auditorium?
10. (Who, Whom) will be the next president of the committee?

● **Writing Sentences**   Use each form as an interrogative pronoun in a sentence of your own.

11. which   **12.** who   **13.** whose   **14.** whom   **15.** what

7 | Demonstrative Pronouns

Pronouns can be used to point out persons, things, or ideas. A pronoun that points out something is called a **demonstrative pronoun**.

SINGULAR: <u>This</u> is her parka. <u>That</u> is his tennis racket.
PLURAL: <u>These</u> are her parkas. <u>Those</u> are his tennis rackets.

This, that, these, and *those* in the sentences above are demonstrative pronouns. Notice that they agree in number with the nouns they point out. *Parka* and *tennis racket* are singular; *this* and *that* are used to refer to them. *Parkas* and *tennis rackets* are plural; *these* and *those* are used to refer to them.

The forms *this* and *these* are used to point to things nearby. *That* and *those* are used to point to things farther away.

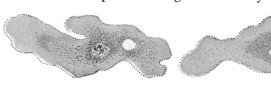

<u>This</u> is a clear specimen under the microscope.
<u>These</u> are amoeba that we are examining.
<u>That</u> is a broken microscope over there.
<u>Those</u> are repaired microscopes in the next room.

The words *this, that, these,* and *those* can also be used before nouns. When they are used in this way, they are used as adjectives rather than pronouns. When they are used alone, they function as pronouns.

ADJECTIVE: I don't want <u>this</u> picture. *(modifies* picture*)*
PRONOUN: I don't want *this. (direct object)*

ADJECTIVE: <u>These</u> shoes are too small. *(modifies* shoes*)*
PRONOUN: *These* are too small. *(subject)*

Avoid expressions like *this here* and *that there. This* already means "the one here," and *that* already means "the one there." Adding the words *here* and *there* is repetitive.

<u>This</u> *(not* this here*)* is an electronic typewriter.
<u>That</u> *(not* that there*)* was my favorite movie.
<u>These</u> *(not* these here*)* are not comfortable shoes.
<u>Those</u> *(not* those there*)* must be Henry's parents.

Try It Out

Choose the correct form to complete each sentence.

1. (This, These) is the house with the fabulous decorations.
2. (These, These here) are my favorite carvings.
3. (That, Those) are the paintings done by my grandfather.
4. (That, That there) is a beautiful old carousel horse.
5. (This, That) must be a portrait of Colonel Flagg on the far wall.

> ▸ A **demonstrative pronoun** points out things, persons, or ideas.
> *This* and *these* point out things that are close.
> *That* and *those* point out things that are farther away.
> *This* and *that* refer to singular nouns or pronouns.
> *These* and *those* refer to plural nouns or pronouns.
> Avoid expressions like *this here* and *those there*.

Written Practice

A. Write the form that correctly completes the sentence.

1. (This, That) is Dr. Spiegler's seat in the far corner.
2. Is (this, that) my seat right here?
3. (This, These) could be the baroness's jewels.
4. (This, These) must be her diamond tiara.
5. (That, Those) cannot be genuine rubies or emeralds.
6. (These, Those) must be her furs in the next room.

B. Rewrite each sentence correctly.

7. I prefer that there.
8. This must be your favorite records.
9. Do you want this here or that?
10. These here are the songs I like to sing.
11. These are my plaid socks under that washing machine.
12. Can that be a tarantula right here?

- **Writing Sentences**   Use each word as a demonstrative pronoun in a sentence.

   13. this   **14.** that   **15.** these   **16.** those

8 | Indefinite Pronouns

Forms

Certain pronouns do not refer to a definite person or thing. Here are some examples.

<u>Everyone</u> will be welcome.   <u>Something</u> is wrong.

Everyone and *something* are used as subjects. *Everyone* refers to any one of a group of people. *Something* refers to a thing that is not identified. A pronoun that does not refer to anyone or anything definite is called an **indefinite pronoun**.

The person or thing referred to by a pronoun like *something* is just one thing, whatever it is. Therefore, it is singular. A pronoun like *many,* on the other hand, refers to more than one person or thing and, therefore, is plural. Other indefinite pronouns may be regarded as singular or plural, depending on how they are used.

Singular			Plural	Singular or Plural
another	everybody	nothing	both	all
anybody	everyone	other	few	any
anyone	everything	one	many	most
anything	neither	somebody	ones	none
each	nobody	someone	others	some
either	no one	something	several	

Some words that can be used as indefinite pronouns can also be used before nouns as adjectives.

ADJECTIVE: <u>Each</u> book has been autographed.
PRONOUN: <u>Each</u> of the books has been autographed.

Try It Out

Identify each indefinite pronoun. Tell whether it is singular or plural.

1. Everybody in the class has been looking for something.
2. Several have been found, but not by anyone here.
3. Someone next door found a few under a desk.
4. Although everyone has searched for the others, no one has found them.

Agreement with Indefinite Pronouns

You know that verbs must agree with their subjects in number. When an indefinite pronoun is the subject, the verb must agree with it.

SINGULAR: <u>Someone</u> **has found** the lost young child.
PLURAL: <u>Many</u> **were searching**.

In most cases, words that come between the subject and the verb will not affect the agreement.

SINGULAR: <u>Everyone</u> in the woods **was** searching.
PLURAL: <u>Several</u> by the truck **were** reporters.

There is an exception to this general rule, however. Some indefinite pronouns can be used as either singular or plural forms. Their number is determined by their meaning in particular sentences. Often, the words that follow the pronoun will tell you the meaning.

SINGULAR: <u>Most</u> of the turkey **has been eaten**.
PLURAL: <u>Most</u> of the passengers **have been rescued**.

In the first sentence, *most* refers to a single, uncountable amount of turkey; it is considered to be singular. In the second sentence, *most* refers to several passengers; it is considered to be plural. A different verb form is used to agree with *most* in each case.

When indefinite pronouns are used as antecedents of other pronouns, the other pronouns must agree with them.

SINGULAR: <u>Everything</u> had been put in **its** place.
PLURAL: <u>Both</u> have been put in **their** places.

Most of the singular indefinite pronouns can refer to either males or females. There is no problem if the gender is clear.

<u>Everyone</u> on the girls' soccer team had **her** eyes on the ball.
<u>Each</u> of the brothers has done **his** homework.

When the gender is not clear, try to avoid too many awkward constructions like this.

<u>Everyone</u> in the classroom had **her or his** assignment.

Where possible, use a plural pronoun instead.

<u>All</u> in the classroom had **their** assignments.

Everyone and *everybody* are singular. Do not use *everyone-their*.

Try It Out

Choose the form that agrees with the indefinite pronoun.

1. All of the work (is, are) completed.
2. All of the jobs (is, are) done.
3. None of the tickets (has, have) been sold yet.
4. Everybody on the flooded highways (was, were) delayed.
5. Few in the last row (was, were) able to see the stage.
6. Has everyone remembered (her, their) uniform?
7. Many in the aisles could not find (his, their) seats.

▸ An **indefinite pronoun** does not refer to a specific person or thing.

Verbs must agree in number with indefinite pronouns used as subjects.

Pronouns must agree with indefinite pronouns used as antecedents.

Written Practice

Copy each indefinite pronoun. Then write the form that agrees with it.

1. Everybody in the room has done (his, their) assignment.
2. All of the beans (was, were) burned.
3. Nobody in the cars (was, were) seriously injured.
4. Someone is singing (her, their) part too loudly.
5. Most of the pears (has, have) been eaten.
6. Most of the watermelon (has, have) been eaten, too.
7. Neither of the girls has found (her, their) helmet.
8. (Do, Does) both of the bats belong to you?
9. Some of the carpeting seems to have stains on (it, them).
10. All of the land (has, have) been developed in the last two years.
11. Has anyone lost (her, their) bags?
12. Has either of the men ever used (his, their) snow blower?
13. Few in the audience had received (his, their) programs.

- **Writing Sentences**   Use each form as an indefinite pronoun in a sentence.

   14. no one   **15.** few   **16.** none   **17.** many   **18.** everything

9 | Reflexive and Intensive Pronouns

There is a set of pronouns that end in *-self* or *-selves*.

	Singular	**Plural**
1st person	myself	ourselves
2nd person	yourself	yourselves
3rd person	herself, himself, itself	themselves

Pronouns ending in *-self* or *-selves* can be used in two different ways in sentences. First, they can be used to refer to the subject. Which underlined pronoun in these sentences refers to the subject?

Burton knows him well.   Burton knows himself well.

In the first sentence, *him* refers to someone other than Burton. In the second sentence, the suffix *-self* tells you that *himself* refers to Burton. A pronoun that ends in *-self* or *-selves* and that refers to the subject is called a **reflexive pronoun**.

REFLEXIVE: Did you hurt yourself?
The tourists found themselves in a charming inn.

A pronoun in *-self* or *-selves* can also be used to emphasize or intensify another word in the sentence. Then it is called an **intensive pronoun**.

INTENSIVE: The famous actress herself answered my letter.
I told the manager about it myself.

In the first sentence, the intensive pronoun *herself* emphasizes or intensifies the noun *actress*. In the second sentence, the intensive pronoun *myself* emphasizes the pronoun *I*. Notice the placement of *myself*. The intensive pronoun need not follow directly the word it emphasizes.

A reflexive pronoun is necessary to the meaning of its sentence and generally cannot be omitted. Intensive pronouns, on the other hand, can be left out without really changing the meaning.

REFLEXIVE: Did you hurt yourself?
Did you hurt? *(yourself cannot be omitted)*
INTENSIVE: I told the manager about it myself.
I told the manager about it. *(myself can be omitted)*

Both reflexive and intensive pronouns always have antecedents.

REFLEXIVE: Liz looked at <u>herself</u> in the mirror.

INTENSIVE: The sink was fixed by Liz <u>herself</u>.

The antecedent of a reflexive pronoun is the subject. The antecedent of an intensive pronoun is the word it emphasizes. The pronouns agree with their antecedents in person, number, and gender.

In casual speech, you may occasionally hear pronouns with *-self* or *-selves* used as personal pronouns. Avoid this usage.

> Ron and I *(not* Ron and myself*)* repaired the lamp.
> This is between you and me *(not* between you and myself*)*.

Use pronouns with *-self* and *-selves* only as reflexive pronouns or as intensive pronouns.

Look again at the list of pronouns on the preceding page. Can you tell how they are formed? Most of the pronouns are made up of a possessive pronoun plus *-self* or *-selves*. *Himself* and *themselves* are the two exceptions: *him* and *them* are not possessive pronouns. Do not substitute *hisself* and *theirselves* for *himself* and *themselves*.

> Mr. Kowak built the house <u>himself</u> *(not* hisself*)*.
> The rabbits didn't cut <u>themselves</u> *(not* theirselves*)* on the fence.

Try It Out

A. Find the antecedent of the underlined pronoun. Tell whether the pronoun is a reflexive pronoun or an intensive pronoun.

   1. Mr. Chopourian <u>himself</u> described the different types of rugs.
   2. Hubert found <u>himself</u> in an unusual situation.
   3. We were introduced to the prima ballerina <u>herself</u>.
   4. The cat washed <u>itself</u> endlessly.
   5. I would rather go <u>myself</u> than send Kate.

B. Correct the error in each sentence.

   6. Why don't you go bowling with Jim and myself?
   7. The skiers had to protect theirselves from the cold.
   8. Mrs. Sullivan and myself found the source of the leak.
   9. He can operate the computer hisself now.
   10. Herself and Russell are leaving for Winnipeg tomorrow.
   11. Karen and myself are starting a club.

C. Complete each sentence with an appropriate reflexive or intensive pronoun.

12. Eleanor _____ told me the good news.
13. My brother has taught _____ to play the guitar.
14. The waiters should see _____ in those straw hats.
15. We _____ aren't sure of the answer.

Pronouns ending in *-self* or *-selves* are used in two ways.
▶ A **reflexive pronoun** refers to the subject.
▶ An **intensive pronoun** emphasizes a certain word or words.
Do not substitute reflexive pronouns for personal pronouns.
Avoid the forms *hisself* and *theirselves*.

Written Practice

A. Rewrite each sentence correctly.

1. Dominic and myself will pick you up at six o'clock.
2. Since the Smiths couldn't come theirselves, they sent us.
3. With great interest, Theodore watched hisself on the TV monitor.
4. The director told Loretta and myself to project our voices.
5. My father taught hisself to play chess.

B. Write the pronoun with *-self* or *-selves* that correctly completes each sentence. Label the pronoun *reflexive* or *intensive*.

6. Scientists _____ are still searching for answers to many puzzles.
7. One scientist may shut _____ in her lab in order to work.
8. Others may make _____ readily available to their coworkers.
9. Dr. Halstend _____ visited my sister's research lab yesterday.
10. The technicians suddenly found _____ and their work on display.
11. Normally the technicians conceal _____ from public view.
12. My sister is a biophysicist _____.
13. Aren't you _____ interested in becoming a research scientist?
14. I think I'd rather be a veterinarian _____.

• **Writing Sentences** Use each pronoun in a sentence.

15. myself 16. himself 17. themselves 18. itself 19. ourselves

10 | Writing Well with Pronouns

Clear Antecedents

Pronouns, as you have seen, allow you to avoid repeating the same nouns over and over again. By using pronouns, you can make your writing more interesting and more direct. You must be sure that your writing remains clear, however. What makes these sentences unclear?

UNCLEAR: They say that trash can be used as a source of energy.
It says that liftoff is at dawn tomorrow.
In the zoo they keep the animals in natural surroundings.

Who are *they*? Who is *it*? You have no way of knowing from these sentences. None of the pronouns has a clear antecedent. Avoid using *they* and *it* without clear antecedents. Use nouns or different constructions instead.

CLEAR: Experts say that trash can be used as a source of energy.
The newspaper says that liftoff is at dawn tomorrow.
or: Liftoff is at dawn tomorrow.
In the zoo, the animals are kept in natural surroundings.

Avoid using *you* as an indefinite pronoun.

UNCLEAR: In certain schools, you are able to learn typing.
CLEAR: In certain schools, students are able to learn typing.

When you use pronouns, also be sure that there is only one clear antecedent. What is the antecedent of *he* in this sentence?

UNCLEAR: Dan wrote to Greg when *he* was in Europe.

Who was in Europe—Dan or Greg? The pronoun can refer to either person. The sentence could be made clearer in one of a number of ways, depending upon the intended meaning.

CLEAR: When he was in Europe, Dan wrote to Greg.
Dan wrote to Greg when Dan was in Europe.
When he was in Europe, Greg wrote to Dan.
Greg wrote to Dan when Greg was in Europe.

When you use pronouns, be sure that the antecedents are clear.

Try It Out

Correct the unclear pronoun antecedents in these sentences.

1. Pearl told Vivian that she had to read *Rosy Is My Relative*.
2. It says in this magazine that skirt lengths are changing again.
3. If a person can't swim, you should not go into the water alone.
4. Ann told Mrs. Bee that she couldn't fold cloth diapers.
5. I heard that they have discovered a new star.
6. My father told my uncle that he was a better pitcher.

Written Practice

Rewrite the passage so that pronouns are used correctly and clearly.

They say that Gerald Durrell had always been fascinated by animals. Eventually, he found hisself a job in a zoo. It tells about that job in *Beasts in My Belfry*. When Teddy the Bear was in his charge, he sang with one paw clasped to his chest. If anyone is interested in animals, you will enjoy this book.

Check Your Writing

Check your passage. Ask yourself these questions, and correct errors.

A. Are my sentences correct?
  1. Have I used subject and object pronoun forms correctly?
  2. Have I used correct pronoun forms in compounds?
  3. Do the pronouns agree with their antecedents?
  4. Have I avoided apostrophes with pronouns except in contractions?
  5. Have I used demonstrative pronouns correctly?
  6. Have I used the *-self* and *-selves* forms correctly?
  7. Do verbs and other pronouns agree with indefinite pronouns?

B. Are my sentences clear?

  Does each pronoun have a single clear antecedent?

- **Writing a Paragraph** Write a passage of about ten sentences about an animal of which you are fond, real or imaginary. Try to use personal, interrogative, demonstrative, indefinite, reflexive, and intensive pronouns. Then ask yourself the questions above. Make needed changes.

Using Words Correctly

Using *we* and *us* with Nouns

Have you ever heard someone use a sentence like this?

NONSTANDARD: Us girls are ready to leave.

You would not say *Us are ready*. Avoid an expression like *us girls* as the subject of a sentence.

Most of the time, the pronoun alone is sufficient as the subject.

STANDARD: We are ready to leave.

Occasionally, you may want to add a noun after the pronoun for identification or special emphasis. You should still use whatever pronoun form you would use if the noun had not been added.

We girls are ready to leave.
You should join us altos in the back row.

We girls is the subject; the subject pronoun *we* is used. *Us altos* is the direct object; the object pronoun *us* is used.

Avoid using expressions like *us boys* as subjects.
If both noun and pronoun are needed for emphasis, use the pronoun form you would use if the noun were not there.

Practice

Tell which sentences are correct. If a sentence is incorrect, tell how it should be corrected.

1. Us orchestra members have been invited to a music workshop.
2. The bus will pick up us violinists near the main entrance.
3. We students will be able to see and listen to professionals.
4. Us amateurs will certainly benefit from the experience.
5. The conductor directed we violinists to our places.
6. Us lucky ones will never forget the workshop.

Naming Yourself Last

When you mention a series of people that includes yourself, it is considered polite to name yourself last.

You, he, and I *(not* I, you, and he*)* need more practice.
These directions are for Thomas and us *(not* us and Thomas*)*.

Remember to use subject pronouns in compound subjects and to use object pronouns in compound objects.

Florence and I *(not* Florence and me*)* have both read the book.
The book fascinated Florence and me *(not* Florence and I*)*.

Mention yourself last when naming a series of people.

Practice

Choose the correct series of forms.

1. Why didn't you tell (me and Todd, Todd and me) the good news about your job?
2. (Me and her, Her and me, She and I) have to make the decision by next week.
3. (Bill, Vera, and I; Bill, I, and Vera; I, Bill, and Vera) have become good friends.
4. The first snowflakes were seen by (me and my sister, my sister and me).
5. The holidays are a special time for (me and my family, my family and me).
6. (Ms. O'Brien and I, I and Ms. O'Brien) attend a lecture on the use of computers every Thursday night.

• **Writing Sentences**   Use each expression in a sentence of your own.

7. we students
8. us members

9. my friends and I
10. Don, Kay, and me

12 | Building Vocabulary

Denotation and Connotation

Words can have two kinds of meanings—**denotation** and **connotation**. *Denotation* refers to the dictionary definition of a word. *Connotation* refers to the feelings associated with a word.

Think slim.   Are you tired of being skinny?

Slim and *skinny* mean just about the same thing. Their denotations are the same. Which word, however, would you use to appeal to people to buy a product? You would probably use *slim,* for it has a positive connotation for most people, bringing to mind high fashion and elegance. *Skinny,* on the other hand, has a negative connotation. It brings to mind scrawniness rather than sleekness.

Not all words have the same connotation for all people. For many, the word *kitten* has a positive connotation, making them think of a soft, furry ball of playfulness. Someone who dislikes or is allergic to cats, however, might not agree.

Think about the connotations of the words you use. They can have an important effect on your writing.

> ▸ **Denotation** refers to the dictionary definition of a word.
> ▸ **Connotation** refers to the feelings associated with a word.

Practice

Decide whether each word has a positive or negative connotation for most people.

1. patriot	**4.** frizzy	**7.** determined
2. mutt	**5.** genuine	**8.** traitor
3. sparkling	**6.** slimy	**9.** dictator

● **Writing Sentences**   Use five of the above words in sentences. Try to convey their positive or negative connotations.

Review

• **Personal Pronouns** *(pp. 183–184)*   Copy each pronoun. Write its person and number. If it is third person singular, write its gender.

  1. He has given all of you his word about it.
  2. Are we taking them to see your great-grandmother in our car?

• **Antecedents of Pronouns** *(pp. 185–186)*   Write the correct pronoun form. Then write its antecedent.

  (3) Mary and Charles must apply one more coat of paint to (his, their) house. **(4, 5)** Then (she, they) will have finished painting (it, them.) **(6)** (It, They) was a difficult job.

• **Subject and Object Pronouns** *(pp. 187–188)*   Write the correct form.

  7. Can that really be (he, him) in that picture?
  8. (We, Us) remember (they, them) every year at this time.
  9. Please send (we, us) a postcard from Hawaii.

• **Compound Subjects and Objects** *(pp. 189–190)*   Write the sentence, substituting the appropriate pronoun for the underlined noun.

  10. Noreen and Joe are the co-chairpersons of the club.
  11. Did you meet Mrs. Trent and Paul at the game?
  12. You, Dawn, and I must draw a picture of an ostrich.

• **Possessive Pronouns** *(pp. 191–192)*   Write the correct form.

  13. The plant toppled from (its, it's) stand.
  14. (Your, You're) sister was standing near it.
  15. My sister and father regarded that plant as (theirs, there's).

• **Interrogative Pronouns** *(pp. 193–194)*   Write the correct form.

  16. (Who, Whom) have you described in your story?
  17. (Who, Whom) is reading the story now?
  18. (Whose, Who's) is that story?

- **Demonstrative Pronouns** *(pp. 195–196)*   Rewrite each sentence correctly.

  19. That there is the new science teacher.
  20. This candle over there should fit the candle holder.
  21. Have you ever seen this here picture before?
  22. These broom in the far corner is for sweeping the porch.

- **Indefinite Pronouns** *(pp. 197–199)*   Copy the indefinite pronoun. Then write the form that agrees with it.

  23. Everyone did (his or her, their) best to arrive on time.
  24. A few of the books (is, are) on our reading list.
  25. All of the milk (was, were) gone by the time I got home.
  26. Most of the coins have fallen out of (its, their) envelopes.

- **Reflexive and Intensive Pronouns** *(pp. 200–202)*   Write the pronoun with *-self* or *-selves* that completes the sentence. Label the pronoun *reflexive* or *intensive*.

  27. Manuel considers _____ ready for the track meet.
  28. Could they possibly have done all this _____?
  29. Joanne Woodward _____ will star in the new play.
  30. Have you ever seen _____ on television?

- **Writing Well with Pronouns** *(pp. 203–204)*   Rewrite the passage so that the antecedent of each pronoun is clear.

  31–33. Angela Thirkell's novels are both humorous and sophisticated. In *Pomfret Towers,* it tells about Alice Barton, a shy young girl. North Americans often enjoy Thirkell's work because you get such a good picture of British life.

- **Using Words Correctly** *(pp. 205–206)*   Rewrite each sentence correctly.

  34. Us eighth graders are going to win the softball game.
  35. The coach encouraged we players to do our best.
  36. Me, Floyd, and Pat are probably the most enthusiastic players.

- **Building Vocabulary** *(p. 207)*   Write *P* or *N* to indicate whether each word has a positive or negative connotation for most people.

  37. clever   **38.** shrewd   **39.** fragrance   **40.** creature   **41.** prejudice

1 | Interviewing

The word *interview* comes from a French word that can be translated as "to look into." When you interview people, you study them and try to find out what they know, what they think, or how they feel about certain topics. Usually the person you interview is special. She or he is an expert on something. Perhaps the person knows something that few people do—such as how to build a dry-stone wall or how to make stained glass the way the masters did or how to letter in gold leaf. Perhaps he or she has witnessed some unique event or lived through an important historical era. In any case, the person you interview is a living reference book full of facts, memories, opinions, and feelings. If your interview is well planned, you can tap all of these resources.

The first step in interviewing is to set up a goal. What is the purpose of your interview? Do you want to question someone about air pollution, volcanic ash, scuba diving, Mozart, calligraphy? Your purpose will in turn set up the topic and focus of your interview.

Secondly, you as an interviewer must plan the interview meeting carefully. An interview is more than just "Hello. My name is ____. Can you tell me something about ____?" In an interview your general aim is to learn something specific. The easiest way to find out what you want to know is to ask questions. Interviews are almost always conducted with a question-and-answer format. The best interview questions require the person being interviewed to elaborate on the subject. The six questions below are not the best kind for an interview. Can you tell why?

1. Do you like scuba diving?
2. Can you dive without wearing a wet suit?
3. Is underwater life very different from other life forms?
4. Is diving alone permitted?
5. Have you ever run out of oxygen on a dive?
6. Are some fish more dangerous than others?

What sort of answer does each question permit? Instead of yes/no questions, try to use questions that look into or probe for reasons, explanations, and specific details. Use questions that begin with *Who, What, When, Where, Why,* and *How.* These five *W*'s plus *How* are the questions that newspaper reporters are taught to ask when they gather information for a story.

Now read these interview questions.

1. How did you first become interested in calligraphy?
2. What exactly is calligraphy?
3. Who first developed this lettering technique?
4. How did you learn to write calligraphic letters?
5. What tools do you use for calligraphy?
6. How do the techniques differ for left-handed calligraphers?

These six questions are well suited for an interview. They draw out information from the speaker. They encourage him or her to supply facts. If you select questions like these, you can sit back during the interview and do what good interviewers should do—listen!

Practice

A. Change the six questions on page 211 into more probing questions that begin with the five *W*'s or *How*.

B. Select an interview topic from the list below or make up one of your own. Write your topic on a piece of paper. Then write six or seven interview questions that will "look into" that topic.

1. Flying a hang-glider
2. Being head cheerleader
3. Organizing a carpool
4. Managing a radio station

The Interview Itself

Conducting an interview is easy if you prepare for it in advance. Once you have written your purpose and your questions, you are ready for the interview itself. Telephone the person you want to interview, or write a note to request an interview appointment. Introduce yourself by giving your name, your school, and your grade. Then explain why you want an interview and how long you think it will take. Let the expert choose the time, date, and place most convenient for the interview.

When the day of the interview arrives, act like a professional.

1. Be on time for your appointment.
2. Bring your list of questions, a pad of paper, and a pencil.
3. Introduce yourself again, and repeat the purpose of the interview.
4. Ask your questions with a voice loud enough to be heard.

5. Listen carefully to what the speaker says. If you do not understand what is being said, ask the speaker politely to explain the point again in a slightly different way or give you an example. Follow up on the speaker's comments in order to get further information.

6. If the speaker strays from the topic, bring him or her back to the question at hand politely.

The following conversation is part of an interview. Read it carefully.

HAL: How long have you worked as a news anchor at Channel 27?

MS. GUERTIN: One year, but I've done other jobs here for almost six.

HAL: How did those other jobs help you to become an anchor?

MS. GUERTIN: When I first was hired, I had no experience at all in media. I began on-the-job training as a camera person for our live programs in the studio. I learned how to cue on-air talent and how to run the character-generator.

HAL: What's a character-generator?

MS. GUERTIN: It's a machine that produces the words you sometimes see on your television screen. For example, during the news we might break away to show a videotape from an early-morning fire in Chelsea. The character-generator could superimpose the words CHELSEA—7 A.M. on the screen.

HAL: What job did you learn next?

MS. GUERTIN: After running a TV camera, I worked on the other side of the camera, interviewing people on my own talk show. Then I became a set director, a director, and eventually a producer. You see, Channel 27 is a small operation. Every staff member has to learn how to work every position—sort of Jacks and Jills of all trades.

- What purpose do you think Hal had in mind during this segment?
- Where does the interview seem to stray from the topic?
- How does Hal bring the conversation back in line?

Practice

Use the interview questions you prepared for page 212, or make up new ones. Choose a partner who will pretend to be the person you want to interview. Your partner should be prepared to make up information. Conduct a full interview. You can begin with the initial telephone conversation if you wish and proceed to the face-to-face interview. Be polite. Keep to your chosen topic and purpose.

2 | Taking Notes

You will be hearing lots of new information during your interview. In order to collect this information properly, you will want to rely on more than just your ears and your memory. You will need to take notes.

Before the interview, you can prepare for the notes that you will take by leaving a space on your paper below each interview question. Thus your notes have an established order even before you take them.

During the interview, you should write a brief note for each answer given by the person you interview. Notes can be single words or abbreviations—just enough to help you remember the point that was made. Try to find a happy medium. Taking too many notes during an interview may prevent you from being a good listener. You may end up with more notes than you want on one aspect of the topic and not enough on another. Similarly, taking too few notes or abbreviating to excess at the interview will leave you puzzling over what really was said.

As soon as possible after the interview, finish your note-taking job. Sit down, and read your notes. Complete any missing parts. Your first aim is to make the notes that you did take easy to understand for later use. Your second aim is to record the ideas and facts that you know are important and are still fresh in your mind but, for some reason, are not yet written down.

Read these interview questions and notes.

Q. Why did you decide to run in the marathon?
  —contest, challenge
  —good comp.
  —historic race
  —"I love running."
Q. How did it go?
  —after the 1st 14 mi, felt tired
  —a strain, uphill
  —sun hotter, feet swollen, ache-y, weak
Q. What was the worst part about this race for you?
  —the start—too many runners, too crowded, bump into them
  —the finish—just exh, in pain, numb, rubber knees
  —1 piece hair kept falling in eyes—annoy

Q. What was the best part of the race for you?
  —finishing!
Q. Why is finishing the marathon important?
  —pers. pride
  —you run so far, then can't quit
  —let down fans, friends, family, self
Q. Your face looked so tormented as you crossed the finish line. Do
  you ever want to run another marathon?
  —too soon to decide, got a yr. to think
  —"I'll need to weigh the physical discomfort, the hours of train-
    ing, and the pressure versus the mental satisfaction, the joy of
    finishing."

- How would you evaluate the interviewer's questions?
- Are the notes brief enough? too brief? Explain.
- Where does the interviewer choose to quote the speaker?
- Why does the interviewer write out every word of the quotations?
- Once the interview has ended, what notes or abbreviations do you
  think the interviewer needs to fill out more completely?

Practice

A. Take notes on the interview shown on page 213.
B. Choose a partner, and conduct a mock interview as you did for page
213. This time take notes. When the interview is over, show your
partner your notes. Discuss whether they are brief yet accurate
enough to be useful and whether or not you used abbreviations
well.

3 | Forming a Working Outline

A **working outline** is a rough plan for what you want to write. In a working outline, you organize your thoughts under a single focus. You design how your interview notes will be transformed later into a report. Outlining is a transitional stage for your writing.

Read this working outline. Notice that it does not use Roman or Arabic numerals and that the items are not necessarily complete sentences.

Topic: How Kit Morris's horse has changed her life

Shelter for the horse
  —found good boarding stable run by reliable people
  —good location for horse's exercise routine

Kit's home
  —too far away from stables, rarely saw horse
  —decided to move out of city to be closer to stables
  —now lives in suburbs and commutes to work
  —close enough to visit stables every day if she wants to
  —before move, could only visit on weekends

Expenses
  —found less expensive place to live
  —can better afford good stable for horse now
  —pays a professional person to feed, exercise the animal

Changes
  —can see and ride horse during the week—not just dream of it
  —happier
  —horse gets more exercise, so does Kit

- How does this working outline keep to its topic?
- What is the rough, four-part organization of this outline?
- Does the order make sense?

Practice

A. Write a topic and a working outline from the interview notes about a marathon given on page 214–215.

B. Then write a topic and working outline from the interview you conducted with your partner for page 215.

4 | Getting Started

You have a bountiful source of knowledge right in front of you. It is people. People live through a great variety of experiences, and most of them enjoy sharing those firsthand experiences with others. Naturally, the person who can supply you with the most complete, accurate information from firsthand experiences is you yourself. Perhaps you have visited a dairy farm, talked to a baker, climbed a mountain, or watched someone work with a jackhammer. Gathering information from these experiences may seem simple, since all you need do is go out and witness an event or visit a place or talk to a person. If you do it on your own, see it with your own eyes, and hear it with your own ears, then it is a firsthand experience.

If you add to your own account the eyewitness report of someone else who saw, heard, and felt the same experience as you, then you have doubled your knowledge. This step requires a bit more work on your part. You will want to interview the person. Collecting information during a face-to-face meeting is in itself a firsthand experience for you. You see a smile; you hear an opinion; you sense a feeling. The result of all of this information-gathering will be a firsthand report.

Practice

A. List five or six firsthand experiences that you have had that would be appropriate for a firsthand report.

B. List one person whom you could interview to find out more about each of the experiences you listed for exercise A.

Steps for Writing a Firsthand Report   Here are the steps for writing a firsthand report. You will follow these steps to write your own firsthand report.

Step One   Choose a topic.
Step Two   Plan your firsthand report.
Step Three   Write your firsthand report.
Step Four   Revise your firsthand report.
Step Five   Proofread your firsthand report.
Step Six   Make a final copy to share.

5 | Step One
Choose a Topic

One important choice a writer makes is deciding which topic to write about. Jamie made a list of some of his first-hand experiences. Beside each one, he wrote the name or title of an expert on that subject.

skiing Burke Mt. — Hans, the ski school director
flying on board a 747 — a pilot or flight
attendant
walking 20 miles for a charity — Mrs. Cotter
visiting U. S. S. Constitution

Jamie read over his list. He looked for one topic that stood out from the rest. Skiing Burke was like skiing a lot of other mountains. Flying aboard a big jet was not very unusual either. Walking twenty miles, however, had been special. He had raised money for charity with each mile he completed, but what stood out in Jamie's memory were his aching muscles and the blisters on his feet. Jamie decided to write about his visit to the *Constitution*. The ship is the oldest commissioned vessel in the world, and Jamie had felt close to all of that history during a recent class trip there. Although he knew the core of his report would depend on his own firsthand experience aboard the ship, Jamie hoped the commander would be available for an interview. If not, he could interview a tour guide or a crew member.

Assignment • Choose Your Topic

A. Read the list of firsthand experiences you made for page 217. Ask yourself these questions about each of them.

   1. How well do I remember the experience?
   2. If my memory is vague, can I arrange to experience it again?
   3. What expert can I plan to interview who knows about this subject from his or her own firsthand experience?

B. Choose one of your experiences as a topic for your firsthand report. Circle it on your paper. Beside it, write the name or title of at least one person you could interview about it.

6

Step Two
Plan Your Report

Preparing Interview Questions

To prepare for writing his first-hand report, Jamie read two encyclopedia articles on the *Constitution*. This helped to refresh his memory and allowed him to think of some possible interview questions to ask the ship's commanding officer. Here is what he wrote.

Jamie's interview questions

1. How did the ship get its nickname "Old Ironsides"?
2. What was the ship's brightest moment?
3. What is your favorite story about "Old Ironsides"?
4. Does "Old Ironsides" look very different from when it was first launched on October 21, 1797?
5. How long have you commanded "Old Ironsides"?

- Which of Jamie's questions will the commander be able to answer with a simple *yes* or *no*?
- Which ones follow the five *W*'s plus *How* line of questioning?
- Which of his questions probe or "look into" the commander's personal or first-hand experience?
- Are Jamie's questions arranged in a logical order? If not, how would you rearrange them?
- What seems to be Jamie's purpose throughout?

Interviewing

Jamie telephoned the office of the commander of the *Constitution*. He introduced himself and explained why he wanted to interview him. He told him that he would like to tour the ship again and then ask him some questions about it. The commander agreed to see him on Tuesday at 4 P.M.

Jamie arrived early enough for the interview so that he could tour the *Constitution* first. Then he walked to the commander's office. It was just 4 o'clock. When the commander greeted him, Jamie introduced himself again and repeated his reason for requesting the interview. He had brought his interview questions, a pencil, and a pad of paper. He asked each of his questions in order, and while the commander was answering, he jotted down some notes. More important, he listened. He followed the points that the commander was making, and he asked a few questions in response, even though they were not on his list.

After the commander had answered his last question, Jamie thanked him for taking the time to let him interview him.

Taking Interview Notes

Here are some of the notes that Jamie took during his interview with the commander of the U.S.S. *Constitution*. Notice that he included some notes about the commander himself.

Some of Jamie's interview notes

Q. What was the ship's brightest moment?
War 1812 battle w. Guerrière (Brit.)
1st time Brit. man-of-war defeated by Amer.
got nickname "Old Ironsides" during battle
Q. What is your favorite story about "Old Ironsides"?
not one, but all of the little-known facts
near mutiny once in the Mediterranean
sailors didn't wear shoes, no reg. uniform
Q. In what ways does ship look different
from when it was first launched?
black-framed glasses, consults his books
ship = over 185; had 3 maj. restor.

- Can you understand all of Jamie's abbreviations?
- Which abbreviations should be written out?
- Do all of the notes make sense?
- Which notes refer to the commander personally?

Forming a Working Outline

As soon as Jamie left the interview, he sat down and filled in the facts and ideas he had not yet recorded. He changed some of his abbreviations to full words. The next step was to decide on a focus for his first-hand report and to write a working outline. Of course, Jamie's report would not simply tell about his interview with the commander. Most of the report would come from his own firsthand impressions of the ship. He would also use information from the tour guide and from the brochure. Here are the main points he put together for a working outline for his report.

The main points of Jamie's working outline

> Topic: The <u>Constitution</u> — its history + personality
> Tradition — how ship got its nickname
> Today — how nickname still fits
> how old ?
> why like iron ?
> How ship looks today
> The ship's "personal" qualities

- Does Jamie keep to his focus?
- Does his outline seem logical?
- Does each item fit?

Assignment • Plan Your Report

A. Write the questions you will ask the person you plan to interview. Put them in a logical order. Use the five *W*'s plus *How*.

B. Set up an appointment with the person you want to interview.

C. Be on time. Ask your questions politely. Take notes. Thank the person for granting you the interview.

D. Complete any notes that seem unfinished. Write out full words instead of abbreviations if necessary.

E. Add any notes that you may have omitted earlier. Then write a focus statement and a working outline.

7 | Step Three
Write Your Report

Jamie had done a lot of preparation to reach this point. He was finally ready to write his report. He based it on his working outline plan and used his interview notes whenever he needed a quotation or details. At this point, he did not worry about making mistakes. Here is the first part of what he wrote.

Part of Jamie's first draft

> "Old Ironsides"
>
> The <u>Constitution</u>'s nickname is "Old Ironsides." The ship earned its nickname in a battle during the War of 1812. A gunner saw shots ~~fall~~ bounce off the ship and said, "Her sides are made of iron." But does that nickname still fit the Constitution?
>
> According to the commanding officer of the ship, it does. The <u>Constitution</u> is very old. It has undergone three major restorations. The commander said, "When we talk of the <u>Constitution</u>, we toss around figures like thirty years here, forty years there. That's all most ships last!" But not "Old Ironsides."
>
> The ship interests many people—including ~~the~~ its commander. "I find it fascinating to learn more and more about her," said the gray-haired officer. He must have read every word ever printed about the <u>Constitution</u>. Almost without effort, he could point out a particular sentence or drawing from among all his reference books. His eyes sparkled as he spoke of his ship.

Although little-known facts about ~~it~~ the <u>Constitution</u> do surface now and again, some parts of its past will always be a mystery.

"Old Ironsides" was not made of iron. It just seemed that way. No shot ever penetrated the twenty-one-inch-thick ~~sides~~ hull. In fact, isn't it strange that one of its captains was named Isaac Hull? The <u>Constitution</u> was built so sturdily that it was the first American ship to defeat a British man-of-war. Today "Old Ironsides" is still afloat, still like iron, and full of 185 years of our history.

- Does Jamie's title fit his report? Why?
- What is his focus?
- Does he keep to it throughout his report?
- How does this part of Jamie's report follow the plan he set up in his working outline? (You may want to look back at the main points of his outline on page 221.)
- Which exact quotations does he use? Do they fit the topic?
- Why did Jamie leave out some of the facts he had learned during his interview?
- What details does Jamie use to describe the commander?

Assignment • **Write Your First Draft**

Write your firsthand report. Keep in mind the focus you have chosen. Let the ideas you have gathered flow onto your paper—ideas from your own firsthand experience, ideas you heard during your interview, and your impressions of the person who spoke with you. Use the speaker's exact words if they help you to make a point or if they reveal a part of the speaker's personality. Include some details about his or her appearance and actions. Refer to your working outline and to your interview notes as needed. Try not to rely on a strict question-and-answer format for your report.

8 | Step Four
Revise Your Report

Jamie put aside his first draft for a day or two. When he read it again, he tried to put himself in the shoes of a reader who knew nothing about the *Constitution*. He decided that his beginning was dull. He needed to reword it so that he could spark some reader interest right from the start.

Jamie could not find any other problems with his report, but he asked Mary Beth to listen to it—just to double check. First, he told Mary Beth what the focus of his report was, and then he read the report aloud to her. He asked Mary Beth to keep the following questions in mind as she listened.

1. What is the best thing about this report?
2. Does the report keep to its focus?
3. Does all of the information fit?
4. Does the report follow a logical order?
5. Do I learn something about the topic and about the person who was interviewed?

When Jamie had finished reading, Mary Beth said, "I like the way you told about the ship and the captain at the same time. It was easy to follow. You wrote that the *Constitution* is very old, but you didn't say how old until your last sentence." Jamie said, "That's true. I should add some more facts about the ship's age closer to the beginning. What other things could I improve?"

"I think some parts don't fit—like the sentence about Captain Hull. It's interesting, but it doesn't prove that the ship was strong." Jamie agreed. "I guess you're right. I just thought his name matched his ship so well. What else?"

Mary Beth said, "I would take out the part about the commander and his reference books, too. It seems to be out of place."

Jamie thanked Mary Beth for her suggestions. He reread the sentences about the commander's books. In some ways, he could understand why Mary Beth thought they did not belong. However, Jamie thought they showed something important about the ship (that there is much to be learned about its history) and about its commander (that he is fascinated by his ship). Jamie decided to keep those sentences in his report.

During their discussion, Jamie came up with some ideas on his own about how he could improve his report. Here are some of those changes.

Part of Jamie's revised report

"Old Ironsides"

A Do you know how the U.S.S. ~~The~~ Constitution's ~~nickname is "Old Ironsides." The~~ *"Old Ironsides?" In* ~~ship~~ earned its nickname ~~in~~ a battle during the War of 1812. A gunner saw shots ~~fall~~ bounce off the ship and said, "Her sides are made of iron." But does that nickname still fit the Constitution?

According to the commanding officer of the ship, it does. The Constitution ~~is very old~~. It has undergone three major restorations. The commander said, "When we talk of the Constitution, we toss around figures like thirty years here, forty years there. That's all most ships last!" But not "Old Ironsides."

A Because of its long history, the ~~The~~ ship interests many people—including ~~the~~ its commander. "I find it fascinating to learn more and more about her," said the gray-haired officer *with black-framed glasses.* He must have read every word ever printed about the Constitution. Almost without effort, he could point out a particular sentence or drawing from among all his reference books. His eyes sparkled as he spoke of his ship.

Although little-known facts about ~~it~~ the Constitution do surface now and again, some parts of its past will always be a mystery.

was one of the first ships built for our navy. It is over 185 years old — the oldest commissioned vessel in the whole world.

"Old Ironsides" was not made of iron. It just seemed that way. No shot ever penetrated the twenty-one-inch-thick ~~sides~~ hull. ~~In fact, isn't it strange that one of its captains was named Isaac Hull?~~ The Constitution was built so sturdily that it was the first American ship to defeat a British man-of-war.

- Why is Jamie's new beginning an improvement?
- What did Jamie write instead of calling the ship *very old*?
- What did he add to the beginning of his third paragraph? Why do these words make the connection between the second and third paragraphs clearer?
- What other changes did he make to his report?

Assignment

- **Revise Your Report**
- **Discuss Your Report**

A. Read your first draft. Ask yourself these questions.

1. Have I kept to my main focus?
2. Have I included details about that person's appearance and actions during the interview?
3. Have I selected a few direct quotations that help me get a point across to my readers?
4. Have I avoided a question/answer set-up that could make my first-hand report seem too stiff?

B. Revise your report. Make changes wherever you think they are necessary. Cross out sentences that do not keep to the focus.

C. Ask a classmate or your teacher to listen to your report. First, tell your listener what your focus is. Then ask him or her to keep in mind the listener questions shown on page 224. Read your report aloud.

D. Discuss your report with your partner.

E. If she or he has given you some helpful suggestions or if you have discovered something on your own while reading your paper aloud or while talking to your partner, make further revisions.

9 | Step Five
Proofread Your Report

Now that Jamie had cleared up the problems with the wording and the organization of his report, he needed to check for possible mistakes in spelling, punctuation, capitalization, and grammar. First, he copied over his report onto another piece of paper. Then he began his job of proofreading. He used a dictionary whenever he was unsure of the spelling of a word. Here is one of the paragraphs he proofread.

Part of Jamie's report after proofreading

At first I could see only the *C*onstitution's masts. The three were made of white pine, and painted white. Black beams crossed each mast at right angles. Obviously the old ship was a square rigger. As I walked closer, I could see the Constitution standing straight and tall—220 feet at the main mast. This was the ship that could *sail* ~~sale~~ faster than thirteen knots. Other ships of the same size did only seven or eight. Wouldn't the Constitution have looked magnificent in the open sea under full sail? With a favorable wind, this vessel must have outdistanced every enemy. There were no sails visible now; There were only miles of rigging that looped in and out in a complicated pattern.

- What word did Jamie need to capitalize? Why?
- Where did he take out a punctuation mark? Why?
- What homophone did Jamie correct? What is the meaning of each word in this homophone pair?
- Which misspelled words did Jamie correct?
- What mark of punctuation did he need to change?

Practice

Proofread the last part of Jamie's report. There are nine errors. Use a dictionary to check on spelling. Write the paragraphs correctly.

When I finlly rounded the corner I caught a full view of the <u>Constitution</u>. The hull was black. I could not tell that the sides were oak. They looked more like armor.

Without a doubt, the <u>constitution</u> was a fighting ship. I stepped from the gangplank onto the top deck. Huge black cannons lined both sides On the gun deck below was more cannons fitted into each gunport. Just imagin firing one of them against the Barbary pirates!

The valiant <u>Constitution</u>, "Old Ironsides" had fought well not only against pirates but against ever foe. after 185 years, it remains undefeated.

Assignment • **Proofread Your Report**

Proofread your report. Keep these questions in mind.

1. Have I made appropriate paragraph breaks?
2. Have I looked up the spelling of any word I am unsure of?
3. Have I punctuated direct quotations correctly?

— Grammar skills checklist —

4. Have I corrected any run-on sentences or sentence fragments?
5. Have I used commas correctly with compound sentences, dependent clauses, and appositives?
6. Have I used the correct form of pronouns?
7. Does the subject of each sentence agree with its verb?

10 | Step Six
Make a Final Copy

Jamie copied his firsthand report in his best handwriting. Then he read it one more time to be sure that he had not made any mistakes in copying. Jamie was proud of his report, but he thought that if he presented it in front of his class, he would need something extra.

He decided to make a collage about the *Constitution*. First, he took a large piece of blue construction paper. Then he found a big color picture of the ship in an old calendar. He cut it out and glued it to the center of the blue paper. At the top of the paper, he printed in black block letters *OLD IRONSIDES*. Then he filled in the rest of the collage by cutting up pages of the brochure the tour guide had given him. He also used snapshots he had taken on the class trip to the *Constitution*. Finally Jamie used the booklet the commander had given him about the *Constitution*'s Fourth-of-July cruise. He cut pictures and articles out of it and glued them onto the collage, too. The finished collage was a great success.

Assignment

- **Make a Final Copy**
- **Share Your Firsthand Report**

A. On a piece of clean paper, copy your firsthand report in your best handwriting.

B. Read your report once more to check that you have not made any copying mistakes.

C. If you have not yet written a title for your report, do so now.

D. Think of a special way to share your report with others.
- You can make a collage the way Jamie did.
- You can draw a picture or make a cartoon sketch of the person you interviewed.
- You can read your report to your class.

Mid-Book Test

- **Sentence Types, Subjects, and Predicates**   Write the correct end punctuation for each sentence, and label it *declarative, interrogative, imperative,* or *exclamatory.* Then find and write each simple subject and predicate.

    1. Answer a question for me
    2. How much television do you watch each week
    3. We don't have a television set
    4. You can't mean that
    5. This is becoming an electronic society
    6. Tell me more, please
    7. Television, computer programs, word processors, and electronic games do occupy more and more of our lives
    8. Are we paying less attention to the spoken and written word

- **Independent and Dependent Clauses**   Write *independent* or *dependent* to describe each clause.

    9. when the show was repeated for the fifth time
    10. after the storm blew down the antenna
    11. we read a lot of books and magazines
    12. unless the television set is repaired
    13. our conversation became far more interesting
    14. if the television set is not repaired

- **Simple, Compound, and Complex Sentences**   Write *simple, compound,* or *complex* to describe each sentence.

    15. When books were copied by hand or were printed from hand-carved blocks, few people could read.
    16. After the printing press was invented in the 1440's, the printed word became available to many people.
    17. More books were written, and reading became widespread.
    18. By 1500, thousands of print shops were operating in Europe and were producing millions of books.
    19. Although print is still our main means of mass communication, the new electronics is rapidly catching up with it.

- **Kinds of Nouns** Divide your paper into six columns. In the first column, list the nouns in the sentences that follow. Head the other columns *common, proper, abstract, concrete,* and *compound.* For each noun, put a check mark in the appropriate columns.

20. Different parts of our planet have different climates and plant life.
21. Every continent in the world has grasslands.
22. Almost a third of the earth's land is covered by forests.
23. In regions of great warmth and humidity, tropical foliage grows.
24. Central America, parts of South America and Africa, Southeast Asia, and the Pacific Islands have such vegetation.

- **Plural and Possessive Nouns** Divide your paper into four columns. Label the columns *singular, singular possessive, plural, plural possessive.* List the nouns given below in the first column. Then complete the other columns.

25. turkey   27. tax   29. leaf   31. story   33. spoonful
26. soprano   28. stimulus 30. Nicholas 32. rash   34. reef

- **Appositives** Write each sentence. Underline each appositive. Add commas where needed.

35. Plasma the part of the blood without the red and white cells has little color.
36. A straw-colored liquid plasma contains water, proteins, salts, and other materials.
37. The centrifuge an important machine separates the blood cells from the blood.
38. The result plasma can be stored longer than whole blood.

- **Kinds of Verbs** Divide your paper in half. Label one half *Linking Verbs* and the other *Action Verbs.* Divide the *Action* section into two columns, *transitive* and *intransitive.* Find the verbs in these sentences, and list each one in the correct column. Underline the main verb.

39. Horacio never stays angry for more than a few minutes.
40. He will return on Thursday evening.
41. Ramona is attending a computer camp this summer.
42. Most of the students do enjoy the new computer.
43. Have you worked on it yet, or are you still waiting?
44. The students did raise the money for it.
45. They even produced a very successful show.
46. The show may become an annual fund-raising affair.

- **Tenses and Forms of Verbs**   Write each verb. Then write *present*, *past*, *future*, *present perfect*, *past perfect*, or *future perfect* to describe its tense. If it is a progressive form, write *progressive*.

  47. The library closes at six o'clock tonight.
  48. At what time will you go?
  49. Felicia has been searching for her pet iguana all day.
  50. The duck had been missing an hour when we found her.
  51. By tomorrow I shall have been waiting for that letter for a week.
  52. Will I be getting it, or has it been lost forever?

- **Agreement**   Find the subject, and write the verb that agrees with it.

  53. The gila monster and the horned toad (is, are) lizards.
  54. Neither the zoo nor the museums (charges, charge) admission on Tuesdays or Sundays.
  55. (Has, Have) the trees in the forest lost any leaves yet?
  56. The home of the Litchfields (is, are) in western Michigan.
  57. There (is, are) no sharp scissors in the top drawer.
  58. Here (comes, come) the glockenspiel player now.

- **Direct and Indirect Objects**   Divide your paper into two columns. Label one column *direct objects* and the other *indirect objects*. Find the objects in these sentences, and list each one in the appropriate column.

  59. Loretta bought herself a new guitar case.
  60. I must give Mr. Lowell a copy of my poem.
  61. Haven't you given the poem to him yet?
  62. Trina has already mailed the gifts to Nigeria.
  63. Pour me some more lemonade, please.
  64. The Hoffmans breed fine Holstein cows.
  65. Do not tell me the rest of the story.
  66. Are you lending Samuel your English notes?

- **Predicate Nouns and Adjectives**   Write each predicate noun and predicate adjective, labeling it *PN* or *PA*.

  67. The animals appear unusually restless tonight.
  68. Can there be an unfamiliar invader in the jungle?
  69. Are you becoming a little nervous?
  70. I have been a resident in this jungle far too long.
  71. Nothing sounds at all strange to me tonight.

- **Direct Object or Predicate Noun?** Look at the verb in each sentence. Is it a linking verb or an action verb? Write *DO* (direct object) or *PN* (predicate noun) to describe the noun that follows it.

72. André is becoming a citizen tomorrow.
73. We are seeing the new show at the planetarium tonight.
74. It will be a presentation about Jupiter.
75. Henry Hudson reached Long Island in 1609.

- **Using Words Correctly** Write the correct form for each sentence.

76. After heavy rains, the river (raised, rose) to a dangerous level.
77. Donald will (leave, let) the bird go free when its wing has healed.
78. Doug is busy every weekday evening (accept, except) Tuesday.
79. Beneath the waterfall (lies, lays) a deep, clear pool of water.
80. The police officer (raises, rises) her arm to stop the traffic.
81. (Lie, Lay) the extra blankets on the sofa.
82. The warm weather had an adverse (affect, effect) on the ski trails.
83. How did the strike (effect, affect) your travel plans?
84. Jeannette (accepted, excepted) the compliment graciously.
85. You (hadn't ought, ought not) to walk alone in those woods.
86. We have a long (way, ways) to go to reach Rockland.
87. Is anyone else tired (beside, besides) me?
88. We could (of, have) been on time if we had hurried.
89. Sam lost his glasses (somewhere, somewheres) in the yard.
90. "We (shall, will) reach the summit," she said firmly.
91. Send a post card to (Pat and me, me and Pat, Pat and I).
92. (Us, We) campers chose a place to put up our tents.
93. (Stan and I, I and Stan, Me and Stan) attend an exercise class.
94. The principal spoke to (us, we) students in the auditorium.

- **Building Vocabulary** Write two synonyms for each noun.

95. happiness 96. belongings 97. journey 98. fear 99. path

Write an antonym of each noun.

100. ease 101. dryness 102. sanity 103. beauty 104. dishonesty

Write a more precise synonym for each verb.

105. talk 106. move 107. create 108. run 109. clean

Write each root. Then add a prefix, suffix, or both to make a new word.

110. spectator 111. retract 112. reverse 113. expire

1 | Using the Dictionary

A **dictionary** contains words, their spellings, meanings, and use. In addition, you can find word pronunciations, syllabications, parts of speech, and etymologies. At the bottom of every dictionary page is a pronunciation guide to help you interpret pronunciation symbols.

Study the following dictionary excerpts and the explanation of the features of an entry.

1. **Guide words** at the top of the page tell you the first and last word defined on that page. *Nonagenarian* and *nonsectarian* are the guide words in the excerpt shown.

2. **Special spellings** follow the entries to show how to pronounce each word. The special spelling for *none* (nŭn) shows a short *u* sound.

3. **Syllabication** is indicated by dots between syllables. Hyphenation is shown by hyphens: *no-non·sense*.

4. **Stress marks** indicate the primary (′) and secondary (′) accents. *Noncom* has the primary accent on *non* and the secondary accent on *com*.

5. **Part-of-speech** labels follow the pronunciations. *None* is a pronoun (*pron.*). Noun (*n.*), verb (*v.*), and adjective (*adj.*) are other common part-of-speech labels.

6. **Definitions** follow the part-of-speech labels and are numbered if there are several. *Nonentity* has two definitions.

7. **Etymologies** or word origins may be shown at the end of an entry. *Nones* is from the Latin *nōnus*.

nonagenarian / nonsectarian

non·a·ge·nar·i·an (nŏn′ə-jə-nâr′ē-ən, nō′nə-) *adj.* Being ninety years old or between ninety and one hundred years old. [From Latin *nōnāgēnārius*, from *nōnāgēnī*, ninety each, from *nōnāginta*, ninety : *novem*, nine + *-gintā*, ten times.] —**non′a·ge·nar′i·an** *n.*

non·cha·lant (nŏn′shə-länt′) *adj.* Cool, carefree, and casually unconcerned. [French, from Old French, from *nonchaloir*, to be unconcerned.] —**non′cha·lance′** *n.* —**non′cha·lant′ly** *adv.*

non·com (nŏn′kŏm′) *n. Informal.* A noncommissioned officer.

non com·pos men·tis (nŏn kŏm′pəs mĕn′tĭs). *Law.* Not of sound mind and hence not legally responsible. [Latin, "not having control of the mind."]

non·con·form·i·ty (nŏn′kən-fôr′mĭ-tē) *n.* **1.** Refusal or failure to conform to accepted customs, beliefs, or practices. **2.** Often **Nonconformity.** Refusal to accept or conform to the doctrines of the Church of England.

none (nŭn) *pron.* **1.** No one; not one; nobody: *None dared to do it.* **2.** Not any: *None of my classmates survived the war.* **3.** No part; not any: *none of his business.* —*adv.* In no way; not at all: *He is none too happy.* [Middle English, from Old English *nān* : *ne*, no + *ān*, one.]

non·en·ti·ty (nŏn-ĕn′tĭ-tē) *n., pl.* **-ties.** **1.** A person of no importance or significance. **2.** Something that does not exist, or that exists only in the imagination.

nones (nōnz) *pl.n.* In the ancient Roman calendar, the seventh day of March, May, July, or October, and the fifth day of the other months. [From Latin *nonus*, ninth.]

none·such (nŭn′sŭch′) *n.* Also **non-such** (nŭn′sŭch′, nŏn′-). A person or thing without equal. —**none′such′** *adj.*

non-Eu·clid·e·an (nŏn′yōō-klĭd′ē-ən) *adj.* Not in accordance with or based on postulates of Euclidean geometry.

no-non·sense (nō-nŏn′sĕns′, -səns) *adj.* Practical; businesslike: *a no-nonsense approach.*

non·pa·reil (nŏn′pə-rĕl′) *adj.* Having no equal; matchless; peerless. —*n.* **1.** Someone or something that has no equal; a paragon. **2.** A small, flat chocolate drop covered with white pellets of sugar. [Middle English *nonparaille*, from Old French *nonpareil* : *non-*, not + *pareil*, equal, from Latin *pār*.]

non·sec·tar·i·an (nŏn′sĕk-târ′ē-ən) *adj.* Not limited to or associated with a particular religious denomination.

ă pat	ā pay	â care	ä father	ĕ pet	ē be	hw which
ĭ pit	ī tie	î pier	ŏ pot	ō toe	ô paw, for	oi noise
ŏŏ took	ōō boot	ou out	th thin	th this	ŭ cut	
û urge	zh vision	ə about, item, edible, gallop, circus				

Dictionary Definitions

If the dictionary gives several meanings for a word, you will have to decide which one fits the context in which the word is used. The part-of-speech label can be a useful clue. How is the word *gilt* used in the following sentence? *The gilt chairs were in front of the windows.* Is the noun, verb, or adjective definition most appropriate for *gilt* in this sentence context? You can go directly to the definitions for the adjective *gilt* and decide which is the one you want.

> **gilt** (gĭlt) *v.* A past tense and past participle of **gild.** —*adj.*
> **1.** Gilded. **2.** Having the appearance of gold. —*n.* **1.** A thin layer of gold or gold-colored material applied to a surface. **2.** Superficial brilliance; glitter.

The numbered definitions of a word such as *gilt* all relate to the same word origin. The meanings all have something in common. However, words sometimes have numbered *entries* as for *guy* below. This means that the word has several origins and very different meanings. These words with the same spellings but different origins are called **homographs.** Look at the etymologies for the homographs *guy* below. What are the origins of the words?

> **guy¹** (gī) *n.* A rope, cord, or cable used for steadying, guiding, or holding. —*tr.v.* To fasten, guide, or hold with a guy. [Prob. of Low German orig.]
> **guy²** (gī) *n. Informal.* A man; fellow. —*tr.v.* To make fun of; mock. [After *Guy* Fawkes (1570–1606), an unsuccessful English regicide whose effigy is ceremonially burned in Britain on Nov. 5.]

Etymologies

Etymologies give the origins of words and show how meanings and spellings have developed over the years. The words are broken into their parts showing prefixes, suffixes, and root words. You can see how a word has come to have its present meaning.

Look at the etymology of *socket.* What is the Old French word that *socket* comes from? What did *soc* mean? How is the meaning related to the word *socket*?

> **sock·et** (sŏk'ĭt) *n.* **1.** An opening or cavity into which an inserted part is designed to fit: *a light-bulb socket.* **2.** *Anat.* **a.** The hollow part of a joint that receives the end of a bone. **b.** A hollow or concavity into which a part, such as the eye, fits. [Middle English *soket,* spearhead shaped like a plowshare, socket, from Norman French *soket,* dim. of Old French *soc,* plowshare.]

The Dictionary as a Reference Aid

The dictionary is also a source of reference material. You can find information about the population, location, and the geographic and historic importance of many places that are listed as entries. Maps and information on size are often included, too. The entries for famous people provide a host of facts about them. You will find their dates of birth and death, their nationalities, and important events or accomplishments in their lives.

What other kinds of information are in dictionaries? Some contain codes such as a table of proofreader's symbols. A variety of alphabets are often included. For example, a dictionary may contain the Braille alphabet, the Morse code, and the Greek, Hebrew, Arabic, and Russian alphabets. Tables and charts with information such as the metric system or alphabet letter histories appear in some dictionaries.

Practice

A. Use the dictionary excerpts on page 235 to answer these questions.

1. Which definition of *none* means "no part"?
2. What part of speech is *nonconformity*?
3. Where is the primary accent in *nonchalant*?
4. Which words are hyphenated?
5. What is the origin of *non compos mentis*?
6. Which words are from Old French?

B. What entry word would you use to answer these questions?

7. When did Henry Thoreau live?
8. How large is the area of Texas?
9. What is bone meal made of?
10. What was Thomas Edison's most important invention?

C. Write the number of the definition for *nonentity* that is correct for each sentence below.

11. The king made even the prime minister feel like a *nonentity*.
12. The child's fears were hard to dispel since what he feared was a *nonentity*.
13. I felt like a *nonentity* when everyone pushed past me to speak to the star of the game.

2 | Using the Library

Most libraries are arranged in a systematic way that makes it possible to locate any book quite easily. All of the books in a library are organized into categories and are then arranged alphabetically within their category. There are two systems for organizing the non-fiction works in most libraries. One is called the Dewey Decimal System, and the other is known as the Library of Congress system. Most of the libraries you use follow the Dewey Decimal System.

Under the Dewey Decimal System, the books are grouped into ten major categories, or subject areas. Each category is assigned a range of numbers, and every book in the category is assigned its own special number within that number range. For example, the science category is assigned the numbers from 500–599. A particular science book might have a number such as 542.16 or 581.42. A science book would never have a number in the 800's or 200's. The number that is assigned to a particular book is its **call number.** The table below gives the numbers assigned to the ten major categories in the Dewey Decimal System.

000–099 General works (encyclopedias and other reference materials)	**500–599 Science** (astronomy, biology, chemistry, mathematics, physics)
100–199 Philosophy (also includes psychology)	**600–699 Technology** (aviation, engineering, hygiene, medicine)
200–299 Religion (includes mythology)	**700–799 The arts** (crafts, hobbies, music, painting, sports)
300–399 Social sciences (communication, economics, education, etiquette, government, law, sociology, transportation)	**800–899 Literature** (essays, plays, poetry)
	900–999 History (biography, geography, travel)
400–499 Language (grammar books, dictionaries)	

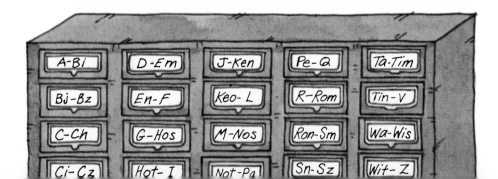

To locate a book easily, you find out what the call number is for the book you want. You can get a book's call number from a library's card catalog. Each library has a set of file drawers called a **card catalog.** The drawers contain three kinds of cards that are filed alphabetically. Each card lists a book's call number.

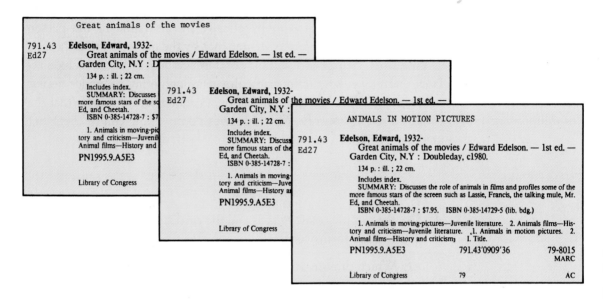

1. The *title card* is filed according to the first word in the title of the book excluding *The, A,* and *An.* You do not need to know the author of the book to locate the title card.
2. The *author card* is filed according to the last name of the author of the book. You do not need to know the title of the book to locate the author card.
3. The *subject card* is filed according to the subject of the book. If the particular subject you have in mind is not listed, try to think of a related subject to look up. You do not need to know the title or author of the book to locate the subject card.

You can locate a book in the library by finding any one of the three cards in the card catalog. Look at the sample cards above. Notice that each one gives the title and author of the book as well as some indication of the subject. Notice also that each card has the same number on it. That is the call number for the book. Make a note of the number before you go to look for the book on the shelves.

Once you know the call number of the book you want, you need to know which shelf to look on. Most libraries will have a sign at the end of each shelf showing the range of call numbers that the shelf contains.

For example, the sign may show 372.18–384.26. If the call number for the book you want is 381.95, would you find it on that shelf?

You should also know that all the fiction books in a library are usually placed in one section. They are arranged in alphabetical order according to the author's last name. Some libraries also group biographies on separate shelves, even though a biography is a nonfiction work. They are arranged alphabetically by the name of the person about whom the biography is written, not by the name of the author.

Your library also has a section of reference books. These include atlases, encyclopedias, dictionaries, almanacs, and other reference books. An *R* or *Ref* above the call number on a catalog card indicates that the book is a reference work. Most libraries do not allow you to check out any of the reference books.

Practice

A. Use the sample catalog cards and the card catalog drawers on pages 238 and 239 to answer the following questions.

 1. Which drawer would contain the sample title card?
 2. Which drawer would contain the sample author card?
 3. Which drawer would contain the sample subject card?
 4. Which drawer would you look in for information on termites?
 5. Which drawer would have an author card for Laurence Yep?
 6. Which drawer would have a title card for *Summer of the Swans*?
 7. Which drawer would you look in for an author card for Barbara Corcoran?
 8. Which drawer would contain a subject card for the Alvin Ailey dancers?
 9. Which drawer would contain a card for a biography of Madame Nehru?
 10. Which drawer would have a subject card for reptiles?

B. Use the card catalog in a library to find answers to the following questions.

 11. What is the title of a nonfiction book about lacrosse?
 12. What is the title of a book written by Scott O'Dell?
 13. Who is the author of *Rabbit Hill*?
 14. What is the title of a nonfiction book about sports cars?
 15. Who is the author of *The Door in the Wall*?

3 | Using Reference Aids

If you want to research a topic or find the answer to a question, you might go to the library. There you will find several different reference aids. Knowing what these reference aids are and what kind of information each contains will make your search more effective.

The Encyclopedia

You already know that an **encyclopedia** is a volume or a set of volumes that contains thousands of alphabetically arranged articles. Each article gives general information about many areas of a subject. For example, an article about newspapers might include facts about how news is gathered and prepared, how a newspaper office is organized, how newspapers are printed, advertising in newspapers, and a history of newspapers in this country. Encyclopedia articles are usually divided by headings and subheadings. By scanning the headings, you can locate specific information quickly. For example, if you wanted to know when the first newspaper was published in America, you would read the material under the heading "History of Newspapers."

Encyclopedia articles also have cross-references to help you locate additional, related information. In the section titled "The Newspaper Library," for example, you might find the cross-reference *See* Microfilm. By looking at the article on microfilm, you could find out how microfilm is prepared, what its advantages are, and when and how it was developed.

To help you find information in a set of encyclopedias, guide letters or words and numbers are printed on the spines of the volumes. The index, with entries arranged in alphabetical order, is often contained in the last volume of the encyclopedia. In place of an index, an encyclopedia may have an outline of its major topics, subtopics, and cross-references.

To use an encyclopedia efficiently, follow these steps.

1. Look up your subject (using a key word) in the index to find out which article or articles may contain the information you need.
2. Use the guide letters or words and numbers on the spines of the volumes to find each article.
3. Scan the headings and subheadings.
4. Use the cross-references to find further information.

The Atlas

An **atlas** is a book of maps that contains information such as land size, climate, population, geographical features, and political boundaries. The indexes tell which map to look at and where to find the feature for which you are looking. Although encyclopedias contain maps, atlas maps are usually more detailed than encyclopedia maps. They also show categories of features, such as weather patterns, streets in a city, historical information, and points of interest.

The Almanac

Where would you look to find the most recently published information about a sport, a country's leaders, or achievements in science? An **almanac** is an annual publication that contains up-to-date information about these and many other subjects. An almanac may include calendars for the coming year showing long-range weather forecasts, phases of the moon, and other information. It also gives facts about historical events, government leaders, achievements and awards in different fields, scientific discoveries and inventions, sports records, and agricultural information. An almanac provides brief descriptions, statistics, and dates, often in the form of lists, tables, and charts.

To find information in an almanac, look in the index. Main topics are usually broken down into subtopics. If you need up-to-date information, use the most recently published almanac. An almanac for 1984 would give information about events in 1983 or before.

The Readers' Guide to Periodical Literature

The *Readers' Guide to Periodical Literature* is a book that lists articles published in magazines and other periodicals. Every few months a paperback volume is published listing recently printed articles and the names of the periodicals in which they appeared. If you are looking for a particular article and know the author's name and the year and month in which the article was published, you can look it up in that year's issue of the *Readers' Guide*. If you are looking for any article by a certain author, or if you want general information on a subject, you can look in several issues of the *Readers' Guide* for what you want. Look at the sample entries from the *Readers' Guide* on the next page.

Notice that there is an entry for William Saroyan listing an article written by him and published in the *Saturday Evening Post* on October 19, 1981. Now look at the entry Saturn (planet). Below is a list of articles about Saturn. There are so many articles that they are organized by the subtopics *Magnetic properties, Ring system, Satellites,* and *Temperature and radiation.* Notice the fourth article under the subtopic Ring system. The title of this article is "Voyager 2: all eyes and ears for Saturn." It was written by J. Eberhart, and it is illustrated. It appeared in the periodical *Science News,* volume 120, pages 106–108 in the August 15, 1981 issue. In the front of the *Readers' Guide* is an explanation of the abbreviations used to describe the magazines and periodicals.

Practice

A. For each question, tell whether you would find the answer in an encyclopedia, an atlas, an almanac, or the *Readers' Guide to Periodical Literature.*

   1. What is the latest information about the magnetic properties of the planet Saturn?
   2. Who is the current prime minister of Canada?
   3. When was William the Conqueror born?
   4. What is a good recipe for barbecue sauce?
   5. What countries border Switzerland?
   6. What is the best route from Philadelphia, Pennsylvania, to San Diego, California?
   7. What is the latest information about whales?

B. Give the title, author's name, periodical name, and date of publication for articles that might contain the answers to questions 1 and 4 above.

4 | The Parts of a Book

There are many occasions when you do not need or have the time to read an entire book just to get some information from it. Also, a book may not contain any of the information you had hoped it might. There are several parts of a nonfiction book that will help you decide if a book has the information you want, and if so, where you can find it.

The **title page** gives you your first clue about the contents of a book. It gives both the title and the author of the book. The **copyright page** is located on the reverse side of the title page. It tells you when the book was published and the name of the publishing company. The copyright date will indicate when the book was written and whether it has been revised and updated since it was first published.

The title and cover of a book usually give you only a very general idea of the book's contents. To get a general overview of the subjects covered in the book, you will want to look at the **table of contents.** The contents page may list only chapter headings, or it may list the subtopics under the chapter titles. Look at the following table of contents. Notice how the subject is subdivided.

The first heading, Part One, in the table of contents gives you the broad area that will be covered in the first chapters. Each chapter is then broken into subtopics that tell you more about what information you will find there. Page numbers for the chapters and subtopics tell you where each section begins. On which page does the section about early railroads begin? How long is it?

Collections of information called **appendixes** are found at the back of some nonfiction books. The information given in appendixes may be in the form of tables or charts, graphs, lists, or diagrams that could not be conveniently located in the main body of the book. Look at the sample table of contents on page 244. Notice where the appendixes are listed and the kinds of information they contain. Which appendix gives information on the Westinghouse brake?

Authors sometimes use books as references when they are writing informational material. These reference books are listed in the **bibliography.** A reference in the bibliography tells you the author, title, publisher, and date. The references listed in the bibliography would be a good place to start if you wanted to read more about the subject of the book. How many bibliographies are there in the sample table of contents? Where is it located? In some books, you will find a bibliography at the end of each chapter. A bibliography may also be helpful in deciding whether the book contains the information you want. If the books listed in the bibliography seem to be about the subject you are investigating, then the book will probably have the information you want.

One of the most useful features for locating information in a book is an **index.** An index is an alphabetical list of specific subjects and people covered in a book. If you want to know about the firing of pottery of North American Indians, you look in the table of contents of a book on North American Indians. You may not find a chapter devoted to the firing of pottery. Instead of looking through the entire book, you can turn to the index and look up pottery. If pottery is not listed, think of a synonym or related subject, such as crafts, or clay products, and look that up instead. Look at the sample index below.

Beads, 122	Oral and written traditions
Clay Products, 124	*See also* Signaling
Dwellings, 192–196	folktales, 252
Food preservation, 197–199	legends, 255
meat processing, 199	Transportation
pemmican, 199	canoe, 54–55
Mound builders, 187*p*	horses, 56

The index entries are followed by the page numbers on which the terms are defined. Some subjects, such as food preservation and transportation, have subtopics. Other entries tell you to see another topic for additional information. This is called cross-referencing. Cross references help you find related information rapidly. What is the cross reference for *oral and written traditions*?

Notice that there is an italicized letter *p* after one page reference for *mound builders*. Indexes may use italicized letters such as *m, p, d, c,* or *t* to indicate where there is a map, picture, diagram, chart, or table.

If you are assigned a report on North American Indian mound builders, you would probably go to the library and find several books on Indians. How will you go about selecting the books that would be most useful without spending too much time? Let the table of contents, index, bibliography, and other special features do some of your work.

Practice

A. Write the answers to the following questions.

1. What part of the book would refer you to other books and articles on the same subject?
2. What part of the book gives you an overview of the contents?
3. What information tells you when the book was published?
4. What part of the book contains charts and tables?
5. What part of the book would tell you the topic of the entire book?
6. What part of the book would give you a list of books the author used as references?
7. How would you locate information about a peace treaty in a history book?

B. Refer to the samples of the table of contents on page 244 and the index on page 245 to answer the following questions.

8. Between what pages would you look to find information on food preservation?
9. On what page is *pemmican* defined?
10. On what page does Chapter 1 begin?
11. On what page would you find a picture?
12. What topic is cross-referenced?
13. What are the subtopics of Chapter 2?
14. What does Appendix A contain?

5 | Scanning for Information

You know that when you want to get the main idea of a selection quickly without reading every word, you use the skill of skimming. However, there are many times each day when you do not want to get the main idea from some reading material. You only want a specific bit of information, and you want it quickly! The kind of information you are looking for may be a date, a phone number, a particular snack on a menu, or the name of a movie theater.

To find such bits of information, you probably scan the material. Scanning is an efficient way of locating some specific information, or detail, without stopping to read any other unrelated facts. In order to scan effectively, you should first figure out the form in which the information will be given. Will it be in numerals, in a special type such as italics, or will it be capitalized? Think of key words that are clues to the information you want. Should you be looking for color words? Names of parks? Names of states? Once you know the form of the information or key words that you should look for, let your eyes move as quickly as possible over the material, looking for those clues. Do not stop and focus on any other information.

Practice

A. Write the forms or the key words you would look for in scanning for the following information about the Civil War.

1. when the Civil War ended
2. the place where the first battle occurred
3. the size of the armies
4. the name of the president at the time

B. Turn to the article on page 248 about Mary McLeod Bethune. Scan to find the answers to these questions. Before you start scanning, think of the form in which the answer will be written or the clue words you should be looking for. Then locate the answers.

5. Where was Mary McLeod Bethune born?
6. Where did she attend college?
7. Whom did she marry?
8. Which president did she advise?

6 | Outlining and Taking Notes

How to organize and remember what you have read are important aspects of good study skills. Outlining is a study skill that will help you to organize and remember facts. An outline organizes information into main topics, subtopics, and details. As you read the article below, try to identify the main topics and subtopics.

Mary McLeod Bethune: A Pioneer in Education

Mary Jane McLeod was born in South Carolina in 1875. Her parents had been slaves, but she was born free. During her childhood, Mary worked in the cotton fields. She wanted to learn to read, but no school in the area would admit blacks. Finally, a missionary opened a school for black children, and Mary attended the school. Later, she won scholarships to colleges in North Carolina and Illinois.

For eight years, until 1903, Mary McLeod taught in mission schools in the South. After her marriage to Albert Bethune and the birth of her son, she made a decision: She would open her own school to ensure that her son and other black children would be well educated. In 1904, she opened the Daytona Normal and Industrial School for Girls in Florida. The school began in a four-room shack in Daytona Beach, Florida.

The school grew quickly. Within two years, 250 students were enrolled. Mary Bethune convinced prominent citizens to support her school so that it could expand even further. In 1923, the school merged with a nearby college, Cookman Institute, with Mary Bethune as president. Eight years later the school was renamed Bethune-Cookman College.

Mary McLeod Bethune earned many awards for her achievements, including the Spingarn medal in 1935. She served as an advisor to President Franklin D. Roosevelt from 1936 to 1943. At the founding of the United Nations, she was an observer for the Department of State. She died in 1955 in Daytona Beach.

On the following page, read over the partial outline of the article you have just read.

Mary McLeod Bethune

I. Early Life
    A. Born 1875 in S. Carolina
        1. Parents slaves
        2. Wanted to go to school; no schools for blacks
    B. Education
        1. Mission school
        2. Scholarships to colleges

The outline shows the correct form. An outline begins with a title. What other title could have been used for this outline? The outline form alternates numbers and letters: Main topics use Roman numerals; subtopics use capital letters; details use Arabic numbers. There are always at least two main topics, subtopics, or details. For example, if you have main topic I, you must have a main topic II. What would main topic II be in the outline above? How many subtopics would be included under that main topic?

An outline can be written in complete sentences or in short phrases, but you should choose one style and be consistent. Capitalize the first word of a phrase. Look at the sample to see where periods are used.

Taking notes is another study skill that will help you to organize and remember facts. When you take notes while reading or listening to a lecture, you write down only the most important ideas and facts. Before a test, you can study your notes, which takes less time than rereading the material. You can also use your notes to prepare reports or essays.

Before taking notes on a selection, read it through once. Notice the main topics and subtopics, as you did when reading the article above. Then reread the selection. Write down the important ideas and facts in sentences, phrases, single words, abbreviations, or symbols. Underline the most important information. Draw lines or arrows to remind yourself how the facts are related. You should write the notes in your own words, but be careful not to change the author's or speaker's meaning. If you think you may want to quote the author or speaker directly, take down his or her exact words, making sure to enclose those words in quotation marks. Your notes should be concise, but they should contain enough information so that they will make sense when you use them.

Practice

A. Complete the outline above for the article on page 248.
B. Take notes on the information in the article on page 248.

7 | Summarizing

Telling a friend the plot of a movie you have seen or a book you have read is a form of **summarizing.** You tell the most important facts and events and the highlights of the story. You may quote what a character said if it was especially important, but for the most part, you tell the story in your own words.

Summarizing can also be a useful study tool. Like note taking and outlining, summarizing helps you to organize and remember information. Sometimes summarizing is a more effective study tool than outlining. In a summary, you can define important terms and tell how ideas and events are related; in an outline, you can only list terms, ideas, and events. Before a test, you might want to summarize your notes. As you think about the information in order to summarize it, you will be able to figure out whether or not you really understand all of the important facts, ideas, and relationships in the material.

There is no one right way to summarize, but these suggestions will help you begin.

1. Start with a clear, brief statement that tells the topic or main idea of the summary. This statement is similar to the title of an outline.
2. Write sentences that add details to support the main idea. These details may include names, dates, places, and a variety of other factual information.
3. If you quote a speaker's or writer's exact words, set off these words with quotation marks.
4. When summarizing a long factual article, such as a chapter in a social studies or science book, write sentences that state the main idea of each paragraph. Then condense these sentences into a summary.

Study the following example of a summary.

The printed book as we know it today has had many forerunners throughout the centuries. The earliest writings were scratched on bark or leather or chiseled in wood, stone, or clay. The early Greeks and Romans used clay tablets for short pieces of writing. A group of such tablets could be joined together with metal rings or leather thongs to form a *codex,* which was an early form of the book. For long pieces of writing, sheets of papyrus were glued together to form rolls up to forty feet long. Such a roll, which was written by hand, was called a *volūmen,* from which our word *volume* derives. Later, writing was done on vellum or parchment sheets, made from animal skins. These sheets were cut to the same size and bound together at the sides with leather ties. Not until the eleventh century was paper used extensively in bookmaking, and not until the fifteenth century were movable type and the printing press invented.

Notice that the first sentence tells what the summary is about. The remaining sentences tell the most important details and include names, dates, terms, and other facts. The summary is a clear and concise statement of all the important information.

Practice

A. Summarize the information below in two or three sentences.

The small wax tablets used by the Greeks and Romans for brief writings were made from small boards. These boards had narrow raised edges. A thin coating of black wax was poured into the frame and allowed to harden. Then letters could be scratched in the wax. The letters were scratched deeply enough so that the light wood of the frame showed through. We are accustomed to seeing black print on white pages, but in this early form of book-making, the page was black and the letters were white.

B. Rewrite the sample summary in your own words. Include the sentences you wrote in part A of the Practice in your summary.

8 | Taking Tests

Have you ever said, "I knew all the answers, but as soon as I started to take the test, I forgot everything." Whether or not you enjoy tests, they are a part of your school life and will be a part of your adult life. Although there is no guarantee of success on every test, there are some ways to do better on most tests. The two major keys to successful test taking are (1) to be prepared and (2) to use common sense and good judgment.

You should begin preparing for school tests as soon as your courses begin. The preparation should include both review and efficient study.

Here are some suggestions for effective review.

1. Review your material daily, both in class and at home.
2. Reread your notes, and try to see the relationships between each week's material. Regular review means that you will not have to learn everything the night before the test. You will have time to understand the important ideas and to see how they are related.

Studying efficiently for a test means beginning your study several days in advance. Here are some suggestions for studying.

1. Read your notes carefully. Summarize the most important ones.
2. Summarize or outline the relevant chapters in your book.
3. Answer the questions at the end of each chapter in your book.
4. Make sure that you understand all the material; ask your teacher for help early, if necessary.
5. Review your quizzes and assignments.

While you are taking the test, think. Read the directions carefully, making sure that you understand what each question asks and what kind of answer you are being asked to give.

The two most common types of tests are the essay test and the objective test. The essay test asks about ideas and events and how they are related. The essay question often includes such words as *explain, describe, list, discuss, contrast,* and *compare.* Use the words in the question to plan your answer. A good way to begin your answer is to use the essay question as your topic sentence. For example, if the question is, "Explain the differences between a dictatorship and a democracy," then your answer might begin, "A dictatorship and a democracy are different in the following ways. ..." The rest of your answer will provide supporting details. Keep in mind the following suggestions as you plan your essay.

- Read the question carefully several times.
- Determine exactly what is being asked.
- Make an outline of the points you wish to cover.
  - **a.** write down the facts
  - **b.** determine the main points
  - **c.** construct a simple outline of the main ideas

Objective tests stress facts and details; they require short answers. There are several types of objective tests: multiple-choice questions, matching questions, true-or-false questions, and sentence completion questions. For objective tests, you need to know important facts, names, terms, and dates. Here are some suggestions to follow when taking an objective test.

- Read the directions carefully to determine what task you are being asked to perform.
- Read the sample questions, and make sure that you understand the answers that are given.
- As you take the test, read all answer choices before making your selection; beware of potential traps that are intended to separate a careful reader from a quick and careless one. Then record your answers accurately.

Practice

A. Write an answer to this essay question, "Explain how an essay test is different from an objective test."

B. Answer each of the following questions.

    1. An objective test is

      a. multiple choice   **d.** matching

      b. sentence completion   **e.** short answer

      c. true or false   **f.** all of the above

    2. To prepare for an objective test, you should learn _____.

    3. To be sure you have time to complete the test, you should read the directions quickly. (true or false)

    4. You should begin preparing for tests in your school courses at the beginning of the course. (true or false)

    5. Before you answer an essay question, you should prepare a simple _____ of the points you wish to cover.

9 | The Parts of a Newspaper

Newspapers contain a wealth of information including reports of local and worldwide news, feature articles about people in the news or people who have won awards for special achievements, classified and other advertising, business reports and analyses, sports news, entertainment listings, and articles about food, travel, and fashions.

Listed below are some of the regular sections and features that most newspapers contain.

- **News stories** are usually located in the front parts of the paper, along with **feature articles.** These stories are given headlines that state the subject of the story. A news story usually begins with a sentence that tells *who, what, where, when, why,* or *how,* followed by supporting sentences that give more details. By reading the headline and lead sentence, you can usually tell which stories will interest you.
- The **Editorial** section gives the opinions held by the paper itself or by its columnists, as well as Letters to the Editor written by readers of the paper.
- The **Living, Life Style,** or **At Home** section contains articles about fashions, hobbies, home repairs, and recipes. It often includes personal advice columns too.
- The **Entertainment** section (also called **Arts and Films**) lists current cultural and entertainment events and often includes a review of one or more such events.
- The **Business** or **Financial** section gives stock reports, analyses of business trends, and current exchange rates of money.
- **Obituaries** are notices of death which include short biographies of well-known people.
- The **Sports** section reports on recent games, teams, and players.

Have you ever wondered how a newspaper gathers so much information every day? There are four major ways. The first is reporters who are stationed in different cities and countries. These people are on the scene to collect and write up news stories as they happen. The second way is the news services, Associated Press and United Press International (AP and UPI). These services have reporters stationed all over the world. Their reporters write stories that the news services sell to different newspapers. The third way is the newspaper syndicates, which supply features such as cartoons, comics, living and fashion articles, and columnists' essays. And the fourth major source of information is the newspaper library, or "morgue." This is a library containing files of newspaper and magazine stories, photographs, reference books, and bound volumes of the newspaper itself. The morgue is used for background information in preparing current stories.

Practice

A. Study the sample newspaper index below, then answer the questions that follow it.

Arts and Films	D38–41	Editorials	B10–15
At Home	C3–7	Obituaries	C13–16
Business	A24–30	Sports	D27–37
Classified	E13–42	TV/Radio	D48
Crossword	B16	Weather	B17

1. In what section would you be most likely to find a review of an art show opening?
2. On what page is the crossword puzzle?
3. In what section would you be likely to find advice about how to fix a leaky roof?
4. What pages would you turn to if you were looking for a job?
5. In what section would you find the newspaper's opinions about a new housing development?
6. In what section would you find news about two firms that were planning to merge?

B. Newspaper headlines must be short and must attract the readers' attention. Write a headline for a story about each of the subjects listed below.

1. A firefighter rescues a small child and her kitten from a burning building.
2. Disarmament negotiations between two major world powers are proceeding slowly.
3. A bill reducing taxes was passed by the House yesterday.

1 | Taking Notes

Sometimes you read information you want to remember. It may be facts you will need to know for a test, for a piece of writing, or for your own information—just to amaze your friends! How can you remember the facts? One way is to take notes. When you take notes to remember something you have read, write key words to help you recall what you want to know. It helps to ask yourself a question and take notes that answer the question.

Read the paragraphs, the question, and notes below.

Scientists have learned that there are two general kinds of sleep. The amount of time spent in each kind of sleep each night affects not only how you feel but also how well you learn and remember.

On a normal night, you will spend about one hundred minutes dreaming. These dream periods are identified by rapid eye movements, or REMs. Sleep during this time is known as REM sleep. Sleep without rapid eye movements and dreams is known as non-REM sleep. The first 1½ to 2 hours that you are asleep is non-REM sleep. This time is followed by about ten minutes of REM sleep. Your body alternates between non-REM and REM sleep all night, with dream periods growing longer and longer. Most REM sleep, therefore, occurs toward morning.

What happens when you sleep only three or four hours in a night and the amount of REM sleep is cut down? Scientists have learned that a reduction in REM sleep can cause forgetfulness. One research study seems to show that new learnings become part of your long-term memory during REM sleep. When REM sleep is reduced, these learnings may not be remembered—at least not for very long. This finding may explain why students who stay up late cramming for a test may not be able to remember the information the next day and certainly not a week later. In fact, when trying to learn a lot of information, it seems to be better to get more sleep rather than less.

What is REM sleep and how does it affect learning?

—period of rapid eye movements and dreaming
—longer periods of REM sleep as night goes on
—REM sleep needed for long-term memory

• What facts were left out of the notes? Why were they left out?

Practice

Imagine that you are writing a report about animal communication. You discover the following curious facts about communication among bees. Take notes to answer the question, *How do bees communicate where to find nectar?*

Scientists have known for a long time that animals communicate with each other. Birds have special calls that warn of danger. Bears and other animals leave a scent to communicate their presence.

Bees, however, can communicate specific information. Have you ever lain in a field of clover on a hot summer day and watched the bees? All the bees probably did not find the field on their own. More than likely, one or two scouts discovered the field and informed the others.

Through various "dances," a bee can tell other bees the direction and distance of food from the hive. The circle dance tells that the food is within a hundred yards. The waggle dance, in which the bee moves in a figure eight, tells that the food is farther away. The speed of the waggle dance indicates how much farther. The faster the bee dances, the closer the food is to the hive.

During the waggle dance, the dancer indicates in which direction the bees must fly to find the food. The dancer crosses from one loop of the eight to the other in the direction of the food.

The other bees smell or touch the dancer to pick up the scent of the bee and the nectar. When they follow the directions, the bees search for that scent. When they find flowers with that smell, they know they have found the right place.

2 | Making an Outline

An **outline** is a simple, effective way of organizing information. If you have taken notes for a piece of writing, an outline helps you organize your notes before you begin to write. When making an outline, you put together the facts and details that tell about each main idea. A carefully planned outline will provide a clear road map for you to follow to write your paragraphs.

An outline has main topics, subtopics, and details. **Main topics** are the main ideas. **Subtopics** are facts that support the main topics. **Details** give specific facts about the subtopics.

When you write an outline from notes, first turn the question your notes answer into a main topic. Look at the information in the notes. What facts support the main topic? Write them as subtopics. What facts tell about a particular subtopic? Write those facts as details under the appropriate subtopic. Give your outline a title.

Read the notes below and the section of outline that follows.

What are the effects of weightlessness?

—eliminates wrinkles   —one or two inches taller
—fills out face   —body in slight crouch when standing
—reduces waistline   —backward lean when sitting
—reduces foot size

      Life in a Space Shuttle   **title**
I. Effects of weightlessness   **main topic**
  A. Changes in body features   **subtopic**
    1. Loss of wrinkles   **detail**
    2. Fuller face
    3. Thinner waist
    4. Smaller feet
    5. Increase in height by one or two inches
  B. Changes in posture
    1. Slight crouch when standing
    2. Backward lean when sitting

- How is a main topic set off in the outline? a subtopic? a detail?
- What words are capitalized in an outline?
- Why are "Changes in body features" and "Changes in posture" appropriate as subtopics?

To write subtopics, you may have to look for several details that, when put together, tell about the main topic in the same way. For example, in the outline on weightlessness, the subtopics are not written in the notes. The subtopics are general headings that state the effects of weightlessness. These effects were described by the details in the notes.

An outline entry must have at least two subentries under it.

It is important for your main topics and subtopics to be in a logical order. Sometimes the order is clear. Look at these main topics.

Abraham Lincoln
I. Early life
II. Legislative career
III. Presidential years

These main topics follow the order of Lincoln's life. There are several ways to arrange main topics and subtopics. Then the order must be made clear in the paragraphs written from the outline.

Practice

Continue the outline about life in a space shuttle, using the notes below. Turn each question into a main topic. Write subtopics that support the main topics. Look at the details to make up the subtopics. Put the main topics and subtopics in a logical order. Be able to give your reasons. Write the details that tell about each subtopic.

What kinds of foods will be on the space shuttle?

—over 100 dehydrated foods
—dehydrated fruits, vegetables, cereals, eggs, soups
—20 kinds of dehydrated drinks
—canned foods—tuna fish, fruit
—some foods in natural forms— crackers
—irradiated food (bacteria killed by radiation)
—irradiated foods—meat, bread

What is a description of the space suit for use outside the shuttle?

—inflatable basic layer to maintain pressure
—restraint layer to keep basic layer from ballooning
—fireproof layers for radiation and temperature protection
—built-in backpack
—backpack contents: oxygen, lithium hydroxide canister to remove dangerous gases, water, water purifier, battery-operated water cooler

3 | Making Transitions

You have learned that an outline provides a plan for a piece of writing. You have also learned that the main topics and subtopics in an outline should be arranged in a logical order. Before you write, review your outline and decide how many paragraphs you will need. Each main topic should have at least one paragraph. Some main topics may have more than one paragraph, depending on the amount of information given.

The connection between one paragraph and the next should be clear to the reader. To make the connections clear, you can use **transition words and phrases.** Transition words and phrases build bridges between paragraphs, and between sentences, so that they read smoothly.

Transition words and phrases are used for different purposes. In the sentences below, the transition words and phrases are underlined. Unless they are part of a longer phrase, transition words and phrases are followed by a comma.

Introduce examples	The red fox deserves its reputation for cleverness. <u>For example</u>, it may play with a stick to arouse the curiosity of nearby ducks. Then it will hide and wait for a curious duck to investigate.
Add another point	The planet Saturn is best known for its colorful rings. <u>In addition</u> to its rings, Saturn has ten to twelve satellites.
Indicate time relationships	Gold was discovered in California in 1849. <u>Before long</u>, thousands of gold seekers were surging west.
Signal results or effects	Charles Lindbergh's wife Anne served as his copilot and navigator on many trail-blazing flights. <u>As a result</u>, she received many aviation awards.
Show comparison and contrast	The Appalachian Mountains are worn down by erosion. <u>In contrast</u>, the Rocky Mountains sport high, jagged peaks.
Connect ideas	Most people know the importance of exercise. <u>However</u>, many people leave it at that.

The chart below lists transition words and phrases that can help you connect the ideas in your sentences and paragraphs.

Introduce examples

for example	in one instance
for instance	in one case
to illustrate	in fact
in one example	as proof

Add another point

in addition	furthermore
also	moreover
another	a second (third, fourth, etc.)

Indicate time relationships

before	since	in the meantime
after	meanwhile	to begin with
next	eventually	at the same time
then	at last	not long after
finally	afterward	as time passed
soon	at this point	first, second, third, etc.

Signal results or effects

as a result	due to
because (of)	for this reason
therefore	in response to
thus	in conclusion
consequently	

Show comparison or contrast

similarly	different from
like	in contrast
unlike	on the other hand
just as	on the contrary
the same as	

Connect ideas

yet	so
however	nevertheless
though	moreover

Another way to make transitions between paragraphs is to refer to a thought from the preceding paragraph in a topic sentence. Read the paragraphs below. Pay special attention to the underlined words and phrases.

A squirrel spends a busy summer gathering nuts and hoarding them. When winter comes, the squirrel has enough to eat.

Is <u>this animal</u> acting intelligently? Is it deliberately planning ahead, as a person plans ahead when he puts money in the bank?

Scientists have performed experiments to try to answer <u>these questions</u>. They have raised squirrels in warm, comfortable laboratories, where they never experience winter and never know a hungry day. Yet when these squirrels are given nuts for the first time, they immediately look for a place to bury them.

<u>The urge to bury nuts</u> is so strong, a squirrel may try to dig a hole in the wire floor of its cage. It will push the nuts into this nonexistent "hole" and will try to "cover them up" by moving its paws rapidly through the air.   –*Russell Freedman and James E. Morris*

You can use the pronouns *this, that, these,* and *those* with a noun repeated from a preceding paragraph to carry over a thought. You may want to substitute a synonym for the first noun, as *animal* is substituted for *squirrel* above. *These questions* in the third paragraph refers to the sentences in the second paragraph.

You can also make a transition by restating an idea. *The urge to bury nuts* restates an idea from the preceding paragraph that is further explained in the new paragraph.

You can use these same techniques to make transitions between sentences within paragraphs as well. Find two examples in the paragraphs above.

Practice

A. Find ten examples of transitional words and phrases in books, magazines, or newspapers. Find at least two examples in which the writer used the pronouns *this, that, these,* or *those.* Find at least two examples in which the writer restated a thought from a preceding paragraph.

B. Write five pairs of sentences. Use a transitional word or phrase to join each pair.

4 | Getting Started

Firsthand reports are based on your own observations, experiences, and interviews. Research reports are based on facts and information given in books, magazines, and other published materials. The library is your main source of information for a research report.

Because the library contains information about thousands of topics, the possible topics for a research report are unlimited. There are so many exciting subjects to learn about. Where should you begin? First of all, think about subjects that interest you. What would you like to know about?

You might think of ideas for report topics by reviewing your favorite subjects in school:

art or music: Would you like to learn about a famous artist, such as Michelangelo, Mary Cassatt, or Andrew Wyeth? a famous musician, such as Mozart or Leonard Bernstein? Perhaps you would like to explore the history of an art form, such as sculpture, or trace the development of a musical instrument.

industrial arts: What tools were used in early America and for what purposes? What are different methods for making furniture?

home economics: How have clothing styles changed in the United States? What are the foods of another country or a particular group?

physical education: How did your favorite sport develop? You might describe the setting of world records in a favorite sport, or report on the life of a famous athlete.

history: If you could ride a time machine, what period of time or event would you like to experience? What was a journey over the Oregon Trail like? How did people live in ancient Egypt? Why was Queen Elizabeth I of England a great ruler?

science: What are the habits of wolves? How do birds' nests differ? How was the computer developed? What are current uses of wind power? How does an oil well work?

language arts: How did the alphabet develop? Read about a famous author, such as Henry David Thoreau or Elizabeth Barrett Browning. Find out about careers in the communications industry, such as public relations, advertising, or radio and television jobs.

There are many other ways to think of topics for research reports. Look around you. Are you curious about natural events, such as earthquakes, volcanic eruptions, or hurricanes? You might research the causes and effects of one of these events.

Special places can be the source of many interesting research topics. To what state, city, or country would you like to travel? What historic place or natural wonder would you like to see?

No matter what your interests, there are many fascinating research report topics just waiting for you to explore them.

Practice

A. List the topics below that would be good topics for a research report.

1. coins of the world
2. an assembly at your school
3. ancient African kingdoms
4. the first computer
5. interview with a business person

6. snow camping
7. your collection of airplane models
8. how solar energy works
9. a club field trip
10. your thoughts about student government

B. Compare your list with a partner's. Discuss the reasons for your choices. Prepare a final list.

C. List five to ten research report topics that interest you. Then meet in a small group with three or four of your classmates. Read your topics to them. Ask them which topics they would be most interested in reading or hearing about. Discuss why some topics may be more interesting than others. Consider their comments. Then circle three or four topics on your list that you think would be the best topics for your report.

Steps for Writing a Report Here are the steps for writing a research report. You will follow these steps to write your own report.

Step One	Choose a topic.
Step Two	Plan your report.
Step Three	Write your report.
Step Four	Revise your report.
Step Five	Proofread your report.
Step Six	Make a final copy to share.

5 | Step One
Choose Your Topic

Pam made a list of eight research report topics that interested her. After discussing her list with three other class members, Pam circled the four topics she liked best.

Egyptian mummies
William Dawes
submarines
events that happened on Sept. 20 (my birthday)

Pam had to consider three questions in choosing her report topic.

1. Does this topic really interest me?
2. Can I find information about it easily?
3. Is this topic narrow enough for a short report?

Pam went to the library to check the availability of information about her four topics. She discovered that information about the life of William Dawes, the man who—like Paul Revere—warned the colonists about the British, was limited. She crossed off that topic. There were several sources of information about her other topics, however.

Pam wondered which of her other three topics she should choose. Pam knew that the topic of submarines was too big for a short paper. She thought of narrowing it to "the first submarine" or "how submarines operate." Egyptian mummies really fascinated her. In the end, however, she decided that the topic about important happenings on her birthdate was even more interesting. Her mother had once said that she had seen a movie being filmed the day Pam was born. Until then, it had not occurred to Pam that something other than her being born might have happened on September 20. She was eager to begin her research.

Assignment • Choose Your Topic

Review the topics you circled on your list in Lesson 4. Add any other topics that interest you. For each topic, answer the three questions to consider when choosing a research report topic. Cross out any topics that you cannot find information about easily. Narrow topics that are too broad. Then circle the topic that interests you the most.

6 | Step Two
Plan Your Report

Pam planned her report before she began her research. If she did not plan first, she might waste time taking notes for facts she would not need. Pam made a working outline, listing facts she wanted to research.

> What was happening on the day I was born —
> Sept. 20, 1972?
>   —in town?
>   —around the state?
>   — in the U.S.a.?
>   — in the world?
> What happened on Sept. 20 in other years?
>   —Who else was born?
>   — What major events have happened?
> What holidays occur on or near Sept. 20?

Pam would use this working outline to begin her research. She could add items to the outline if she found other information. She could cross off items if she could not find certain facts. She could also rearrange the order of the outline. For now, though, she had a rough plan.

Pam found several reference books in the library that had some information. When she told the librarian her research topic, she learned that the library had many years of old news magazines bound into books. The library also had old issues of the local newspaper, *The Montrose Daily Press,* on microfilm. Pam could request the issues of magazines and newspapers for September 20.

Whenever Pam found a fact that answered one of her questions, she took notes about the fact on a note card. She wrote one card for each fact. At the top of the card, she wrote the question the fact answered. At the bottom of the card, she wrote a number and circled it. The circled number matched a number on Pam's bibliography card. The number on the bibliography card identified the source where Pam found the fact. Next to the circled number on her note card, Pam also wrote the page number(s) where she found the fact. Here is one of Pam's note cards and part of her bibliography card.

What holidays occur on or near Sept. 20?
— Sept. 14: National Anthem Day
— Francis Scott Key wrote words to "The Star-Spangled Banner"

① p. 838

1. Hatch, Jane M. The American Book of Days. New York: The H. H. Wilson Co., 1978, p. 838.
2. "New Junior High School Opens Doors," The Montrose Daily Press, September 20, 1970, pp. 1, 6.

- What kind of source is the first entry in the bibliography for? How is the author's name written? What other information is given?
- What kind of source is the second entry for? What information is given?
- What punctuation marks and abbreviations are used?

When she had gathered all her facts, Pam sorted her note cards into three piles, one pile for each main question in her working outline. In each pile, she grouped the cards for each point underneath the main question. Pam discovered that she had not found any interesting facts about events in her state on her birthday. In addition, she had not recognized the names she had found of other people born on September 20. She decided to leave out those two points.

Pam organized her notes into a final outline. She had a main topic for each main question in her working outline. She filled in the subtopics and details. Part of her outline is shown on the next page.

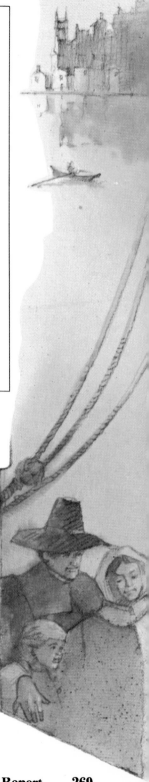

III. Holidays around Sept. 20
    A. Sept. 14
       1. National Anthem Day
       2. 1814 — British attack on Fort McHenry
       3. During attack, words written for "The Star-Spangled Banner" by Francis Scott Key
    B. Sept. 16
       1. Mayflower Day
       2. 1620 — Pilgrims left Plymouth, England
    C. Sept. 17
       1. Citizenship Day
       2. Constitution signed
       3. Honors new voters and new citizens

Assignment

- **Make a Working Outline**
- **Take Notes**
- **Make a Final Outline**

A. Make an informal working outline to direct your research.

B. Find sources of information—books, reference materials, magazines, newspapers, pamphlets—that provide answers to your questions. Take notes to remember the facts. Follow these steps.

    1. Write one fact on a card. At the top, write the question the fact answers. At the bottom, write the number from the bibliography card of the source. Write the pages where you found the fact.

    2. Make a bibliography card. For a book or unsigned newspaper article, follow the models on page 268. Models for magazine and encyclopedia entries are shown on page 273.

C. Sort your fact cards. Make a pile for each main question in your working outline. In each pile, group the cards for each point underneath the main question. Pull out any cards that do not fit.

D. Write a final outline. Arrange your topics and subtopics logically.

7 | Step Three
Write Your Report

You have already completed some of the most difficult steps of writing a research report—choosing an interesting topic, narrowing it, searching out informative sources, taking careful notes, and making a well-structured outline. Having all your facts clearly in order will make the next step—writing your first draft—much easier.

A report has an introduction, a body, and a conclusion. The introduction may begin with the general subject of the report, then move to the specific topic. It may begin with an anecdote, or little story, that illustrates the topic of the report. However it is written, the introduction should present the topic of the report in a way that attracts the reader's interest. An introduction for a short report of several pages is usually one paragraph.

The body presents the factual information about the topic. It includes as many paragraphs as necessary to explain the main ideas. Before you begin your report, review your outline. Decide how many paragraphs you will need for the body.

The conclusion sums up the main ideas and finishes the report. In a short report, the conclusion is usually one paragraph.

Pam thought of several introductions for her report. She wrote them on a piece of paper so that she could compare them. Read Pam's introductions on this page and the next.

Pam's introductions

Every day someone is born and being born is the most important thing for that person. Maybe it doesn't matter to other people, but it matters to you because if you aren't born, who or where are you?

I was born on September 20, 1970. In this report, I will tell about things that have happened on that day and about holidays around that day.

Just 154 years and six days after Francis Scott Key wrote the words to "The Star-Spangled Banner," I was born "by the dawn's early light." Sometimes many special events happen on the same day. What important events have happened in United States history on or about September 20?

- Which introduction does not tell the topic of the report?
- Which introduction states the topic but is very boring?
- Which introduction is the best? Why?

Pam decided that her third introduction was the best. It introduced the topic of the report in an interesting way.

Pam then wrote the first draft of the body of her report. She followed the order of the main topics and subtopics in her outline. She wrote several paragraphs for her first main topic telling what happened on her birthday, September 20, 1970, in her town, in the United States, and in the world. Then she wrote several paragraphs for her second main question about happenings on September 20 in other years. Last, she wrote the final section of her report about holidays that occur on or around September 20.

Pam just tried to get all the facts and ideas on paper. She knew that she would go back and polish her report later.

At the very end of her report, Pam wrote a conclusion.

Read the final section and conclusion of Pam's report on the next page.

Final section and conclusion of Pam's first draft

~~Around~~ There are many holidays around September 20. September 14 is National Anthem Day. Francis Scott Key wrote the words to "The Star-Spangled Banner." He had watched the United States Flag fly over Fort McHenry while the British attacked it and tried to capture it and make the Americans surrender, but they never sucseeded. The sight of the flag flying all threw the night made him write the beautiful words which became our national anthem. Mayflower Day is ~~when~~ September 16. The Pilgrims left Plymouth, England, on the <u>Mayflower</u> on September 16, 1620. We can think of their leaving England as the beginning of the United States.

Citizenship Day is Sept. 17. It honors people who have become old enough to vote during the year and people from other ~~places~~ countrys who have become United States Citizens. This was the day the United States constitution was signed in 1787. Sept. 22 is Nathan Hale Day in Connecticut. Nathan Hale was a spy who was caught and hanged by the British. He said the famos words I only regret that I have but one life to loose for my country.

Many things have happened around Sept. 20. That's probably true for all the other days, too. I checked out Sept. 20 because it is my birthday.

- What is the topic sentence in the paragraph about holidays?
- How many paragraphs should Pam use to present the facts about holidays? Why?
- What are possible topic sentences for the new paragraphs?
- Where could Pam use transition words and phrases?
- Did Pam leave out any information from her outline on page 269? Did she add any information on the three holidays shown there?
- What parts of the report does Pam need to explain more clearly?
- Did Pam write a good conclusion? Why or why not?

When Pam finished her first draft, she wrote a bibliography page. The page listed all the sources Pam had used. She took the information from her bibliography card. Pam wrote the entries in alphabetical order. Here is part of her bibliography.

"Nathan Hale." Collier's Encyclopedia. 1974 ed.

Scovel, C. "Oh Say Can You Sing?" The Atlantic

    Monthly, January, 1975, pp. 54–55.

Assignment   • Write Your First Draft

Write your first draft, following these steps. You may want to skip a line when you write to leave room for revisions.

1. Write an introduction for your report. Lead into your report by moving from the general subject of your report to the specific topic. Write your introduction in a way that will interest a reader.
2. Review your final outline. Decide how many paragraphs you will write for each main topic. Remember to include only one main idea in each paragraph. Write a topic sentence for each paragraph. Write the facts in the outline in sentences that support that main idea.
3. Write a conclusion to finish your report and sum up the main ideas.
4. Write a bibliography page. List the sources in which you found facts about your topic. List the entries in alphabetical order. For a book and unsigned newspaper article, follow the models on page 268. For an encyclopedia, a magazine article, or a signed newspaper article, follow the models above.

8 | Step Four
Revise Your Report

When Pam reread her report, she noticed that her paragraph about holidays was too long. Her topic sentence stated the main idea, but each holiday needed a paragraph of its own. Pam inserted signs for new paragraphs on her draft. Then she wrote a topic sentence for each new paragraph. She remembered to use transition words and phrases to help tie sentences and paragraphs together.

Pam decided her conclusion did not sum up the main ideas very well. She wrote a new conclusion and taped it over her first one.

Pam asked Ramón to listen to her report and make suggestions. When Pam finished, Ramón said he liked the part about holidays. He liked the way they all had something in common.

"What do they have in common?" asked Pam.

"Those special days you talk about are all—well, American. Maybe you should write that part in red, white, and blue!" explained Ramón.

"Hey, that's it!" exclaimed Pam. "That's a great way to tie all these holidays together. I didn't know how to do it."

"When was 'The Star-Spangled Banner' written?" asked Ramón. "And whom did Nathan Hale spy for?"

Pam jotted down a few notes on her paper to remember Ramón's ideas. She thanked Ramón, then made the changes she liked. Pam also used more exact words in a few places to make her facts clearer.

Pam's revision

> The week of Sept. 20 is a good time to wear red, white, and blue. Many holidays during this week commemorate important events in U.S. history.
> ~~Around~~ To begin with, ~~There are many holidays around September 20.~~ September 14 is National Anthem Day. On this day in 1814, Francis Scott Key wrote the words to "The Star-Spangled Banner." He had watched the United States Flag fly over

Fort McHenry while the British attacked it and tried

to capture it. ~~and make the Americans surrender, but~~

However
they never succeeded. The sight of the flag flying all

 inspired   to
threw the night ~~made~~ him write the beautiful words

 ¶ An especially important day in our history is
which became our national anthem. Mayflower Day ~~is~~,

~~when~~ September 16. The Pilgrims left Plymouth,

England, on the Mayflower on September 16, 1620.

We can think of their leaving England as the begin-

ning of the United States.

A third holiday is   on
Citizenship Day ~~is~~ Sept. 17. It honors people who

have become old enough to vote during the year and

people from other ~~places~~ countrys who have become

 In addition t
United States Citizens. This was the day the United

 ¶ The last holiday during this week, Nathan Hale
States constitution was signed in 1787. ~~Sept. 22 is~~

Day is celebrated in Connecticut on Sept. 22.
~~Nathan Hale Day in Connecticut.~~ Nathan Hale was a

for the colonists during the Revolutionary War. He
spy ~~who~~ was caught and hanged by the British. He

said the famos words I only regret that I have but one

life to loose for my country.

In conclusion, September 20 has been an important day in my town, the United States, and the
world. Also, it is part of a week that includes
four days honoring important events in our
history. Now I understand my place in history, too!

- Why is Pam's new introduction better? her conclusion?
- Where did Pam add transition words and phrases?
- Where did Pam add information to make a part clearer?
- Where did Pam use more exact words?

Assignment

- **Revise Your Report**
- **Discuss Your Report**

A. Reread your report after a few days. Ask yourself these questions.

1. Does the introduction lead into the topic in an interesting way?
2. Is the information in the report clear and complete?
3. Does each paragraph lead logically to the next?
4. Does the conclusion sum up the report?

B. Follow these steps to revise your report.

1. Write another introduction for your report. Then choose the introduction which you think is better.
2. Check each paragraph to be sure that it includes only one main idea. Begin new paragraphs if necessary.
3. Underline the topic sentence in each paragraph. If the topic sentence is dull or weak, write a new one. If there is no topic sentence, write one. Write a topic sentence for any new paragraphs you may have made.
4. Add or change words or phrases to make your facts clearer and your sentences more interesting.
5. Add transition words and phrases where they are needed to show the connection between sentences and paragraphs.
6. Write another conclusion. Choose the one you like better.

C. Read your report to a classmate or your teacher. Ask your listener to answer the questions in part A above. Take notes to help you remember your listener's suggestions. Make any changes your listener suggests that you like. If the discussion or oral reading of your paper makes you aware of other changes you think are good, make those changes, too.

9 | Step Five
Proofread Your Report

Pam was really pleased with her revised report. She had made so many revisions, though, that she had difficulty reading it. She decided to copy over her report before proofreading it.

Pam checked her punctuation, capitalization, and spelling. When she was unsure of a spelling, she looked it up in a dictionary. As Pam proofread, she noticed she had used some abbreviations in the report. She knew that reports should not include contractions or most abbreviations. She replaced the abbreviation with the full name. Finally, Pam checked to be sure she had used the correct forms of nouns, verbs, pronouns, and other parts of speech.

Part of Pam's proofread report

> The week of ~~Sept.~~ *September* 20 is a good time to wear red, white, and blue. Many holidays during this week com*m*emorate important events in ~~U.S.~~ *United States* history.
>
> To begin with, September 14 is National Anthem Day. On this day in 1814, Francis Scott Key wrote the words to "The Star-Spangled Banner." He had watched the United States *f*lag fly over Fort McHenry while the British attacked it and tried to capture it. However, they never suc*c*eeded. The sight of the flag flying all ~~threw~~ *through* the night inspired him to write the beautiful words which became our national anthem.

- Why did Pam make the changes in capitalization?
- Why did she add a comma?
- What spellings did she correct?
- Why did she spell out *September*?

Practice

Proofread the paragraphs from Pam's report below. Copy them correctly on a piece of paper. If you are unsure of a spelling, check a dictionary. There are twelve mistakes.

A third holiday is Citizenship Day on Sept. 17. It honors people who have become old enough to vote during the year and people from other countrys who have become United States Citizens. In addition this was the day the United States constitution was signed in 1787.

The last holiday during this week, Nathan Hale Day is celebrated in Connecticut on Sept. 22. Nathan Hale was a spy for the colonists during the Revolutionary War. He was caught and hanged by the British. He said the famos words I only regret that I have but one life to loose for my country.

Assignment • **Proofread Your Report**

Proofread your own report for capitalization, punctuation, spelling, and other grammar errors. Use the questions below as guidelines.

1. Have I made appropriate paragraph breaks?
2. Have I looked up the spellings of any words I am unsure of?

Grammar skills checklist

3. Have I corrected any sentence fragments or run-ons?
4. Have I used capital letters correctly?
5. Have I used commas correctly with appositives, the parts of a compound sentence, dependent clauses?
6. Have I written plural and possessive nouns correctly?
7. Have I used the correct forms of verbs and pronouns?

10 | Step Six
Make a Final Copy

Pam made a final clean copy of her report. She gave her report the title "A Most Important Day." Then Pam checked her report one last time for errors. Finally, she attached her bibliography page.

The students in Pam's class decided to present their reports to each other in small groups of three or four. Pam decided to make a collage showing pictures and other items of different events mentioned in her report. Her collage included a copy of her birth certificate, a picture of herself taken the day she was born, headlines (which she handprinted) from newspapers published September 20, a little flag she had received at a parade, and a picture of the *Mayflower II* from a travel brochure, among other items. She drew a few pictures herself to show certain events. She arranged all the items for her collage on a large piece of poster board. At the top, she wrote, "What Happened on or about Your Birthday?" When Pam presented her report to her group, she pointed to the pictures and items as she read about them.

Assignment
- **Make a Final Copy**
- **Share Your Report**

A. Copy your proofread report neatly on a clean piece of paper. Give your report a title if you have not already done so.

B. Check your final copy to be sure you corrected all mistakes and made no new errors in copying.

C. Attach your bibliography page to your final copy.

D. Think of a special way to share your report.

- Present your report orally to several people, as Pam did.
- Bring to class books that show illustrations of your report topic.
- Make a collage or another art project to accompany your report. Then display your picture and report so that interested students can learn about your topic.

13 Modifiers

1 | Adjectives

Identifying Adjectives

When you speak or write, you usually want to convey a clear picture, feeling, or idea.

> A cat was on our doorstep.
> A trembling, scrawny gray cat was on our doorstep.

The first sentence states the bare fact. The second sentence paints a picture of a particular cat. *Trembling, scrawny,* and *gray* put details into the picture. They describe, or modify, the noun *cat.* A word that modifies a noun or pronoun is called an **adjective**.

Adjectives like *trembling, scrawny,* and *gray* tell *what kind* about a noun or pronoun. Other words used as adjectives can tell *how many* or *which one.*

WHAT KIND: young, happy, deserted, yellow, aging, uneven, famous
HOW MANY: three, several, few, half, many, eight million
WHICH ONE: the, that, those, other, my, which

You have studied some of these words before. You learned about words like *several, few, that, those,* and *my* when you studied pronouns. You learned about words like *deserted* and *aging* when you studied verbs. When words like these are used to modify nouns or pronouns, they are considered adjectives.

PRONOUN: <u>That</u> must be Oliver's drawing.
ADJECTIVE: <u>That</u> drawing must be Oliver's.
VERB: The top was <u>spinning</u> fast.
ADJECTIVE: The <u>spinning</u> top amused the children.

If a word tells *what kind, how many,* or *which one* about a noun or pronoun, it is being used as an adjective.

Here are some of the types of words that can be used as adjectives.

DEMONSTRATIVE PRONOUNS: this, that, these, those
INDEFINITE PRONOUNS: each, several, many, some
POSSESSIVE PRONOUNS: their, my, your, our
NOUNS: cardboard, student, town
VERB FORMS: spinning, grinning, completed, torn

The words *a*, *an*, and *the* are special adjectives called **articles**. *A* and *an* are **indefinite articles** because they can refer to any one of a group of things. *The* is a **definite article** because it refers to a specific thing.

A dog can be short-haired or long-haired.
The dog by the door is short-haired.

An adjective formed from a proper noun is called a **proper adjective**. Like proper nouns, proper adjectives are capitalized.

North American history   Mexican art   British flag

Most adjectives precede the noun or pronoun they modify.

that long, dark alley   an exciting new book

Sometimes, however, an adjective may follow the modified word.

The runners were hot and flushed from their efforts.

The adjectives *hot* and *flushed* come after the linking verb *were* and refer back to the subject, *runners*. An adjective used in this way is a **predicate adjective;** it occurs in the predicate part of the sentence.

Adjectives are given special emphasis when they immediately follow a noun or pronoun. Such adjectives are set off by commas.

The runners, hot and flushed, rested in the shade of a tree.

Adjectives used in this way can also come before the noun.

Hot and flushed, the runners rested in the shade of a tree.

Try It Out

Identify each word used as an adjective. Which word does it modify?

1. A serious young man waited in the outer room of the imposing office.
2. Her photographs are exhibited in our neighborhood library.
3. Rich, kind, and generous, he sponsored many college scholarships.
4. You were calm and patient with those children.
5. This new drugstore carries your favorite French shampoo.
6. Several Mexican tourists took pictures of the towering structure.
7. The child, lovable but mischievous, wore out every sitter.
8. Each meal at that hotel was fresh, attractive, and delicious.
9. The six enthusiastic players discussed their next few games.
10. The mirrored wall reflected her bouquets of fresh flowers.

Commas with Adjectives

You have seen that two or more adjectives can modify a noun or pronoun. Usually, the adjectives are separated by commas.

> The <u>tired,</u> <u>thirsty</u> hikers decided to rest.

This sentence says that the hikers were tired and thirsty. The adjectives are of equal rank, and they are separated by commas.

> The <u>tired</u> <u>British</u> tourists decided to rest.

This sentence does not say the tourists were tired and British; it says that the British tourists were tired. *British* and *tired* are not equal in rank, and therefore they are not separated by commas.

There are two tests that can help you decide whether to use commas. First, try reading the adjectives with the word *and*. If *and* sounds awkward, a comma should probably *not* be used.

> tired and British tourists *(awkward—no comma)*
> tired and thirsty hikers *(not awkward—use comma)*

You can also try reversing the order of the adjectives. If they sound awkward when reversed, a comma should probably not be used.

> British, tired tourists *(awkward—no comma)*
> thirsty, tired hikers *(not awkward—use comma)*

A series of three or more adjectives is often joined by a conjunction like *and, but,* or *or.* Use a comma before the conjunction.

> The <u>hot,</u> <u>tired,</u> and <u>thirsty</u> hikers decided to rest.

Articles, numbers, possessives, and words like *this* and *several* are not used with commas.

<u>Those</u> <u>two</u> red shoes are mine.   <u>His</u> lucky catch was a big tuna.

Try It Out

Where are commas needed in these sentences?

1. A raw gray rainy day greeted several cheerful foreign visitors.
2. The busy vendor was selling red blue and gold balloons.
3. Those three large gifts are from my favorite uncle.
4. The hungry exhausted dog finally wandered home.
5. The snow was beautiful deep and wet.

> ▸ An **adjective** describes, or modifies, a noun or a pronoun.
> ▸ An adjective formed from a proper noun is a **proper adjective**. Proper adjectives are capitalized.
>
> Adjectives usually but not always precede the modified word.
>
> ▸ A **predicate adjective** follows a linking verb and refers back to the subject.
>
> Two or more equally ranked adjectives are separated by commas.

Written Practice

A. List each word used as an adjective and the word it modifies.

1. Handwritten manuscripts were the main records of human history until the fifteenth century.
2. Then, printing became common.
3. In ancient times, many manuscripts were written on papyrus.
4. Papyrus was made from a tall, needlelike Egyptian plant.
5. Connected papyrus sheets were formed into long rolls.
6. Most rolls were six meters in length, but some rolls were longer.
7. Parchment, another ancient writing material, was made from animal skin.
8. Vellum, smooth and precious, is parchment of high quality.
9. This parchment was made from the skin of lambs, calves, or other young animals.
10. Other people, especially in Greek and Roman societies, wrote with special instruments on wax tablets.
11. This sharp, pointed instrument was called a *stylus*.

B. Copy each sentence, adding commas where needed.

12. Our four devoted friends stayed with us.
13. This has been a bright crisp invigorating day.
14. Moe's two yapping dogs are careful observant watchdogs.
15. That lonely deserted junkyard looks like a ruined city.
16. Tina was alert watchful and cautious during the first match.

● **Writing a Paragraph** Write a paragraph of at least eight sentences describing a spring, summer, fall, or winter scene. Use different kinds of adjectives in your description.

2 | Adverbs

Identifying Adverbs

There are only two basic kinds of modifiers in English. The adjective, as you have learned, modifies nouns and pronouns. The other kind of modifier is the adverb. The **adverb** modifies a verb, adjective, or another adverb.

> The queen ruled <u>wisely</u>, <u>kindly</u>, and <u>well</u>. *(modify verb)*
> She became <u>quite</u> popular with her subjects. *(modifies adjective)*
> She handled her duties <u>remarkably</u> well. *(modifies adverb)*

Adverbs tell *where, when, how,* and *to what extent.*

> The bats flew <u>everywhere</u>. *(flew where?)*
> We had heard the same rumor <u>earlier</u>. *(heard when?)*
> He listened <u>carefully</u> to the words. *(listened how?)*
> I was <u>very</u> concerned. *(concerned to what extent?)*

Many of the adverbs that tell *to what extent* are words like *very, really,* and *too.*

Homero felt <u>very</u> tired.   Had he worked <u>too</u> hard?

An adverb like *very* or *too* intensifies the meaning of the adjectives and adverbs it modifies. This type of adverb is called an **intensifier**. Here is a list of common intensifiers.

awfully	less	quite	so	too
extremely	more	rather	terribly	very
least	most	really		

You may have noticed from the example sentences that many adverbs end in *-ly*. In fact, some adverbs are formed by adding *-ly* to adjectives: *wise-ly, slow-ly, kind-ly.* Not all words that end in *-ly* are adverbs, however. *Lovely, lonely, friendly, ugly,* for example, are used as adjectives.

Try It Out

Identify each adverb, and tell which word it modifies. Which of the adverbs are intensifiers?

1. Yesterday it rained constantly.
2. The day was so gloomy that I stayed indoors.
3. It was very hard to find really interesting things to do.
4. I worked quite diligently on my miniature train collection.
5. I exercised rather vigorously here and there.
6. I ran up and down repeatedly and rested afterward.

Position of Adverbs

Adverbs that modify verbs can often be placed in different positions.

<u>Cautiously</u>, Mr. Schultz approached the snorting bull.
Mr. Schultz <u>cautiously</u> approached the snorting bull.
Mr. Schultz approached the snorting bull <u>cautiously</u>.

Notice that an introductory adverb usually has a comma after it. Not all adverbs can be shifted around in this way. Sometimes the meaning of a sentence changes if the position of the adverb is changed. Do these sentences have the same meaning?

<u>Only</u> Samantha works there.
Samantha <u>only</u> works there.
Samantha works <u>only</u> there.

The first sentence says that Samantha is the only one who works there. The second sentence says that Samantha is only a worker there; she does not just visit the place or own it. Finally, the third sentence says Samantha works only in that place and nowhere else.

Be very careful when you use adverbs like *only*. They should be placed as close as possible to the words they modify. Other such adverbs include *almost, even, hardly, just, nearly, merely.*

Most adverbs that modify adjectives and adverbs should also be placed close to the words they modify.

MISPLACED: <u>Deeply</u>, Hiram Higglebottom was grateful.
CORRECTED: Hiram Higglebottom was <u>deeply</u> grateful.

Try It Out

Tell which adverbs can be shifted without causing a change in meaning. Then shift those adverbs to another part of the sentence.

1. That insignificant little item costs almost forty dollars.
2. Morton Haines searched frantically through his pockets.
3. The newborn calf slept peacefully.

▶ An **adverb** modifies a verb, an adjective, or another adverb. Adverbs usually tell *where, when, how, to what extent.*
▶ An adverb that tells *to what extent* is usually an **intensifier.** Intensifiers intensify the meanings of adjectives and adverbs.
Adverbs that modify verbs can often be placed in different positions in a sentence. Other adverbs should be placed as close as possible to the modified words.

Written Practice

A. Write each adverb and the word or words it modifies. Label each intensifier.

1. H. G. Wells is noted for his brilliantly written science fiction.
2. He was a very widely read writer in his time.
3. Many people today still read Wells's works enthusiastically.
4. Initially, Wells worked mainly on fiction writing.
5. He then developed rather naturally into a bold forecaster.
6. In the 1930's, Wells became quite deeply involved in world events.
7. He went everywhere and spoke continuously against the forces he firmly believed were driving humanity steadily downward.

B. If an adverb can be shifted without changing the meaning of the sentence, rewrite the sentence with the adverb in a different position. Otherwise, write *no change.*

8. Only three people bought tickets.
9. The bluejay scolded the cat noisily.
10. Mr. Hartwell skates only on the pond.

● **Writing Sentences** Write five sentences with adverbs.

3 | Comparing with Adjectives and Adverbs

Degrees of Comparison

Adjectives and adverbs can be used to compare two or more persons, places, things, ideas, or actions. The adjectives and adverbs change form, depending upon how many things are being compared. There are three different forms, or **degrees,** of comparison: positive, comparative, and superlative.

The **positive** degree is the basic form of the adjective or adverb. It is the form used when no comparison is being made.

ADJECTIVE: This is a long train.
ADVERB: This train travels fast.

The **comparative** degree is used when two things are compared.

ADJECTIVE: This is a longer train than the other one.
ADVERB: This train travels faster than the other one.

The **superlative** degree is used to compare three or more things.

ADJECTIVE: This is the longest train of the five in the station.
ADVERB: This train travels fastest of all.

Did you notice how the adjective and adverb changed as the degree of comparison changed? To form the comparative, *-er* is added to the adjective or adverb. To form the superlative, *-est* is added.

Try It Out

Give the correct form of the adjective or adverb in parentheses. Then tell whether the form is positive, comparative, or superlative.

1. The tan puppy was the ____ one in the litter. (small)
2. We shall have to eat dinner ____ tonight than last night. (late)
3. Ammonia has the ____ odor I have ever smelled. (strong)
4. My brother gets up ____ every weekday morning. (early)
5. Marlene seemed to be the ____ of the three girls. (young)
6. Ethan skates ____ than anyone else on the team. (fast)
7. Which of the two pencils is ____? (sharp)

Forms of Comparison

All adjectives and adverbs of one syllable form the comparative by adding -*er* and the superlative by adding -*est*.

	Positive	**Comparative**	**Superlative**
ADJECTIVE:	tall	taller	tallest
ADVERB:	slow	slower	slowest

Some adjectives of two syllables also add -*er* or -*est*.

Positive	**Comparative**	**Superlative**
heavy	heavier	heaviest

Most adjectives and adverbs of two syllables or more show comparison in a different way. They add the word *more* to form the comparative and *most* to form the superlative.

	Positive	**Comparative**	**Superlative**
ADJECTIVE:	famous	more famous	most famous
	beautiful	more beautiful	most beautiful
ADVERB:	quickly	more quickly	most quickly
	frequently	more frequently	most frequently

A few spelling changes occur. In one-syllable words that end in a single vowel and consonant, the consonant is doubled before -*er* or -*est*: *thin, thinner, thinnest*. In words that end in a consonant and -*y*, the *y* is changed to *i* before -*er* or -*est*: *happy, happier, happiest*.

You may sometimes have to check your dictionary to decide whether to use -*er*/-*est* or *more*/*most* with an adjective of two syllables. In many cases, your ear and eye will tell you which form is correct: *more precious*, rather than *preciouser*, for example. In a few cases, you will find that either form is correct: *gentler, more gentle*.

Avoid double comparisons. Do not use *more* with -*er* or *most* with -*est*.

INCORRECT: Ann is <u>more happier</u> now.   Ira is <u>most happiest</u> of all.
   CORRECT: Ann is <u>happier</u> now.   Ira is <u>happiest</u> of all.

When the comparison is meant to show less rather than more, use *less* to form the comparative and *least* to form the superlative.

	Positive	**Comparative**	**Superlative**
ADJECTIVE:	warm	less warm	least warm
ADVERB:	quickly	less quickly	least quickly

The examples below summarize the ways in which adjectives and adverbs change form to show comparison.

Adjectives

One Syllable   great
Comparative: Add *-er*   great**er**
Superlative: Add *-est*   great**est**

Two Syllables   pretty   famous
Comparative: Add *-er* or *more*   prett**ier**   **more** famous
Superlative: Add *-est* or *most*   prett**iest**   **most** famous

Three Syllables or more   independent
Comparative: Add *more*   **more** independent
Superlative: Add *most*   **most** independent

Adverbs

One Syllable   soon
Comparative: Add *-er*   soon**er**
Superlative: Add *-est*   soon**est**

Two Syllables or more   clearly
Comparative: Add *more*   **more** clearly
Superlative: Add *most*   **most** clearly

A few important adjectives and adverbs have irregular forms.

Positive	Comparative	Superlative
good, well	better	best
bad, badly	worse	worst
many, much	more	most
little (quantity)	less	least
far	farther	farthest

Try It Out

A. Give the correct form of each adjective or adverb.

1. Which do you like ____, the blue jacket or the green one? (well)
2. Does Harris, Liu, or Ruiz run ____? (fast)
3. Perez is running ____ of all. (smoothly)
4. I think he is ____ likely to win than Liu. (little)
5. Eliza has ____ courage than I do. (much)
6. Who in this class has the ____ cold? (bad)

B. Correct each sentence.

   7. Mrs. Lekach has the least practicalest approach of all.
   8. Is Loring, her brother, or her sister the better singer?
   9. You are the speedyest typist of anyone here.
  10. Who throws farer, you or he?

> ▸ The **comparative degree** of an adjective or adverb is used to compare two things.
> ▸ The **superlative degree** is used to compare three or more things.
> Form the comparative degree with *-er* or *more*.
> Form the superlative degree with *-est* or *most*.
> Avoid double comparisons.

Written Practice

A. Write the correct form of each word in parentheses.

   1. Reading can be the _____ adventure in the world. (wonderful)
   2. It can sometimes be _____ than real life. (exciting)
   3. Your imagination can roam _____ than your feet. (far)
   4. You can travel _____ than on a supersonic jet. (quickly)
   5. The places you visit can be the _____ anywhere. (unusual)
   6. Which city is _____, Cairo or Shanghai? (interesting)
   7. If you like Cairo _____, you can return there. (well)
   8. You can join the _____ mammals of all in the ocean. (big)
   9. You can see the _____ and _____ homes. (shabby, fancy)
  10. You can go to _____ places than actual travelers. (good)

B. Rewrite each sentence correctly.

  11. The puppy behaved gooder today than yesterday.
  12. Wasn't yesterday more hoter than today?
  13. Tuesday was the least warmest of any day this week.
  14. The catcher can throw farer than anyone on the team.
  15. If you do that, you're more brave than I am.

● **Writing Sentences**   Use each form in a sentence.

  16. more clever   **18.** less graceful   **20.** neatest
  17. busiest   **19.** bigger   **21.** least harmful

4 | Negatives

A word that says "no" or "not" is called a **negative**. The words *no* and *not* themselves are negative words, but they are not the only ones. Here is a list of the most common negatives.

neither	nobody	not (n't)
never	none	nothing
no	no one	nowhere

The word *not* is often used as an adverb to make a verb negative.

We could <u>not</u> find any more pencils.

When *not* is used as an adverb, it frequently forms a contraction that is joined to the verb. The contraction is still considered negative.

We <u>couldn't</u> find any more pencils.

Other adverbs that are considered to be negative are *barely*, *hardly*, and *scarcely*.

The car is <u>barely</u> moving.
They can <u>hardly</u> see anything through the dense fog.
There are <u>scarcely</u> any cars on the road.

One negative word is enough to express a negative idea. A construction with two negative words rather than one is called a **double negative**. Avoid double negatives.

NONSTANDARD: They don't want no more pets.
     CORRECT: They <u>don't</u> want <u>any</u> more pets.
NONSTANDARD: We can't hardly refuse that offer.
     CORRECT: We <u>can hardly</u> refuse that offer.

Try It Out

Change each sentence to avoid a double negative.

1. I didn't see nothing I liked in the store.
2. Ms. Stern hasn't none of the records with her.
3. There wasn't scarcely any water in the pool.
4. Because of my sore arm, I can't hardly swim today.
5. There isn't nothing more to say on the subject.

> ▸ A **negative** word or contraction says "no" or "not."
> *Barely*, *hardly*, and *scarcely* are considered negative words.
> Two negatives used to express one negative idea are called a
> **double negative**. Avoid double negatives.

Written Practice

Rewrite each sentence correctly.

1. There isn't scarcely any firewood left.
2. Didn't nobody bring some in?
3. Without wood, we can't cook nothing.
4. We can't keep warm neither.
5. I've never been nowhere that's colder than this.
6. You can't hardly expect it to be warm here.
7. There isn't nothing we can do without help.
8. Won't nobody get some wood?
9. There isn't none in the shed.
10. You can't barely see in there.
11. Won't nobody come with me?
12. We haven't hardly begun to bring in the wood.
13. No one said nothing this morning.
14. Haven't you never heard of electricity?
15. Of course, but we don't have no electricity in this cottage.

● **Writing Sentences**   Use each negative in a sentence.

16. hardly	**18.** neither	**20.** won't	**22.** scarcely
17. never	**19.** can't	**21.** nowhere	**23.** barely

5 | Adjectives or Adverbs?

Because adjectives and adverbs are both modifiers, they are sometimes confused. You can avoid confusing them if you remember what they do. Adjectives modify only nouns or pronouns and tell *what kind, how many,* or *which one.* Adverbs modify verbs, adjectives, or other adverbs and tell *when, where, how,* or *to what extent.*

ADJECTIVE: My friend Allan has a <u>soft</u> voice. *(modifies noun; tells what kind)*

ADVERB: My friend Allan speaks <u>softly</u>. *(modifies verb; tells how)*

Remembering the difference between adjectives and adverbs will help you avoid sentences like these.

INCORRECT: Martina sings bad.
Mr. Shea feels badly about the accident.

Sings is an action verb. To describe how someone sings, an adverb is needed. The word *bad,* however, is an adjective.

Feels, in the second sentence, is used as a linking verb. A modifier following a linking verb refers back to the subject. The modifier, then, should be an adjective. *Badly,* however, is an adverb.

CORRECT: Martina sings <u>badly</u>. *(adverb)*
Mr. Shea feels <u>bad</u> about the accident. *(adjective)*

The modifiers *good* and *well* usually follow the same rules as other adjectives and adverbs. The adjective *good* is used after a linking verb, especially a verb that refers to the senses, like *taste, feel, smell.* The adverb *well* is used to modify an action verb.

ADJECTIVE: Brendan's bread both smells <u>good</u> and tastes <u>good</u>.
ADVERB: He certainly bakes <u>well</u>.

The word *well* can be used as an adjective when referring to health.

Doesn't Ms. Crowell feel <u>well</u>?   I feel very <u>well</u> today.

Real-really and *sure-surely* are other pairs that are often confused. Remember the differences between adjectives and adverbs, and you will use these words correctly.

INCORRECT: I am real sorry.   You sure are kind.
CORRECT: I am <u>really</u> sleepy.   You <u>surely</u> are kind.

Try It Out

Choose the correct form.

1. It's (real, really) hard to believe that Albert Einstein didn't do (good, well) in school as a boy.
2. He did particularly (bad, badly) in history and languages.
3. However, mathematics and science became (easy, easily) for him.
4. By the time he was sixteen, he had grown (sure, surely) of his mathematical abilities.
5. He (sure, surely) developed into a brilliant mathematician.

> Use *good, bad, sure,* and *real* as adjectives to modify nouns or pronouns and after linking verbs.
> Use *well, badly, surely,* and *really* as adverbs to modify verbs, adjectives, or other adverbs.
> Use *well* as an adjective to refer to health.

Written Practice

Rewrite each incorrect sentence correctly. If the sentence is already correct, write *C.*

1. The book has a real good description of Africa.
2. Irwin felt surely he had done good on the geography test.
3. It sure makes a lot of sense to ride your bicycle there.
4. Sonya looked bad tonight, but she said she felt well.
5. The family is real excited about living on a houseboat.
6. Ms. Lorne did good to find one on such short notice.
7. I knew Bobby didn't feel good when he turned pale.
8. Do you really feel badly about missing the trip?
9. Karen did not perform badly in the first selection.
10. She did sound rather bad in the second piece, though.
11. The tomato sauce didn't look very well, but it tasted good.
12. I felt surely that that was not a real snake.

- **Writing Sentences**   Use each word in a sentence of your own.

13. sure	**15.** good	**17.** real	**19.** bad
14. surely	**16.** well	**18.** really	**20.** badly

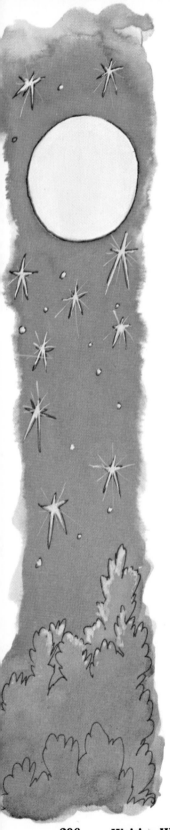

6 | Writing Well with Modifiers

Using Modifiers for Variety

You can sometimes use modifiers to combine sentences with adjectives in an interesting way.

TWO SENTENCES: The night was bright and clear.
It revealed all its stars.
COMBINED: Bright and clear, the night revealed all its stars.

Modifiers set off by commas in this way give added emphasis and force to your writing.

You will recall that many adjectives and adverbs can be placed in different positions within a sentence. Use this fact, when you can, to make your sentences more varied and interesting.

ADJECTIVE: <u>Bright and clear</u>, the night revealed all its stars.
The night, <u>bright and clear</u>, revealed all its stars.

ADVERB: <u>Slowly</u>, the snake slithered toward Sam.
The snake <u>slowly</u> slithered toward Sam.
The snake slithered <u>slowly</u> toward Sam.
The snake slithered toward Sam <u>slowly</u>.

Try It Out

Revise each sentence or pair of sentences in two ways, changing the position of one or more adjectives or adverbs. Remember to combine sentences.

1. Carefully, Mr. Sanders placed the necklace back in its box.
2. The wolf was huffing and puffing. It blew the house down.
3. The smoke rose from the towering chimneys. It was thick and dark.
4. The beaming director graciously accepted the Oscar.
5. A small, furry shape darted out of the bushes suddenly.
6. The dog was loyal and obedient. The well-trained dog marched brightly by its master's side.
7. Loudly and clearly, the cathedral bells announced the time of day to everyone in the village.
8. Michael felt tired and hot. He slipped into the cool cathedral gratefully.

Written Practice

Rewrite the passage, using adverbs and adjectives in a correct and interesting way. Correct capitalization and punctuation errors.

Sacajawea, also known as Bird Woman, was a shoshone indian woman. She has the most memorials in her honor than any other North american woman. Sacajawea was brave strong and intelligent. She traveled thousands of miles through the wilderness as guide and interpreter for the Lewis and Clark expedition. Throughout the trip, she carried even her infant son on her back. Sacajawea was a memorable figure, certainly. Because the facts are not clear, however, historians can't never be real sure of what is truth and what is legend in her life.

Check Your Writing

Review your passage about Sacajawea. Make any needed changes.

A. Are my sentences correct?

1. Have I capitalized all proper adjectives?
2. Have I used commas between adjectives that are equally ranked?
3. Have I used commas correctly in a series of adjectives?
4. Have I used commas with modifiers that are set off?
5. Have I used commas with introductory adverbs?
6. Have I used comparative and superlative forms correctly?
7. Have I avoided double negatives?
8. Have I used adjectives like *good, bad, real, sure*, correctly?
9. Have I used adverbs like *well, badly, really, surely*, correctly?

B. Are my sentences clear and direct?

Have I placed modifiers so that they clearly refer to the words modified?

C. Are my sentences interesting?

1. Have I used modifiers to fill in details?
2. Have I varied the position of adjectives and adverbs?

- **Writing a Paragraph**   Remember or imagine a person you have seen on a bus, in a car, or on a street. In about ten sentences, describe that person's appearance and actions in detail. Then review your paragraph, asking yourself the questions above. Make any needed changes.

7 | Using Words Correctly

fewer, less; farther, further

Fewer and *less* are the comparative forms of *few* and *little*. In careful English, *few* and *fewer* are used to modify plural nouns. *Little* and *less* are used to modify singular nouns.

> Machines allow people to spend <u>fewer</u> **hours** in the kitchen.
> Machines allow people to spend <u>less</u> **time** in the kitchen.

Farther and *further* also have different uses in careful English. *Farther* is used to refer to actual physical distance. *Further* is used in all other cases.

> They traveled fifty miles <u>farther</u> that afternoon.
> She ran <u>farther</u> than I did.
>
> There is no reason to discuss this <u>further</u>.
> Nothing could be <u>further</u> from my mind.

Use *fewer* to modify plural nouns. Use *less* to modify singular nouns.

Use *farther* to refer to physical distance. Use *further* in all other cases.

Practice

Decide which sentences are incorrect, and correct them.

1. It is further than I thought.
2. I'd like fewer meat, please.
3. Let's discuss this farther.
4. Today there were less people.

5. I made less errors than he.
6. Shall we walk any farther?
7. We have a mile further to go.
8. Does that have less calories?

• **Writing Sentences**   Use each word in a sentence of your own.

9. fewer   10. less   11. farther   12. further

Building Vocabulary

Adjective Suffixes

Many adjectives are formed by adding certain suffixes to other words. Being familiar with some of these suffixes can help you both to recognize and create adjectives. Here is a list of common adjective suffixes.

-able	acceptable	-ic	tragic
-al	comical	-ish	childish
-an	suburban	-ive	assertive
-ant	tolerant	-less	helpless
-ar	molecular	-like	childlike
-ary	fragmentary	-ly	lovely
-en	wooden	-ous	miraculous
-ent	confident	-some	loathsome
-ful	helpful	-y	hairy
-ible	horrible		

Notice that adjectives as well as adverbs can end in *-ly*: *lovely, homely*.

Adjective suffixes can help you recognize and form adjectives.

Practice

Add suffixes to form adjectives. Use your dictionary when necessary to check spelling changes.

1. gold	**6.** wind	**11.** hope
2. disrupt	**7.** fear	**12.** rely
3. friend	**8.** fever	**13.** revere
4. agree	**9.** Colombia	**14.** spectacle
5. tire	**10.** atom	**15.** glory

- **Writing Sentences** Use five of your adjectives in sentences.

Review

- **Adjectives** *(pp. 281–284)* List adjectives and words they modify.

  1. Automobile races can be fast and exciting.
  2. His many virtues include a friendly, open personality.
  3. Several Canadian specialties are served at every meal.
  4. The ten little dogs belong to Ken's big brother.
  5. That green scarf matches both new dresses.

  Write the passage, adding commas where needed.

  6–12. The long narrow canoe glided along the smooth waters. Silent and serious the two men concentrated on their smooth movements. They dipped their paddles in a slow steady rhythm. The shore forested dark and unfriendly appeared at last.

- **Adverbs** *(pp. 285–287)* List the adverbs and the words they modify. Label intensifiers.

  13. The day had begun very satisfactorily.
  14. Only two hours had passed, and his chores were nearly done.
  15. Now the breakfast smells floated outdoors enticingly.
  16. He sniffed appreciatively as he walked homeward.
  17. He suddenly felt terribly hungry, and he rushed in and sat down.

  Rewrite only those sentences in which an adverb can be shifted.

  18. She told only me, for I'm her closest friend.
  19. They stumbled clumsily over the trail.
  20. Quickly, the car came to a stop.

- **Comparing with Adjectives and Adverbs** *(pp. 288–291)* If a sentence is incorrect, rewrite it correctly. Otherwise, write *C*.

  21. I did more better than I expected.
  22. This is the most happiest day of my life.
  23. Which of these two motors is most efficient?
  24. The St. Bernard seems to have grown thinner.
  25. The other dog gets more big every day.

- **Negatives** *(pp. 292–293)*   Rewrite each sentence correctly.

    26. We had hardly never seen such a storm.
    27. Wouldn't it never end?
    28. By afternoon, we didn't have no power.
    29. Nobody had no light or heat.
    30. There isn't a warm place nowhere in the house.
    31. I couldn't hardly stand the cold.

- **Adjectives or Adverbs?** *(pp. 294–295)*   Correct any errors.

    32. Tim looks especially well today in that suit.
    33. His suit is really smart-looking.
    34. He surely has good taste in clothes.
    35. Does he feel badly about having gotten tomato sauce on his jacket?
    36. He certainly doesn't feel well about it.
    37. Isn't Sue feeling good today?
    38. Her face looks real pale.

- **Writing Well with Modifiers** *(pp. 296–297)*   Rewrite each sentence, changing the position of a modifier.

    39. Dark and thick, his hair flattered his face.
    40. The unexpected visitor knocked loudly on the door.
    41. Slowly but determinedly, the caterpillar made its way up the tree.
    42. Lithe and graceful, the dancers swayed to the music.
    43. The car carefully approached the intersection.

- **Using Words Correctly** *(p. 298)*   Write the correct word.

    44. This book has (fewer, less) illustrations than that one.
    45. I shall have nothing (farther, further) to say on the subject.
    46. Mr. Bidwell gave us (fewer, less) homework tonight.
    47. The watermelon seems to have (fewer, less) seeds than usual.
    48. She can see (farther, further) without her glasses.

- **Building Vocabulary** *(p. 299)*   Add an appropriate suffix to each word to form an adjective.

    49. form
    50. bird
    51. sheep
    52. trouble
    53. danger
    54. Puerto Rico
    55. custom
    56. wash

Maintain

- **Personal Pronouns** *(pp. 183–190)*   List each personal pronoun. Write its person *(1, 2, 3)*, number *(singular, plural)*, and, where appropriate, gender *(masculine, feminine, neuter)*. Label it *subject* or *object*. Finally, if it has an antecedent, write that.

  1. The family and I are driving to the fair, and we are really looking forward to seeing it.
  2. Boris is going, too, but he will meet us there.
  3. Boris will bring Sue and me home, and we shall try to be prompt.
  4. In the afternoon, you, Sue, and I will view the cattle judging.
  5. The cows look good, and they should win some prizes.
  6. When the Evanses saw Boris, they gave him and me extra tickets.
  7. Sue has the tickets, but I don't see her now.
  8. Before Sue loses them, I had better get the tickets.

- **Other Pronouns** *(pp. 193–202)*   Rewrite each sentence correctly.

  9. Who did you meet in the produce aisle?
  10. Whom put the Brussels sprouts in my shopping cart?
  11. Who's are these oranges?
  12. Is that there the best buy?
  13. This here is the new brand of detergent.
  14. That must be the sale price right here.
  15. Everyone has their own idea about what to buy.
  16. None of the boxes seems to have been opened.
  17. Each of the boxes have their own design.
  18. Brendan cut hisself on the edge of the cart.
  19. They can get the rest of the groceries theirselves.

- **Writing Well with Pronouns** *(pp. 203–204)*   Rewrite each sentence to make it clearer.

  20. They say that there will be a storm tomorrow.
  21. When he arrives, Barney will tell Bill the news.
  22. In the office, they turn off the heat at five.
  23. It says in the paper that the thieves have been caught.

- **Adjectives / Adverbs** *(pp. 281-287)*   List the adjectives and adverbs in separate columns. Next to each, write the word that it modifies.

  24. The small, graceful gazelle lives on open plains and semideserts.
  25. Gazelles live in herds that usually have only a few members.
  26. Most gazelles are alert and attractive.
  27. They are brownish in color, with white underparts.
  28. The dama is the largest North African gazelle.
  29. Its coat can be reddish, brown, or white.
  30. The horns curve up and forward at their tips.

- **Comparing with Adjectives and Adverbs / Negatives / Adjectives or Adverbs?** *(pp. 288-295)*   Rewrite each sentence correctly.

  31. Which is the best of the two?
  32. That dog has the most beautifulest coat I've ever seen.
  33. Can you jump farer than Mindy?
  34. No one hasn't answered the door yet.
  35. I can't hardly believe what you're saying.
  36. It is real considerate of you to help me.
  37. How good did you do on today's quiz?
  38. The kitchen smells especially well today.

- **Writing Well with Modifiers** *(pp. 296-297)*   Rewrite each sentence, changing the position of a modifier or modifiers.

  39. Loudly the trombones declared themselves.
  40. Cold and damp, the skiers huddled by the fire.
  41. Mrs. Grossman explained the problem patiently.

- **Using Words Correctly** *(pp. 205-206, 298)*   Write the correct form.

  42. (We trombonists, Us trombonists) sound especially good today.
  43. (Me and him, He and I, him and me) have become good friends.
  44. Show (Dolly and me, me and Dolly) how to do that, please.
  45. Let's not drive any (farther, further) tonight.
  46. (Fewer, Less) people are building houses this year.
  47. There seems to be (fewer, less) demand for new homes.

- **Building Vocabulary** *(p. 299)*   Add a suffix to form an adjective.

  48. America   **49.** sense   **50.** brown   **51.** live

Writing a Story

1 | Plot

The plot of a story is its action—what happens and the order in which it happens. A plot is not just a string of events, however. It always involves a problem or a conflict of some kind: Will the men in the lifeboat survive? Will the missing bracelet be found? Will Brad realize he really cares about Jocelyn? Will the dark horse win the race? Every plot raises some question in the mind of the reader and then answers it in one way or another.

A plot does not need to be exciting or dramatic. Look at this plot summary.

> A young boy always challenges his father to wrestle with him. As the boy gets older, they continue to wrestle occasionally on the living room floor. One night when the boy is in high school, he realizes that they have not done this for over a year. He challenges his father. After a long, fairly even struggle, the boy pins his father. The father laughs afterward and says the boy must wait till next time. They both know there won't be a next time. The boy goes outside and discovers that there are tears running down his cheeks.
>
> *–from "The Cub," by Lois Dykeman Kleihauer*

The basic problem in a plot is called the **conflict.** The most tense point of the action is called the **climax.** At this point, it is not certain how the problem is going to be solved. The working out of the problem is called the **resolution.**

In the plot summary above, the conflict is both physical and emotional. The boy thinks he wants to win, but does he really? The climax is the last wrestling match. The resolution is the boy's victory and his feelings about it afterward.

Practice

Think of a story you know or have read recently.

1. Write one or two sentences describing the basic problem or conflict in the story.
2. Write one or two sentences describing the climax.
3. Write one or two sentences describing the resolution.

2 | Setting

The setting is the background against which the action of a story takes place. In some stories you read, you are probably barely aware of the setting. In others, the setting is so dramatic and important that you may remember it, and the mood it created, better than anything else in the story.

The setting and the way it is described can have a very important overall effect on a story. Stories set in places such as the Yukon, a barren planet, or the open sea can give you very powerful feelings of loneliness and strangeness. On the other hand, a story set in a small town or a farmhouse can make you feel happy and secure.

Look at these two very different descriptions of settings.

> The drugstore was maybe old-fashioned, but it was large and dark and cool; during summer months there was no pleasanter place in town. At the left, as you entered, was a tobacco-magazine counter. . . . Beyond this counter stood the beautiful soda fountain. It was very antique and made of fine, yellowed marble, smooth to the touch but without a trace of cheap glaze.   —*Truman Capote*

> And now on the right was a wrinkled, dusty plain, and on the left, its ramparts and terraces rising mile after mile into the sky, was a wall of mountains that marched into the distance until its peaks sank from sight below the rim of the world. There was no sign that men had ever explored this land, but once they passed the skeleton of a crashed rocket, and beside it a stone cairn surmounted by a metal cross.   —*Arthur C. Clarke*

- What feeling do you get from the first description?
- What kind of mood does the second setting create?

Practice

Write two setting descriptions. In one of them, try to create a mood of lightness and happiness. In the other, try to create a mood of loneliness or suspense. You may want to use the same place for both descriptions but make it seem entirely different by choosing different details or by changing the weather or the time of day.

3 | Character

Although the characters in a story are usually people, they may be animals or machines or whatever the author creates. In a famous story by Ray Bradbury, the character is a house and all the computerized machinery in it that carries on with little everyday routines.

How do you get to know the characters in a story? You know them through what they say and how they say it; through what they do; and often, through what the author tells you about them directly.

> He was a stranger in town. At least no one could recall ever having seen him before. He said he lived on a farm a mile past Indian Branches; told us his mother weighed only seventy-four pounds and that he had an older brother who would play the fiddle at anybody's wedding for fifty cents. He claimed that Appleseed was the only name he had and that he was twelve years old. But his sister, Middy, said he was eight. His hair was straight and dark yellow. He had a tight, weather-tanned little face with anxious green eyes that had a very wise and knowing look. He was small and puny and high-strung, and he wore always the same outfit: a red sweater, blue-denim britches and a pair of man-sized boots that went clop-clop with every step.   –*Truman Capote*

In the story, "Jug of Silver," Appleseed comes and stares every day at a jug of nickels and dimes that is to be given to anyone who guesses correctly how much money is in it. Finally he announces that he has the answer. Nobody believes him, but he turns out to be right.

- What details about Appleseed let you know how important the money might be to him?
- What details tell you that he might be the kind of person who would really try to count all that money?

Practice

Make up a character. Then make a list of details about him or her. What does the character look like? What do the character's looks tell you about him or her? What are the character's likes and dislikes? Where does the character live?

4 | Point of View

Your point of view is the way you look at things—your own interpretation of what you see and hear. When two people are involved in the same incident and then describe it, they rarely tell exactly the same story. Each sees it from his or her own point of view.

Here is the same incident described from two different points of view.

Around midnight I suddenly woke up. It was pitch dark. Then I heard a branch snap. Something was moving in the woods! I held my breath. A dark shadow was coming slowly towards me. "Corinne!" I said in a loud whisper. There was no answer. The shadow was now so near that I could hear it breathing. I reached out and punched Corinne's sleeping bag. She wasn't there! My heart began to pound. I fumbled in the darkness for the flashlight. It was gone. The dark shape was moving closer and closer. I leaped out of my sleeping bag and raced towards the barn. As I rounded the corner, I crashed head on into something. I fell down with a thud with something heavy on top of me. It was Corinne. Behind us, the dark shape lifted its huge head and moaned, "Moooooooooooooooooooooo!"

In the middle of the night, I woke up feeling really hungry. I crawled out of my sleeping bag very quietly, crept back to the house, and made myself some cheese sandwiches and poured a glass of milk. I was walking back to the grove, carrying my snack, when Sherri came tearing around the barn. Her eyes were popping out of her head like ping-pong balls, her face was as white as a picket fence, and her hair was standing up straight! She looked as though she'd been electrocuted! She charged right into me, knocking me over and sending the milk and sandwiches flying into the air. We fell down in a heap. Just then I heard a loud "Moo." *That* was what had scared Sherri out of her wits—Blossom, our old milk cow!

- What was Sherri's feeling about the incident?
- What was Corinne's feeling?

Every story is told from some point of view. Sometimes it is the point of view of someone outside the action, watching what happens to the other characters. Sometimes it is the point of view of one of the main characters. Sometimes the writer takes an all-knowing point of view and tells what all the characters are thinking and feeling.

If you are writing a story and decide to tell it from the point of view of one person only, you will probably want to call yourself "I." A story told by an "I" character is in the **first person.** If there is no "I" character, but only "he" and "she" and "they," the story is in the **third person.**

Usually you can tell from the beginning of the story what the point of view will be.

> He came in without a word. I was stropping my best razor. And when I recognized him, I started to shake.   *–Hernando Tellez*

> What woke Lida was being hit on the nose with a pajama button. She opened her eyes abruptly.   *–Miriam Allen deFord*

- Which story will be told in the third person?
- Which story will be told in the first person?
- Which story will probably be told by an all-knowing narrator?

Practice

A. Think of something that happened to you but involved one or more other people—perhaps a contest, an accident, a misunderstanding, or a narrow escape. Pick one very small part of it—a one- to five-minute period. Write four or five sentences in the first person describing this incident from your own point of view.

B. Now pretend you are one of the other people involved in the same incident. Write four or five sentences in the first person, describing what took place from that person's point of view.

5 | Dialogue and Monologue

A dialogue is a written conversation between the characters in a story. Some stories are written almost entirely in dialogue. The setting, the action, and who the characters are can all be revealed by having the characters talk.

"Is it there, Marvin?"

"I can't tell for sure. It's so dark in here–"

"*You* were supposed to bring the lantern. I can't——Hey! What was that?"

"What was what, Ben?"

"That–that sound. Like a buzzer or something."

"I didn't hear anything."

"Listen! There it goes again. And it's getting louder."

"I *told* you we shouldn't come!"

"Let's get out of here!"

- How old do you think the characters are?
- What might the setting be?
- What action takes place?

When you speak, your feelings are revealed by your tone of voice, by your facial expressions, and by your gestures. Do you speak very, very slowly in order to show someone how serious you are? Do you wrinkle your nose in disgust, lift your eyebrows in surprise, or shrug your shoulders with impatience?

In dialogue, words alone are not always enough to reveal a speaker's feelings. Sometimes it is important to show *how* something is said.

"Oh, come on, don't play innocent with me."

"What are you talking about?" Kate asked, looking bewildered.

Ray clenched his fists. "I know you're the one who told."

Kate's face paled. "I did not!" she cried hotly. "If you think for one minute that I'd give away a surprise like that. I——."

Ray looked puzzled. "I didn't think you would," he said, more softly. "But somebody did. And Brad thinks——"

"Oh, Brad——" said Kate scornfully.

Notice that when you are writing dialogue, it is not necessary to have people speak in complete sentences. Your dialogue should sound like the way people really speak. People start sentences without finishing them, interrupt each other, and use informal language.

Sometimes an entire story is told as though someone were speaking. The language is usually informal, and the reader is aware of the speaker's individual voice. This kind of story is called a **monologue.**

Here are two sections of monologue from stories that are told by an "I" character. Do they give you the sense that you are listening to a person speaking directly to the reader?

> The man on the loudspeaker is calling everyone over to the track and I'm on my back looking at the sky trying to pretend I'm in the country, but I can't, because even grass in the city feels hard as sidewalk and there's just no pretending you are anywhere but in a "concrete jungle" as my grandfather says.   – *Toni Cade Bambara*

> Wait a minute while I dry my hands and get away from this hot stove. There! You'd never believe to look at me that I am president of Rolling Scones, Inc. I mean, how many presidents do you discover in a kitchen? Not many, I can tell you. Now let me stir this soup once more, and then I'll tell you how all this happened.
>
> – *Jane Williams Dugel*

Practice

A. Write a dialogue to replace one of the following statements. Try to show your characters' feelings as well as the situation.

1. Grandpa Asher revealed a secret to Lois.
2. The pilot and co-pilot realized the plane was in trouble.
3. Pam and Lisa tried to figure out who had left the mysterious package.

B. Write a short monologue for one of these situations. Think about the kind of person you want the character to be. Try to show what the character is like, as well as the character's feelings and thoughts, through his or her "voice."

1. A boy or girl loses his or her dog.
2. A racecar driver is a few minutes away from the finish line.
3. A trapped miner hears rescuers nearby.
4. Someone is being tried for a crime she or he did not commit.

6 | Beginnings and Endings

The beginning of a story does not have to be the same as the beginning of the action. Many stories start near the end of the action and then go back and explain how the situation came about.

> I am very sorry, now that it's too late, that I never got to know Vladimir Surov.   *–Arthur C. Clarke*

No matter where you decide to begin a story, your first few sentences should get your readers' interest.

Good beginnings and good endings both should *show* the reader what is happening. Compare these two endings for the same story.

> I knew that my big brother was sorry and he knew that I had forgiven him when he carried me piggyback up the stairs.

> He squatted down. "Give us a kiss."
> I kissed him.
> "Okay. Climb up. I'll give you a ride. Hold on, now."
> He carried me piggyback up the stairs.   *–James Baldwin*

- Which ending explains and sums up the action instead of showing it?
- Which is the better story ending?

Practice

Here is the plot of a story by Saki called "The Interlopers." Decide where you would begin if you were writing the story. Write two possible beginning sentences. Then write two different ending sentences.

For many years two rich families had each claimed a section of forest. One stormy night both men were hunting there with their servants. Suddenly they met face to face. At that moment a tree crashed in the storm and pinned them both to the ground. Lying there wounded they first threatened each other and then made peace. They shouted together for their servants. They saw figures running toward them and felt great relief. Then they saw that the figures were wolves.

7 | Getting Started

Suppose you could find a storyteller who would write a story just for you. What kind of story would you ask for? mystery? science fiction? high adventure? Would you prefer a story about the kind of people you see every day? Where would you like the story to take place? in a city? on a farm? in a jungle? in outer space? Would you like the story to be funny or serious? You *can* find a storyteller who will write precisely what you order. That storyteller is you.

When you write about yourself, you try to remember what actually happened. When you write a story, however, you can invent everything. You create fiction. In stories, anybody can do anything. Anything can happen anywhere. From first to last, the storyteller has control.

How do you get your story rolling? Try the following warm-up.

Practice

Work with one classmate to answer these questions about the photograph on page 304. Let your imaginations run free!

1. What is the name of each person?
2. What is one personality trait of each person?
3. Are these people strangers, or do they know one another? If they are not strangers, what is their relationship?
4. What has happened just before the moment of this photograph?
5. What is happening now? What problem are they dealing with?
6. How will the problem be solved?
7. What will be the feelings of two of these people afterward?

Steps for Writing a Story Here are the steps for writing a story. You will follow these steps to write your own story.

Step One	Choose a story idea.
Step Two	Write your story.
Step Three	Revise your story.
Step Four	Proofread your story.
Step Five	Make a final copy to share.

8 | Step One
Choose a Story Idea

Story ideas can come from almost anywhere. You can sit in a shopping mall and find yourself getting curious about people passing by. You can glimpse a headline at a newsstand: BLIZZARD TRAPS HIKERS IN ABANDONED MINE.

Sometimes you hear snatches of conversation that you could build on for a story.

"I told her I didn't care *what* she thought!"

"But aren't you afraid to go?"

"The funny thing is that he doesn't know that I know!"

Bryan had three story ideas. He made some notes about them to help him decide which he would most like to write about. If he wasn't sure how he would work something out, he wrote a question about it.

---

setting: far in the future when people have space colonies

characters: young man and woman who try to find a colony that has not been heard from for a few hundred years

plot: They find it, but the people have made laws that are completely different from the laws on Earth. They keep breaking the laws without meaning to.

Do they see the point of the new laws in the end? Do they help the people get back to the laws on Earth? Are they imprisoned?

setting: volcano that is about to erupt

character: a scientist who is very daring and brave

---

plot: He visits the volcano secretly, although he has been warned not to. It erupts and he is buried. He manages to survive and come back with new information.
What does he want to find out? How could he survive this?

setting: a race in a small town
character: Tony Rabitini, "Rabbit" for short — a junior high student a lot like me
plot: Rabbit thinks he is going to win the race because his chief rival has hurt his foot and can't run. Then he runs after all, but a lion gets loose from the circus and gets in the race behind my character. My character sets a record!

It was hard for Bryan to decide which idea to write about. For the space colony story he tried to think of some laws that would be really different and still make sense. He decided to save this story for when he was ready to write something really long. The second idea he liked too. He would have to do a lot of research, however, and he was very unsure about how he would end the story. The last idea seemed almost to be writing itself in his head. He had gotten it from a newspaper story, and his imagination had been running wild ever since. Bryan chose this story idea.

Assignment

- **Make a List**
- **Choose a Story Idea**

A. Use all the sources for story ideas you can—photographs, headlines, bits of conversation. Let your imagination run away with you.

B. Make notes on your story ideas. Follow the pattern of Bryan's notes. Write who the character or characters are. Briefly describe the setting. Write down the main part of the plot, and write questions about the parts you need to work out.

C. Look over your ideas, and choose the one you will write about.

9 | Step Two
Write Your Story

Bryan thought about what point of view he should use for his story. He thought it would be interesting to be able to see into the minds of all the characters and tell what his character felt like, what the coach thought, and even perhaps what the lion felt. However, he decided there would probably be more suspense if he stuck to the point of view of his character.

Bryan began writing his first draft. He filled in the details of the plot and characters and setting as he wrote. He didn't worry about making mistakes at this point. There would be time to go back and correct them later.

Bryan's first draft

Rabbit was really looking forward to the big Fourth of July race. Sam Fox had won it for the last three years ~~running~~, and Rabbit thought he might have a chance this year.

One night at supper, his sister Tammy ~~told~~ said Sam's ankle was better and that he was going to run after all. Rabbit was very upset.

At last the day of the big race came. Crowds lined Main Street. The lamp posts were hung with red, white and blue streamers. Everyone was shouting, shoving, and horsing around, trying to get a front row place to stand. A circus was camped by the river two blocks away and clowns and acrobats wandered through the crowd in their costumes.

~~A policeman~~ Officer Blackwell was talking through his bullhorn, asking everyone to please stand back.

One by one, the runners were ~~getting~~ assembling at the starting line. Rabbit peeled off his sweatshirt. He was wearing his new blue and gold track suit.

Then he saw Sam Fox. Sam was holding his hands over his head in a victory sign. He was that sure of himself. Rabbit was really annoyed.

Thud, thud. Thud, thud. Rabbit could hear the other runners' feet pounding on the ashpalt pavement. Now they were crossing Fifth Street, all straggled out. Sam Fox was eight or ten yards in front of him. The rest of the runners were behind. Sixth Street was coming up. Officer Blackwell had his patrol car parked on the left side of the intersection to block the traffic.

All at once the red light on the patrol car flashed. Then Rabbit heard the siren. Everybody seemed to be running off to the right. What was up? Then he saw his dad at the curb, pointing up Sixth Street. It sounded like he was shouting, "Line! Line!" but the finish line was still six blocks away. He wasn't about to stop now.

Then Rabbit saw something out of the corner of his eye. There coming past the patrol car was the biggest dog he had ever seen. No, it wasn't a dog. It was—it couldn't be, but it was—a lion! Thud, thud. Now all he could hear were his own two feet, the siren, and this funny sound behind him. It sounded like "Wheeze-puh." It was a lion for sure.

- What point of view did Bryan choose for his story?
- Did he use the first or the third person?
- How could his beginning be improved?
- Where could he add dialogue to make the story more interesting and realistic?
- What details does Bryan give about the setting? Where could he add more?

Assignment • **Write Your First Draft**

Your plan for your story is a jumping-off point. You will probably get new ideas as you write. One way to get started is to write two or three different beginnings and see which makes the best take-off point. Be sure to decide on your point of view before you begin writing. Keep these points in mind.

1. Try to get inside the minds of your characters and figure out why they do what they do.
2. Give details about the characters. What actions can help your readers see them?
3. Help your readers see your setting. Include details about how things look, feel, taste, smell, feel.
4. Use dialogue wherever you can.

Don't worry about mistakes as you write. You will have a chance later to correct them and make any other changes.

10 | Step Three
Revise Your Story

As Bryan read over his story the next day, it seemed to him that it got better as it went on. As he had gotten more excited about the action and felt more as though he were inside Rabbit's mind, his writing seemed to improve.

Bryan decided that he needed a new beginning that would be as good as the rest of his story. He wrote a new beginning, using dialogue, and taped it on top of his first two paragraphs.

Bryan's new beginning

Rabbit's enthusiasm about the Fourth of July took a nosedive when he heard his sister's news.

"I saw Sam Fox today," said Tammy. "He wasn't limping."

"Oh no!" groaned Rabbit. "Does that mean he's going to run after all?

"Don't let it upset you, Rabbit," said his father. Didn't you just beat your best time by three seconds? And remember all that training!"

"Yes," said Rabbit, but I still think that if Sam Fox is going to run I don't have a chance."

Then he read his story to Dale. Dale was very impressed.

"I felt like I really was Rabbit," he said. "You made everything seem very real. I wasn't sure when the race began, though."

Bryan thanked Dale for his comments. He agreed that the beginning of the race needed to be clear. It could help increase the suspense. He marked that place on his paper. Then he went back to his desk and made that change. He also added some details about Sam Fox.

part of Bryan's revision

Then he saw Sam Fox. Sam was holding his hands over his head in a victory sign. He was that sure of himself. ~~Rabbit was really annoyed.~~ "You haven't won yet," Rabbit said to himself.

Mr. Sprint stepped up to the starting line. "Runners, take your mark!" he shouted. Rabbit dropped down into starting position. The crowd grew silent. "Get set," came the command. The gun barked. Now!

- Compare Bryan's first two opening paragraphs on page 316 with his new beginning on the previous page. Find all the information in the new beginning that is the same. Find the new information.
- What did Bryan write instead of *Rabbit was annoyed*?
- What did Bryan do to make the start of the race seem real?

Assignment
- **Revise Your Story**
- **Discuss Your Story**

A. Read your story, keeping these questions in mind.

1. Does the plot make sense?
2. Do the characters seem real? Where could I add more details about them?
3. What details could I add about the setting?
4. Have I stayed with the point of view I chose?

B. Revise your story. Cross out sections you can improve. Write between the lines and in the margins.

C. Write a new beginning and a new ending, even though you like the ones you have now. Make your beginning catch the readers' attention. Make your ending show rather than tell what happened. Decide on your best beginning and ending.

D. Read your story to someone—a classmate or your teacher. Discuss your story. Make more changes if your listener had good suggestions or if you got any new ideas while reading your story out loud.

11 | Step Four
Proofread Your Story

Your story is now complete. You should have a beginning and an ending that you like. Your reader should be able to follow the plot easily and to picture the characters and the setting.

It is time now to focus your attention on your spelling, punctuation, and capitalization. When you proofread, you should also look for words you may have left out or repeated. To make sure your dialogue is punctuated correctly, check page 466 of the Handbook at the back of this book. Remember to start a new paragraph when you change speakers. Use the dictionary to check any words you are unsure of.

Here are the next two paragraphs of Bryan's story, with his proofreading marks.

Part of Bryan's story after proofreading

> Rabbit thought his lungs would burst. His legs were numb. Out of the corner of his eye he could see people falling all over themselves trying to get out of the way. Up ahead, the rope, with it's dangeling gold penants, stretched across the finish line. He pumped his legs furiously, he didn't dare look back over his shoulder but he knew the lion was still there.
>
> Now he could see Tammy on the far side of the rope jumping up and down, waving her arms and yelling "Rabbit, Rabbit, Rabbit! Then the lion groweled. Rabbit heard a sharp whip crack and then immediately afterward a snap as he hit the the rope and felt it give way.

- What misspelled words did Bryan correct?
- Give a reason for each punctuation mark Bryan added.

Proofread Your Story   321

Practice

Here is the last part of Bryan's story. Proofread it carefully. Use a dictionary to check any words you are unsure about. Then copy the paragraphs over correctly. You should find seven errors to correct.

Tammy almost knocked him over with hugs. "Incredible, said Mr. Sprint, pinning a gold ribbon on his shoulder strap.

A cheer went up from the side lines.

Rabbit blinked tears and sweat from his eyes. Behind him, in the middle of the street, a man in a red coat and riding pants snapped a chain to the lions collor. The lion sat quietly, it was breathing heavily. It looked for all the world as though it had won something, too.

Assignment • **Proofread Your Story**

Proofread your own story, checking carefully for errors in spelling, capitalization, and punctuation. Can you find any other errors? Use these questions to guide you.

1. Have I made paragraph breaks where appropriate?
2. Have I spelled all my words correctly and looked up any words that I am unsure of?

Grammar skills checklist

3. Have I corrected any sentence fragments or run-ons?
4. Have I written plural and possessive nouns correctly?
5. Have I used commas correctly with compound sentences, appositives, and clauses?
6. Have I used correct verb tenses?
7. Have I used the correct forms of pronouns?

12 | Step Five
Make a Final Copy

When your story is as good as you can make it and you have corrected your spelling and punctuation and other errors, it is time to make a final copy.

Bryan decided to make a booklet of his story and make a pen drawing for every page of words. He was not really an artist, but his drawings were like cartoons, and they were funny. He made a separate drawing for the cover. He wrote the title on the cover: "The Rabbit, the Fox, and the Lion."

Assignment

- **Make a Final Copy**
- **Share Your Story**

A. Copy your revised and proofread story neatly on a clean piece of paper. The kind and size of paper you will use will depend on how you want your finished story to look. Give your story a title if you have not already done so.

B. Check your final copy to make sure that you have corrected all your errors and not introduced any new ones.

C. Think of a special way to share your story.

- You could take turns with a small group of classmates reading your stories aloud.
- You could tape your story so that your classmates could listen to it when they had free time.
- You could make a booklet and illustrate it with pencil or pen drawings, paintings, or even woodcuts or some other kind of print.
- You could pretend your story was going to be made into a movie and make a poster advertising it to go with your story.

Prepositions and Their Objects

Prepositions and Objects

Here are some sentences in which only one word has been changed. What does changing the word do to the meaning of the sentence?

My dog lies <u>on</u> my bed.   My dog lies <u>beside</u> my bed.
My dog lies <u>under</u> my bed.   My dog lies <u>behind</u> my bed.

When you change the word *on* to *under, beside,* or *behind,* you change the relationship between the bed and where the dog lies. A word that shows a relationship between a noun (*bed*) and another word (*lies*) is called a **preposition**.

Some words commonly used as prepositions are listed below. Notice that a preposition can be more than one word.

about	at	by	instead of	through
above	because of	down	into	to
according to	before	during	like	toward
across	behind	except	next to	under
after	below	for	of	until
against	beneath	from	off	up
along	beside	in	on	with
among	besides	in back of	over	within
around	between	in front of	since	without

A preposition is never used alone. It is always followed by a noun or a pronoun. The noun or pronoun that follows a preposition is called the **object of the preposition**. *To* and *with* are prepositions in the sentences that follow. Which words are their objects?

Mr. Swenson drove <u>to</u> **school**.   He drove <u>with</u> **care**.

Modifiers often accompany the object of a preposition.

He drove <u>to</u> the new **school**.   He drove <u>with</u> great **care**.

The object of a preposition can be compound.

Mr. Swenson drove <u>to</u> the **school** and the **store**.
He drove <u>with</u> **care** and **patience**.

Try It Out

Find each preposition and its object.

1. The opera *Lohengrin*, by Richard Wagner, is based on legends of the Middle Ages.
2. The events of the complicated plot take place in the tenth century.
3. During the first act, a boat drawn by a swan comes into view on the stage.
4. According to legend, a marriage takes place between Lohengrin and Elsa.
5. The famous melody of the "Wedding March" from this opera is traditionally played at weddings.
6. Because of Elsa's curiosity about Lohengrin's identity, Lohengrin must leave her forever.

Pronouns as Objects of Prepositions

The object of a preposition, like the object of a verb, can be a pronoun.

Sit next to <u>him</u>.   Brett hasn't heard from <u>them</u>.

You have learned that object pronouns, not subject pronouns, are used as the objects of verbs. Object pronouns are also used as the objects of prepositions.

> Please hold this for <u>me</u> *(not for I)*.
> During assembly, a firefighter spoke to <u>us</u> *(not to we)*.

You need to be especially careful to use the correct pronoun when the object of a preposition is compound.

> The candidate spoke to my friend and <u>me</u> *(not to my friend and I)*.
> Between you and <u>me</u> *(not between you and I)*, we have fifty cents.

When you studied compound objects of verbs, you learned that separating the parts of the compound can help you choose the correct pronoun. Use the same technique with compound objects of prepositions.

> Henry sent letters to <u>you</u>.   Henry sent letters to <u>her</u> *(not to she)*.
> Henry sent letters to you and <u>her</u>.

> I heard from Ina.   I heard from <u>him</u> *(not from he)*.
> I heard from Ina and <u>him</u>.

Try It Out

Choose the correct pronoun to complete the sentence.

1. Have you sent the invitation to (she, her) yet?
2. Was this painting done by you or (he, him)?
3. Between you and (I, me) there are no secrets.
4. Instead of Trudy, Scott, or (I, me), Ms. Contreras chose Benny.
5. The play cannot go on without you and (I, me).

> ▸ A **preposition** is a word that shows a relationship between a noun and another word in the sentence.
> ▸ The **object of the preposition** is the noun or pronoun that follows the preposition.
>
> When the object of a preposition is a pronoun, it is always in the form of an object pronoun.

Written Practice

A. Write the sentence, completing it with the correct pronoun.

1. Jessica has not heard from (he, him) in a long time.
2. There is a real bond between you and (I, me).
3. Everyone except Ronald and (she, her) is a good swimmer.
4. The game will be won by the Titans or (we, us).
5. In front of Pilar and (I, me) walked Mr. Tierney.
6. I cannot go skating with you and (he, him) tomorrow.

B. Copy every preposition. Next to it, write its object or objects.

(7) *The Hobbit*, by J.R.R. Tolkien, appeals to readers of all ages. (8) Readers are fascinated by the story and its deeper meaning. (9) Tolkien, an authority on myth, uses that knowledge in his work. (10) He writes of Middle Earth as though he were writing about the land of his birth. (11) Bilbo Baggins is the hero of *The Hobbit*. (12) He is a quiet creature, with just a touch of a wild streak in him. (13) Bilbo shows that the seeds of heroism can lie within the ordinary person. (14) If you were in *The Hobbit*, would you act like a hero?

- **Writing Sentences**   Write ten sentences, using ten different prepositions.

2 | Prepositional Phrases

Phrases

Some groups of words act like single words. Compare the following sentences.

Irene passed the test <u>easily</u>.   Irene passed the test <u>with ease</u>.

The words *with ease* are used in the same way as the single word *easily*. A group of words that is used like a single word is a **phrase**. A phrase like *with ease*, which begins with a preposition and ends with the object of the preposition, is a **prepositional phrase**.

Several prepositional phrases can occur in one sentence. In fact, one prepositional phrase can directly follow another. How many prepositional phrases are there in this sentence?

At the end of the concert, the people in the audience applauded with enthusiasm.

Try It Out

Identify each prepositional phrase. Where is the preposition, and where is the object?

1. The piece of ice melted slowly in the glass of lemonade.
2. Across the hot, dusty plains moved the wagons in a long line.
3. Because of the bees among the blossoms, I moved with caution.
4. We have not seen Erica since our last visit to Puerto Rico.
5. After forty hours and heavy floods, the rain stopped.
6. During the day, the cars on the street were covered with snow.
7. Everyone except Donald had walked up the stairs to the library.
8. Next to the horse stood a man with a saddle in his hands.
9. A bunch of grapes lay beside the pears on the table.
10. Is that a letter from Tahiti in the mailbox?

As Modifiers

A phrase is a group of words that is used like a single word.

She drove <u>carefully</u>.   She drove <u>with care</u>.

In these sentences, the word *carefully* and the prepositional phrase *with care* are used in the same way. *Carefully* is an adverb that modifies the verb *drove*. The prepositional phrase *with care* is also an adverb that modifies the verb *drove*.

Now compare these two sentences.

<u>Klee's</u> paintings are on exhibit.   Paintings <u>by Klee</u> are on exhibit.

The possessive noun *Klee's* and the prepositional phrase *by Klee* are used in the same way. *Klee's* is used as an adjective that modifies the noun *paintings*. The prepositional phrase *by Klee* is also used as an adjective that modifies *paintings*.

Prepositional phrases are always modifiers. A prepositional phrase that modifies a noun or pronoun is an **adjective phrase.** A prepositional phrase that modifies a verb, adjective, or adverb is an **adverb phrase.**

Adjective Phrases
Take the path <u>on the left</u>. *(modifies noun* path*)*

One <u>of the puppies</u> is barking. *(modifies pronoun* one*)*

Adverb Phrases
We went <u>on a photographic safari</u>. *(modifies verb* went*)*

The area is famous <u>for its wildlife</u>. *(modifies adjective* famous*)*

Can you meet us later <u>in the afternoon</u>? *(modfies adverb* later*)*

In the examples above, the prepositional phrases follow the words they modify. This is not always the case, however. Sometimes another word or phrase comes between the modified word and the prepositional phrase. Other times, the phrase precedes the word it modifies.

The lone runner jogged steadily <u>along the deserted beach</u>.

<u>At that moment</u>, the alarm sounded.

<u>For four years</u>, Twain toiled <u>on the river</u> <u>as a steamboat worker</u>.

Notice that when a prepositional phrase begins a sentence, it is followed by a comma.

Try It Out

A. Find each *adjective* phrase and tell which word it modifies.

1. All of the audience applauded the members of the jazz group.
2. One reason for their popularity is their interest in education.
3. They discuss the development of jazz from its roots in Africa.

B. Find each *adverb* phrase, and tell which word it modifies.

4. The jazz concert is scheduled for tomorrow.
5. If you are interested in jazz, please remain after the concert.
6. Later in the day, the performers will talk with students.

- A **phrase** is a group of words that acts like a single word. Phrases never contain subjects and verbs.
- A **prepositional phrase** begins with a preposition and ends with a noun or a pronoun that is its object.
- An **adjective phrase** modifies a noun or a pronoun.
- An **adverb phrase** modifies a verb, adjective, or adverb.

Written Practice

A. Copy each adjective phrase and the word it modifies.

1. Martha's Vineyard is an island off the coast of Massachusetts.
2. It is an area with beautiful views of sand and sea.
3. Most of the residents have homes for the summer.
4. Year-round residents must make preparations for winter.
5. The months from October to May can be a time of isolation.

B. Copy each adverb phrase and the word it modifies.

6. Martha's Vineyard lies not far from Cape Cod.
7. The island was discovered in 1602 and claimed by New York.
8. After some years, it was ceded to Massachusetts.
9. Many people who are famous in the arts vacation on the island.
10. People travel to the island by ferry or plane.
11. Because of the weather, few vacationers arrive in the winter.

- **Writing Sentences**   Write eight sentences about a place you have visited or would like to visit. Use prepositional phrases.

3 | Verbals

Read the following sentence, paying particular attention to the underlined words.

The excited hiker enjoys walking, but he has decided to rest.

All of the underlined words are formed from verbs. However, only two of the forms, *enjoys* and *decided,* are actually used as verbs in these sentences. The other words are verb forms, but they are not used as verbs here.

A word that is formed from a verb but is used in another way is called a **verbal**. There are three kinds of verbals—**participles**, **gerunds**, and **infinitives**.

Participles

When you studied the principal parts of verbs in Unit 5, you learned about present participles like *crying* and past participles like *trained.* These forms are used with helping verbs to form verb phrases.

The baby is crying. *(helping verb* be + *present participle)*
I have trained my parakeet. *(helping verb* have + *past participle)*

Now look at the way the same forms are used in the sentences below.

The crying baby kept everyone awake.
The trained parakeet responded to our questions.

Here, *crying* and *trained* function as adjectives, not as verbs. *Crying* modifies the noun *baby; trained* modifies the noun *parakeet.* When a form ending in either *-ing* or *-ed* is used as an adjective, it is called a **participle**.

Irregular verb forms, which do not end in *-ed,* may also be used as participles.

The forgotten letter lay on the desk.

Participles can follow as well as precede the nouns or pronouns they modify.

The person singing is Ms. Amram.
The rescuers, chilled and exhausted, returned to their homes.

Try It Out

Look at the underlined words in each pair of sentences. Identify each sentence in which the word is used as a participle. Tell which word is modified by the participle.

1. (a) Someone is <u>frying</u> bacon. (b) I smell the <u>frying</u> bacon.
2. (a) The <u>cracked</u> dish has been repaired. (b) Who <u>cracked</u> the dish?
3. (a) The dog <u>barking</u> is Peanut. (b) The dog has been <u>barking</u> all day.
4. (a) Have you <u>lost</u> the tickets? (b) The <u>lost</u> tickets have been found.

Gerunds

You have seen that verb forms ending in *-ing* can be used as participles. These forms can also be used in still another way. Study the *-ing* form in this sentence.

<u>Bowling</u> is a very old sport.

Bowling is the subject of the sentence. It is an *-ing* form used as a noun. When an *-ing* form acts as a noun, it is called a **gerund**. Gerunds are used in sentences in the same way nouns are used.

<u>Walking</u> is my favorite exercise. *(subject)*
I enjoy <u>walking</u>. *(direct object)*
Today is a good day for <u>walking</u>. *(object of preposition)*
My favorite exercise is <u>walking</u>. *(predicate noun)*

To determine whether an *-ing* word is a verb, a participle, or a gerund, you will have to determine how it is used in the sentence.

Cora and Andy are <u>whispering</u>. *(verb, used with helping verb* be)
The breeze made a <u>whispering</u> sound. *(participle, modifies* sound)
The <u>whispering</u> disturbed the class. *(gerund, subject)*

Try It Out

Identify each gerund. Is it used as a subject, direct object, object of a preposition, or predicate noun? Not every sentence has a gerund.

1. Do you like fishing?
2. A growing plant needs care.
3. She exercises by swimming.
4. Her hobby is painting.
5. I am painting a portrait.
6. Sketching is fun for me.
7. I care most about reading.
8. Traveling comes second or third.

Infinitives

You have learned about two kinds of verbals: participles (*-ing* or *-ed* forms) and gerunds (*-ing* forms). The third kind of verbal is the **infinitive**. Infinitives are formed with the word *to* and the basic form of the verb.

Paul likes <u>to skate</u>.   It is necessary <u>to leave</u> now.

You know that participles are used as adjectives, and gerunds are used as nouns. Infinitives can be used as nouns, adjectives, or adverbs.

Used as Noun

<u>To leave</u> would be rude. *(subject)*
I want <u>to leave</u> now. *(direct object)*
His decision is <u>to leave</u> now. *(predicate noun)*

Used as Adjective

Now is the time <u>to leave</u>. *(modifies noun* time*)*

Used as Adverb

We are ready <u>to leave</u>. *(modifies adjective* ready*)*
<u>To leave</u>, use the back door. *(modifies verb* use*)*

Do not confuse infinitives with prepositional phrases introduced by *to*. The infinitive *to* is used with a basic verb form. The preposition *to* is used with a noun or pronoun.

INFINITIVE: Is this the road <u>to **take**</u>?
PREPOSITIONAL PHRASE: Is this the road <u>to the **store**</u>?

Try It Out

A. Find each infinitive. Tell whether it is used as a noun, an adjective, or an adverb.

1. To succeed requires hard work and talent.
2. The best book to read is *Jane Eyre* by Charlotte Bronte.
3. The bandits did not want to sleep, for their aim was to flee.
4. Sometimes it is difficult to relax.
5. Can you help to rake the leaves today?

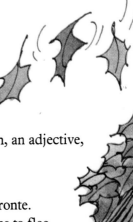

B. Tell which of the underlined terms are infinitives and which are prepositional phrases.

6. Are you going <u>to the store</u>? **8.** I want <u>to go</u> <u>to the concert</u>.

7. What do you plan <u>to buy</u>? **9.** <u>To win</u>, you must concentrate.

> ▸ A **verbal** is a verb form that is not used as a verb.
> ▸ A **participle** is an *-ing* or *-ed* form used as an adjective.
> ▸ A **gerund** is an *-ing* form used as a noun.
> ▸ An **infinitive** is the basic verb form preceded by *to*. It may be used as a noun or as a modifier.

Written Practice

A. Divide your page into three columns labeled *verb*, *participle*, *gerund*. Write each underlined word in the appropriate column. Next to each participle, write the noun or pronoun it modifies. Next to each gerund, tell how it is used—as subject, direct object, predicate noun, or object of a preposition.

1. My cousin Alvin is <u>yodeling</u> tonight at the talent contest.

2. Alvin, a <u>determined</u> person, has been <u>practicing</u> every night.

3. By <u>practicing</u>, he has become an <u>accomplished</u> yodeler.

4. <u>Yodeling</u> is a kind of <u>singing</u>.

5. The person <u>singing</u> changes his or her voice to falsetto.

6. The <u>changed</u> tone quickly starts <u>changing</u> back to normal.

7. This rapid and <u>continuing</u> alternation of tone is <u>yodeling</u>.

8. <u>Yodeling</u> singers are usually from Switzerland or the United States.

B. Copy each infinitive and tell if it is used as a noun, an adjective, or an adverb.

9. To sing is Alvin's goal in life.

10. He learned to yodel when he traveled to Kentucky.

11. His uncle wanted to teach the technique to Alvin.

12. It was difficult to learn.

13. The way to learn is to practice.

● **Writing Sentences** Write three sentences of your own with participles, three with gerunds, and three with infinitives.

4 | Participial Phrases

Identifying Participial Phrases

Recall that a participle is a verb form used as an adjective.

The person speaking is an expert chess player. *(modifies person)*

The dictated examples were helpful. *(modifies example)*

A participle accompanied by other words forms a **participial phrase**. Participial phrases are used in the same way as participles.

The person speaking to our club is an expert chess player.

The examples dictated by the teacher were helpful.

Sometimes you may not be sure the first time you look at a sentence which is the verb and which is the participial phrase.

I saw the robin building a nest.

First find the subject and predicate. In the sentence above these are clearly *I saw. Robin* is the direct object, and *building a nest* is a participial phrase that modifies *robin*.

Remember that participial phrases *describe* nouns and pronouns.

Dressed for the party, she left.

Being a secretary, Walt typed very fast.

Try It Out

Locate each participial phrase. Tell which word each phrase modifies. Do not confuse the participial phrases with the verb phrases.

1. Alerted to a possible story, the reporters waited impatiently.
2. The police were keeping them separated from the building.
3. Expecting a famous passenger, the reporters ran to a limousine.
4. A green van, tearing out of the driveway, raced down the hill.
5. In the van, a man accused of espionage was concealed.
6. Mystified by the van, the reporters ran to their cars.

Using Commas

You will have noticed that participial phrases can precede as well as follow the words they modify.

Shattered by the storm, the window offered no protection.

An introductory participial phrase is always set off with a comma. Other participial phrases may or may not require commas. If a participial phrase is necessary to the meaning of the noun or pronoun, then no commas are used. If it just gives added information about the noun or pronoun, then commas are used.

IDENTIFYING INFORMATION: The woman waving good-by is Emily.
ADDED INFORMATION: Emily, waving good-by, drove away.

The first sentence tells us that Emily is the woman who is waving good-by. It is her waving that identifies her as Emily. Without the participial phrase, we would not know which woman was being referred to. No commas are used. The second sentence tells us that Emily is driving away and also waving good-by. Her waving is added information. Commas are used.

Try It Out

Locate the participial phrases. Tell whether they need commas.

1. Stepping quickly out of the van the two men walked to the plane.
2. One man concealed by a large hat seemed to walk awkwardly.
3. The man concealed by the large hat was a foreign diplomat.
4. Stealing secrets from many countries the spy had operated for years.
5. The man captured last night is undoubtedly the infamous spy.
6. The brilliant deceiver captured at last remained sullen and silent.

> ▸ A participle can be accompanied by other words to form a **participial phrase**.
>
> A participial phrase, like a participle, is used as an adjective.
>
> A comma is used with an introductory participial phrase and with a participial phrase that gives added information.
>
> A comma is not used with a participial phrase that gives identifying information.

Written Practice

A. Copy each participial phrase. Write the word it modifies.

1. Abigail Adams, wed to John Adams, was unusual for her time.
2. Married for 54 years, the Adamses were a close couple.
3. Because of the long absences demanded by John's public service, Abigail and John communicated a great deal by letter.
4. The letters written between them have been published.
5. Expressing strong feelings about the education and freedom of women, the letters reveal much about Abigail and her times.
6. The political advice given in her letters was usually sound.
7. Abigail, separated from her husband for years at a time, managed the farm, business, and family.

B. Copy each sentence. Underline each participial phrase. Add commas where needed.

8. The horse tied to the tree belongs to Sumner Fielding.
9. The gray horse tied to the tree for hours is growing restless.
10. Tied to the tree for hours the gray horse is growing restless.
11. Weakened by the storm the limb has finally fallen.
12. The only thing given to me by my aunt was a lace collar.
13. The lace collar yellowed with age is being cleaned carefully.
14. The man tying his shoe is a trapeze artist.
15. Tracy knitting furiously finished the sweater in a week.
16. The tree lying across the path is a pecan tree.

• **Writing Sentences**   Use each participle as part of a participial phrase in a sentence.

17. carrying   18. hidden   19. crying   20. ruined

5 | Gerund Phrases

A gerund, like a participle, can be accompanied by other words to form a **gerund phrase**.

> <u>Wearing heavy boots</u> can protect your feet.
> He likes <u>singing in the rain</u>.
> His goal is <u>being a ballet dancer</u>.

Gerund phrases, like gerunds, are used as nouns in sentences. Like nouns, they can function as subjects, as objects, or as predicate nouns.

As Subjects

In the sentences below, you can see how a gerund phrase can function as a subject in the same way that a noun or pronoun can.

Noun or Pronoun	**Gerund Phrase**
Ian seems silly.	<u>Standing on one foot</u> seems silly.
It creates a nice effect.	<u>Painting a mural</u> creates a nice effect.

A gerund phrase used as a subject often comes at the beginning of a sentence. However, an introductory participial phrase can also begin a sentence. Do not confuse the two.

> GERUND PHRASE: Wishing for the impossible is a waste of time.
> PARTICIPIAL PHRASE: Wishing for the impossible, they wasted time.

First, look for the main verb of the sentence. Then determine whether or not the *-ing* phrase is the subject of the verb. If it is, it is a gerund.

Try It Out

Which sentence in each pair has a gerund phrase as its subject? Identify the phrase.

1. (**a**) Guiding its master, the seeing-eye dog led the way.
   (**b**) Guiding its master is the task of a seeing-eye dog.
2. (**a**) Tracking animals requires special skills.
   (**b**) Tracking animals, they use their special skills.
3. (**a**) Using modern equipment, the factory expanded its output.
   (**b**) Using modern equipment helped the factory expand its output.

As Objects

Like nouns, gerund phrases can be used as objects. A gerund phrase can act as the direct object of a verb or as the object of a preposition.

> Lane began <u>practicing for the concert</u>. *(direct object of* began*)*
> Stop him from <u>making a serious mistake</u>. *(object of* from*)*

Once again, do not confuse a gerund phrase with a participial phrase. Look carefully at the sentence to see what function the phrase has.

> GERUND PHRASE: The girl stops <u>tossing the ball</u>. *(object of* stops*)*
> PARTICIPIAL PHRASE: The girl <u>tossing the ball</u> is Pat. *(modifies* girl*)*.

Try It Out

Identify each gerund phrase, and tell if it is used as a direct object or the object of a preposition. Not all sentences have gerund phrases.

1. I hate getting up on cold mornings.
2. The woman climbing the hill is my aunt.
3. Faced with earning a living, the hero learned a trade.
4. After a while, he enjoyed working at his trade.
5. Boris received the prize for being the fastest runner on the team.
6. Anyone knowing Dorita's whereabouts should notify me.
7. Before mailing the packages, try weighing them.
8. He went on his paper route after eating breakfast.

As Predicate Nouns

A gerund phrase can also be used as a predicate noun. That is, it can follow a linking verb to rename the subject of the sentence.

> My favorite activity **is** <u>weaving rugs</u>.
> His greatest skill **was** <u>laying bricks rapidly and evenly</u>.

Do not confuse these gerund phrases with verb phrases.

> GERUND PHRASE: My uncle's hobby is <u>weaving rugs</u>.
> VERB PHRASE: My uncle <u>is weaving</u> rugs now.

Is my uncle doing the weaving in the second sentence? Yes. Then *is weaving* is a verb phrase. Is his hobby doing the weaving in the first sentence? No. *Is* is a main verb. *Weaving rugs* is a gerund phrase.

Try It Out

Identify the gerund phrases used as predicate nouns.

1. Katerina's assignment was describing the parts of the eye.
2. The hardest part of the experiment is describing the results.
3. Alma's favorite activity is riding her horse.
4. Their great concern is missing five days of school.
5. The challenge will be making up the work.

> ▸ A gerund plus accompanying words forms a **gerund phrase**.
>
> A gerund phrase is used in the same way a noun is used—as a subject, direct object, object of a preposition, or predicate noun.

Written Practice

Copy each gerund phrase, underlining the gerund. Then write how the gerund is used in the sentence—*subject, direct object, object of a preposition,* or *predicate noun*.

1. A program of encouraging young artists has begun.
2. Providing students with a chance to draw or paint is its goal.
3. Few question the desirability of encouraging young talent.
4. The problem is obtaining the needed money.
5. The program's supporters try different ways of raising funds.
6. Soliciting funds has become an important activity for them.
7. They must continue advertising the program.
8. Now the organization will try campaigning on a large scale.
9. Mounting such a campaign is a challenging task.
10. Their strategy will be requesting funds from large corporations.
11. Contacting firms is the director's role.
12. Companies find different ways of being supportive.

● **Writing Sentences**   Write a sentence using each form in a gerund phrase.

13. wearing *(subject)*
14. talking *(object of preposition)*
15. playing *(direct object)*
16. swimming *(predicate noun)*
17. listening *(direct object)*
18. trying *(object of preposition)*

6 | Possessives with Gerunds

When a noun or pronoun precedes a gerund, the noun or pronoun is in the possessive form. Try substituting a regular noun for the gerund. You will see that a possessive form is needed in that position.

GERUND: **His** leaving was a disappointment.
NOUN: **His** departure was a disappointment.
GERUND: It is wonderful to think of **your** being chairperson.
NOUN: It is wonderful to think of **your** job.

Try It Out

Choose the word that correctly completes the sentence.

1. The tension was relieved by (Joe, Joe's) making a grand entrance.
2. I warned Gino about (them, their) being late all the time.
3. No one appreciated (him, his) saying such a thing.
4. (Fran, Fran's) leaving will solve the problem.
5. (Me, My) being there was a help.

> Use a possessive noun or pronoun before a gerund.

Written Practice

If a sentence is correct, write *C*. Otherwise, rewrite it correctly.

1. My dad buying a new car was quite an event.
2. Because of him wanting bright red, we all discussed the color.
3. Dad patiently listened to our arguing.
4. Everyone was cheered by Mom's offering to help.
5. Us deciding to vote on the color was the best solution.

- **Writing Sentences**   Write a sentence using each form in a gerund phrase.

6. Dan's cooking   8. my driving   10. Jan's sighing   12. our racing
7. my knowing   9. Al's rowing   11. their helping   13. his tying

7 | Infinitive Phrases

Identifying Infinitive Phrases

An **infinitive phrase** includes the infinitive and the words that accompany it.

> I am determined <u>to make a spectacular dive from that board.</u>
> <u>To make a good dive from the board</u> is not easy.
> It is important <u>to be calm and concentrate.</u>

Infinitive phrases usually can be recognized by the word *to* that precedes the verb form. Remember that this is not the same *to* that occurs in prepositional phrases.

> INFINITIVE PHRASE: Please ask them <u>to organize the party.</u>
> PREPOSITIONAL PHRASE: Please ask them <u>to the party.</u>

The preposition *to* always has a noun or pronoun as its object. The infinitive *to* is always followed immediately by a verb form.

Try It Out

Identify each infinitive phrase. Not every sentence has one.

1. The watt is a unit used to measure power.
2. The name was given to this unit in honor of a Scottish engineer and inventor, James Watt.
3. People most often relate this measurement to electric power.
4. Have you ever stopped to look at the number on a light bulb?
5. The number is there to show the power requirement in watts.
6. I am going to the store to buy a powerful 200-watt bulb.
7. I plan to use it in the floor lamp my sister gave to me.
8. To read more comfortably, I need a stronger light.

As Modifiers

Like infinitives, infinitive phrases can be used as modifiers. Infinitive phrases used as adjectives modify nouns or pronouns.

> Now is the time <u>to speak out.</u> *(modifies noun* time*)*

> He is the one <u>to ask for help.</u> *(modifies pronoun* one*)*

Infinitive phrases used as adverbs usually modify verbs or adjectives.

She called them to announce her decision. *(modifies verb* called*)*

They are all eager to hear about it. *(modifies adjective* eager*)*

Try It Out

Find each infinitive phrase. Tell which word it modifies. Is the infinitive phrase used as an adjective or an adverb?

1. Jessie is anxious to know his grade in science.
2. It is an idea to be considered carefully.
3. To be certain of the facts, Beth checked them in the library.
4. Everyone to be tested should report to the office.
5. His remark was intended to be funny.

As Nouns

Infinitive phrases acting as nouns may be used as subjects, as direct objects, and as predicate nouns.

To present both sides of the issue is necessary. *(subject)*
We wanted to present both sides of the issue. *(direct object)*
Our aim is to present both sides of the issue. *(predicate noun)*

Try It Out

Find each infinitive phrase used as a noun. Tell whether it acts as a subject, a direct object, or a predicate noun.

1. The officials decided to postpone the game.
2. Our goal was to solve the problem in five minutes.
3. To give one's time to a good cause is admirable.
4. I don't want to throw those things away.
5. To be completely honest is to avoid disaster.

> ▸ An infinitive plus accompanying words forms an **infinitive phrase**. Infinitive phrases can be used as modifiers or as nouns.

Written Practice

A. Copy each infinitive phrase. If the sentence does not contain an infinitive phrase, write *none*.

1. The point of the dictation exercise was to train your ear.
2. Because of the storm, we cannot go to the library now.
3. To achieve one's goal is a satisfying thing.
4. To the top of the mountain went the climbers.
5. Let's go to Ann's house to practice our scene in the play.
6. The squirrel was eager to reach the acorn.
7. The bucket dropped all the way to the bottom of the well.
8. Your objective should be to finish the job today.
9. They hope to travel to South America this summer.
10. Ms. Guzman promised to review equations today.

B. Copy each infinitive phrase. Then label it *noun, adjective,* or *adverb* to tell how it is used in the sentence.

11. The story to read tomorrow is "The Garden Party" by Katherine Mansfield.
12. I was planning to call you this afternoon.
13. To think about such a thing makes me shudder.
14. Do you want to plan the talent show now?
15. Our hope is to reach Vancouver by midnight.
16. In that town there is not much to do.
17. The raccoon waited until dark to invade the garbage.
18. Lyle does not plan to miss the rehearsal tonight.
19. That piano piece is not easy to play fast.
20. To stop at this point would be to admit failure.

- **Writing Sentences** Use each infinitive in an infinitive phrase, and include the phrase in a sentence of your own. Use the phrase as a noun, adjective, or adverb, as shown in each case.

21. to stir *(noun)*
22. to become *(noun)*
23. to read *(adverb)*
24. to hear *(adjective)*
25. to learn *(adverb)*
26. to whistle *(noun)*

8 | Writing Well with Phrases

Placing Phrases for Clarity

If you read this headline in a newspaper, what picture would you get?

> Man Rescues Dog in Tuxedo

How many dogs in tuxedos have you seen? It is far more likely that the man was the one in the tuxedo. The problem with the headline, of course, lies in the placement of the prepositional phrase. It should follow the noun it modifies, *man*. *Man **in Tuxedo** Rescues Dog* might not arouse as much curiosity, but it would certainly be clearer.

When you use modifying phrases, place them so they refer clearly to the words they modify.

Try It Out

Change these sentences to make them clearer.

1. Stefanie builds bookcases for her friends with three shelves.
2. Newspapers carried the story of the flood in every part of the world.
3. Mr. Wilson made it clear that rudeness was unacceptable on Friday.
4. Ribs were served to the guests covered with sauce at the picnic.
5. The low attendance was the result of a flu epidemic at the meeting.

Placing Phrases for Variety

Certain phrases can be used in various positions without changing the meaning of the sentence. Take advantage of this fact to vary your sentences and make them more interesting.

> <u>In the personnel office</u>, two people were taking applications.
> Two people were taking applications <u>in the personnel office</u>.
> <u>Waiting for help</u>, the stranded motorist sat by the roadside.
> The stranded motorist, <u>waiting for help</u>, sat by the roadside.
> The stranded motorist sat by the roadside, <u>waiting for help</u>.

Try It Out

Change each sentence by moving a phrase to either one or two different positions as indicated in parentheses. Add commas where needed.

1. Dr. Martinez checked the records thoroughly before examining her patient. (2)
2. All five of us, chattering noisily, left and went home. (2)
3. The dark clouds had begun to gather before noon. (1)
4. At thirteen, Isaac Stern was already a brilliant violinist. (2)
5. Divide mass by volume to find the density of a substance. (1)

Using Phrases to Combine Sentences

You know that a series of short sentences, all beginning with the subject, can become monotonous. A good writer thinks about creating longer sentences to get a more interesting and direct flow of words. You can often make use of phrases to combine short sentences into longer, more effective ones.

Study the following sets of sentences to see how you can use phrases of different kinds to combine sentences.

TWO SENTENCES:	I saw Elsie. She was at the library.
PREPOSITIONAL PHRASE:	I saw Elsie <u>at the library</u>.

TWO SENTENCES:	I saw Ivan. He was skating on the pond.
PARTICIPIAL PHRASE:	I saw Ivan <u>skating on the pond</u>.

TWO SENTENCES:	I am building model planes. That's my hobby.
GERUND PHRASE:	<u>Building model planes</u> is my hobby.

TWO SENTENCES:	I want to own a horse. That's my dream.
INFINITIVE PHRASE:	My dream is <u>to own a horse</u>.

There is often more than one way to combine a pair of sentences. The combination you choose will depend on what you want to emphasize and on how the sentence fits in with the sentences around it.

Study the different ways in which these two sentences are combined.

TWO SENTENCES:	Play more often. You will improve your skills.
PARTICIPIAL PHRASE:	<u>Playing more often</u>, you will improve your skills.
GERUND PHRASE:	<u>Playing more often</u> will improve your skills.
INFINITIVE PHRASE:	<u>To improve your skills</u>, play more often.

Try It Out

Use the phrase or phrases in parentheses to combine the sentences in either one or two ways. Use commas correctly.

1. My only short story is about five friends. It is entitled "Jewels." *(participial phrase)*
2. I want to show the importance of friendship. That is my aim. *(infinitive phrase; gerund phrase)*
3. Last night my father telephoned his sister. She lives in Mexico. *(prepositional phrase)*
4. His sister was feeling lonely. She was glad to hear from us. *(participial phrase)*
5. We shall be visiting my aunt next month. That is our plan. *(gerund phrase; infinitive phrase)*
6. We shall travel by plane. We shall be in Mexico City in only a few hours. *(participial phrase)*
7. Joshua looked out of the window. It helped him concentrate on the problem. *(gerund phrase)*
8. There was something Sarah wanted to learn. It was to ride a horse really well. *(infinitive phrase)*

Written Practice

Rewrite the passage to make it more direct and interesting. Use phrases to combine sentences. Vary the position of the phrases. Be careful, however, to place the phrases so that the sentences are clear.

Willa Cather is known for her portrayals of frontier life. She was born in Virginia in 1873. She moved to Red Cloud, Nebraska, when she was nine. She went with her family. There she grew up. She lived among hard-working European immigrants. They were farming the Great Plains.

Willa Cather was at the University of Nebraska. She showed great talent for writing. She worked on a magazine for several years. She eventually became the managing editor. Then she left. She was going to devote herself to her writing.

Her novel *O Pioneers!* was published in 1913. It told of the spirit and courage of frontier women. She described the hardships and beauty of prairie life. That became her specialty. In 1923 this talented, sensitive writer won the Pulitzer Prize for a book. It was entitled *One of Ours.*

Check Your Writing

Review your passage about Willa Cather, asking yourself these questions. Make any needed changes in the passage.

A. Are my sentences correct?

1. Have I used object pronouns as objects of prepositions?
2. Have I used commas after introductory phrases?
3. Have I used commas correctly with participial phrases?
4. Have I used possessive nouns and pronouns before gerunds?

B. Are my sentences clear?

Have I placed phrases so that it is clear which words they modify?

C. Are my sentences direct?

Have I used phrases instead of separate sentences where this was appropriate?

D. Are my sentences interesting?

1. Have I placed phrases in different places in sentences for variety?
2. Have I used phrases to avoid boring sequences of short sentences?
3. Have I used different kinds of phrases where appropriate?

● **Writing a Paragraph** What special things do you dream of doing? Do you want to go on a safari? pitch a no-hitter? write a hit song? Do you want to discover an ancient city or find a new source of energy?

Write a passage of eight to ten sentences describing one or more of your dreams. Use different kinds of phrases in your sentences. When you have finished, review what you have written, asking yourself the questions above. Make appropriate changes, and rewrite the passage if necessary.

9 Using Words Correctly

between, among

Between is generally used with two people or things. *Among* is used with more than two people or things.

> A treaty was signed <u>between</u> the two countries.
> The four bricklayers split the work <u>among</u> them.

If two groups are being talked about, *between* is used, even though many people or things may be involved.

> The dealings <u>between</u> the actors and the directors were cordial.

The distinction between *between* and *among* is almost always made in formal English. In informal spoken English, it is not always observed.

Practice

Choose the correct word in each sentence.

1. You'll have to choose (between, among) the sweater and the shirt.
2. (Between, Among) all of you, someone must be interested in the part.
3. The correspondence (between, among) my pen pal and me has been active.
4. The inheritance will be divided (between, among) several cousins.
5. There is real affection (between, among) our dogs and our cats.
6. The hammock was hung (between, among) the two walnut trees.

from, off

From and *off* both have several meanings. One of the meanings of *from* is "out of the possession of." Never use *off* in this sense.

> I took the catcher's mitt <u>from</u> *(not* off*)* her.

Do not use *of* with *off*.

> A button has come <u>off</u> *(not* off of*)* her coat.

Practice

Choose the correct word in each sentence.

1. I borrowed some money (off, from) Susan and paid her back today.
2. Since it was my turn to pitch, I took the ball (off, from) Eli.
3. The patch has come (off, off of) my jeans.

beside, besides

Beside and *besides* are two different words with different meanings. *Beside* means "next to." *Besides* means "in addition to."

Who sits <u>beside</u> you in science class?
<u>Besides</u> you, who is going to the library?

Use *between* with two persons or things.
Use *among* with more than two persons or things.
Use *from*, not *off*, to mean "out of the possession of."
Do not use *of* after *off*.
Beside means "next to." *Besides* means "in addition to."

Practice

A. Choose the correct word in each sentence.

1. Harry sat (beside, besides) the window all afternoon.
2. No one (beside, besides) you has complained about that.
3. Put the fertilizer (beside, besides) the garage.

B. If a sentence is incorrect, correct it. One sentence is correct.

4. Please take your books off of the table.
5. The blue chair looks good besides the couch.
6. Don't borrow the skates from Denise.
7. The matter should be discussed between all the family members.

• **Writing Sentences** Use each word in two sentences of your own.

8. between 9. among 10. off 11. from 12. beside 13. besides

10 Building Vocabulary

Homophones and Homographs

If you have ever wondered whether to write *their* or *there*, or *pane* or *pain*, you know that different words can sound alike. Such words are called **homophones**. Here are some examples of common homophones. Do you know what each of these words means? If not, check your dictionary.

aisle, isle	compliment, complement	principal, principle
bare, bear	peace, piece	stationary, stationery

Homographs are words that are spelled alike but have different meanings. They may also be pronounced differently. *Désert* is a noun meaning "a dry, barren place," while *desért* is a verb meaning "to abandon." Can you think of two meanings for *kind? bow? present?*

> ▸ **Homophones** are words that are pronounced alike but are spelled differently and have different meanings.
> ▸ **Homographs** are words that are spelled alike but have different meanings and often different pronunciations.

Practice

A. Choose the correct word from each pair in parentheses.

1. Who is the new (principle, principal) of the school?
2. The pet (bare, bear) had a (piece, peace) of watermelon.
3. I wrote the invitations on my new (stationary, stationery).

B. Write two meanings for each word. Use a dictionary if you need to.

4. content 5. mine 6. minute 7. object 8. check 9. draft

- **Writing Sentences** Use each word in a sentence.

10. meat 11. meet 12. plane 13. plain 14. alter 15. altar

Review

- **Prepositions and Their Objects** *(pp. 325–327)* Copy each preposition. Next to it, write its object.

  1. Harry and his family are traveling across the country by car.
  2. To me that seems like a dreadfully long drive.
  3. They will spend about three weeks on their trip.

  If a sentence is incorrect, rewrite it. If it is correct, write *C.*

  4. That book has been lent to everyone except you and me.
  5. Between Camilla and I, we have collected fifty cans for recycling.
  6. Mr. Belansky has received a few letters from Elliot and her.

- **Prepositional Phrases** *(pp. 328–330)* Copy the passage. Underline each prepositional phrase. Draw an arrow to the modified word.

  7–15. Everyone should prepare for everyday emergencies. Cases of injuries at home are common. Keep on hand bandages of all sizes, ointments with antibiotics, and band-aids for minor wounds. For a burn, place the burned area under cold running water.

- **Verbals** *(pp. 331–334)* List the verbals. Identify each one as a participle, a gerund, or an infinitive.

  16–26. A group of children had come to visit the zoo in Melbourne. Staring, they stood around the caged animal. Was it a wild dog, a captured wolf, or something unknown? Fascinated, the children kept staring. They were looking at Oscar, a dedicated polar husky. No longer able to work, the dog retired to the zoo. Relaxing and preening were his main activities now.

- **Participial Phrases** *(pp. 335–337)* Copy each participial phrase, adding commas where needed. Write the modified word.

  27. Standing on the hilltop we could see the entire town below us.
  28. The cure recommended for that disease sounds simple.
  29. Phoebe waiting for the school bus was smiling at the bright sky.
  30. The music performed by that group is original.

- **Gerund Phrases** *(pp. 338-340)*   Copy each gerund phrase. Write whether it is used as a subject, direct object, object of a preposition, or predicate noun.

    31. Waiting for buses can be tiresome.
    32. The worst thing about being sick is feeling so terrible.
    33. I began sealing the letter, but then I read it once more.

- **Possessives with Gerunds** *(p. 341)*   If a sentence is incorrect, re-write it. If it is correct, write *C.*

    34. We enjoyed his singing.
    35. You joining us is wonderful.
    36. They disliked me being late.
    37. Iris being there surprised us.

- **Infinitive Phrases** *(pp. 342-344)*   Copy each infinitive phrase. Write whether it is used as a noun, an adjective, or an adverb.

    38. That is not easy to do well.
    39. To go back was not possible.
    40. Now is the time to act fast.
    41. Do you want to wait longer?

- **Writing Well with Phrases** *(pp. 345-348)*   Revise each sentence or sentence pair by shifting or creating phrases.

    42. She gave crackers to the children with sesame seeds.
    43. The holiday crowds seemed cheerful walking along the streets.
    44. Geraldo was fascinated by the spider web. He drew a picture of it.
    45. She wanted to finish the race. That was the important thing.

- **Using Words Correctly** *(pp. 349-350)*   Write the correct word.

    46. (Between, Among) the three of us, we should be able to do the job.
    47. What are you taking with you (beside, besides) sport clothes?
    48. Did you get the red pen (from, off) Dennis?
    49. The pile of books toppled (off, off of) the desk.

- **Building Vocabulary** *(p. 351)*   Write the correct word.

    50. On what (principle, principal) is your argument based?
    51. Mavis dropped her (stationary, stationery) in the (aisle, isle).

    Write the meaning of the underlined word in each sentence.

    52. The dog's bark was harsh.
    53. The bark sailed away at high tide.
    54. The bark of the white birch is quite beautiful.

1 | Facts and Opinions

Have you ever seen an opinion poll published in a magazine or newspaper? Have you ever been asked to give your opinion for a poll on the theme of the class party, a new food product at the local supermarket, or some other issue?

An opinion poll seeks to find out what people feel or think about a certain issue—what their opinions are. There is no right or wrong response to an opinion poll. Everyone is entitled to his or her own opinion.

Facts, on the other hand, can be proven right or wrong. They can be verified by observation or by consulting a reference of some kind.

Read the two statements below.

Smooth Spread margarine tastes better than Golden Glow.
Smooth Spread maragarine is made from 100 percent corn oil.

- Which statement above is a fact? How do you know? How could it be verified?
- Which statement is an opinion?

Practice

A. Tell whether each of these statements is a fact or an opinion. How do you know?

1. Seventy-eight students attended the party.
2. The band was too loud.
3. Frances won a prize for the most original costume.
4. Olympio wore the funniest costume!

B. Conduct an opinion poll in your class. Ask your classmates' opinions on one of the following issues or one of your own choice.

1. What is your favorite television show or movie?
2. What does our school need most?
3. What is the best way to study for a test?
4. What is the greatest problem facing the world today?

Write a fact or facts stating the results of your opinion poll.

2 | Supporting Details and Topic Sentences

To be persuasive, a written argument should provide evidence, or facts and reasons, to support the opinion being presented. Evidence that is exact, specific, and relevant (related to the topic) is most convincing.

Read these two endorsements. Which student would you vote for? Why?

1. I think that Kristin James would make a good class president. She has friendly eyes and a nice smile. She has had experience being a class officer, and she comes from a big family. She has the skills to do the job.

2. As class treasurer last year, Joe McCormack ran two highly successful fundraising events—the talent show and the car wash. His work on these projects proves his qualifications to be an excellent class president. He is dedicated, hard-working, creative, and well organized. Joe McCormack is my choice for class president!

- Which paragraph presents evidence that is clearer and more specific? Give examples.
- Give examples of details in the other paragraph that are too vague.
- Which details are not relevant?

In a well-organized argument, each paragraph presents evidence that supports one main idea. That main idea is stated in the topic sentence. Look at the two endorsements for class president above.

- What is the topic sentence of the first paragraph?
- What is the topic sentence of the second paragaph?
- Does the topic sentence always have to be the first sentence in the paragraph?

An argument may have supporting details that are clear, specific, and relevant, but without a strong topic sentence the reader is left wondering exactly what he or she is being persuaded about.

Read the paragraph below.

The tomato sauce in pizza is a source of vitamin C. Protein is provided by the meat and cheese. You can add vegetables such as onions, peppers, mushrooms, or even carrots and broccoli, to pizza.

- Does the paragraph have a topic sentence?
- What is the main idea?
- Think of a topic sentence for the paragraph. Decide where in the paragraph you would put it.

Practice

A. For each underlined topic sentence, tell which detail is most persuasive. Tell why you think so.

1. We should feed the birds in the winter.
   They don't eat much.
   The snow covers up their usual food.
   They have such pretty feathers.
2. That old, abandoned building should be torn down.
   It doesn't look very nice.
   It's dangerous.
   There could be a serious accident if someone were to step on a rotten floor board.

B. Think of a good topic sentence for the group of supporting details below. Then write the sentences as a paragraph. Arrange the sentences in the way that you think will be most persuasive.

For the last two years I have baby-sat for my next-door neighbors, and they will recommend me.
I am available every afternoon after school, as well as Friday and Saturday evenings.
I have recently completed a Red Cross course in first aid.

C. Look in newspapers or magazines for examples of persuasive writing, such as advertisements, letters to the editor, editorials, or reviews. Bring the examples to class. Use these questions to help you share each example with your classmates.

1. What does the writer want readers to do or think? How do you know?
2. What reasons are given?
3. Is every reason exact? specific? relevant? Explain. Point out any that are not.
4. Which of your examples do you think is most persuasive? least persuasive? Why?

3 | Using Connotations

A writer's choice of words is an important factor in persuasive writing. You have already learned the value of using strong, exact words in writing details. Another aspect of word choice to consider is the connotation of a word, or the feelings people associate with it.

Look at the words used on page 356 to describe Joe McCormack, candidate for class president: *dedicated, hard-working, creative, well-organized.* What connotation do these words have for you? How do they make you feel about Joe?

Suppose we were to say that Joe was *single-minded, drudging, impractical,* and *rigid,* words with similar meanings to the ones above, but with very different connotations. How do these words make you feel toward Joe?

Examine the use of connotation in the following sentences.

The Sultan is a first-class luxury car.
The Sultan is an expensive car.

Their vegetables are saturated in a heavy, calorie-laden sauce.
Our vegetables are enhanced by a rich, full-bodied sauce.

- Which words in each pair of sentences have positive connotations? negative connotations?
- How did the writers use connotation to persuade?

Because connotation is related to *feelings,* the same words can have different connotations for different people. What connotations would a forecast of *drenching rain* have for farmers during a drought? for vacationers planning a picnic? Why is it important for writers to keep their audience in mind?

Practice

Use the examples of persuasive writing that you found for Practice C on page 357, or find other examples. Underline words and phrases that have strong connotations, either positive or negative. Discuss with a group of classmates how each underlined word makes you feel. Is the connotation the same for everyone?

4 | Openings and Closings

An argument needs more than evidence to be persuasive. It needs a strong opening and closing in order to get readers interested, let them know what the writer's position is, and let them know what the writer wants them to do.

A good opening for an argument should do the following.

1. get readers' attention
2. clearly state the main point of the argument

The owner of Island Paradise wanted to persuade people to visit his vacation resort. He wrote this opening for a brochure.

> Warm sun, sailboats scudding across the clear blue water, delicious gourmet meals—all this awaits you at Island Paradise. A scenic ferry ride will transport you to the vacation spot of your dreams.

- What is the main point of the resort owner's argument?
- Does the opening capture your attention? How?
- Does the writer make use of word connotation? Explain.

A good closing should do the following.

1. Let the readers know what the writer wants them to do.
2. Give them the information they need to do it.
3. Make them *want* to do it.

Read this closing for the Island Paradise brochure.

> Call your travel agent today, or dial our toll-free number, 1-800-XXX-XXX-XXXX. Forget your cares, and relax at Island Paradise!

- What does the writer want you to do? How do you know?
- Does the closing include all the necessary information? Explain.
- Does it make you *want* to do what the writer asks? Explain.

Practice

Write a persuasive opening and closing for an advertisement. Keep in mind the points listed above about what a good opening and a good closing should do.

5 | Getting Started

Suppose you want to persuade your class to raise money for new uniforms for the band. Do you have a good idea for fundraising? Should those who damage or destroy school property be made to clean it, fix it, or pay for it? Do you think you should get your money back for the "waterproof" boots you bought that leak like a pair of sieves?

You can try to persuade others to see things your way by writing a letter to the editor of your school or community newspaper, to a public official, or to an official of an organization or company.

If your letter includes specific, relevant evidence to back up your argument, if it is well organized with an attention-getting opening and a strong closing, you may be successful in persuading your reader or readers to agree with you.

Practice

A. Take turns with three or four other students orally composing a persuasive letter. You can use one of the topics suggested above or an opinion of your own. Listen carefully to each other. Ask yourself these questions about each "letter."

1. What is the speaker's position?
2. What evidence is given? Is it clear? specific? relevant?
3. What other evidence could the speaker use?

B. Discuss which arguments seemed most persuasive. What made them persuasive?

Steps for Writing an Argument   Here are the steps for writing an argument. You will follow them to write your own argument.

Step One	Choose a topic.
Step Two	Plan your argument.
Step Three	Write your argument.
Step Four	Revise your argument.
Step Five	Proofread your argument.
Step Six	Make a final copy to share.

6 | Step One
Choose a Topic

Carlotta thought about some things she wished she could persuade others to do. She made this list.

Collect waste paper from school and business offices to use for writing first drafts and notes.

Close off the hilly paths in the city park for roller skaters and skateboarders to use.

Get the principal to let students plan one school assembly each month.

Oppose the 9:00 P. M. closing at the city's playgrounds.

Carlotta looked at her list. The third and fourth topics both seemed like good ideas, but she could not think of enough reasons to make a strong argument for either of them.

The idea of putting trash to good use was appealing to Carlotta. Because she loved to zip around on anything on wheels, she was also very interested in the second topic. She could think of good reasons to support each of these. However, she realized that she cared more about the problem of roller skates and skateboards in the park, so she chose that as her topic.

Assignment
- **Make a List**
- **Choose a Topic**

A. Make a list of several topics for a persuasive letter. Use these suggestions to help you.

1. Pick issues that matter to you.
2. Pick real issues about which there is genuine disagreement.
3. Pick issues that you know something about or can find out about.

B. Choose the topic on your list that seems best.

7 | Step Two
Plan Your Argument

Carlotta's next step was to decide *what* to write. First she thought about writing a letter to the editor of the local newspaper. She was sure that if her letter were printed in the newspaper, she might be able to persuade a lot of people to agree with her. What she really needed to do, however, was to persuade whoever was in charge of the park.

Since Carlotta was not sure which department of the city government would be responsible for roping off a section of the park, she called City Hall. She found that the Department of Parks and Recreation had authority over the park. She also found that Ms. Carol Winters was the director of that department. She decided to write a letter to Ms. Winters about her idea for the park.

Before Carlotta began to write, she planned her argument. First she wrote a sentence stating her opinion: *The department of parks and recreation should rope off the hilly section of the park for roller skaters and skateboarders to use.*

Below it she listed all the reasons she could think of to support her opinion. Then she looked over her list, trying to put herself in the position of Ms. Winters, who would read the letter. Were her reasons good? She decided that two of them were not relevant. She crossed them out.

Next Carlotta planned how she would organize her argument. She wanted the opening to catch Ms. Winters's interest. The director of the Park Department would probably be most concerned about safety in the park. Carlotta decided to make her opening argument focus on the fact that it was dangerous for the skaters to be using the same paths as people on foot. She marked a *1* next to the items on her list that related to the main topic of safety.

She decided that the topic of the second paragraph would be fairness. She marked a *2* next to the sentences that related to the rights of skaters to use the public park.

In her closing, she wanted to make it clear to Ms. Winters exactly what she was asking the department to do: to close off the hilly section of the park so she and her friends could enjoy their sports without endangering themselves or others. She marked a *3* next to the details that would be included in her closing. The next page shows Carlotta's list after she had finished planning.

3 The department of parks and recreation should rope off the hilly section of the park for roller skaters and skateboarders to use.

1 Everybody could have fun and be safe.

2 Walkers and joggers can use the mane roads.

1 Someday there's going to be a bad accident — I've ~~saw someone~~ even seen people get knocked down.

1 People walking in the park get mad when roller skaters whizz by them or bump into them.

2 There are bycicle paths for people on bikes. ~~Roller skating is good exercise.~~

3 Skateboarders need hills to practice on, but people don't need hills to walk on. ~~Some people walk so slowly!~~

3 It would show that the department cares about kids.

Assignment

- **Explore Your Topic**
- **Plan Your Argument**

A. After you have selected your topic, decide what kind of persuasive writing you will use.

B. Make a list of reasons to support your argument. Write down all the reasons you can think of.

C. Now put yourself in the place of your readers. Look back over your list. Try to decide if the reasons are persuasive. Use these questions to help you.

1. Is each reason relevant to the argument? Cross out any that are not.

2. Is any further information needed to support the argument? If so, use reference books or ask an expert to obtain it. Add the information to your list.

D. Plan the organization of your argument. Decide how many paragraphs you will write and what the topic of each paragraph will be. Decide what details from your list will be in each paragraph.

8 | Step Three
Write Your Argument

Carlotta used her notes and her plan for organizing them to help her write a first draft. She tried to state her position clearly and to support it with facts and reasons. She tried to use exact, specific language and to pay attention to the connotations of the words she used. She did not worry about mistakes at this point. She knew that she could go back to revise her letter.

Carlotta's first draft

Dear Ms. Winters:

People walking in the park get mad when roller skaters and ~~kids on~~ skateboarders whizz by them or bump into them. Someday there's going to be a bad accident. I've even seen people get nocked down. We need our own place in the park so everybody can have fun and be safe.

Bycicle riders have their own special place in the park. They have bike paths just for them. Skaters and skateboarders don't so that's why we bump into people. Walkers and joggers can use the mane roads.

The department of parks and recreation should rope off the hilly part of the park just for skaters and skateboarders. Skateboarders need the hills to practice on but other people don't need the hills to walk on. This would prove that the department of parks and recreation cares about kids.

- What words in Carlotta's opening are intended to catch the reader's attention? What connotation would the words *bad accident* have for a city official who is responsible for the park? Could this paragraph be made stronger? How?
- What is the main topic of each paragraph Carlotta wrote? Which paragraph needs a topic sentence?
- Is every supporting detail relevant? If any details are not relevant, which are they?
- Does the closing clearly state what Carlotta wants her reader to do? Could it be made clearer? How?
- Does the closing make the reader *want* to do what Carlotta asks? Explain.

Assignment • Write Your First Draft

Review your list of details and your plan for organizing them. Then write a first draft of your argument. Do not worry about spelling and punctuation at this point. You can go back and make changes later.

Keep these points in mind as you write your draft.

1. Concentrate on organizing your evidence into a strong, persuasive argument.
2. For each paragraph, write a strong topic sentence that states the main idea. Then back it up with your supporting details.
3. Use strong, exact words and specific examples; avoid vague words and generalities.
4. Pay attention to the connotation of the words you use, keeping in mind your audience.
5. Make sure your opening includes details that will grab your readers' attention and that your closing clearly states what you want your readers to do.

9 | Step Four
Revise Your Argument

Because she had planned her argument, Carlotta's opinion was stated clearly and supported by specific, relevant evidence. However, when she read over her draft, Carlotta thought of some improvements she could make.

In her opening, she was hoping to grab Ms. Winters's attention by focusing on safety, but her topic sentence said that the skaters caused people to *get mad.* She changed this phrase so that the sentence more clearly stated her main topic.

The second paragraph, she realized, presented good evidence for the fairness of her proposal, but it did not have a topic sentence. She thought of a sentence to state the main idea and wrote it at the end of the paragraph. She also crossed out one detail that seemed weak.

When she read the third paragraph, she decided to cross out the sentence about skateboarders needing hills more than other people. She realized that it was not relevant to the topic stated in her first sentence—the action she wanted the Park Department to take.

These changes helped, Carlotta thought, but she still wanted to know how persuasive her argument would be to someone else. Carlotta read her letter to Denise. She asked Denise to imagine that she was the Director of Parks and Recreation. Would this letter persuade her?

"I think you have a good idea," said Denise, "and I hope Ms. Winters goes along with it. Playing up the danger of accidents in the first paragraph *is* attention-getting. Maybe you could make it even stronger. How about giving an example of an accident you've seen?"

"I saw a man get knocked down by a roller skater last week," said Carlotta. "I'll add that example."

"A lot of people walk through that part of the park to get to work during the week," continued Denise, "and it's mostly on weekends that we want to skate. Maybe you'd have a better chance if you asked her to rope it off just on Saturdays and Sundays."

That seemed like a reasonable compromise to Carlotta. She thanked Denise for her good ideas and made the changes she had suggested.

When she read her letter aloud, Carlotta realized that some adults enjoy wheel sports, too, so she changed *kids* in the last paragraph to *all citizens,* a phrase that would include more people and would probably be more persuasive to a city official.

Carlotta's revision

Dear Ms. Winters:

People walking in the park ~~get mad when~~ *are indangered by* roller skaters and ~~kids on~~ skateboarders *who* fly by them or bump into them. ~~Someday there's going to be a bad accident.~~ *Last week I saw a man* I've even seen people get nocked down. ~~We need our own place in the park so everybody can have fun and be safe.~~

Bycicle riders have their own special place in the park. They have bike paths just for them. ~~Skaters and skateboarders don't so that's why we bump into people.~~ Walkers and joggers can use the mane roads.

The department of parks and recreation should rope off the hilly part of the park *on Saturdays and Sundays* just for skaters and skateboarders. ~~Skateboarders need the hills to practice on but other people don't need the hills to walk on.~~ This would prove that the department of parks and recreation cares about *all citizens of our city, on feet and on wheels.* ~~kids.~~

by a skater who couldn't stop in time. Before a serios accident happens skaters and skateboarders should have their

People on skates and skateboards have just as much right to enjoy the public park as everybody else.

- What changes did Carlotta make to her first paragraph? Why? Do they make her opening more attention-getting? Explain.
- Why did she add a new last sentence to the second paragraph?
- What changes did she make in the third paragraph? Why did she make each one? Do you agree with the changes? Why or why not?
- What other changes would improve Carlotta's letter?

Assignment

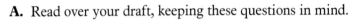

- Revise Your Argument
- Discuss Your Argument

A. Read over your draft, keeping these questions in mind.

1. Will my opening capture my readers' attention?
2. Does each paragraph have a strong topic sentence? Does every detail in the paragraph support the topic sentence? Are there any weak or irrelevant details I could cross out?
3. What other details or specific examples could I add to make my argument stronger?
4. Have I used strong, exact language? Are there any vague words or generalities I could change?
5. What connotations will my words have for the person to whom my argument is directed? Are they likely to make the reader agree with my position?
6. Does my closing state clearly what I want my readers to do? Will it make them *want* to do it?

B. Use your answers to the questions above to help you revise your draft. Add details by writing new sentences above the lines, or write the sentences at the bottom of the page if they are long. Cross out weak, vague words and write more specific ones above them. Cross out any irrelevant sentences. Use arrows to move words, phrases, and sentences around.

C. Read your argument aloud to a classmate or to your teacher. Ask your partner to listen from the point of view of the person to whom your argument is directed. Would he or she be persuaded? What suggestions can your listener offer to improve your argument?

D. Discuss your partner's suggestions. If you agree with the suggestions, make the changes on your paper. If you had any other good ideas as you read your argument aloud, make those changes as well.

10 | Step Five
Proofread Your Argument

Now that your argument is as clear and convincing and easy to follow as you can make it, you can check for mistakes such as errors in spelling, capitalization, and punctuation.

Carlotta copied her letter over because it was so difficult to read. She added the heading, inside address, closing, and signature, following proper business letter form. Then she proofread it, using a dictionary to help with spelling.

Last part of Carlotta's letter after proofreading

> *Bicycle*
> ~~Bycicle~~ riders have their own special place in the
> park. They have bike paths just for them. Walkers and
> joggers can use the ~~mane~~ *main* roads. People on skates and
> skateboards have just as much right to enjoy the pub-
> lic park as everybody else/ *does*.
> The department of parks and recreation should rope
> off the hilly part of the park on Saturdays and Sun-
> days just for skaters and skateboarders. This would
> prove that the department cares about all citizens of
> our city, on feet and on wheels.
>
> Sincerely,
>
> Carlotta Harris

- What spelling errors did Carlotta correct?
- What punctuation did she add? Why?
- What verb did she add? Why? Could she have corrected that sentence another way? Explain.
- What other corrections did she make? Why?

Practice

Proofread the beginning of Carlotta's letter. You should find seven errors. Use a dictionary to check the spelling of any words you are unsure of. Refer to page 469 of the Handbook to check proper business letter form. Copy the portion of the letter correctly.

Ms. Carol Winters, Director

Department of parks and recreation

50 City Hall Square

St. Louis, MO 63103

Dear Ms. Winters:

People walking in the park are indangered by roller skaters and skateboarders who fly by them or bump into them. Last week I saw a man get nocked down by a skater who couldnt stop in time. Before a serios accident happens skaters and skateboarders should have their own place in the park.

Assignment • Proofread Your Argument

Proofread your argument. Ask yourself these questions.

1. Have I made appropriate paragraph breaks?
2. Are all the words spelled correctly? Have I looked up any word I am unsure of?

Grammar skills checklist

3. Have I corrected all fragments and run-on sentences?
4. Did I begin each proper noun with a capital letter?
5. Have I used apostrophes to write contractions and possessive nouns correctly?
6. Have I used commas to set off appositives?
7. Have I used the correct forms of verbs and pronouns?

11 | Step Six
Make a Final Copy

Carlotta typed her letter neatly, being careful to use correct business letter form. She checked it to be sure she had made no errors and that she had used the correct address for Ms. Winters's office.

Then she wondered if there was anything she could do to make her argument clearer and more persuasive. She decided to make a map of the park, showing the area she was requesting for skaters, as well as the bike paths and roads that would not be affected by her proposal.

Carlotta went to the park and made sketches, then came home and drew her map. She used a red pencil line to mark the area that would be roped off on weekends. She indicated the bike paths in green and the main roads in plain black pencil. The map, she felt, would make it clear that her plan would affect only a small area of the park, leaving plenty of space for people to walk and bicycle in safety.

Carlotta also wanted to show Ms. Winters that her idea was supported by others beside herself. She asked her classmates and other friends who used the park to sign a petition in support of her plan.

On a business-size envelope, Carlotta typed Ms. Winters's address and her own return address. She put her letter, the map, and the petition in the envelope and took it to the post office. It was so heavy that she had to use two stamps, but it would be worth every cent if it persuaded Ms. Winters to grant her request!

Assignment
- **Make a Final Copy**
- **Share Your Argument**

A. Make a final copy of your argument, either typewritten or in your best handwriting. Check to make sure you have not made any errors in copying.

B. Think of an appropriate way to share your writing.

1. If it is a letter, refer to the Handbook (page 469) for correct business letter form, address and stamp an envelope, and mail your letter.
2. If it is an essay, you might want to present it orally to your class.
3. You might want to make a map, chart, diagram, or other illustration to accompany your writing, as Carlotta did.

Clauses

Independent and Subordinate Clauses

In Unit 1, you learned about clauses. A **clause** is a group of words that has a subject and a predicate. There are two major types of clauses.

INDEPENDENT CLAUSE: When the sun set, <u>the air grew cool</u>.
DEPENDENT CLAUSE: <u>When the sun set</u>, the air grew cool.

An **independent clause** expresses a complete thought. *The air grew cool* can stand alone as a sentence. A **dependent clause** does not express a complete thought. *When the sun set* cannot stand alone. A dependent clause needs an independent clause to complete its meaning. A dependent clause and an independent clause form a complex sentence.

A dependent clause is also called a **subordinate clause**. *Sub-* means "below." Subordinate clauses are "ordered below" independent, or **main**, clauses. From now on, we shall use the term *subordinate clause*.

Subordinate clauses can be introduced by some of the same words that introduce prepositional phrases—such words as *before, after, until, since*. Do not confuse phrases and clauses. A clause always includes a subject and predicate; a phrase never does.

CLAUSE: I'll see you <u>before the sun sets</u>.
PHRASE: I'll see you <u>before sunset</u>.

CLAUSE: She read a magazine <u>while she waited for you</u>.
PHRASE: <u>Waiting for you</u>, she read a magazine.

Try It Out

A. Tell whether each clause is subordinate or independent.

1. when Cary arrives
2. when will he arrive
3. soon Carry will be here
4. at first I didn't like it
5. after he came
6. since you aren't going

B. Tell whether the underlined group of words is a phrase or a clause.

7. You'll have to wait here <u>until the act ends</u>.
8. You'll have to wait here <u>until the end of the act</u>.
9. <u>After the signal</u>, the coach kept his eye on the ball.
10. <u>Watching from the sidelines</u>, the coach monitored every play.

Independent and Subordinate Clauses   373

> ▸ A **clause** is a group of words that has both a subject and a predicate.
> ▸ An **independent,** or **main, clause** expresses a complete thought. It can stand alone as a sentence.
> ▸ A **dependent**, or **subordinate**, **clause** needs an independent clause to complete its meaning. A dependent clause does not express a complete thought.

Written Practice

A. Write either *subordinate* or *independent* to describe each of the following clauses.

1. when will Ella arrive
2. before the cord breaks
3. because a bird told me
4. on the deck stood Marvin
5. as the cow stared at us
6. skiing is exhilarating
7. in July, it becomes very hot
8. the boat didn't sink
9. when the roof fell
10. if you are right
11. to stay would be a mistake
12. after the plane lands

B. Copy each underlined word group. Then label it *phrase* or *clause.*

(13) Although it is often called the teddy bear of Australia, the koala bear is not really a bear at all. (14) The koala, belonging to the marsupial family, is a small, furry animal with a broad face. (15) Koalas are highly selective in their choice of food, since they eat only certain kinds of eucalyptus leaves. (16) A koala baby, after remaining in the mother's pouch for five or six months, clings to its mother's back until it is weaned. (17) Until some years ago, koalas were hunted for their fur. (18) Millions were killed before a law was passed to protect them.

- **Writing Sentences** Write *phrase* or *clause* to identify each group of words. Then use the phrase or clause in a sentence of your own. Use a comma after a phrase or clause that begins a sentence.

19. lifting its head high
20. after she had danced
21. after the last test
22. to swim in the ocean
23. when the robins return
24. as the car approached
25. before the prices change
26. watched by the zebra
27. although no one asked
28. before the first of April

2 | Adjective Clauses

Subordinate clauses, like phrases, can be used like single words in sentences. You know that a word that modifies a noun or pronoun is an adjective. You also know that a phrase that modifies a noun or pronoun is an adjective phrase. You can probably guess, then, that a clause that modifies a noun or pronoun is an **adjective clause**.

ADJECTIVE: The <u>bright</u> sun cheered us.
ADJECTIVE PHRASE: The sun, <u>shining brightly,</u> cheered us.
ADJECTIVE CLAUSE: The sun, <u>which was shining brightly,</u> cheered us.

Adjective clauses are subordinate clauses. *Which was shining brightly* cannot stand by itself. To complete its meaning, it needs the independent clause *the sun cheered us*. Notice, as in the above example, that the adjective clause can interrupt the independent clause.

An adjective clause usually follows the word it modifies.

There must be someone <u>who can give us that information.</u>
The pineapple, <u>which was grown in Puerto Rico,</u> was delicious.
The animals <u>that escaped from the zoo</u> have been recaptured.

Words like *who, which,* and *that* introduce adjective clauses. These words are called **relative pronouns**. Relative pronouns relate the adjective clause to the modified word. For example, the relative pronoun *who* in the first of the three sentences above refers to the pronoun *someone. Which* in the second sentence refers to *pineapple. That* in the last sentence refers to *animals*.

Who, which, and *that* are the most common relative pronouns. *Who* is usually used to refer to people. *Which* usually refers to animals or things. *That* may be used to refer to animals, things, or people.

Where and *when* may also be used to introduce adjective clauses.

This is the classroom <u>where we meet.</u>
She came at a time <u>when we were very busy.</u>

You can use adjective clauses to help you write smoother sentences. Often, two sentences can be combined into one sentence with an adjective clause.

TWO SENTENCES: We bought a computer. It has proven useful.
ADJECTIVE CLAUSE: We bought a computer <u>that has proven useful.</u>

Try It Out

A. What noun or pronoun is modified by the underlined adjective clause? Find the relative pronoun in each clause.

   1. Mr. Ortega, <u>who is an electrical engineer</u>, comes from South America.
   2. The story <u>that we are discussing in class</u> is set in England.
   3. Stratford is the town <u>where the Shakespeare Festival is held</u>.
   4. The first thing we noticed was the painting, <u>which hung crookedly</u>.
   5. The woman <u>who is running for state senator</u> is our neighbor.

B. Identify each adjective clause. Tell which noun or pronoun it modifies. A sentence may have more than one adjective clause.

   6. A purebred dog is a dog that has a mother and father of the same breed.
   7. The American Kennel Club, which registers purebred dogs, lists more than 120 breeds.
   8. Those who own purebred dogs often receive pedigree papers from the club.
   9. A dog that has a pedigree must have ancestors that are known and registered.
   10. At the Animal Rescue League, where stray dogs are cared for, my friend found a dog that looks like a beagle, which is a type of hound.

C. Combine each pair of sentences into one sentence with an adjective clause. Use the relative pronoun given.

   11. The doctor lives next door (who). She has a noisy dog.
   12. It barks at anyone. Anyone passes by (who).
   13. My other neighbors have a dog. It never barks (that).
   14. A breed of dog does not bark (that). It is the basenji.

▸ An **adjective clause** is a subordinate clause that is used to modify a noun or a pronoun.

A **relative pronoun** such as *who*, *which*, or *that* usually introduces an adjective clause. The pronoun relates the clause to the word modified.

Written Practice

A. The adjective clauses in the following passage are underlined. For each clause, write the relative pronoun and the word modified.

(1) Australian Aborigines are members of tribes that once populated the entire continent of Australia. (2) Their ancestors were the first people who lived in Australia. (3) Those who study the culture of the Aborigines estimate that there were 300,000 at the time when the first European settlers arrived. (4) That number, which was reduced by more than half, is now on the increase again. (5) The different tribes, which are usually identified by a common language and common cultural patterns, numbered about 500. (6) In certain places where Aborigines lived long ago, there remain cave paintings that can still be seen and appreciated.

B. Copy each adjective clause. Write the word it modifies.

7. The dog breeds that are recognized by the American Kennel Club are divided into six groups.
8. The sporting group consists of dogs that were bred as bird dogs, which include pointers, setters, spaniels, and retrievers.
9. The nonsporting group, which is a miscellaneous category, covers dogs that are kept for show and companionship, such as the poodle.
10. People who like trailing game may have a dog of the hound group, which includes dogs that hunt by smell or sight.
11. Herders, guard dogs, sled dogs, and farm dogs are included among those that are classified as working dogs.
12. Anyone who likes smallish wire-haired dogs with busy whiskers and eyebrows will like the terrier group.
13. Toy dogs, which were named for their small size, include fifteen breeds that are kept as pets.

C. Rewrite each pair of sentences as a single sentence with an adjective clause. Use either *who* or *that* as the relative pronoun.

14. People like tiny dogs. Those people may own a Chihuahua.
15. Someone has a Saint Bernard. The person must like big dogs.
16. The breed has the tallest dogs. It is the Irish wolfhound.
17. There are wolfhounds. They stand 91 centimeters high.

● **Writing Sentences**   Write five sentences with adjective clauses.

3 | Adjective Clauses with *who, whom,* and *whose*

Notice the relative pronoun used in each of these sentences.

> Emily Dickinson, **who** lived in the 1800's, was a poet.
> She was influenced by the English writer Emily Brontë, **whom** she admired.
> Ralph Waldo Emerson was also a writer for **whom** she had great respect.
> Dickinson, **whose** life was spent alone, wrote with great intensity.

The choice of *who, whom,* or *whose* depends on how the relative pronoun is used *within its clause*. When the relative pronoun is the subject of the clause, then *who* is used.

> who lived in the 1800's *(subject of the verb* lived*)*

When the relative pronoun is the object of a verb or preposition, then the object pronoun *whom* is used.

> whom she admired *(object of the verb* admired*)*
> for whom she had great respect *(object of the preposition* for*)*

When a relative pronoun shows possession or a close connection, the possessive form *whose* is used.

> whose life was spent alone *(modifies* life*)*

Remember that it is the use of the relative pronoun *within its own clause* that determines which form is used. Nothing outside the adjective clause has any effect on the choice of *who, whom,* or *whose*. Look carefully at the clauses in these sentences.

> The poet **who** wrote those beautiful lines is Emily Dickinson.
> The poet **whom** I admire most is Emily Dickinson.

The sentences have the same independent clause: *The poet is Emily Dickinson.* The adjective clause in each sentence modifies the noun *poet.* The relative pronouns, however, are different because they are used differently *within the adjective clauses.*

> who wrote those beautiful lines *(subject of verb* wrote*)*
> whom I admire most *(object of verb* admire*)*

Try It Out

Complete each sentence with *who*, *whom*, or *whose*. Identify the subordinate clause.

1. Everyone _____ knows Mr. Arno enjoys his company.
2. Mr. Arno, _____ has five brothers, has only one sister.
3. He lives next door to his sister, _____ children he adores.
4. The children, for _____ he writes poems, are very fond of their uncle.
5. He has become a serious poet _____ work is being published.
6. A person _____ everyone likes, he is amusing, creative, and kind.

Use *who* when the relative pronoun is the subject of the adjective clause.

Use *whom* when the relative pronoun is the object of a verb or preposition in the adjective clause.

Use *whose* when the relative pronoun is possessive.

Written Practice

A. Write the adjective clause, adding *who*, *whom*, or *whose*.

1. Poe is a writer _____ tales of terror are often dramatized.
2. There are many to _____ such stories appeal.
3. Elliot, _____ is from England, came here only recently.
4. Do you know the name of the composer _____ wrote this piece?
5. The people _____ he represents support his policies.
6. Ariadne, _____ was the daughter of King Minos, aided Theseus.
7. Is she the astronomer _____ you met at the planetarium?
8. The artists _____ work I prefer use bold colors.

B. Rewrite each pair of sentences as a single sentence. Make the underlined sentence an adjective clause with *who*, *whom*, or *whose*.

9. We introduced ourselves to the guests. <u>They had just arrived.</u>
10. Mr. Lawrence was the speaker. <u>I heard him at the meeting.</u>
11. Ms. Lorenzo is the firefighter. <u>Her picture was in the paper.</u>
12. Christo is a friend. <u>I have great respect for him.</u>

• **Writing Sentences** Use *who*, *whom*, and *whose* in two sentences each.

4 | Restrictive and Nonrestrictive Clauses

You may have noticed that some adjective clauses are set off with commas while others are not.

> The girl <u>who will sing next</u> is Brian's sister.
> Laura, <u>who will sing next,</u> is Brian's sister.

When an adjective clause is needed to *identify* the word it modifies, no commas are used. When an adjective clause supplies *additional information* about the word it modifies, then it is set off with commas.

In the first example above, *who will sing next* identifies Brian's sister. No commas are used. In the second example, the same clause tells us that Brian's sister happens to be singing next. The name *Laura* identifies her, not the clause. Commas are used.

Sometimes the use of commas with an adjective clause changes the meaning of a sentence.

> The doctor treated the children <u>who had measles.</u> *(Only some of the children had measles. The doctor treated only those children.)*
> The doctor treated the children, <u>who had measles.</u> *(All of the children had measles. The doctor treated all of them.)*

A clause that is needed to identify a noun or pronoun is called a **restrictive clause**. A clause that gives added information about the noun or pronoun is called a **nonrestrictive clause**. Nonrestrictive clauses are set off with commas; restrictive clauses are not.

Compare the restrictive and nonrestrictive clauses in these sentences.

> RESTRICTIVE: Al showed me the letter **that** <u>he had just read.</u>
> NONRESTRICTIVE: Al showed me her letter, **which** <u>he had just read.</u>
>
> RESTRICTIVE: The house **that** <u>is painted green</u> is ours.
> NONRESTRICTIVE: Our house, **which** <u>is painted green,</u> is the next one.

The relative pronoun *that* is used in the restrictive clause, while *which* is used in the nonrestrictive clause. This is a distinction that is usually observed in careful or formal English. You will sometimes see *which* used with a restrictive clause. To practice careful writing, however, use *that* with restrictive clauses in the exercises here.

Try It Out

A. Identify the adjective clause as restrictive or nonrestrictive. Tell whether commas should be added.

1. The people who are buying our house are from Minneapolis.
2. Dickens whose books I enjoy lived in the eighteenth century.
3. Gilbert's which is a fine restaurant is on State Street.
4. The broccoli that you cooked was delicious.

B. Choose the correct relative pronoun for careful writing.

5. The window, (which, that) was open, looked out on a meadow.
6. The one window (which, that) was open looked out on a meadow.
7. The plane (which, that) we took to Ireland arrived on time.

▸ A **restrictive clause** identifies the noun or pronoun it modifies. It is not set off with commas.
▸ A **nonrestrictive clause** gives added information about the noun or pronoun it modifies. It is set off with commas.

Written Practice

A. Copy each adjective clause. Add commas if it is nonrestrictive.

1. Here are the notes that you wanted.
2. The Carlsons who were moving to Iowa were the guests of honor.
3. The herbs that grow in his garden are parsley, thyme, and basil.
4. Aunt Eleanor who is my mother's sister is the attorney general.
5. The attorney who is drawing up the contract is Mr. Swenson.

B. Rewrite each sentence, making the adjective clause nonrestrictive.

6. We visited the bazaar that was a few blocks from the hotel.
7. The book that Monty gave me was a perfect choice.
8. The dancers who were rehearsing wore leg warmers.
9. I sent a card to my cousin who was traveling in Scandinavia.

• **Writing Sentences** Write three sentences with restrictive clauses and three with nonrestrictive clauses.

5 | Adverb Clauses

An **adverb clause** is a subordinate clause that is used as an adverb.

ADVERB: The first snow fell <u>today</u>.
ADVERB CLAUSE: The first snow fell <u>while I was sleeping</u>.

Most adverb clauses modify verbs. Some clauses, however, modify adjectives and other adverbs.

Check your equipment <u>before you do the experiment</u>. *(modifies verb)*

The ring was less valuable <u>than we had hoped</u>. *(modifies adjective)*

I walked faster <u>than I normally do</u>. *(modifies adverb)*

An adverb clause is introduced by a **subordinating conjunction** such as *before*, *while*, and *than*. You learned about subordinating conjunctions in Unit 1, when you studied complex sentences.

Adverb clauses can usually take different positions in sentences.

They began to shiver <u>when the cold rain fell</u>.
<u>When the cold rain fell</u>, they began to shiver.

A comma is used after an adverb clause that begins a sentence.

Often you can use adverb clauses to combine short sentences and make your writing smoother. One of the sentences becomes an adverb clause when a subordinating conjunction is added.

TWO SENTENCES: The cold rain fell. They began to shiver.
ADVERB CLAUSE: **When** <u>the cold rain fell</u>, they began to shiver.

Try It Out

A. Identify each adverb clause.

1. Stephen Vincent Benét's first book was published when he was only seventeen years old.
2. Before he turned twenty, he had published a second volume.
3. Recognition came as soon as *John Brown's Body* appeared.
4. In this work, Benét described the Civil War as it was seen by people of both the North and the South.
5. After this was published, it received the Pulitzer Prize.

B. Where are commas needed in these sentences?

    6. Until April comes we shall wear thermal underwear.
    7. Since they give light candles are useful as well as decorative.
    8. Wherever you go today take your umbrella with you.

C. Combine the sentences. Use the subordinating conjunction given.

    9. Horace walked away from the dog. It growled at him (after).
    10. We waited (while). We read every word of the newspaper.
    11. We biked all the way home. The rain stopped (when).

▸ An **adverb clause** is a subordinate clause used as an adverb.
▸ An adverb clause is introduced by a **subordinating conjunction**.
▸ Introductory adverb clauses are followed by commas.

Written Practice

A. Copy the adverb clauses.

    1. Since the Sears Tower was built, I have visited it often.
    2. From the top, one can see for miles if the day is clear.
    3. Chicago spreads out below as though it were built of blocks.
    4. When you move around the deck, you see different views.
    5. The city view is especially spectacular after the sun goes down.

B. Write each sentence, adding commas where needed.

    6. Unless everyone cooperates the project will fail.
    7. Although it seemed impossible the climbers reached the top.
    8. When the events were set in motion no one could stop them.
    9. They visit their grandparents whenever they can.

C. Combine the sentence pairs. Use the subordinating conjunction given. Add commas where needed.

    10. The doors open at 6 o'clock (when). We will be there.
    11. We talked for an hour. Everyone else had left (after).
    12. Josh has two copies (since). He will give us one.

● **Writing Sentences**   Write five sentences with adverb clauses.

6 | Subordinating Conjunctions

Choosing the Right Conjunction

You have seen that subordinating conjunctions introduce adverb clauses. When a subordinating conjunction is used with a clause, it makes that clause subordinate to, or dependent on, another clause.

The game ended. *(complete thought)*
<u>when</u> the game ended *(incomplete—what happened when the game ended?)*

<u>When</u> the game ended, the crowd left. *(complete thought)*

Here is a list of common subordinating conjunctions.

after	before	till
although	even though	unless
as	if	until
as if	in order that	when
as long as	provided (that)	whenever
as soon as	since	where
as though	so that	wherever
because	than	while

Different subordinating conjunctions express different kinds of relationships between the clauses.

Whenever I hear music, I want to dance. *(when)*
My little brother wants to go **wherever** I go. *(where)*
You talk **as though** it were my fault. *(how)*
The door squeaks **because** the hinges need oiling. *(why)*
Cathy is better at this **than** I am. *(comparison)*

When you use a subordinating conjunction, think about the meaning you intend. Then choose the conjunction that best expresses that meaning. Notice how the meaning can change with the conjunction.

<u>Whenever</u> I listen to my favorite song, I cry.
<u>Until</u> I listen to my favorite song, I cry.
<u>Unless</u> I listen to my favorite song, I cry.
<u>After</u> I listen to my favorite song, I cry.
<u>Even though</u> I listen to my favorite song, I cry.

Try It Out

Supply an appropriate subordinating conjunction to relate the clauses.

1. Negotiations began _____ the workers walked off the job.
2. The jurors asked for the trial records _____ they could review the testimony.
3. _____ people would cooperate, this land could become productive.
4. He picked up the flute _____ he were going to play.
5. _____ the waves were high, the lifeguard raised a red flag.
6. _____ I'm scared, I'm going to jump.

Pronouns After *as* and *than*

In comparisons with *as* and *than*, the adverb clause is often shortened. What word can be left out of the sentence below?

> Emily is younger than Bea is.

The sentence could also read, *Emily is younger than Bea.* In a shortened clause, be careful to use the right form of the pronoun after *than* or *as.*

> INCORRECT: Stuart is taller than him.
> **CORRECT**: Stuart is taller than <u>he</u> (is).

Would you say *than him is?* The verb *is* can be left out, but the pronoun *he* doesn't change. If you complete the clause in your mind, you should have no problem with the form of the pronoun.

Now look at this sentence.

> I know Stuart better than (I know) her.

Here, not only the verb but also the subject can be omitted, leaving only the object pronoun *her.* Again, complete the sentence in your mind, and you will know which form of the pronoun to use.

The form of the pronoun can affect the way you understand a sentence.

> I know Stuart better than (I know) <u>her.</u>
> I know Stuart better than <u>she</u> (knows Stuart).

Remember to complete the clause in your mind, and you will know which pronoun form to use.

Try It Out

Give the missing part of the adverb clause, and choose the right pronoun. If there are two possibilities, give both.

1. Hillary can do this better than (I, me).
2. Do you admire Catherine more than (he, him)?
3. I certainly trust William as much as (she, her).
4. Pat was even more surprised than Yoshi and (I, me).

► A **subordinating conjunction** relates the subordinate clause to the independent clause.

In an incomplete clause with *as* or *than*, use the pronoun you would use if the clause were complete.

Written Practice

A. Write two subordinating conjunctions that relate the clauses in an appropriate way.

1. ____ it becomes colder, we shall have to light a fire.
2. The new bottling plant will open ____ the road is completed.
3. ____ Miriam joined the game, the score didn't change.
4. He will sew the button on ____ he has time.
5. ____ they watch too much television, their eyes look glazed.
6. Trent will skip his lunch hour ____ he can leave early.

B. Write each sentence, filling in the missing words in the adverb clause and supplying the correct pronoun. If a sentence can be completed in *two* ways, write both alternatives.

7. No one could be more certain than (he, him).
8. Ronald wrote as much of the report as (she, her).
9. Ms. Stiglitz knows Derek better than (I, me).
10. The captain praised Eleanor as much as (we, us).
11. They are certainly as capable as Larry and (I, me).

● **Writing Sentences**   Use each word to introduce a subordinate clause.

12. since   13. than   14. while   15. as if   16. if

7 | Noun Clauses

After having learned about adjective and adverb clauses, you can probably anticipate what a noun clause is. A **noun clause** is a subordinate clause that acts as a noun in a sentence.

Nouns and noun clauses are used in the same way. In each pair of sentences below, the underlined noun or pronoun and its modifiers are replaced by a noun clause.

SUBJECT:	The story is probably true.
	What you say is probably true.
DIRECT OBJECT:	I don't know his number.
	I don't know how he can be reached.
INDIRECT OBJECT:	Give Claire the message.
	Give whoever asks the message.
OBJECT OF PREPOSITION:	I sent the notice to everyone.
	I sent the notice to whoever was interested.
PREDICATE NOUN:	That is my request.
	That is what I would like to do.

A variety of words can be used to introduce noun clauses. Here are some of them.

how	what	where	which	whoever
if	whatever	wherever	whichever	why
that	when	whether	who	

Notice that many of the words that are used to introduce other types of subordinate clauses are also used to introduce noun clauses. Consider the clauses in these sentences.

NOUN CLAUSE: The frog noticed that a fly was approaching.
ADJECTIVE CLAUSE: The fly that was approaching avoided the frog.

In the first sentence, the clause with *that* is the object of the verb *noticed*; it is a noun clause. In the second sentence, the clause with *that* modifies the noun *fly*; it is an adjective clause. To tell such clauses apart, you have to determine how they are used in the sentence.

Try It Out

A. Tell how each underlined noun clause is used—as a subject, direct object, indirect object, object of a preposition, or predicate noun.

1. <u>What we heard this morning</u> is <u>what we heard yesterday morning.</u>
2. The police learned <u>that the criminal was still in the city.</u>
3. We're prepared for <u>whatever happens.</u>
4. Ask <u>whoever answers the first question</u> another question.

B. Identify the noun clauses in these sentences. How are they used?

5. What you just said does not explain why you are late.
6. Send whoever is interested an invitation.
7. The problem is that the shoe is on the wrong foot.
8. I shall mail the information to whoever requests it.

> ▶ A **noun clause** is a subordinate clause that acts as a noun.

Written Practice

Copy each noun clause, and label it *subject, direct object, indirect object, object of a preposition,* or *predicate noun.*

1. When the train will arrive is what we want to know.
2. In this case, things are what they appear to be.
3. The chairperson suggested that the committee meet more often.
4. Those gloves are what I would like for my father.
5. Offer whoever arrives first the seats in the front row.
6. The captain insisted that the passengers go below.
7. The petition will be signed by whoever supports the issue.
8. The silver cup belongs to whoever wins the race.
9. Tell whoever arrives early that the doors open at nine o'clock.
10. That the tree survived the storm was a great relief.

● **Writing Sentences** Write five sentences with noun clauses. The noun clause in each sentence should have a different function—subject, direct object, indirect object, object of a preposition, and predicate noun.

8 | Noun Clauses with *who* and *whom*

When you worked with adjective clauses, you learned how to use the relative pronouns *who* and *whom*. *Who* is used as a subject within the clause, and *whom* is used as an object within the clause. The pronouns *who* and *whom* are used in the same way in noun clauses. Look carefully at these sentences.

> **Who** will go is not clear. *(subject of* will go*)*
> **Whom** you meant is not clear. *(object of* meant*)*

In both sentences, the independent clause is the same. The independent clause has no effect on the choice of *who* or *whom* in the subordinate clause. To decide between *who* and *whom*, look only within the noun clause.

Do not confuse the use of the pronoun in the clause with the use of the clause in the sentence.

> I know **who** is going. *(clause is a direct object;* who *is the subject of its clause)*
> **Whom** you meant is not clear. *(clause is the subject;* whom *is an object in its clause)*

Whoever and *whomever* are also used in noun clauses, and they are distinguished in the same way. *Whoever* is used as a subject within its clause. *Whomever* is used as an object within its clause.

> **Whoever** is ready can begin. *(subject of* is*)*
> **Whomever** you called did not receive the message. *(object of* called*)*

Pay special attention when noun clauses are used as the objects of prepositions.

> Give the library book to **whoever** wants it. *(*whoever *is subject of* wants*)*
> Give the library book to **whomever** you choose. *(*whomever *is object of* choose*)*

Neither *whoever* nor *whomever* is the object of *to*. The whole noun clause is the object of *to*.

Try It Out

Identify the noun clause, and choose the correct pronoun.

1. (Who, Whom) they will nominate is still a mystery.
2. (Whoever, Whomever) they choose will probably accept.
3. Tell me (who, whom) is likely to run for that office.
4. I'll vote for (whoever, whomever) will do the best job.
5. The candidate chosen was exactly (who, whom) you predicted.
6. Give my congratulations to (whoever, whomever) chose her.

> Use *who* and *whoever* as subjects in noun clauses.
> Use *whom* and *whomever* as objects of verbs or prepositions in noun clauses.

Written Practice

A. Write each noun clause, using the correct pronoun.

1. All calls will be taken by (whoever, whomever) is home.
2. Tell (whoever, whomever) calls the reason for my absence.
3. (Whoever, Whomever) you called must live out of town.
4. Did the operator say (who, whom) was calling?
5. I can't imagine (who, whom) would call from that city.
6. Give the message to (whoever, whomever) you choose.
7. (Who, Whom) he called yesterday is a secret.

B. Complete each sentence with *who, whom, whoever,* or *whomever.*

8. _____ is interested in marine life will enjoy the aquarium.
9. Did the principal say _____ she would see next?
10. The block party is for _____ wants to come.
11. _____ you saw is gone now.
12. The article indicated _____ was involved in the rescue attempt.
13. Tell _____ is going on the tour the history of the town.
14. The suit will be bought by _____ it fits.

● **Writing Sentences** For each word, write two sentences using the word in a noun clause.

15. who   16. whom   17. whoever   18. whomever

9 | Writing Well with Clauses

Deleting Pronouns

The deletion of only one word can sometimes improve the flow of a sentence. What word has been deleted in the second adjective clause in each sentence pair below?

> The art exhibit **that** we attended was crowded.
> The art exhibit we attended was crowded.
> The people **whom** we met there were art lovers.
> The people we met there were art lovers.

Relative pronouns used as objects can sometimes be deleted to create smoother, more direct sentences.

Some words that introduce noun clauses can also be deleted.

> Mr. McCoombs did not realize **that** we were standing there.
> Mr. McCoombs did not realize we were standing there.

Only certain words that introduce clauses can be omitted. Pronouns that act as subjects in their clauses can never be deleted. Relative pronouns that follow prepositions cannot be deleted either.

> The exhibit featured artists **who** work with metal.
> Give it to **whomever** you like.

Try It Out

Find the adjective clause or noun clause in each sentence. Then tell whether the introductory word can be deleted.

1. The pictures that you took turned out well.
2. They show some of the other tourists who accompanied us.
3. Several of those whom we met are planning to visit us.
4. I am certain that the Chuns will arrive soon.
5. Do you know whose house they will visit first?
6. I am looking forward to seeing the new friends that we made.
7. I know that they will enjoy visiting our area.

Using Clauses

When you add a phrase or a clause to a sentence, you are adding a related idea to the main idea.

MAIN IDEA: Our neighbor fixed the faucet.
ADDED IDEA: Our neighbor is a plumber.
COMBINED IDEAS: Our neighbor, who is a plumber, fixed the faucet.

If you put each idea into its own sentence, your writing will be monotonous and unclear. You force your reader to guess how your ideas are related.

Our kitchen sink developed a bad leak. We called our neighbor. He is a plumber.

When you combine the sentences, the relationships become clearer and your writing becomes more interesting.

When our kitchen sink developed a bad leak, we called our neighbor, who is a plumber.

Often sentences can be combined in different ways. How you combine them will often depend upon the meaning you want to convey. You have already seen how the meaning can change when ideas are combined with different subordinating conjunctions.

Before the tide began to rise, we loaded the boat.
As soon as the tide began to rise, we loaded the boat.
We loaded the boat because the tide began to rise.

Adjective clauses, too, can be used to combine ideas in different ways.

TWO SENTENCES: The film is in the camera.
It has been exposed.

ONE SENTENCE: The film that has been exposed is in the camera.
The film, which has been exposed, is in the camera.
The film, which is in the camera, has been exposed.
The film that is in the camera has been exposed.

Learning to write well involves learning to combine ideas. Subordinate clauses allow you to combine ideas in different ways. The proper use of these clauses can help you achieve variety, interest, and clarity in your writing.

Try It Out

A. Combine each group of sentences into a single sentence with one or more subordinate clauses. Use the connecting words given. Where should commas be used?

1. It had grown late (although). Everyone was still awake.
2. Tourists visit the island (who). They seldom want to leave.
3. The mystery story held me in its grip. I had started to read it after dinner (that). The clock struck midnight (until).
4. The old factory had lain neglected for years (which). It has been visited by thousands of people. It was converted into a shopping mall (since).

B. Using subordinate clauses, combine each group of sentences in two ways to form two different sentences. Use different subordinate clauses or different combining words or both. Indicate where commas should appear. The first sentence group has been done for you.

5. Clara raised the goat. The goat won first prize.
   Clara raised the goat that won first prize.
   The goat that Clara raised won first prize.
6. The storm ended. We left the cottage.
7. The rabbit was eating the berries. It did not notice me.
8. I did my Latin homework. I waited for Chet. He is always late.
9. The curtain opened. The audience saw only a spotlighted stool. The audience had been growing restless.

Written Practice

A. Using subordinate clauses, rewrite each group of sentences as a combined sentence in two different ways. Use different subordinate clauses, different combining words, or both. Add commas where needed.

1. I had read the last chapter. I did not know the murderer.
2. Her hair was pulled back tightly. It was the color of copper.
3. Franklin is Walter's cousin. He rented the house next door. He and his family moved here from Phoenix.
4. The Wus brought the flowers. The flowers are on the hall table.
5. The bassoon player felt nervous. She played in public. She always appeared confident.

B. Rewrite the passage, using adjective or adverb clauses to combine related ideas. Where appropriate, delete the word that introduces a subordinate clause.

Some persons believe that the name butterfly comes from the bright yellow color of many butterflies. The monarch butterfly is common in the Americas. It has vivid orange and black coloring. That monarchs taste bad to birds and insects is known to scientists. These scientists study butterflies. Birds and insects see the vivid colors of the monarch. They stay away. A butterfly takes advantage of this fact. It is the viceroy. The viceroy is quite edible. Its enemies stay away from it. It looks like the monarch.

Check Your Writing

Review your passage about butterflies. Ask yourself these questions.

A. Are my sentences correct?

1. Is every subordinate clause used with an independent clause?
2. Have I used *who* as a subject and *whom* as an object within clauses?
3. Have I distinguished between *that* and *which*?
4. Have I used commas with nonrestrictive clauses?
5. Have I used commas after introductory adverb clauses?
6. Have I used the correct form of the pronoun after *as* and *than*?

B. Are my sentences clear?

1. Have I used subordinate clauses to join related ideas?
2. Have I used appropriate subordinating conjunctions?

C. Are my sentences direct?

Have I deleted words that introduce clauses where appropriate?

D. Are my sentences interesting?

1. Have I used subordinate clauses to combine and vary my sentences?
2. Have I used adverb clauses to begin some sentences?

• **Writing a Paragraph**   Write a passage about someone with an occupation that interests you—a mechanic, a pilot, a magician, a teacher, for example. Use five or more subordinate clauses. Then review your passage. Ask yourself the questions above, and make all needed changes.

10 Using Words Correctly

like, as if; where, that; whether

Remember that a preposition introduces a phrase, while a subordinating conjunction introduces a clause.

The word *like* is a preposition. Do not use it to introduce a clause. Instead, use a subordinating conjunction like *as if* or *as though*.

CORRECT: They move <u>like</u> ballet dancers.
INCORRECT: They move like they were ballet dancers.
CORRECT: They move <u>as if</u> (<u>as though</u>) they were ballet dancers.

When *where* introduces a noun clause, it should refer to place. It should not be used instead of the introductory word *that*.

CORRECT: I see <u>where</u> the car is parked.
INCORRECT: I see where you have a new car.
CORRECT: I see <u>that</u> you have a new car.

Also avoid using *as* instead of *whether* to introduce a noun clause after a verb like *know*.

INCORRECT: I don't know as I can go with you.
CORRECT: I don't know <u>whether</u> I can go with you.

Use *like* as a preposition. Use *as if* and *as though* as subordinating conjunctions.

Avoid using *where* instead of *that* to introduce a noun clause.

Avoid using *as* instead of *whether* to introduce a noun clause.

Practice

A. Tell which sentences are correct. Revise the sentences that are not correct.

1. We heard where we're going to have a lot of work today.
2. The ballerina's arms fluttered like they were the wings of a swan.
3. The ballerina's arms fluttered like the wings of a swan.
4. We don't know as we'll be able to hear the president speak.
5. It appears as if we're going to be very busy today.
6. I don't know whether we'll have time to go shopping.
7. I read where the play is an excellent one.
8. Yesterday Cory sounded like he had something on his mind.
9. He felt like he was getting a cold.
10. Sam didn't know as he would sing with the chorus this year.

B. Choose the correct word for each sentence.

11. I heard (where, that) you did well on the science test.
12. Manuel isn't sure (as, whether) he's interested in the play.
13. He doesn't know (as, whether) he really wants to try out for the part.
14. The skunk looked (like, as if) it was leaving at last.
15. It appears (like, as though) the plane will be delayed.
16. I read (where, that) Bonnie entered the science contest.
17. Don't you think the puppy looks (like, as if) a panda?
18. His fur feels (like, as if) a soft piece of velvet.
19. I don't know (as, whether) it's supposed to rain today or not.
20. Did you hear (where, that) we may have a major storm tonight?
21. It certainly doesn't look (like, as though) it's going to snow.
22. It looks (like, as if) she will be the winner.

- **Writing Sentences**   Write a sentence each for *like, as if, where, that, whether.*

Building Vocabulary

Idioms

Imagine that you are new in this country and do not know English well. You ask someone for directions. That person says: "Pay attention. First, take a bus." You are very confused. "Pay attention? I can pay money, but how do I pay attention? And why should I steal a bus?"

Expressions like *pay attention* and *take a bus* are idioms. An **idiom** is a phrase whose meaning cannot be understood from the meanings of the individual words. Every language has its own idioms.

Think about the word-for-word meanings of these phrases. Then think about the meanings of the idioms.

take a drive	keep an eye on	put up with
dress up	have your heart set on	give yourself away

Many prepositions are used idiomatically. In such cases, you must be sure to use the right preposition.

run out of (something)	angry with (someone)	agree with (someone)
run out on (someone)	angry about (something)	agree to (something)

> ▶ An **idiom** is a phrase whose meaning cannot be understood from the meanings of the individual words.

Practice

Substitute a word that is not an idiom for the underlined idiom.

1. Carlos <u>made up his mind</u> to leave early.
2. You can <u>get in touch with</u> him after the holiday.
3. The alarm <u>went off</u> at six o'clock.
4. Ms. Eboli <u>dropped in on</u> us yesterday.

• **Writing Sentences**   Write a sentence for each idiomatic expression.

5. agree with   6. come about   7. spill the beans   8. take charge of

Review

- **Independent and Subordinate Clauses** *(pp. 373–374)* Copy the underlined word group. Label it *phrase, subordinate,* or *independent.*

  (1) The gnu, <u>known also as the wildebeest</u>, is an African antelope. **(2)** <u>Because of its massive shoulders, thick neck, and long head</u>, the gnu is a big animal. **(3)** Despite its large body, <u>the gnu stands on thin legs</u>. **(4)** It can travel fast <u>since it takes long strides</u>.

- **Adjective Clauses** *(pp. 375–377)* Copy each adjective clause, underlining the relative pronoun. Write the word it modifies.

  (5) Sir Isaac Goldsmid, who was a financier, was England's first Jewish baronet. **(6)** His efforts brought about the passage of a bill that granted civil and political rights to English Jews. **(7)** His son became England's first Jewish barrister, which means trial lawyer.

- ***Who, Whom, Whose* in Adjective Clauses** *(pp. 378–379)* Write *who, whom,* or *whose* to correctly complete each sentence.

  8. The person ____ left these gloves has not come back for them.
  9. The singer ____ we heard last night captivated the audience.
  10. I wonder ____ books these are.

- **Restrictive and Nonrestrictive Clauses** *(pp. 380–381)* If the sentence is punctuated correctly, write *C.* Otherwise, write it correctly.

  11. The Canadian Eskimos who live in igloos do so only in winter.
  12. In summer, they live in tents that are made of sealskin.
  13. The igloos which are made from blocks of snow are dome-shaped.

- **Adverb Clauses** *(pp. 382–383)* Write the adverb clauses, adding commas where needed.

  (14) Since they were considered great delicacies oranges have been cultivated since ancient times. **(15)** Orange cultivation probably spread as the Romans marched on their conquests. **(16)** Before Columbus sailed orange trees were common in the Canary Islands.

- **Subordinating Conjunctions** *(pp. 384–386)* Write two subordinating conjunctions to complete each sentence.

   17. ____ we arrived home, the snow began.
   18. Helene practices the guitar ____ she has time.
   19. ____ the chorus finishes rehearsing, we shall leave.

   Write the pronoun that correctly completes each sentence.

   20. Carolla is taller than (he, him).
   21. They got fewer hits than Betsy and (I, me).
   22. Kenneth sings as well as (she, her).

- **Noun Clauses** *(pp. 387–388)* List every noun clause. Write *subject, direct object, indirect object, predicate noun,* or *object of preposition.*

   23. Why anyone wants to go there is a mystery to me.
   24. That is what I wanted.
   25. Take whatever you need and give the rest to whoever wants it.

- ***Who* and *Whom* in Noun Clauses** *(pp. 389–390)* Write *who, whom, whoever,* or *whomever* to correctly complete each sentence.

   26. He was appointed by ____ was in charge at the time.
   27. Do you know ____ they hired for the position?
   28. ____ they choose will appreciate the job.
   29. I wonder ____ painted that picture.

- **Writing Well with Clauses** *(pp. 391–394)* Rewrite this passage as two sentences, using subordinate clauses.

   30–31. A parachute is an umbrella-like apparatus. It is used to slow a body falling through the air. Parachutes have many uses today. They were originally used only to escape from damaged planes.

- **Using Words Correctly** *(pp. 395–396)* Rewrite each sentence correctly.

   32. I heard where Mike's class had a surprise quiz today.
   33. I don't know as I'm ready to take the exam.
   34. You sound like you're really worried.

- **Building Vocabulary** *(p. 397)* Write the meaning of each idiom.

   35. drop a line   **36.** now and then   **37.** give up   **38.** hand out

Maintain

- **Prepositional Phrases** *(pp. 328–330)* Copy each prepositional phrase. Underline the object of the preposition. Then write the word the phrase modifies.

  1. The trees on the mountains change color in the autumn.
  2. By the end of October, giant buckets of brilliant paint seem to have been splashed over the mountains.
  3. Every year we drive to Vermont to see the autumn colors.
  4. During the winter, we think about the beauty of the autumn.

- **Verbals / Participial, Gerund, and Infinitive Phrases** *(pp. 331–340, 342–344)* Copy each verbal or verbal phrase and label it *participle, gerund,* or *infinitive.*

  5. Lying in bed, I could smell the bacon frying.
  6. Waiting for the results is the hardest part of the exam.
  7. The exhausted and frightened climbers radioed to get help.
  8. One way to attract attention is to put up interesting posters.

- **Possessives with Gerunds** *(p. 341)* Write the form that correctly completes the sentence.

  9. (His, Him) not finishing the report is unusual.
  10. No one understands (me, my) wanting to play the cello.
  11. We appreciated (Gerald, Gerald's) changing the tire for us.
  12. (Me, My) going to sleep was not a great move.
  13. I'll never forget (them, their) coming out at midnight.
  14. Do you think (our, us) putting out all that effort will pay off?

- **Writing Well with Phrases** *(pp. 345–348)* Rewrite each pair of sentences as a single sentence, using the kind of phrase indicated.

  15. The kitten is named Rosie (participial). It is bright orange.
  16. To climb that mountain (infinitive). That is my goal.
  17. Kay will write a hit song (gerund). That is her ambition.
  18. Wilhelm is visiting his aunt. She lives in Austria (prepositional).

- **Independent and Subordinate Clauses** *(pp. 373–374)* Write *phrase, dependent clause,* or *independent clause* for each group.

   19. before the play
   20. before we go
   21. to do well is my goal
   22. when you leave

- **Adjective Clauses** *(pp. 375–381)* Write the adjective clause, supplying the correct relative pronoun. Add commas where needed.

   23. The representative _____ introduced the bill is from our district.
   24. The train _____ is already late will be delayed further by the storm.
   25. The person on _____ we rely most is Mr. Van der Kroef.

- **Adverb Clauses** *(pp. 382–386)* Write the adverb clause, supplying an appropriate subordinating conjunction.

   26. _____ you change your mind, you can remain here.
   27. The plane bounced _____ it traveled through the stormy area.
   28. _____ we saw it happening, we couldn't believe it.

- **Noun Clauses** *(pp. 387–390)* Choose the correct form, and write the noun clause.

   29. I don't know (who, whom) will be there.
   30. Tell (whoever, whomever) is interested that the storm is over.
   31. (Who, Whom) I met yesterday is my secret.

- **Writing Well with Clauses** *(pp. 391–394)* Use a subordinate clause to combine each pair of sentences.

   32. Bennet grew the chrysanthemums. They won the prize.
   33. Marcello had had a tiring day. He left the party early.

- **Using Words Correctly** *(pp. 349–350, 395–396)* Write the correct form.

   34. Please choose (between, among) the red and the blue pens.
   35. I got the recipe (off, from) Gene.
   36. The car sounded (as if, like) something was wrong.

- **Building Vocabulary** *(p. 351)* Choose the correct word.

   37. The rocky (aisle, isle) was (bare, bear) of vegetation.
   38. The deer stood (stationary, stationery) as we passed.

UNIT 18

Literature

1 | Plot and Foreshadowing

In this story, Nasr-ed-Din Hodja proves a point to his friends in a humorous and surprising way.

One Candle Power

Perhaps Nasr-ed-Din Hodja[1] had been sitting too long in the warm house, swapping yarns with his friends. The boasts were growing bigger and bigger. None was bigger than the Hodja's.

"I could stand all night in the snow without any fire to warm me," the Hodja declared.

"No one could do that!" One of the men shivered as he looked through the window at the falling snow.

"I could!" The Hodja spread his hands over the open pan of burning coals. "I'll do it this very night."

"You can't!"

"I will! If I have so much as a glow of fire to warm myself, I'll—I'll—I'll give a feast for you all at my house tomorrow!"

The wager was on.

The friends of Nasr-ed-Din Hodja went home to their warm beds, while he stood alone in the snow-draped market square. He had never realized how much longer the hours were at night than in the daytime. He had never realized how many hours there were in the night. Once in a while, a prowling dog or an adventuring cat would sniff at him and then slink off to a snugger spot. The cold snow swathing his feet and tickling his neck was hard enough to bear. Harder still was the sleepiness that plagued him. It would never do to fall asleep in the snow. He must keep awake to stamp his cold feet and beat his cold arms. He found that it was easier to fight off sleep if he fastened his eyes on the flickering candle in Mehmet Ali's house across the market square. There was something cheering about the wavering of that tiny flame, which helped his tired eyes stay open.

Morning came at last. Curious men met the shivering and yawning Hodja on his way home. They asked about his night and marveled at what he had done.

---

[1] NASR-ED-DIN HODJA (nä′sred din′hō jä′): the name of the clever man in this story.

"How did you keep awake all night?" they asked.

"I fixed my eyes on a flickering candle in Mehmet Ali's house," he answered.

"A candle?"

"A burning candle?"

"Did you say a candle?"

"Of course!" The Hodja saw no harm in watching a candle.

"A lighted candle gives flame. Flame gives heat. You were warming yourself by the heat of that candle. You have lost your wager."

At first, the Hodja tried to laugh at their joke, but he soon found that they were not joking. For once, the Hodja was too tired to argue successfully. Try as he would, he could not convince his friends that a candle in a distant house could give no warmth to a cold man standing in a snowy market square.

"What time shall we come for the feast at your house tonight?" The laughing men gathered about the Hodja, insisting that they had won the wager.

"Come at sunset," said the Hodja. He plodded drearily toward home. He was cold and very tired, but he was thinking—and thinking hard.

Just after the muezzin's[1] musical voice sent the sunset call to prayer trilling over Ak Shehir[2], a group of men knocked at Nasr-ed-Din Hodja's street gate. It creaked open for them. They walked across the courtyard and left their shoes in a row beside the house door. They entered the Hodja's house and sat cross-legged on the floor.

"Dinner is not quite ready." It was the Hodja's voice from the kitchen.

"Oh, that's all right," called the men. "We are in no hurry."

They waited. There was an occasional footstep in the kitchen, but no sound of clattering dishes. They sniffed the air to guess what the feast might be, but they could smell no cooking food. They waited—and waited—and waited.

"I hope you are not hungry," called the Hodja from the kitchen. "Dinner is not quite ready yet."

"Perhaps we could help," suggested a hungry guest.

"Fine," called the Hodja. "You might all come out in the kitchen to help."

The men, glad of anything to do, stretched their cramped legs. As each man entered the kitchen, there passed over his face a look of surprise and then a sheepish grin.

---

[1] MUEZZIN (myo͞o ez′ in): in Moslem countries, a crier who calls the faithful to prayer.
[2] AK SHEHIR (äk′shə hēr′): a town in Turkey.

There stood the Hodja earnestly stirring the contents of a big copper kettle which was suspended high in the air. Far below it burned one flickering candle.

"Just a few minutes!" The Hodja, standing a-tiptoe, peered into the cold kettle. "It should boil before long. A candle gives so much heat, you know!"

Alice Geer Kelsey

For Discussion

1. What bet did the Hodja make with his friends? What did he promise to do if he lost the bet?
2. Why do you think the Hodja used a candle to heat the large copper kettle? What does this action tell you about this man?
3. The arrangement of events in a story is called the **plot.** It is the bare outline of what happens in the order that each event occurs. What is the plot in this story?
4. Sometimes a writer will give a clue, perhaps mention an object, early in the story that will have importance later on. This technique is called **foreshadowing.** Good foreshadowing is an excellent way to keep a reader interested and involved in the plot. When is the candle first mentioned in this story? How do the Hodja's friends make use of the candle? When did you first suspect that the Hodja would use the candle to outsmart his friends?

Activities

Write the plot for a story in which the main character outsmarts someone because of some wrong he or she did. The following plot is an example:

A woman borrows a kettle from a man and returns it along with a smaller one. She explains that while she had the kettle, it gave birth to the smaller one. By rights, therefore, both kettles belong to the man. The man knows that this explanation is ridiculous but agrees with it because he wants both kettles. At a later date, the woman once again borrows the kettle, but this time she keeps it. The man asks for the kettle's return; the woman replies that she cannot return it as it died. The man protests that kettles cannot die. Whereupon the woman explains that if something can give birth, it can die. Because of his greed, the man is minus his kettle.

2 | Simile and Metaphor

In these poems, Eve Merriam uses comparison in an original way.

Simile: Willow and Ginkgo

The willow is like an etching,
Fine-lined against the sky.
The ginkgo[1] is like a crude sketch,
Hardly worthy to be signed.

The willow's music is like a soprano,   5
Delicate and thin.
The ginkgo's tune is like a chorus
With everyone joining in.

The willow is sleek as a velvet-nosed calf;
The ginkgo is leathery as an old bull.   10
The willow's branches are like silken thread;
The ginkgo's like stubby rough wool.

The willow is like a nymph with streaming hair;
Wherever it grows, there is green and gold and fair.
The willow dips to the water,   15
Protected and precious, like the king's favorite
    daughter.

The ginkgo forces its way through gray concrete;
Like a city child, it grows up in the street.
Thrust against the metal sky,
Somehow it survives and even thrives.   20

My eyes feast upon the willow,
But my heart goes to the ginkgo.

          Eve Merriam

Metaphor

Morning is
a new sheet of paper
for you to write on.

Whatever you want to say,
all day,   5
until night
folds it up
and files it away.

The bright words and the dark words
are gone   10
until dawn
and a new day
to write on.

          Eve Merriam

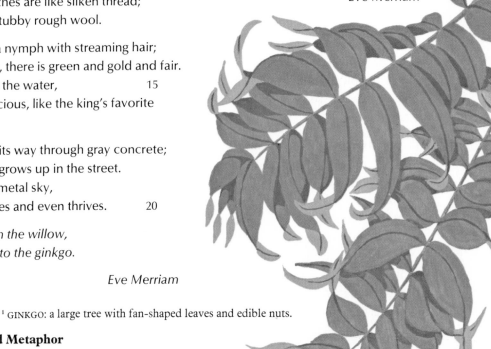

[1] GINKGO: a large tree with fan-shaped leaves and edible nuts.

For Discussion

1. What things are the willow and ginkgo like?
2. In the first three stanzas, the poet uses the same pattern, two lines to describe the willow and two for the ginkgo. How does she change the pattern in stanzas four and five? How is the last stanza different from the others? Why is it in italic type?
3. A **simile** is a comparison between two essentially different things. *Like* or *as* is always used to make the comparison. In line 1, Merriam says, "The willow is like an etching." A tree and an etching are dissimilar objects, but the poet sees, and enables us to see, that they are alike in the fine craftsmanship that produced each. Pick out three or four other similes in the poem, and explain how the two objects compared are alike.
4. Like a simile, a **metaphor** is a comparison, but without the use of *like* or *as*. It simply states or implies that one object *is* another. For example, in the metaphor "The light is dancing on the water," light is compared to a dancer. The two things compared are different, but the writer or speaker who sees the similarity provides a fresh way for us to see it. In the poem "Metaphor," the poet compares a day to a sheet of paper. In what ways are they alike?

Activities

1. Write a poem in which you use a series of similes to compare two essentially different objects. Choose your subject carefully. What original comparison can you make that will give readers a new way of seeing something? For example, at first glance, a building and a person have little in common. However, one might make a series of comparisons between the two showing that each is born, lives through successive stages, serves a particular function, and dies.
2. Write a short poem that consists of one basic metaphor as Merriam did in "Metaphor." You might begin it as a kind of equation, A = B. Choose your own subject or you may use one of these: life is a book, trees are hands, raindrops are tears.
3. Pair up with another student. Make each of the images below into a simile or metaphor. Your partner will identify whether you have made a simile or metaphor. Then switch roles.

haunted house	basketball player	canoe in the water
rush hour traffic	cat stalking its prey	jet at takeoff

3 | Free Verse

Read these poems that have no regular rhyme or rhythm.

Primer Lesson

Look out how you use proud words.
When you let proud words go,
   it is not easy to call them back.
They wear long boots, hard boots;
   they walk off proud; they can't
   hear you calling—
Look out how you use proud words.

Carl Sandburg

A Song of Greatness

When I hear the old men
Telling of heroes,
Telling of great deeds
Of ancient days—
When I hear that telling,   5
Then I think within me
I, too, am one of these.

When I hear the people
Praising great ones,
Then I know that I too—   10
Shall be esteemed;
I, too, when my time comes
Shall do mightily.

Traditional Chippewa Song
translated by Mary Austin

For Discussion

1. What is a primer?
2. In your own words, state the meaning of "Primer Lesson." Why is it a lesson for everyone?
3. Explain the metaphor in line 3.
4. What impression do the stories and praise of heroes make on the young Chippewa in "A Song of Greatness"?
5. Though completely different in subject matter, these poems are alike in verse form. They have no rhyme or regular rhythm. They are written in **free verse.** They have rhythm, of course, but it is more like that of speech, not a rhythm that repeats a regular pattern. Poets may use free verse because they feel that it allows them to focus on meaning without the restrictions of following a regular pattern. How would each of these poems be different if the poets had used a set pattern?
6. Explain why each of the following quotations is or is not free verse.

   a. And still on a winter's night, they say, when the wind is in the trees,
      And the moon is a ghostly galleon tossed upon cloudy seas,

   b. I am the people—the mob—the crowd—the mass.
      Do you know that all the great work of the world is done by me?

   c. once
      forgotten by tourists
      a bicycle joined
      a herd
      of mountain goats

Activities

1. Write a poem in free verse. It may be a lesson or a song like one of those you just read.
2. Draw an illustration for "proud words."
3. Imagine that you have been asked to set "A Song of Greatness" to music. What kind of music would be appropriate? Consider the instrument you would use, the rhythm, pace, and mood. Describe to others the kind of music you would compose.

4 | Fable

See if you recognize yourself or someone else you know in the characters in Thurber's fable.

What Happened to Charles

A farm horse named Charles was led to town one day by his owner, to be shod. He would have been shod and brought back home without incident if it hadn't been for Eva, a duck, who was always hanging about the kitchen door of the farmhouse, eavesdropping, and never got anything quite right. Her farmmates said of her that she had two mouths but only one ear.

On the day that Charles was led away to the smithy, Eva went quacking about the farm, excitedly telling the other animals that Charles had been taken to town to be shot.

"They're executing an innocent horse!" cried Eva. "He's a hero! He's a martyr! He died to make us free!"

"He was the greatest horse in the world," sobbed a sentimental hèn.

"He just seemed like old Charley to me," said a realistic cow. "Let's not get into a moony mood."

"He was wonderful!" cried a gullible goose.

"What did he ever do?" asked a goat.

Eva, who was as inventive as she was inaccurate, turned on her lively imagination. "It was butchers who led him off to be shot!" she shrieked. "They would have cut our throats while we slept if it hadn't been for Charles!"

"I didn't see any butchers, and I can see a burnt-out firefly on a moonless night," said a barn owl. "I didn't hear any butchers, and I can hear a mouse walk across moss."

"We must build a memorial to Charles the Great, who saved our lives," quacked Eva. And all the birds and beasts in the barnyard except the wise owl, the skeptical goat, and the realistic cow set about building a memorial.

Just then the farmer appeared in the lane, leading Charles, whose new shoes glinted in the sunlight.

It was lucky that Charles was not alone, for the memorial-builders might have set upon him with clubs and stones for replacing their hero with just plain old Charley. It was lucky, too, that they could not reach the barn owl, who quickly perched upon the weather vane of the barn, for none is so exasperating as he who is right. The sentimental hen and the gullible goose were the ones who finally called attention to the true culprit—Eva, the one-eared duck with two mouths. The others set upon her and tarred and unfeathered her, for none is more unpopular than the bearer of sad tidings that turn out to be false.

Moral: Get it right or let it alone. The conclusion you jump to may be your own.

James Thurber

For Discussion

1. When Charles returned wearing new shoes, why were the animals most angry with Eva?
2. Why did Eva so seldom get anything right?
3. What characteristic of the hen and of the goose made them eager to help build the memorial?
4. Which three characters did not take part in building the memorial? Why did each refuse to participate?
5. A **fable** is a short narrative that teaches a lesson or points out some truth about human experience. The characters are often animals or birds that speak and act like human beings. Why is the fable a good form for teaching a lesson?

Activities

1. Look carefully at some group of which you are a part—a team, a class, a club. Think of a situation in which the group acted unwisely, foolishly, or ridiculously—or just the opposite. Write a fable that will show your lesson or observation of human experience. Use animals as characters, and conclude with a statement of the moral, as Thurber did.
2. Pair up with a classmate. Each of you read your fable to the other, omitting the moral. Each of you provide a moral for your partner's fable.
3. Read another of Thurber's fables and tell the story to your class. Look in the library for Thurber's *Fables for Our Time* and *Further Fables for Our Times*.

5 | Alliteration and Onomatopoeia

Read how the poet uses sound to help create an image and mood.

Onomatopoeia

The rusty spigot
sputters,
utters
a splutter,
spatters a smattering of drops,   5
gashes wider;
slash,
splatters,
scatters,
spurts,   10
finally stops sputtering
and plash!
gushes rushes splashes
clear water dashes.

Eve Merriam

For Discussion

1. What action is the poet describing in the poem?
2. The repetition of consonants in words close together is called **alliteration.** Alliteration is pleasing to hear and is often used to help create a mood by having the sound echo the meaning of the words. For example, in the lines "In that *muffled monotone*" and "Over the *mountains* / Of the *moon*" the *m* sound is soft, in keeping with the meaning of the words. What examples of alliteration do you find in this poem?
3. Another device that helps create images and mood through sound is **onomatopoeia.** When the sound of a word imitates its meaning, the word is onomatopoetic. Examples of such words are *whiz, bang, clang, murmur,* and *crack.* This quotation shows how effective such words can be: "The buzz-saw snarled and rattled in the yard." What words does Merriam use to create the effect of water coming from a rusty faucet?

Activities

1. Think of a game that you know well. It might be baseball, tennis, or chess. Write a description of the game in prose or poetry. Use several examples of alliteration and onomatopoeia to add "sound" to your description.
2. In a sentence or two, describe the situations below using alliteration and onomatopoeia.

   a hungry animal   a ball being hit
   a traffic jam   a musical instrument

6 | Characterization

This story shows how a flute became more than just a fine musical instrument.

The Flute

Doretha didn't know just what it was, but there was something different about Mrs. Anderson today. Maybe her plump brown hands were lying extra still in her lap, or maybe her eyes were looking too far away. Whatever it was made Doretha pause before disturbing her.

"Mrs. Anderson?"

"Yes? Oh, hello, Doretha, I didn't see you come up. How are you today?"

"Fine. Mama said Mr. Anderson wanted to see me."

"He certainly does. Go right on in. I think he's in the living room."

Mr. Anderson met Doretha at the door. "I thought I heard you, Doretha," he said. He was cheerful, smiling behind his rimless glasses and under his thin, mixed-gray mustache, but the house seemed to have taken on Mrs. Anderson's mood. He led Doretha into the front room. "Sit right down there in the big chair. I have a present for you."

"But my birthday's not until February," Doretha said.

"Now, could I forget when your birthday is?" Mr. Anderson said. He pushed at the sides of his glasses. "The way your father was bragging the day you were born? But this is something I want you to have now." He slid a long black leather case from behind the sofa, opened it, and took out the silver instrument. He put it in Doretha's lap.

"Your flute?" she said. She held the flute with one hand to keep it from rolling off her lap.

"I want you to have it," Mr. Anderson said. He stood with his back swayed like a man with a big stomach, but he had hardly any.

Doretha was too surprised to think of being glad. She couldn't imagine Mr. Anderson without his flute. "You giving me your flute?"

"I have to go away soon, and I can't take many things with me. I know you'll take good care of it."

"I will!" Doretha said. Now she felt the excitement of the cool metal in her hands. "But why you *giving* it to me? You need it when you get back."

"I won't be coming back," Mr. Anderson said. "I can't come back this time."

"Oh."

"Here, let me put it back in the case for you, so you can take it home. And if your mother says it's all right, I'll give you a lesson every Saturday until I go away."

"I know Mama'll say okay," Doretha said. "Can we start this Saturday?"

"This Saturday is fine."

Doretha stood up. Through the window she saw Mrs. Anderson sitting just the way she had left her. "Is Mrs. Anderson sick?" she asked.

"No, she's worried. She's worried about my trip. She was always with me when I traveled before, and I'll be going alone this time."

Going home, Doretha carried the flute up in her arms, instead of by the handle. She would take care of her flute the way her mother took care of the piano. She would love it as much as she loved Mr. Anderson.

He hadn't told her very much about his trip. She wondered when he was leaving. And where he was going all by himself. And why he couldn't ever come back.

And then she knew.

She held the flute tighter, but she kept walking and didn't cry. When she got near home, she saw her mother watching her from the porch, frowning. Doretha smiled a little and waved, and the frown disappeared.

Eloise Greenfield

For Discussion

1. The next to the last paragraph contains only four one-syllable words. Its abruptness may startle you, just as certain knowledge startled Doretha. What had she discovered?

2. Point to details throughout the story that finally make clear to Doretha what is really happening.

3. **Characterization** is the means by which writers create lifelike characters. We come to know the characters by what they do, say, and think, by what others say about them, and by what the writer directly says about them. What do we know about Doretha and Mr. Anderson? How does Greenfield give us that information?

Activity

Write a short story paying particular attention to characterization. Limit your characters to two or three as the author does in "The Flute." Place your characters in a situation where their actions and speech can reveal their characteristics.

Language History

1 | The Life of a Word

Our language constantly changes to meet our needs. We adopt words from other languages and maintain their meanings. We adapt words from languages by altering their meanings slightly. Sometimes we completely change the meaning of a word when we take it for our own. Words have origins and histories, many of which are fascinating. The study of words is called **etymology.**

Consider the word *canary,* which originally comes from the Latin word for *dog, canis.* What do dogs and canaries have in common? The Romans named a group of Islands off northwest Africa, Canaria Insula, or Dog Island, because of all the dogs that they found there. Songbirds also inhabited the islands. Later, when the birds were exported to Europe, they were called canaries, after their home, the Canary Islands.

Another word that got its name from a place is *mayonnaise.* According to a legend, the town of Mahón on the island of Minorca in the Mediterranean once had a shortage of milk products. Consequently, the usual cream sauces could not be made. One chef began experimenting with eggs and oil. The result was a sauce that took the name of the city, Sauce Mahónnaise. Eventually, the word changed to *mayonnaise.*

Word change is unpredictable. For instance, the word *silly* in Old English was *seely,* meaning "blessed." The Normans were considered *seely,* because they had idle time for hunting and playing. Over time, *seely* came to mean "idle." In contrast, the word *knight* was originally the Anglo-Saxon word for youth, *cniht.* Later, it came to mean "servant," then "servant of a noble." Finally, the meaning was elevated to mean a person who served a noble with great chivalry and daring.

Many dictionaries give whole or partial etymologies. Some dictionaries list the early meanings of a word before its current meanings. Check your dictionary for its etymologies. You may also want to look at the *Oxford English Dictionary* which provides extensive etymologies.

Practice

A. Create your own etymology for each of these words: *mathematics, study, gymnasium, vacation.* What are their real etymologies?

B. What is the etymology for the name of your state, the month of your birth, and the days of the week?

2 | The Long Road to Our Alphabet

Early Systems of Writing

Compared to spoken language, writing is young. Linguists, the scientists of language, have determined that the earliest examples of writing are probably close to 10,000 years old. These early records are preserved in the caves where primitive people found shelter from the cold and from wild animals.

Writing developed slowly over thousands of years in different parts of the world. No one just sat down one day and thought up the idea of an alphabet. Our alphabet, for example, evolved in stages beginning with pictographs and ideographs.

Early cave dwellers drew a great variety of human and animal figures on the walls of their caves. Many of the pictures were probably just for decoration. However, there is no doubt that many of them had meaning: to tell a story, to portray the animals they hunted, or to pass on a message. The earliest drawings were elaborate and detailed. Eventually, the pictures became simplified. Instead of drawing a cat with head and body, the cave-writers eventually drew only the head of the cat. The cat's head became a kind of shorthand symbol for *cat*.

These simplified pictures are called **pictographs.** Their meanings are easy to decipher, because each pictograph stands for one concrete thing. Look at the pictographs in the margin.

One problem with pictographs is how to draw a picture for something you cannot see. What if you wanted to show *heat* or *sadness* or *walking* or *night*? To solve this difficulty, ancient people began to use their pictographs to stand for ideas or concepts. The symbol for the sun might also mean heat. The symbol for foot could also stand for walking, and a star could stand for night. These early inventors of writing also *combined* symbols. Two or more horses might stand for a herd. A pictograph of a human being with a spear could mean a hunter. An eye with water running through it could stand for crying.

Pictures that stand for ideas are called **ideographs.** The step from pictographs to ideographs was an important one. At last, a picture could stand for an idea, not just a concrete thing. Ideography is a sophisticated kind of writing. In fact, the Chinese still use an ideographic alphabet. A Chinese dictionary has over 40,000 entries.

The need for so many ideographs probably led some ancient people to experiment. The next step was to use a symbol to represent a sound. The symbol for an eye might stand for the sound of the syllable *see* whenever it was written. Using this system, you could combine the symbol for the syllable *see* with the symbol for the syllable *sun* to make the word season.

This development was an advance over ideographs. The person who wrote the early ideograph for crying did not link the picture with the *sound* of the word—only with the *idea* of the word. An alphabet that is made of symbols that stand for the sounds of syllables is called a **syllabary.** The Japanese write with a syllabary. A syllabary, however, still requires hundreds of symbols for all the syllables in a language.

Gradually, ancient writers developed the idea of an alphabet. In an alphabet, one letter stands for one sound. Each language has a limited number of sounds. That means that you need only a limited number of symbols, or letters, to build an alphabet. Alphabetic writing is the simplest form of writing, because it requires fewer symbols than other forms use.

Ancestors of the English Alphabet

The earliest ancestor of our English alphabet was the Egyptian's. Over 3,000 years ago, the Pharaohs, great kings, built pyramids. Inside, the walls were covered with writing. The dry climate helped preserve the contents of the pyramids, including the Egyptian **hieroglyphics.** Egyptian hieroglyphics include ideographs, but they also include symbols that stand for sound.

Within trading distance of Egypt lived the seafaring Phoenicians. The Phoenicians borrowed some of the Egyptian signs to name sounds in their own language, but they dropped ideographs from their alphabet. All of the Phoenician symbols stood for consonants; they had no letters to represent vowels. The first two letters of the Phoenician alphabet were *aleph* and *beth.* These letters remind us that the Phoenician "alephbeth" was our alphabet's important ancestor.

The Phoenicians sold their goods throughout the Mediterranean world and carried their "alephbeth" with them. The Greeks, who traded with the Phoenicians, made an important change in the Phoenician alphabet. They used the Phoenician symbols to create vowel sounds. They changed the names of some of the Phoenician letters to make them sound more familiar, and they added some new letters. *Aleph* and *beth,* for example, became *alpha* and *beta.* As you can guess,

Phoenician and Greek Alphabets

	Sound	ʾ	b	g	d	h	w	z	ḥ	ṭ	y	k	l	m	n
Phoenician	Name	ʾāleph	bēth	gīmel	dāleth	hē'	wāw	zayin	ḥēth	ṭēth	yōdh	kaph	lāmedh	mēm	nūn
	Sign														

	Sound	s	'	p	ṣ	q	r	sh	t
	Name	sāmekh	ayin	pēh	ṣadhē	qōph	rēsh	shīn	tāw
	Sign								

	Sound	a	b	g	d	e	w	dz	h	th	i	k	l
Greek	Name	alpha	beta	gamma	delta	epsilon	(digamma)	zeta	eta	theta	iota	kappa	lambda
	Sign												

	Sound	m	n	x	o	p	s	q	r	s	t	u	ph	ch
	Name	mu	nu	xi	omikron	pi	san	koppa	rho	sigma	tau	upsilon	phi	chi
	Sign													

the names of these letters joined to make our English word *alphabet*. Compare the Greek and Phoenician alphabets above.

The Greeks passed on their alphabet to the Romans. The Romans adapted it to their own language by adding new symbols and changing some letters. The Roman alphabet then evolved into a form that is similar to our own. Many of our modern letters look like these ancient ones. However, the letters do not necessarily sound the same.

The Romans had invaded England in 55 B.C. They remained there for about 400 years, however, their language was not adopted. Around A.D. 600, Christian missionaries from Rome came to England, and their monasteries became centers of learning. The clergy copied their religious manuscripts in the Latin, or Roman alphabet. From them, the knowledge of the alphabet eventually passed to the common folk.

Practice

A. Pair up with a partner. Write a message in pictographic writing. Then write a message in ideographic writing. Try to translate your partner's message. What are some of the problems with these forms of writing?

B. Make up a symbol for each syllable below. What are some of the problems with syllabaries?

sunny   childhood   hearty   sunlight   snowflake

3 | The History of English

Anglo Saxon and the Vikings

The history of the English language is the story of migrations, invasions, and conquests among different tribes and nations. Around A.D. 450, the Angles, Saxons, and Jutes, three Germanic tribes, left Northern Europe and invaded Britain from across the English Channel. The Celts, the people in Britain, were conquered, and the invaders settled in. Eventually, the Celts surrendered their own language and adopted the language of these Germanic tribes. Their new tongue was Anglo-Saxon or Old English. While Old English is the base of modern English, they are vastly different. Look below at the Old English lines and their modern translation.

> When I then this all remembered, then wondered I exceedingly
> *Ðā ic þā ðis eall gemunde, ðā wundrade ic swīðe swīðe*

> of the good wise men who formerly were throughout England.
> *þāra gōdena wiotona þe gīu wǣron giond Angelcynn.*

Within a few hundred years, the Vikings invaded Britain and settled into the areas they conquered. After years of fighting, a treaty was signed in A.D. 878. The agreement turned over a large portion of Britain to the Vikings. These Danes and Norwegians probably communicated fairly easily with the Anglo-Saxons because their languages were similar. Many Viking words came into English. Notice below that many Viking words had to do with everyday things and actions.

Viking Words

thrive	her	he	they	their	nose	point	fellow	odd
happy	calf	sky	flat	spring	lug	scream	gate	leg

Practice

Match each English word below with its Anglo-Saxon source.

bleach   show   speed   craft   heavy   steep

1. craeft: strength, sorcery
2. hefe: weight
3. steap: tall, high, deep
4. blac: white
5. sceawian: to look out for
6. sped, spaed: success, good

Middle English and the Normans

The last great invasion of England was led by the Norman king, William, known as "the Conqueror," in A.D. 1066. Normandy is part of what is now France. The Normans took control of England, and French became the ruling language. As a result, many of the French words in English have to do with government and business.

Words from French

government	sovereign	state	reign	nobility
obedience	authority	rent	interest	cash

English was not abandoned during the Norman reign. It was still spoken openly among the common folk. In fact, English eventually became the language of business, education, and literature. The Old English language had changed however. It had acquired a huge body of French words. Through the French rulers, considerable Latin and Greek had come into English as well. Read the sample below of Middle English and its modern version. These lines are by Geoffrey Chaucer, a fourteenth century English writer who also spoke French fluently.

> A *Knyght* ther was, and that a worthy man,
> That fro the time that he first bigan
> To riden out, he loved chivalrie,
> Trouthe and honour, fredom and curtesie.

> There was a *Knight*, a most distinguished man,
> Who from the day on which he first began
> To ride abroad had followed chivalry,
> Truth, honor, generousness and courtesy.

Practice

A. Which of the following words came into English from the Vikings? Which came from the French? How do you know?

parliament	money	ball	politics	ski
master	bait	noble	mansion	skin

B. Write your version of these Middle English lines of Chaucer's.

1. With him ther was his sone, a yong Squier
2. Wel koude he sitte on hors and faire ryde
3. He sleep namoore than dooth a nyghtyngale

4 | Our Language Family

Today an estimated 5,000 languages are spoken across the globe. Every language is complex, having the capacity to express any idea, feeling, event, or situation. All languages have parts of speech and ways to ask questions, make statements, and show surprise.

Most languages belong to one of 25 language families. A **language family** is a group of languages that have words in common. They also share a common ancestor, just as relatives of a human family do. English is one of 130 languages that make up the Indo-European language family. Nearly half of the world's population speak an Indo-European language, but Indo-European itself is no longer spoken. In fact, no written records of Indo-European exist because people spoke it so long ago.

Linguists, people who study the nature and structure of language, found their first clues about our Indo-European ancestors in modern languages. Since the late 1700's, they have been making systematic comparisons between the languages of Europe and Asia. Linguists discovered that these modern languages share many similar words. Look at the chart below.

English	Portuguese	Italian	French	Russian	Norwegian	Spanish
night	noite	notte	nuit	nochy	natt	noche
mother	mãe	madre	mère	maty	moder	madre
two	dois, duas	due	deux	dua	to	dos

On the basis of many similarities, linguists deduced that these languages must be related. To find the nearest ancestors of these modern languages, linguists went to written records of "dead" languages, languages no longer spoken. Look below at what they discovered.

Middle English	Old English	Latin	Greek	Sanskrit
nyht	niht	nox	nyx	nakta
moder	moder	mater	meter	mater
two	twa	duo	dyo	dvau

Because of the similarities they found in these dead languages, linguists went back even further in history. They wanted to find out about the root language of them all—Indo-European. There were, however, no written records. As a result, linguists had to reconstruct what the language was probably like. Based on words the modern and dead languages had in common, linguists were able to figure out many of the words that came from Indo-European. Also, they used information about how languages change over time. In this way, linguists drew conclusions about what Indo-European words were probably like. For example, linguists believe that *one* was *oinos*, *two* was *dwo*, and *three* was *treies*.

Indo-European Family of Languages (simplified)
MAJOR BRANCHES

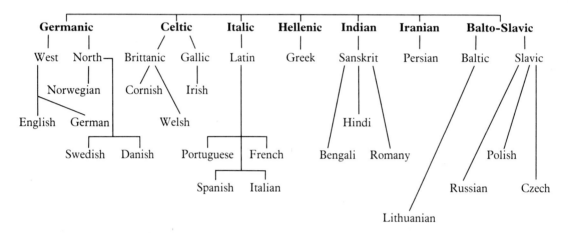

Practice

Refer to the Indo-European language tree above to answer the following questions.

1. English belongs to what major branch of Indo-European?
2. To what modern language is English most closely related?
3. Is Swedish more closely related to Danish or Norwegian? to English or Irish?
4. Is English more closely related to German or Irish?
5. What modern languages "grew" directly out of Sanskrit?
6. To what other Old Slavic languages is Russian related?
7. What modern languages "grew" directly out of Latin?
8. To what major branch of Indo-European does Persian belong?
9. Is Greek the root of Latin? Why or why not?
10. Is the French word *nuit* more closely related to the Italian word *notte* or to the Old English word *niht*? All three words have the same meaning—"night."

5 | Modern English

By the late 1400's, all of the different groups that had settled in Britain had begun to think of themselves as English people. Their language was close to the modern form we speak today. On the mainland of Europe, a similar process of "nation-forming" was underway. Their French, Dutch, Swedish, German, Portuguese, and Spanish neighbors all spoke different languages. It was not apparent that all of these languages were related and that they all shared a common ancestor.

British merchants began trading with their European neighbors. Along with their wares, the traders brought back new ideas about art, music, architecture, and writing, and also many new words. English more than any other language is a great borrower of foreign words. Many borrowed words often come into English in their original form.

As English explorers and traders sailed the globe, they were exposed to many new places and experiences: exotic plants and animals, new forms of art, strange and different ways of living. Rather than making up new words, these English people usually just absorbed the native vocabulary. Consequently, English has a rich assortment of words from virtually every country on the globe, and the process has not stopped in modern times.

English Words from Across the Globe

Norwegian: troll	French: restaurant
Spanish: tornado	Italian: opera
Hebrew: jubilee	Czechoslovakian: robot
Arabic: algebra	Indian: shampoo
Chinese: silk	Malay: bamboo
Australian: boomerang	African: chimpanzee
German: waltz	Native American: raccoon

Practice

Write the language from which each of these words came into English. Use your dictionary to help you.

veranda	koala	opossum	kimono	soprano
almanac	yoga	gingham	mammoth	model
tomato	picnic	hurricane	syrup	blank

End-of-Book Test

- **Sentences and Clauses**   Copy each sentence. If it contains more than one clause, draw a slash mark between the clauses. Within each clause, underline the simple subject once and the simple predicate twice. Write *simple*, *compound*, or *complex* to describe the sentence.

    1. Is Stockholm the capital city of Sweden?
    2. Kris's grandparents live in Sweden, and he is visiting them.
    3. Because Stockholm is built on sixteen islands, you can get a good view of the city from a boat.
    4. The boat winds through the city and stops at places of interest.
    5. You can leave the boats at any of the stops if you wish.
    6. Stockholm is a modern city, but its history goes back to the thirteenth century.

- **Plurals of Nouns**   Write the nouns in each sentence. Then write their plural forms.

    7. On the beach, a child threw sand on Morris's radio.
    8. The mouse's foot has no hoof.
    9. Why is there a patch on your mother-in-law's piano?
    10. The basis of the story is a mystery to Jones.
    11. Is that a chip on the glass's edge?
    12. A turkey, a deer, a sheep, an ox, and a monkey met in the zoo.

- **Verb Agreement and Tense**   Choose the correct verb form. Then write the entire verb phrase. Label its tense (*present, past, future, present perfect, past perfect, future perfect*).

    13. Neither the washing machine nor the dryer (works, work).
    14. The skaters on our hockey team (will leave, is leaving) tomorrow.
    15. The team certainly (seems, seem) in good shape for the match.
    16. Faith (practices, had practiced) on the guitar for an hour before she joined the band on stage.
    17. Sebastian (weared, wore) his softball uniform to the dinner.
    18. By the time the clouds in the sky (has, have) cleared, it will be too late to go swimming.
    19. By the time the program ends, we (left, shall have left).
    20. *Engines and Motors* (has, have) been checked out of the library.

- **Principal Parts**   Write the four principal parts of each verb.

  21. choose   **23.** aim   **25.** tap   **27.** break   **29.** do
  22. catch   **24.** state   **26.** worry   **28.** ride   **30.** sit

- **Completing the Predicate**   Determine whether the verb is an action verb or a linking verb. Then write *DO* (direct object), *IO* (indirect object), *PN* (predicate noun), or *PA* (predicate adjective) to describe what follows the verb.

  31. My uncle is a lapidary.
  32. Lapidaries cut gems into different shapes.
  33. They also polish the stones and sometimes make jewelry.
  34. My uncle does not sell customers his gems directly.
  35. He sells them to jewelers all over the world.
  36. My uncle bought me a lapidary wheel, and I polish dolomite and other stones on it.

- **Kinds of Pronouns**   List the pronouns. Next to each, write *personal, interrogative, demonstrative, indefinite, intensive,* or *reflexive* to describe it. (List a pronoun only once.)

  37. The larynx is also called the *voice box* because it contains the vocal cords.
  38. Has anyone found one blue glove under her or his desk?
  39. Neither can be my glove, for both are green.
  40. That is the weirdest-looking hat I have ever seen.
  41. Who would wear it?
  42. The ducklings found themselves in a strange pond.
  43. Whose is the big straw hat?
  44. Those are definitely not Gordon's shoes.
  45. I prepared the entire dinner myself.
  46. Aren't those the books you wanted?
  47. Whom will everybody stay with in Des Moines?
  48. None of the boats lost its way when the storm arose.

- **Subject and Object Pronouns**   Write the correct pronoun, and label it *subject* or *object.*

  49. Neither (he, him) nor (I, me) will want to leave early.
  50. Mr. Cargill has asked Barney and (I, me) to be co-captains.
  51. The sun was setting, and both (she, her) and (I, me) had to leave the lovely, peaceful beach.
  52. The new class officers are (she, her) and (I, me).

- **Agreement with Indefinite Pronouns**   Write the correct form.

   53. All (has, have) complained about (his or her, their) treatment.
   54. Not everyone (has, have) handed in the assignment.
   55. Each of the actresses (has, have) accepted (her, their) award.
   56. None of the waiters (has, have) picked up (his, their) order.
   57. Some of the butter on the shelves (seems, seem) spoiled.

- **Adjectives and Adverbs**   Divide your paper into two columns labeled *Adjectives* and *Adverbs*. List each modifier once in the correct column. (Do not list *a, an,* or *the*.)

   58. Certain North American pioneers built log cabins.
   59. Actually, the first English colonists did not know about log cabins, and instead they lived in rough shelters.
   60. Probably, Swedish settlers built the first American log cabins in the 1600's.
   61. Logs were not cut carelessly, for their size was quite important.
   62. Carefully, the builder fit the split and notched logs together.
   63. Few people could afford costly glass panes in their windows.
   64. Instead, greased paper or animal skins covered the openings.

- **Comparing with Adjectives and Adverbs**   Write the correct comparative or superlative form of the adjective or adverb in parentheses.

   65. That is the (big) lemon I have ever seen.
   66. It looks (large) than a grapefruit to me.
   67. Of all the paintings, I like Picasso's (good).
   68. Let's bicycle (far) today than we did yesterday.
   69. I think a diamond is (precious) than an emerald.
   70. Who of the three of them practices (often)?
   71. Which of the two is a (famous) drummer?

- **Prepositional Phrases**   Write each prepositional phrase. Underline the preposition once and the object or objects twice.

   72. On Tuesday of next week, the porch around the front of the house will be painted by Mrs. Bellini and her son.
   73. Because of the shade and the cool dirt under the porch, both of the dogs rest there in the summer.
   74. According to today's paper, the competition between the two players was created by the coach.
   75. Up the hill struggled the hikers from the camp below.

- **Participles and Participial Phrases**   Write each participle and participial phrase and the word or words it modifies.

   76. We did not notice anyone fishing in the stream today.
   77. The unknown singer captured the hearts of the people sitting in the audience.
   78. The completed poem was read to the audience by the talented poet himself.
   79. The airplane, landing on an icy runway, skidded very slightly.
   80. Perspiring in the heat, we walked into the steaming subway.
   81. Impressed by the qualified applicant, they hired her immediately.

- **Gerunds and Gerund Phrases**   Write each gerund and gerund phrase.

   82. His mistake was challenging the struggling champion.
   83. The real challenge will be winning the match.
   84. Going to the movies will be impossible for us today.
   85. We can make up for it by attending the afternoon class.
   86. Their job will be planting seven shade trees.
   87. Do you prefer arriving at six rather than at five? ·

- **Infinitives and Infinitive Phrases**   Write each infinitive and infinitive phrase.

   88. To forgive is not always an easy thing to do.
   89. The problem was to get to the Martinezes' without getting lost.
   90. We all decided to try harder to get to rehearsals on time.
   91. Everyone was determined to put on a good performance.
   92. The baby didn't want to go back to her crib.

- **Adjective Clauses**   Write each adjective clause. Underline the relative pronoun.

   93. The police officer who was directing traffic in the busy intersection wore bright orange gloves.
   94. The tablecloth that Marion bought was a hideous color.
   95. *Madama Butterfly*, which is an opera about Japan, was written by an Italian composer whose name was Giacomo Puccini.
   96. *The Girl of the Golden West*, which is an opera about the Old West, was written by the same Italian composer.
   97. Puccini also wrote *La Bohème*, which takes place in Paris.

- **Adverb Clauses** Write each adverb clause. Underline the subordinating conjunction.

    98. Unless the traffic is very heavy, we should arrive on time.
    99. The Causeys have moved to Detroit so that they can be closer to their family.
    100. A cuckoo emerges whenever the clock strikes the hour.
    101. If it thunders, the cows will come home.
    102. We shall leave as soon as the taxi arrives at the door.

- **Noun Clauses** Write each noun clause.

    103. I have heard that the field trip must be postponed.
    104. The award will go to whoever earns it.
    105. How the prisoner escaped remains a mystery.
    106. The problem is that the pitcher is being careless.
    107. Why do you think that the biology test will be easy?

- *Who* or *Whom* **in Clauses** Write the correct word.

    108. Do you know (who, whom) will lead the discussion?
    109. Everyone is talking about (who, whom) will get the job.
    110. Constance called the woman (who, whom) installed the phone.
    111. Henry Harper, (who, whom) everyone admires, has returned.
    112. Monique will audition after (whoever, whomever) goes next.

- **Using Words Correctly** Write the correct form for each sentence.

    113. That ship has (lain, laid) at the bottom of the sea for centuries.
    114. Deirdre (raised, rose) her eyes to look at the ceiling.
    115. The noise (effected, affected) Jean's ability to concentrate.
    116. Yesterday, they (lay, laid) the new carpet on the living room floor.
    117. The huge curtain (raised, rose) and the performance began.
    118. Don't (let, leave) go of the kite string.
    119. The researchers studied the (effects, affects) of the storm.
    120. You (ought, had ought) to be home if you're not feeling well.
    121. Jimmy likes all kinds of music (accept, except) choral music.
    122. Who (shall, will) win the election?
    123. We can't go (anywhere, anywheres) this weekend.
    124. The candidate said emphatically, "I (shall, will) win."
    125. You should (of, have) let me know that you weren't coming.
    126. The shelter is a long (way, ways) from here.
    127. (Besides, Beside) photography, Jill has no other hobbies.
    128. The child could not (accept, except) the fact that her cat was lost.

129. There will be (further, farther) discussion about this matter.
130. (Wayne and I, I and Wayne, Wayne and me) will go to a concert.
131. There are (fewer, less) paintings on the museum's second floor.
132. The lifeguard watched (us swimmers, we swimmers).
133. (Us, We) students will all graduate in June.
134. Save a seat for (Claudia and me, me and Claudia, Claudia and I).
135. Jake was too tired to run any (further, farther).
136. Ellie took the newspaper (off, from) the delivery boy.
137. Did you hear (where, that) Pam will be getting married soon?
138. Janet doesn't know (as, whether) she will attend the wedding.
139. The painting hung (between, among) the two windows.
140. She acted (like, as though) she knew all the answers.
141. The friendship (between, among) the four of us is close.
142. The vase fell (off, off of) the shelf.

- **Building Vocabulary**   Write two synonyms for each noun.

143. anger   **144.** road   **145.** building   **146.** sound   **147.** strength

Write an antonym of each noun.

148. cleanliness   **149.** height   **150.** justice   **151.** happiness

Write a more precise synonym for each verb.

152. write   **153.** look   **154.** walk   **155.** like

Write the root of each word. Then make a new word from each root by adding a new prefix, suffix, or both.

156. nonsense   **157.** joyous   **158.** dictate   **159.** scientist

Add suffixes to these words to form adjectives. Check spelling changes in a dictionary, if necessary.

160. child   **161.** help   **162.** suburb   **163.** miracle   **164.** wonder

Write the correct homophone.

165. They walked down the (aisle, isle) of the theater to their seats.
166. Are you going to New York by bus or by (plain, plane)?
167. The helicopter hovered in a (stationary, stationery) position.

Write two meanings for each homograph. Use a dictionary, if you need to.

168. bank   **169.** row   **170.** minute   **171.** lead   **172.** object

Language Handbook

Parts of Speech

Nouns

Definition   A **noun** names a person, place, thing, quality, act, or feeling.

Fred, woman   hill, Ohio   glue, stick   shininess   jump   sorrow

Kinds of Nouns   A **proper noun** names a particular thing and is capitalized.

Spaniards   Rover   Flag Day   Lincoln High School   Dave

A **common noun** is any noun that is not a proper noun.

people   dog   holiday   place   brother

A **concrete noun** names a thing that can be touched and seen.

friend   lamp   trout   excavation   television

An **abstract noun** names a thing that cannot be touched and seen.

friendship   idea   history   truth   grief

A **compound noun** is a noun made up of more than one word.

bathtub   mother-in-law   guidance counselor

Practice   Copy each noun and write whether it is common or proper, concrete or abstract, and compound.

1. hatred   **2.** Miami Beach   **3.** computer   **4.** baseball   **5.** stinginess

Singular and Plural Nouns   A **singular noun** names one person, place, thing, quality, act, or feeling.

child   hotel   expense   beauty   drink   arrogance

A **plural noun** names more than one.

children   hotels   expenses   beauties   drinks   arrogances

To form the plural of most nouns, add -*s.*

books   stores   Stuarts   dads   rations   ideas

For nouns ending in -*s, -x, -z, -sh,* or -*ch,* add -*es.*

masses   foxes   buzzes   washes   watches

For nouns ending in -*o,* add -*s* or -*es.*

vetoes   torpedoes   potatoes   silos

For nouns ending with a vowel and -*y,* add -*s.* For nouns ending with a consonant and -*y,* change *y* to *i* and add -*es.*

turkeys   monkeys   berries   tries

For some nouns ending in -*f* or -*fe,* add -*s.* For others, change *f* to *v* and add -*es.* Check your dictionary.

proofs   reefs   lives   calves

For most compound nouns, add -*s* to the most important word.

sisters-in-law   chiefs of staff   station wagons

For letters, numbers, symbols, and words considered as words, add -*'s:*

e's   3's   +'s   *if's*

See page 65 for examples of nouns that change from singular to plural in irregular ways.

Practice   Write the plural form of each noun.

1. George   **3.** *maybe*   **5.** cupful   **7.** datum   **9.** upset   **11.** safe
2. tomato   **4.** donkey   **6.** alto   **8.** leaf   **10.** 7   **12.** sheep

Possessive Nouns   A **possessive noun** shows ownership.

Dan's hat   children's playground   Williamses' car

To form the possessive of a singular noun, add an apostrophe and -*s.*

tooth's   sister-in-law's   grandmother's   family's

For a plural noun that ends in -*s,* add an apostrophe only.

sisters'   families'   Robins'   hound dogs'

For a plural noun that does not end in -*s,* add an apostrophe and an -*s.*

stimuli's   women's   mice's   sisters-in-law's

Practice Write the singular and plural possessive of each noun.

1. e **3.** grandmother **5.** cupful **7.** moose **9.** maid of honor
2. Deb **4.** Lorenzo **6.** high jump **8.** man **10.** Atlas

Appositives An **appositive** is a noun, with or without accompanying words, that identifies or explains another noun. An appositive is set off with commas unless it is needed to identify the other noun.

My favorite book, *Huckleberry Finn,* is in the library.
The novel *Huckleberry Finn* was written by Mark Twain.

Practice Write the sentences. Underline each appositive. Add commas if needed.

1. That tale is based on an old fable "The Boy Who Cried Wolf."
2. Of my two sisters Emily and Laura Emily is taller.
3. The composer Bach will be featured at the concert.
4. One of my aunts Aunt Helen is a writer.
5. My favorite short stories were written by the author Willa Cather.
6. Sam a resident of New York City does not own a car.

Verbs

Definition A **verb** expresses action, either physical or mental, or it expresses a state of being.

The workers demanded higher wages.
The inventor thought about the problem.
The dog feels tired.

Main Verbs and Helping Verbs A **verb phrase** includes a main verb and one or more helping or auxiliary verbs.

You could have worked harder.

The **main verb** expresses the action or state of being.

You could have worked harder.
I will have been working for three years by next June.

The **helping** or **auxiliary** verb or verbs help complete the meaning of the main verb.

Could he have seen that movie already?
That antique may have become valuable in a few years.

Practice   Copy each verb phrase, underlining the main verb. After the verb phrase, write *action* or *being* to tell what it expresses.

1. Would he have graduated in June?
2. Grandmother has not been feeling well.
3. A visit to the aquarium will be interesting.
4. She will have been in school since eight o'clock this morning.

Verb Tenses   Every verb has four **principal parts:** the verb, the present participle, the past, and the past participle.

start	starting	started	started
forget	forgetting	forgot	forgotten

The principal parts of a verb are used to show different time, or **tense.** Verbs have six tenses, three simple and three perfect. The **present tense** is formed from the basic verb form. The letters *-s* or *-es* are added with *he, she, it,* or a singular noun. The **past tense** is formed with the verb plus *-d* or *-ed.* The **future tense** is formed with *will* plus the verb.

Every day she practices the violin. (*present tense*)
She practiced last Tuesday. (*past tense*)
She will practice tomorrow. (*future tense*)

The three **perfect tenses**—the **present perfect, past perfect,** and **future perfect**—are formed with *have* and the past participle.

I have started my report. (*present perfect*)
I had started it by Monday. (*past perfect*)
I shall have started the conclusion by next week. (*future perfect*)

Irregular verbs do not add *-d* or *-ed* to form the past and past participle. The principal parts of each irregular verb must be learned. See page 461 for a list of common irregular verbs.

I chose a book.   I have chosen a book.   (choose)

Practice   Write each sentence, using the verb form indicated.

1. He ___ his homework before dinner. (do, *past perfect*)
2. Every day she ___ school. (teach, *present*)
3. Soon the pilot ___ over sixty transatlantic flights. (fly, *future perfect*)
4. I ___ today was Wednesday. (think, *past*)
5. We ___ dinner at six. (eat, *future*)
6. They ___ him for ten years. (know, *present perfect*)

Progressive Forms   Each tense has a **progressive form** to express continuing action. The progressive is formed with *be* and the present participle.

> Dave <u>is talking</u> now. (*present progressive*)
> Dave <u>was talking</u> earlier. (*past progressive*)
> Dave <u>will be talking</u> later. (*future progressive*)
> They <u>have been talking</u> all day. (*present perfect progressive*)
> They <u>had been talking</u> all week. (*past perfect progressive*)
> They <u>will have been talking</u> for two hours. (*future perfect progressive*)

Practice   Write the six progressive forms of each verb and subject.

1. She finishes.   **2.** They forget.   **3.** I begin.   **4.** He loses.

Linking Verbs   A **linking verb** expresses being. It links the subject with an adjective or a noun in the predicate that refers to the subject.

> The apple <u>tasted</u> sour.   Grandpa <u>is</u> an avid reader.

Practice   List each verb and write *action* or *linking* beside it.

1. Tina grew worried when Beth was late.
2. He felt angry.
3. His face became red and his hands shook.

Transitive and Intransitive Verbs   A **transitive verb** expresses action that is sent to a noun or pronoun in the predicate.

> The spectators <u>watched</u> the football game.
> The quarterback <u>kicked</u> the ball.

The word that receives the action is the **object** of the verb.

> Valerie grew <u>tomatoes</u> in the garden.
> He drives a <u>sports car</u>.

An **intransitive verb** does not have an object. Linking verbs are always intransitive.

> They <u>watched</u> silently.   They <u>are</u> overjoyed.

Practice   List each verb. Label it *transitive* or *intransitive*.

1. The crowd watched eagerly as the cars raced around the track.
2. The lead car drew the attention of the spectators.
3. The rain began again, and we took shelter.
4. The race was over before the clock struck twelve.

Active and Passive Voices A verb is in the **active voice** if the subject performs the action. A verb is in the **passive voice** if the subject receives the action.

> Molly <u>placed</u> the books on the shelf. (*active voice*)
> The books <u>were placed</u> on the shelf by Molly. (*passive voice*)

Practice Rewrite each active sentence in the passive voice. Rewrite each passive sentence in the active voice.

1. The tomatoes were planted in the garden by the children.
2. The winning basket was made by the star player.
3. Frank accidentally dropped the valuable vase.
4. An army of ants invaded our picnic basket.

Pronouns

Definition A **pronoun** is a word that takes the place of a noun.

> My grandmother is ill, and <u>she</u> is in the hospital.

Personal Pronouns and Antecedents **Personal pronouns** have different forms depending on their person (1st, 2nd, 3rd) and number (singular, plural). See page 184 for a list of personal pronouns.

> <u>I</u> asked <u>my</u> mother for permission. (*first person singular*)
> <u>They</u> spent <u>their</u> money on a new car. (*third person plural*)

Third person singular pronouns have different forms depending on their gender (masculine, feminine, neuter).

> <u>He</u> is driving.   <u>She</u> is working.   <u>It</u> is my dog.

The noun or nouns to which a pronoun refers are its **antecedents.** Pronouns agree with their antecedents in number and gender.

> Bill and Tina are my cousins, and <u>they</u> will visit in July.
> The dog and <u>her</u> puppies are in <u>their</u> beds.

Practice Write each personal pronoun. Next to it, write its antecedent.

1. No one knows where Ron is, but Drai and Vera reported that they had seen him in the gym.
2. Sam, Mother says that she will let you go to baseball practice.
3. When it was dropped, the glass broke.
4. Betty and Harold watched the game together, and they enjoyed it.

Subject and Object Pronouns   Pronouns that are used differently have different case forms. A pronoun used as a subject is in the **nominative case.** It is called a **subject pronoun.**

He composed many works for the piano.

A pronoun used as an object is in the **objective case.** It is called an **object pronoun.**

Clyde collected old coins and sold them. (*direct object*)
Let's share these bananas with them. (*object of preposition*)
She gave him a choice. (*indirect object*)

Use subject pronoun forms after linking verbs.

I am she.   It is he who got the job.   The members are they.

Use subject pronouns in compound subjects and in compounds following linking verbs.

He and I were elected to the student council.
The people elected to the student council were he and I.

Use object pronouns in compound objects.

Give the directions to Beth and him.   Watch Tim and me.

Practice   Write the correct pronoun to complete each sentence.

1. The people who made that poster are (he, him) and (I, me).
2. Who sent (we, us) these flowers?
3. Was it really (he, him) you saw at the show?
4. His friends or (we, us) will meet (they, them) at the airport.
5. (They, Them) asked (she, her) to join the club.

Possessive Pronouns   A **possessive pronoun** can replace a possessive noun. Possessive pronouns are in the **possessive case.** Possessive pronouns never use apostrophes.

This is their car.   Are you our friend?   Show me your report.
This pen is mine.   This hut is ours.   This dog is theirs.

Practice   Write the correct possessive pronoun for each blank.

1. The Williamses have a large cat. The cat is ____.
2. We have an idea. The idea is ____.
3. Fran lives in an apartment. It is ____ apartment.
4. The dog has a sore paw. ____ paw needs a bandage.

Interrogative Pronouns   **Interrogative pronouns** like *who, which, what, whom,* and *whose* introduce questions. *Who* is used as a subject, *whom* as an object, and *whose* as a possessive.

> <u>Who</u> called? <u>Whom</u> did you call? <u>Whose</u> is this?

Do not confuse *whose* with the contraction *who's.*

> <u>Whose</u> shoes are these?   <u>Who's</u> the star of that show?

Practice   Write *who, whom,* or *whose* to complete each sentence.

1. ____ has seen my jacket?
2. ____ have you seen?
3. ____ did they elect?
4. ____ jacket is this?
5. ____ dog is that?
6. ____ is your guest?

Demonstrative Pronouns   A **demonstrative pronoun** points out things, persons, or ideas. *This* (singular) and *these* (plural) point out things that are close.

> <u>This</u> is my homework.   <u>These</u> are my friends.

That (singular) and *those* (plural) point out things that are farther away.

> <u>That</u> must be the place.   <u>Those</u> must be the players.

Avoid expressions like *this here* and *those there.*

Practice   Write the form that correctly completes the sentence.

1. (This, That) is the island that has a lighthouse.
2. (This, These) are the missing pieces to the puzzle.
3. (These, Those) are the chairs from the other room.
4. (That, Those) are the stars that form the Big Dipper.
5. (That, That there) was the sleigh made by my grandfather.

Indefinite Pronouns   An **indefinite pronoun** does not refer to a specific person or thing. Verbs must agree in number with indefinite pronouns used as subjects.

> <u>Everyone</u> is invited. (*singular*)   <u>Several</u> were invited. (*plural*)
> <u>Neither</u> is here. (*singular*)   <u>Many</u> are here. (*plural*)
> <u>All</u> is well. (*singular*)   <u>All</u> were accounted for. (*plural*)

Pronouns must agree with indefinite pronouns used as antecedents.

> <u>Each</u> has <u>its</u> own name.   <u>Others</u> forgot <u>their</u> books.
> <u>Everyone</u> has <u>his or her</u> own ideas.

Practice Copy each indefinite pronoun. Then write the form that agrees with it.

1. Everyone waited in (his or her, their) place.
2. Several (was, were) absent from school.
3. Both (has, have) (his, their) skates.
4. Neither (is, are) my brother, but both (is, are) my friends.

Reflexive and Intensive Pronouns Pronouns ending in *-self* or *-selves* are used in two ways. A **reflexive pronoun** refers back to the subject.

Brad can see himself in the mirror.   Did you cut yourself?

An **intensive pronoun** emphasizes a certain noun in the sentence.

The children wrote the play themselves.

Do not substitute reflexive pronouns for personal pronouns.

Dan and I (not *myself*) are responsible for refreshments.

Avoid the forms *hisself* and *theirselves*.

Practice Write the pronoun with *-self* or *-selves* that correctly completes each sentence. Label the pronoun *reflexive* or *intensive*.

1. They ____ built the house.
2. Dana and Mark did not hurt ____ in the game.
3. Did you three draw that mural ____?
4. The dog cut ____ on a piece of broken glass.

Adjectives

Definition An **adjective** describes, or modifies, a noun or pronoun.

There is a moderate amount of water in the pool.
The three tired, grumpy children were sent to bed.

A, an, and *the* are special adjectives called **articles.** *The* refers to a specific item or items. *A* and *an* refer to any one in a group of items.

The storm raged throughout the day.   An airplane landed in a field.

An adjective formed from a proper noun is a **proper adjective.** Proper adjectives are capitalized.

We ate at a Hungarian restaurant.   She is French.

Adjectives usually, but not always, precede the modified word.

> The <u>bright</u>, <u>cozy</u> room welcomed us.
> The room, <u>bright and cozy</u>, welcomed us.

Two or more equally ranked adjectives are separated by commas.

> The <u>fresh</u>, <u>ripe</u> fruit was placed in a bowl.

Practice Copy each sentence, underlining each adjective. Capitalize proper adjectives. Add commas where needed. (Do not underline *a, an,* or *the.*)

1. On a dark snowy winter day, everyone stayed indoors and listened to records of spanish songs.
2. The four australian visitors took pictures of historical sites.
3. An ancient north american legend tells how the world was created.
4. All multi-colored shirts were on sale during the grand opening.

Adverbs

Definition An **adverb** modifies a verb, an adjective, or another adverb. Adverbs usually tell *where, when, how, to what extent.*

> They finished their meal <u>very</u> <u>quickly</u>.
> <u>Yesterday</u> a storm <u>suddenly</u> blew in from the east.
> That is an <u>awfully</u> good drawing.

Adverbs that modify verbs can often be placed in different positions.

> <u>Today</u> it is raining.   It is raining <u>today</u>.

Other adverbs should be placed close to the modified words.

> It was a <u>terribly</u> frightening movie.   She was <u>deeply</u> embarrassed.

An adverb that tells *to what extent* is usually an **intensifier.** Intensifiers modify adjectives or other adverbs.

> It is <u>quite</u> warm today.   This is a <u>very</u> fast roller coaster.

Practice Write each adverb and the word or words it modifies. Label each intensifier.

1. It rained rather suddenly, and soon we stopped the game.
2. No one is more popular than the person with a friendly smile.
3. Very cautiously, we stepped into the fun house.
4. Yesterday I acted quickly and wisely.

Comparing with Adjectives and Adverbs The **comparative degree** of an adjective or adverb is used to compare two things. Form the comparative with *-er* or *more*.

> This plant is <u>taller</u> than this one.   It grew <u>more quickly</u>.

The **superlative degree** is used to compare three or more things. Form the superlative degree with *-est* or *most*.

> This plant is the <u>tallest</u> of the three.   It grew <u>most quickly</u>.

Avoid double comparisons.

> She is a <u>better</u> (*not* more better) skier than he.
> This is the <u>deepest</u> (*not* most deepest) snow I have ever seen!

Practice Write the correct form of each word in parentheses.

1. Skiing is the _____ sport I have ever tried. (exhilarating)
2. This tooth is in _____ condition than that one. (serious)
3. Of the three diseases, this one is the _____ contagious. (less)
4. Who ran _____, you, Harry, or Wendy? (far)
5. Today the rain fell _____ than yesterday. (heavily)

Prepositions

Definitions A **preposition** shows a relationship between a noun or pronoun and another word in the sentence. A preposition can be more than one word. See page 325 for a list of prepositions.

> A cat sits <u>in</u> the chair.   <u>Because of</u> the rain, we ran.

The **object of the preposition** is the noun or pronoun that follows the preposition.

> The cat was <u>between</u> two <u>chairs</u>.   The bus stopped <u>in front of us</u>.

When the object of a preposition is a pronoun, it is always in the form of an object pronoun.

> She gave the notebook <u>to him</u>.   He is standing <u>behind her</u>.

Practice Write each preposition and its object or objects.

1. The yard is in back of the house.
2. The car drove into the drive and stopped near the fence.
3. According to that book, the ship sank after dark.
4. Please walk toward the front of the room without any noise.

Sentence Structure

The Sentence

Definition A **sentence** is a group of words that expresses a complete thought.

> The city has an excellent museum of natural history.

Kinds of Sentences A **declarative sentence** makes a statement and ends with a period. An **interrogative sentence** asks a question and ends with a question mark. An **imperative sentence** gives a command or makes a request and ends with a period. An **exclamatory sentence** expresses strong feeling and ends with an exclamation mark.

> Everyone in the school will visit the museum. (*declarative*)
> Will everyone in the school visit the museum? (*interrogative*)
> Please let me go to the museum. Get on the bus now. (*imperative*)
> What a wonderful museum! I saw a dinosaur skeleton! (*exclamatory*)

Practice Write each sentence, adding end punctuation. Write *declarative, interrogative, imperative,* or *exclamatory* after it.

1. How dark and threatening the sky is
2. Do you think there will be a storm
3. Please go upstairs and close the windows
4. The wind is blowing and the rain is starting to fall

Simple and Compound Sentences A **simple sentence** has one complete subject and predicate. Either or both may be compound.

> The lecturer and his assistant told us about penguins.

A **compound sentence** is made up of two or more related simple sentences. The sentences are usually joined by a comma and a **coordinating conjunction.**

> The lecturer told us about penguins, and his assistant showed a film.
> Penguins live in the southern hemisphere, but polar bears live in the northern hemisphere.

Practice Write each pair of sentences as one compound sentence. Use the conjunction in parentheses. Add commas where necessary.

1. The sun melted the snow. The daffodils bloomed. (and)
2. I will leave today. I would rather leave tomorrow. (but)

Complex Sentences An **independent clause** has a subject and a predicate and can stand alone.

I wrote a book report and Bernice read it.

A **dependent clause** has a subject and a predicate but cannot stand alone. Many dependent clauses begin with **subordinating conjunctions.**

When the wind blew, leaves rustled in the trees.

A sentence with one or more dependent clauses and an independent clause is a **complex sentence.**

I wrote a book report after I read *Tom Sawyer.*
When the wind blew, leaves rustled in the trees.

Practice Write each complex sentence. Underline the dependent clause. Draw a circle around each subordinating conjunction.

1. If it rains before noon, we will not have a picnic.
2. Ships cannot travel through the straits until the ice melts.
3. Since we are hungry, let's have lunch early.
4. I will pick the blueberries after they have ripened.

Sentence Fragments and Run-ons A **sentence fragment** is a word group that lacks a subject or a predicate or does not express a complete thought.

seeing the game on Tuesday   only Janet and Bill   when I arrived

A **run-on sentence** is a series of two or more sentences that are run together with commas or with no punctuation.

The elevator was crowded, we waited for the next one.

To correct a run-on, rewrite it as separate sentences, as a compound sentence, or as a complex sentence.

The elevator was crowded. We waited for the next one.
The elevator was crowded, and we waited for the next one.
Because the elevator was crowded, we waited for the next one.

Practice Correct the fragments and run-ons.

1. Even after I had finished my homework.
2. The teacher explained the homework, I did not understand.
3. I misplaced my umbrella I am getting wet in this rain.
4. Since Timmy had to go home early.

Subjects

Complete and Simple Subjects Every sentence has a subject and a predicate. The **complete subject** tells what the sentence is about.

Fourteen-year-old Amy has been practicing for the track meet.

The **simple subject** is the key word in the subject. It is usually a noun or a pronoun.

Fourteen-year-old <u>Amy</u> has been practicing for the track meet.

In most sentences the subject comes before the predicate. In sentences in **inverted order,** all or part of the predicate comes before the subject.

There are three <u>people</u> in line.   Under the tree sat a shaggy <u>dog</u>.

To find the subject, arrange the subject and predicate in their natural order, or ask <u>who</u> or <u>what</u> about the predicate.

Three <u>people</u> are in line.   A shaggy <u>dog</u> sat under the tree.

The subject of imperative sentences is understood to be *you*.

(<u>You</u>) Stand up, please.   Roberto, (<u>you</u>) let in the dog.

A **compound subject** is made up of two or more simple subjects with the same predicate.

The <u>singer</u>, the <u>actors</u>, and the <u>dancers</u> will rehearse today.

Practice Copy each sentence, and underline each simple subject.

1. Behind the stage stood the manager, the producer, and the director.
2. Here are my Aunt Sally and her poodle.
3. Three weeks have passed since my graduation.

Predicates

Complete and Simple Predicates The **complete predicate** tells something about the subject.

Karl has become an excellent athlete.

The **simple predicate** is the key word or words in the predicate. It is always a verb.

Karl <u>has become</u> an excellent athlete.

A **compound predicate** is made up of two or more simple predicates with the same subject.

George <u>has saved</u> his money and <u>bought</u> a new bicycle.

Practice   Copy each sentence. Then underline the simple predicates.

1. Sean practiced every day, worked hard, and finally won the contest.
2. Climbing the tree were two small kittens.
3. Shelly trained the bears, but did not perform with them.
4. Are you doing your homework or watching television?

Direct Objects and Indirect Objects   The **direct object** is a noun or pronoun in the predicate that receives the action of the verb.

The carpenter built a new <u>staircase</u>.
She asked her <u>mother</u> or her <u>father</u> for a loan.

The **indirect object** is a noun or pronoun in the predicate that tells to or for whom or what the action is done. It comes between the verb and the direct object.

Have you taught <u>Steven</u> the alphabet?
Judith told <u>Billy</u> and <u>Sam</u> a horrifying tale.

Practice   Write each direct and indirect object. Label it *DO* or *IO*.

1. The mail carrier handed me a letter from Japan.
2. Have you asked Tom or Jan for help?
3. The insurance agent sold the family a better policy.
4. Anyone can give her advice.

Predicate Nouns and Adjectives   A **predicate noun** identifies or renames the subject. Predicate nouns follow linking verbs.

The major ingredient of bread is <u>flour</u>.

A **predicate adjective** describes the subject. Predicate adjectives follow linking verbs.

Heating oil is both <u>necessary</u> and <u>expensive</u>.

Practice   Label each predicate noun and predicate adjective.

1. The tar became hot and sticky in the broiling sun.
2. She worked for many weeks on the short story, and it was publishable.
3. After months of drought, the river became a sun-cracked desert.

Phrases

Definition   A **phrase** is a group of words that acts like a single word.

   with difficulty   playing baseball   tossed by the waves

A **prepositional phrase** begins with a **preposition** and ends with a noun or pronoun that is the **object of the preposition.** See page 442 for information on prepositions and their objects.

   in the afternoon   for the present   beside the dead tree

An **adjective phrase** modifies a noun or a pronoun.

   The music by Bach was performed beautifully. (*modifies* music)

An **adverb phrase** modifies a verb, adjective, or adverb.

   At ten o'clock the visitors arrived. (*modifies* arrived)
   Maria is popular among her classmates. (*modifies* popular)
   Early in the morning we caught the bus. (*modifies* early)

Practice   Copy each prepositional phrase and the word it modifies. Write whether each phrase is an adjective phrase or an adverb phrase.

1. The apple was divided between Deb and me.
2. The cabin near the shore was destroyed during the storm.
3. A horse galloped spiritedly along the trail.

Verbals   A **verbal** is a verb form that is not used as a verb.

   The howling dog kept everyone awake.
   Do you like singing?
   To point is rude.

A **participle** is an *-ing* or *-ed* verb form used as an adjective.

   The screaming children annoyed everyone.
   The tamed rabbit was fun to watch.

A **gerund** is an *-ing* form used as a noun.

   Growing vegetables is both interesting and economical.

An **infinitive** is the basic verb form preceded by *to.* It may be used as a noun or as a modifier.

   To scream was forbidden. (*noun*)
   This is the way to go. (*adjective*)
   The vegetables are ready to sprout. (*adverb*)

Practice Write *participle, gerund,* or *infinitive* to describe each verbal.

1. <u>To protest</u> was useless.
2. That <u>dangling</u> wire is dangerous.
3. <u>Cooking</u> is a challenging profession.
4. Francine, a <u>frightened</u> person, needs more self-confidence.

Participial Phrases A **participle** is an *-ing* or *-ed* verb form used as an adjective. A participle accompanied by other words forms a **participial phrase.** A participial phrase is used as an adjective.

Sam, <u>being a painter,</u> has fulfilled his ambition. (modifies *Sam*)

A comma is used with an introductory participial phrase and with a participial phrase that gives added information.

<u>Explained by the teacher,</u> the directions were clear.
The dog, <u>coming home at last,</u> was a welcome sight.

A comma is not used with a participial phrase that gives identifying information.

The woman <u>entering the building</u> is the mayor.

Practice Copy each participial phrase. Write the word it modifies.

1. The boat, tied to the dock, was safe from the storm.
2. Watched day and night, the prisoner could not escape.
3. Being an excellent painter, Alex wants to go to art school.
4. Carmen, excited by the performance, decided to study ballet.

Gerund Phrases A gerund plus accompanying words forms a **gerund phrase.** A gerund phrase is used in the same way a noun is used.

<u>Buying the groceries</u> is Henry's job. (*subject*)
Henry started <u>buying the groceries.</u> (*direct object*)
Henry knows all about <u>buying the groceries.</u> (*object of a preposition*)
Henry's favorite job is <u>buying the groceries.</u> (*predicate noun*)

Practice Copy each gerund phrase, underlining the gerund. Then write how the gerund is used in the sentence—*subject, direct object, object of a preposition,* or *predicate noun.*

1. We began looking for the lost cat.
2. His only ambition is becoming a doctor.
3. Campaigning all over the county was necessary for the candidate.
4. He must do his chores before practicing the piano.

Possessive with Gerunds   Use a possessive noun or pronoun before a gerund.

> Your winning the championship is a remarkable achievement.
> The fair was a success because of Molly's organizing it so well.

Practice   Choose the word that correctly completes each sentence.

1. (Joe, Joe's) skating on the pond was safe because the pond is frozen.
2. My (sister, sister's) graduating from high school was a joyous event.
3. Lee's best feature is (him, his) being willing to help anyone in need.

Infinitive Phrases   An **infinitive** is the basic verb form preceded by *to*. It may be used as a noun or as a modifier. An infinitive plus accompanying words forms an **infinitive phrase.** Infinitive phrases can be used as modifiers or as nouns.

> To be courageous in the face of adversity is a virtue. (*subject*)
> He tried to be courageous in the face of adversity. (*direct object*)
> A virtue is to be courageous in the face of adversity. (*predicate noun*)
> The place to go fishing is Lake Manitoba. (*adjective*)
> That map is not easy to follow without a compass. (*adverb*)

Practice   Copy each infinitive phrase. Then label it *noun, adjective,* or *adverb* to tell how it is used in the sentence.

1. Did they decide to sell the house?
2. To give him a gift would be a nice gesture.
3. He is studying to become an electrician.
4. There wasn't much to do on that rainy day.
5. They hope to see the Eiffel Tower in Paris.

Clauses

Definition   A **clause** is a group of words that has a subject and a predicate.

> when I went home   my dog was standing on the doorstep

An **independent,** or **main,** clause can stand alone.

> My dog was standing on the doorstep.

A **dependent,** or **subordinate,** clause needs an independent clause to complete its meaning.

> When I went home, my dog was standing on the doorstep.

Practice   Write *subordinate* or *independent* to describe each clause.

1. whenever it snows

2. in the nest were three eggs

3. where the pasture begins

4. to listen to music is a pleasure

Subordinating Conjunctions   A **subordinating conjunction** relates the subordinate clause to the independent clause.

> Whenever I read a sad book, I cry.

In an incomplete clause with *as* or *than,* use the pronoun you would use if the clause were complete.

> She is taller than he (is).
> Do you respect George more than (you respect) him?

Practice   Copy each sentence, underlining the subordinating conjunction. Choose the correct pronoun to complete one sentence.

1. Sal was even better-dressed than (they, them).

2. We can go wherever you like.

3. As soon as everyone is quiet we can begin.

Adjective Clauses   An **adjective clause** is a subordinate clause that is used to modify a noun or a pronoun.

> The book that I just finished reading was excellent. (*modifies* book)

A **relative pronoun** such as *who, which,* or *that* usually introduces an adjective clause. The pronoun relates the clause to the word modified.

> My dad, who is an electronics engineer, found a new job.

Practice   Copy each adjective clause. Write the word it modifies.

1. Mom bought me the sweater that I wanted.

2. He is the man who fixed our car.

3. The car, which is ten years old, often breaks down.

Who, Whom, and Whose in Adjective Clauses   Use *who* when the relative pronoun is the subject of the adjective clause. Use *whom* when the relative pronoun is the object of a verb or preposition in the adjective clause. Use *whose* when the relative pronoun is possessive.

> Eleanor Roosevelt is the woman who is my model. (*subject*)
> Is that the person whom you meant? (*object of verb*)
> I know to whom I spoke. (*object of preposition*)
> I wonder whose paper this is. (*possessive*)

Practice   Write the adjective clause, adding *who, whom,* or *whose.*

1. Can you tell me to ____ you gave the message?
2. Bergman was the director ____ movie I saw.
3. I received a letter from Molly, ____ I had called just yesterday.
4. Hank is the person ____ rescued the cat from the tree.

Restrictive and Nonrestrictive Clauses   A **restrictive clause** identifies the noun or pronoun it modifies. It is not set off with commas. A **nonrestrictive clause** gives added information about the noun or pronoun it modifies. It is set off with commas.

> I met the singer who recorded that song. (*restrictive*)
> I picked the vegetables, which were ripe. (*nonrestrictive*)

In careful writing, *that* is used in a restrictive clause, and *which* is used in a nonrestrictive clause.

> Jorge gave me the bread that he had baked yesterday. (*restrictive*)
> Jorge gave me the bread, which he had baked yesterday. (*nonrestrictive*)

Practice   Make each adjective clause nonrestrictive.

1. The jacket that I borrowed from Timmy had a hole in it.
2. I received a letter from my aunt who lives in Paris.
3. All of the actors who are rehearsing today must be at the theater at eleven o'clock.
4. Today I wrapped the present that I bought yesterday.

Adverb Clauses   An **adverb clause** is a subordinate clause used as an adverb.

> Whenever he races competitively, Sean always does his best.

An adverb clause is introduced by a subordinating conjunction.

> Let's paint the room before we bring in the carpet.

Introductory adverb clauses are followed by commas.

> If I don't miss the bus, I'll be home by six.

Practice   Copy the adverb clauses, adding commas where needed.

1. Since I lost my book I cannot do my homework.
2. When the temperature dropped the pond froze.
3. Dad told us the news after we had finished dinner.

Noun Clauses   A **noun clause** is a subordinate clause that acts as a noun.

> <u>What we need to know</u> is <u>when dinner will be served.</u>
>   *(subject)*   *(predicate noun)*
> You may give <u>whoever asks</u> <u>what is in the box.</u>
>   *(indirect object)*   *(direct object)*
> Ask him about <u>what happened.</u> *(object of preposition)*

Practice   Copy each noun clause, and label it *subject, direct object, indirect object, predicate noun,* or *object of preposition.*

1. How the accident happened was what the police wanted to know.
2. I can't imagine why the whale beached itself.
3. He told the interviewer that she could type.
4. Send whoever is on the mailing list a discount coupon.
5. Tell whoever asks what happened.
6. Whether it will snow tomorrow is what the forecaster will announce.
7. Tell me about who was at the party.
8. Whoever called had hung up before I answered the phone.
9. The letter is from whichever child is at camp.
10. Why the fire started was investigated by the arson squad.

Who and Whom in Noun Clauses   Use *who* and *whoever* as subjects in noun clauses.

> I know <u>who</u> will attend the party. (subject of clause)
> <u>Whoever</u> wants to go should sign up in the office. (subject of clause)

Use *whom* and *whomever* as objects within their clauses.

> <u>Whom</u> they will select is not known. *(object of* select*)*
> <u>Whomever</u> you spoke to is gone now. *(object of* to*)*

Practice   Write each sentence, completing it with *who, whom, whoever,* or *whomever.*

1. I know ____ wrote that poem.
2. You should believe ____ seems to be telling the truth.
3. ____ I talked to earlier is not working in that department now.
4. Assign that job to ____ you think best.
5. ____ they will elect is unpredictable.
6. You can tell me ____ is most likely to win the prize.
7. Please don't ask me ____ I called.

Usage

Agreement

Compound Subjects   A compound subject with *and* takes a plural verb.

Jason, Kelly, <u>and</u> Wonda <u>have</u> new dictionaries.

A compound subject with *or* or *nor* takes a verb that agrees with the nearer noun.

She <u>or</u> her <u>cousins</u> <u>are</u> ready to help.
Her cousins <u>or</u> <u>Paula</u> <u>is</u> ready to help.

Practice   Select the correct verb form from the pair in parentheses.

1. Neither Jackson nor his friends (has, have) the address.
2. Seiji and his sisters (go, goes) to California every summer.
3. Sue or Bob (writes, write) to their grandmother every week.
4. Either the dogs or the cat (likes, like) broccoli.
5. The swimmer and his coaches (is, are) well prepared for the race.

Titles, Names, and Collective Nouns   A title or name of a single thing takes a singular verb.

McNally, Doyle, and Hennessey <u>is</u> a stockbroking firm.
Star Wars <u>is</u> playing at the theater.

A collective noun takes a singular verb unless the group's members are referred to.

The committee <u>is</u> meeting at eight o'clock.
The committee <u>have</u> different opinions about that issue.

A noun referring to an amount usually takes a singular verb unless the individual units are referred to as individuals.

Ten dollars <u>is</u> too much to pay for that shirt.
Those ten coins <u>are</u> yours.

Practice   If the underlined verb form is correct, write *correct*. If it is not correct, write the correct form.

1. Akmajian Brothers <u>are</u> our moving company.
2. "The Hare and the Tortoise" <u>are</u> a famous fable.
3. Four pounds <u>is</u> what it weighs.

Inverted Order and Interrupted Order   Subject and verb must agree, no matter where the subject is. First find the subject, then make the verb agree with it.

In the pond <u>was</u> a <u>frog</u>.   In the pond <u>were</u> several <u>frogs</u>.
The <u>road</u> to town <u>is</u> blocked.   All <u>roads</u> to town <u>are</u> blocked.

Practice   If the underlined verb form is correct, write *correct*. If it is incorrect, write the correct form.

1. The plants in the garden <u>needs</u> more sun and rain.
2. When <u>is</u> Dad and the boys going to the game?
3. Here <u>is</u> the book and the pencil on the desk.
4. All the rooms in the house <u>are</u> large.

Negatives

A negative word or contraction says "no" or "not." *Barely, hardly,* and *scarcely* are considered negative words. Two negatives used to express one negative idea are a double negative. Avoid double negatives.

NONSTANDARD: I didn't hardly have enough time.
   CORRECT: I <u>hardly had</u> enough time.
NONSTANDARD: There wasn't barely enough food.
   CORRECT: There <u>was barely</u> enough food.

Practice   Rewrite these sentences, correcting the double negatives.

1. Haven't you seen that movie neither?
2. They weren't hardly strong enough to lift the crates.
3. Didn't nobody hear the thunder?
4. She hasn't never seen a live elephant.

Prepositions

beside, besides   *Beside* means "next to." *Besides* means "in addition to."

He is sitting <u>beside</u> me.   Who, <u>besides</u> him, was invited?

between, among   Use *between* to refer to two people or things. Use *among* to refer to more than two.

Just <u>between</u> the two of us, this is a secret.
The stew was divided <u>among</u> four campers.

from, off   Use *from,* not *off,* to mean "out of the possession of."

I got the pen <u>from</u> (*not* off) my friend.

in, into   *In* means "located within." *Into* means "movement from the outside to the inside."

The garbage is <u>in</u> the trash can.
Throw that garbage <u>into</u> the trash can.

of, at   Avoid using *off of.* Avoid using *at* in questions with *where.*

The bowl fell <u>off</u> (*not* off of) the counter.
<u>Where</u> is my dog (*not* at)?

Practice   Write each sentence correctly.

1. The horse was led (in, into) the stable after the workout.
2. I got this idea (from, off) my friend Kim.
3. This argument is just (between, among) us three.
4. Place the chair (beside, besides) the table.
5. Who, (beside, besides) us, is in the play?
6. The life jackets are (in, into) the boat.
7. The barn is located (between, among) the house and the river.

Problem Words

a, an, the   Use *a* and *an* before singular nouns. Use *a* before words that begin with a consonant. Use *an* before words that begin with a vowel or a vowel sound. Use *the* with both singular and plural nouns to point out a particular person, place, or thing.

This is <u>an</u> opportune moment.
It's <u>the</u> best chance we'll have.

accept, except   Do not confuse the verb *accept* ("to receive") with the preposition *except* ("excluding") or the verb *except* ("to exclude").

She was <u>accepted</u> at college.
He was <u>excepted</u> from gym yesterday.

affect, effect   Do not confuse the verb *affect* ("to influence") with the verb *effect* ("to cause to happen") or the noun *effect* ("result").

The weather <u>affects</u> our plans.
The politician <u>effected</u> a change in the committee's rules.
What <u>effect</u> will the weather have?

and, but, or   The conjunctions *and, but,* and *or* are used to join the parts of compound sentences, compound subjects, and compound predicates. *And* means "in addition to." *But* means a difference or contrast. *Or* states an alternative.

> She and I ski and skate well.
> Rita and Bob skate well, but they do not ski at all.
> Rita or Bob will try to learn to ski.

anywhere, everywhere, nowhere, somewhere   Do not add an *-s* to the end of *anywhere, everywhere, nowhere,* or *somewhere.*

> The cat was nowhere (*not* nowheres) to be found.

are, our   *Are* is a verb. *Our* is a possessive pronoun that means "belonging to us."

> Are these our coats?   Are you ready?
> This is our car.   They are here.

bad, badly   *Bad* is an adjective. It may be used after the linking verbs *look* and *feel. Badly* is an adverb.

> It's been a bad day.   The horse looks bad.   Karen sings badly.

fewer, less   Use *fewer* or *fewest* to make comparisons with nouns in the plural. Use *less* or *least* to make comparisons with nouns in the singular.

> Fewer students are absent today.   I have the least money.

farther, further   Use *farther* to refer to physical distance. Use *further* in all other cases.

> Grandma's house is farther from here than I thought.
> The further you read, the more interesting the story becomes.

good, well   *Good* is an adjective. It may be used after linking verbs such as *feel* and *look. Well* is an adverb in most cases. *Well* is used as an adjective only when it refers to health.

> The day looks good.   She swims well.   She feels well.

lend, loan   *Lend* means "to give something temporarily." *Loan* means "the act of lending" or "the thing lent." *Lend* is a verb; *loan* is a noun.

> Please lend me some money.   I appreciate the loan of your pencil.

like, as if, as though   Use *like* as a preposition. Use *as if* and *as though* as subordinating conjunctions.

I look <u>like</u> Dad.   It looks <u>as if</u> (*or* <u>as though</u>) it might rain.

than, then   *Than* is a conjunction used in comparisons. *Then* is an adverb meaning "at that time, soon after, next in time."

She is thinner <u>than</u> her sister.   Finish breakfast, and <u>then</u> leave.

their, there   *Their* means "belonging to more than one person or thing." *There* can begin a sentence. *There* also means "in or at the place." To find whether the subject and the verb agree in a sentence beginning with *there,* drop *there.* Then rearrange the sentence.

<u>Their</u> house is over <u>there</u>.   <u>There</u> are two cars in the driveway.

to, too, two   *To* means "in the direction of." *Too* means "also" and "more than enough." *Two* is a number.

These <u>two</u> books are <u>too</u> long.   <u>Two</u> of us walked <u>to</u> the dance.

where, that   Avoid using *where* to introduce a noun clause.

I see <u>that</u> (*not* where) they have gone on vacation.

whether, as   Avoid using *as* to introduce a noun clause.

I don't know <u>whether</u> (*not* as) it will rain.

Practice   Write the word that correctly completes each sentence.

1. Would you like (a, an) orange to eat?
2. Many people do not like to (accept, except) advice.
3. The jury was greatly (affected, effected) by the witness's statement.
4. Carlos looked (everywhere, everywheres) for his umbrella.
5. Since (are, our) house looks so (bad, badly), it will be painted.
6. Are you taking (fewer, less) days of vacation this year?
7. After thinking about it (further, farther), I have decided to travel (further, farther) for my vacation next year.
8. Lillian plays the violin very (well, good).
9. Please (lend, loan) Phil your jacket, (to, too, two).
10. Did you read (where, that) it looks (like, as though) the conference will be canceled?
11. Because (their, there) isn't any wind, today is more pleasant (than, then) yesterday.
12. Tina doesn't know (whether, as) she will go to (an, the) party.

Pronouns

I, me   *I* is used as a subject. *Me* is used in other parts of a sentence. *I* and *me* come last when used with a noun or another pronoun.

Jan and I are going to the show.   She lends the book to Jill and me.

its, it's   *Its* is a possessive noun. *It's* is a contraction of *it is.*

The show had its own announcer.   It's cold today.

we, us   To use the pronouns *we* or *us* correctly with a noun in a sentence, first look at the noun. If the noun is the subject of the sentence or if it follows a linking verb, use the pronoun *we* with it.

We students are proud.   It is we students who are proud.

If the noun is the object after an action verb or a preposition, use the pronoun *us.*

She gave us students a lecture.   She gave the book to us students.

who, whom   Use the pronoun *who* as a subject. Use the pronoun *whom* as a direct object or object of a preposition.

Who was the surprise guest?   Whom did you ask?

whose, who's   *Whose* is an interrogative pronoun. *Who's* is a contraction for *who is.*

Whose tickets are these?   Who's your friend?

their, they're   *Their* is a possessive pronoun. *They're* is a contraction of *they are.*

Their car is in the driveway.   They're preparing for a trip.

theirs, there's   *Theirs* is a possessive pronoun. *There's* is a contraction of *there is.*

This dog is theirs.   There's his tag.

they, this, these   Avoid using *them* as a demonstrative pronoun. Do not use *here* or *there* after a demonstrative pronoun.

They (*not* them) are mine.   This (*not* this here) is yours.

your, you're   *Your* is a possessive pronoun. *You're* is a contraction for *you are.*

Are these your glasses?   You're late again.

Practice   Write the correct word or words.

1. You and (I, me) should share this sandwich.
2. Is this the person (who, whom) you called?
3. (Us, We) detectives are anxious to find out if this stereo is (theirs, there's).
4. (Whose, Who's) cutting (your, you're) hair these days?
5. (They, Them) are my boots, and I need them because (its, it's) going to snow today.

Verb Usage

be, have, do   *Be, have,* and *do* can be used as main verbs and as helping verbs. They are irregular in form. See pages 110–111 for the forms.

I <u>am</u> happy.   I <u>am</u> walking.   I <u>have</u> them.   I <u>have</u> tried.

borrow, lend   Borrow means "to take." Lend means "to give."

You may <u>borrow</u> my pen.   I will <u>lend</u> it to you.

let, leave   *Let* means "to permit" or "to allow." *Leave* means "to go away from" or "to let stay in a certain place."

Please <u>let</u> me go swimming, Mom.   I want to <u>leave</u> at ten o'clock.

lie, lay   *Lie* means "to rest, recline, remain in one place." *Lay* means "to put, place (something)."

The dog <u>lies</u> in its bed.   Please <u>lay</u> the books here.

raise, rise   *Raise* means "to move something up, to increase something, to grow something." *Rise* means "to get up, to go up."

The crane will <u>raise</u> that beam.   We <u>rise</u> at seven in the morning.

shall, will   *Shall* is used with *I* and *we* in very careful usage.

I <u>shall</u> leave now.   We <u>shall</u> be home early.

teach, learn   *Teach* means "to give instruction." *Learn* means "to receive instruction."

She <u>taught</u> science to high school students.   I <u>learned</u> about history.

set, sit   *Set* means "to place, to put." *Sit* means "to rest, to stay in one place."

<u>Set</u> the vase on the windowsill.   Please <u>sit</u> in this chair.

Practice   Choose the correct word to complete each sentence.

1. We'll be awake before the sun (raises, rises) tomorrow.
2. I (shall, will) send in my resignation.
3. Ms. Fishbein (teaches, learns) junior high school students.
4. Martha will (lay, lie) down to rest.
5. I think that I will (let, leave) Jim (borrow, lend) my bike.
6. Please (sit, set) the dishes on the counter before you (set, sit) down.

Verb Phrases   Avoid using *could of, might of, should of, must of.* Use *could have, might have, should have, must have.*

> She <u>could have</u> (*not* could of) arrived earlier.

Avoid using phrases like *had ought* or *hadn't ought.* Use *ought, ought not,* or *should, should not.*

> You <u>ought</u> (*not* had ought) to arrive at school on time.

Practice   Write the verb phrase that correctly completes the sentence.

1. He (ought not, hadn't ought) to have tried to climb that mountain.
2. He (must of, must have) been frightened before he was found.

Verb Tenses   Avoid unnecessary shifts from one tense to another.

> The trains <u>stopped</u> suddenly, and everyone <u>was</u> (*not* is) surprised.

Use the past perfect to discuss the earlier of two related past actions and the past tense to express the later action.

> Brenda <u>had studied</u> hard, but she <u>failed</u> the test anyway.

Use the future perfect to express the earlier of two related future actions and the present to express the later action.

> I <u>will have finished</u> the book before the movie <u>comes</u> out.

Use the present perfect to express an action that occurred at an unspecified time in the past.

> She <u>has ridden</u> a horse only once.

Practice   Correct all unnecessary shifts in tense.

1. Before I finish this book, it is due back at the library.
2. You could have been on time if you take the bus.
3. It had begun to rain before we will get home.
4. I should have worn my raincoat when I will leave this morning.

Irregular Verbs Irregular verbs do not add *-ed* or *-d* to form the past participle. The principal parts of these verbs must be memorized. Following are the present, past, and past participles of some common irregular verbs. Use *have* when you are learning the past participle.

Verb	Past	Past Participle	Verb	Past	Past Participle
begin	began	begun	let	let	let
blow	blew	blown	make	made	made
break	broke	broken	put	put	put
bring	brought	brought	ride	rode	ridden
catch	caught	caught	ring	rang	rung
choose	chose	chosen	run	ran	run
come	came	come	say	said	said
cost	cost	cost	see	saw	seen
do	did	done	shrink	shrank	shrunk
drink	drank	drunk	sing	sang	sung
drive	drove	driven	sit	sat	sat
eat	ate	eaten	speak	spoke	spoken
fly	flew	flown	steal	stole	stolen
freeze	froze	frozen	swim	swam	swum
give	gave	given	take	took	taken
go	went	gone	tear	tore	torn
grow	grew	grown	think	thought	thought
know	knew	known	throw	threw	thrown
leave	left	left	wear	wore	worn
lend	lent	lent	write	wrote	written

Practice Write the past or past participle form to complete each sentence.

1. I ____ my homework before six. (begin)
2. She ____ on that track many times before the meet. (run)
3. They ____ about the problem for a long time. (think)
4. We ____ many vegetables in the garden. (grow)
5. The wind had ____ shingles from the roof. (blow)
6. Rafael ____ me his jacket. (lend)
7. People applauded after Amanda had ____. (speak)
8. How long have you ____ in the chorus? (sing)
9. The pond ____ last winter. (freeze)
10. The telephone ____ ten times. (ring)

Punctuation and Capitalization

Abbreviations Abbreviations are shortened forms of words. Most abbreviations begin with a capital letter and end with a period.

Titles

Mr. (Mister) Mr. Juan Albino   Sr. (Senior) John Helt, Sr.
Mrs. (Mistress) Mrs. Frances Wong   Jr. (Junior) John Helt, Jr.
Dr. (Doctor) Dr. Janice Dodds

Words Used in Addresses

St. (Street)   Blvd. (Boulevard)   Pkwy. (Parkway)
Rd. (Road)   Rte. (Route)   Mt. (Mount or Mountain)
Ave. (Avenue)   Apt. (Apartment)   Expy. (Expressway)
Dr. (Drive)

Words Used in Business

Co. (Company)   Corp. (Corporation)   Inc. (Incorporated)

Some abbreviations are written in all capital letters, with a letter standing for each important word.

P.D. (Police Department)   P.O. (Post Office)
M.P. (Member of Parliament)   R.N. (Registered Nurse)
J.P. (Justice of the Peace)   U.K. (United Kingdom)

Some abbreviations have neither capital letters nor periods.

mph (miles per hour)   hp (horsepower)   ft (feet)

Abbreviations of government agencies or national organizations do not usually have periods.

SBA (Small Business Administration)
OAS (Organization of American States)
PBS (Public Broadcasting Service)
NATO (North Atlantic Treaty Organization)

The United States Postal Service uses two capital letters and no period in each of its state abbreviations.

CA (California)   OH (Ohio)   NJ (New Jersey)
IN (Indiana)   SC (South Carolina)

Practice Write abbreviations where you can for the items below.

1. Southeast Expressway   3. West Cedar Street
2. 14 feet   4. Doctor Deborah Rennant

5. Eucalyptus Boulevard
6. Oslo Furniture, Incorporated
7. North Atlantic Treaty Organization
8. Mister Walter Robins
9. 70 horsepower
10. Sarah Nelson, Registered Nurse

Titles   The important words and the first and last words in a title are capitalized. Titles of books, magazines, and newspapers are underlined.

<u>Oliver Twist</u>   <u>Better Homes & Gardens</u>   <u>The Phoenix Express</u>

Titles of short stories, articles, songs, poems, and book chapters are enclosed in quotation marks.

"The Necklace" (*short story*)
"Primate Physiology: An Introduction" (*article*)
"Home on the Range" (*song*)

Practice   Copy these sentences, writing the titles correctly.

1. Gilda could not remember the words in the second verse of in flanders fields.
2. Our English teacher assigned the book moby dick.
3. Please read the chapter titled the scientific method before the quiz on Monday.

Punctuation

End Punctuation   There are three end marks. A **period (.)** ends a declarative or imperative sentence. A **question mark (?)** follows an interrogative sentence. An **exclamation mark (!)** follows an exclamatory sentence.

The scissors are on my desk. (declarative)
Look up the spelling of that word in the dictionary. (imperative)
How is the word spelled? (interrogative)
I was sure there was an *e* on the end! (exclamatory)

Practice   Write these sentences with the correct end punctuation.

1. How I wish I had an apple
2. Marci, Oliver's cousin, won the lead in a play
3. How do you make bran muffins, Alan
4. Learn how to use the fire extinguisher
5. Do you hear the thunder
6. Please close the window

Apostrophe   Use an apostrophe in the following ways.

1. Use an apostrophe to show possession.

   Doug's rabbit   girls' shoes   women's talents

2. Use an apostrophe in contractions in place of one or more dropped letters.

isn't (is not)	wasn't (was not)	I'm (I am)
can't (cannot)	we're (we are)	they've (they have)
won't (will not)	it's (it is)	they'll (they will)

Practice   Write a contraction or a possessive for each item.

   1. cage of the mice   **6.** he is
   2. you are   **7.** they will
   3. I have   **8.** sails of the boat
   4. books of the boys   **9.** we have
   5. is not   **10.** fur of the foxes

Colon   Use a colon after the greeting in a business letter.

   Dear Mrs. Trimby: Dear Realty Homes:

Practice   Write two possible greetings for a business letter to the Palmer Doorbell Company.

Comma   A comma tells the reader to pause between the words it separates. Use commas in the following ways.

1. Use a comma to separate words in a series.

   Clyde asked if we had any apples, peaches, or grapes.

2. Use a comma to separate simple sentences in a compound sentence.

   Some students were at lunch, and others were studying.

3. Use commas to set off an appositive from the rest of the sentence.

   Charles Dickens, the author, lived most of his life in London.

4. Use commas after introductory words such as *yes, no, oh,* and *well.*

   Well, it's too cold out.   No, it isn't six yet.

5. Use a comma to separate a noun in direct address.

   Jean, help me fix this tire.   How was your trip, Grandpa?

6. Use a comma to separate the month and day from the year. Use a comma to separate the year from the rest of the sentence.

   On July 4, 1776, our nation was born.

7. Use a comma between the names of a city and a state.

   Chicago, Illinois   Miami, Florida

8. Use a comma after the greeting in a friendly letter.

   Dear Deena,   Dear Uncle Rudolph,

9. Use a comma after the closing in a letter.

   Your nephew,   Sincerely yours,

10. Use a comma before or after a direct quotation to separate it from the statement that tells who is speaking.

    "Bring a map," said Eli.   Joyce said, "I must go."

11. Use a comma to set off the word *too* when it means "also."

    Michael has a new haircut, too.

12. Use a comma following an introductory participial phrase and with a participial phrase that gives added information.

    Looking through the binoculars, he located a warbler.
    The bird-watcher, using his binoculars, spotted a heron.

13. Use a comma following introductory adverb clauses.

    While we're waiting, let's think of names for the new puppy.

14. Use commas with a nonrestrictive clause that gives added information about the noun or pronoun it modifies.

    This book, which I got at the library today, is about whales.

Practice   Write each item, adding commas where necessary.

1. Jackson avoiding his guard made the basket.
2. Harold Rubin a well-known scientist has written a book.
3. Clint do we have any apples peaches or grapes?
4. "Please close the barn door" said Mrs. Olson.
5. Smiling broadly Nellie said "I took pictures of the cabin the lakes and the mountain.
6. Dear Uncle Bert

7. Sincerely yours
8. Since we have time let's go to the museum too.
9. The painting which Clara just finished will be in an exhibit that begins March 25 1984.
10. Yes I will help clean up the beach and Joe will help too.

Punctuating Dialogue   **Dialogue** is written conversation. **Quotation marks** are used to set dialogue apart from the rest of the sentence. The first word of a quotation begins with a capital letter. Punctuation belongs inside the closing quotation marks. Commas separate a quotation from the rest of the sentence.

> "Where," inquired the mysterious-looking stranger, "is the post office?"
>
> "Please put away your books now," said Mr. Emory.
>
> Linda replied, "I don't know what time it is."

Practice   Write each sentence, punctuating and capitalizing the quotations correctly.

1. Who in the world asked my mother could be calling at this hour?
2. I don't believe in vampires scoffed Edwardo.
3. The critic raved it was a marvelous performance!
4. Reconstruction explained the teacher followed the Civil War.
5. I'm sure, Anna, that the party will be fun I said or at least it will be interesting.

Capitalization

1. Capitalize the first word of every sentence.

   What an unusual color the roses are!

2. Capitalize the pronoun *I*.

   On April 14, I will fly to London.

3. Capitalize every important word in the names of particular people, places, or things.

   Emily G. Shenk   Edon, Ohio   Lincoln Memorial

4. Capitalize titles or their abbreviations when used with a person's name.

   Governor Bradford   Ms. Ida Lee   Mr. Max Souda

5. Capitalize the names of months and days.

My birthday is on the last <u>M</u>onday in <u>M</u>arch.

6. Capitalize the names of organizations, businesses, institutions, and agencies.

<u>N</u>ational <u>H</u>ockey <u>L</u>eague   The <u>S</u>tatus <u>C</u>ompany

7. Capitalize names of holidays and other special events.

<u>F</u>lag <u>D</u>ay   <u>H</u>alloween   <u>F</u>ourth of <u>J</u>uly

8. Capitalize the first word of a direct quotation.

David shouted, "<u>B</u>uckle your seat belts!"

9. Capitalize the first and last word and all important words in the titles of books, newspapers, stories, songs, poems, reports, and outlines.

<u>F</u>rom the <u>E</u>arth to the <u>M</u>oon   "<u>T</u>he <u>R</u>ainbow <u>C</u>onnection"
<u>T</u>he <u>N</u>ew <u>Y</u>ork <u>T</u>imes   "<u>G</u>rowing <u>U</u>p"

10. Capitalize the first word of each main topic and subtopic in an outline.

   I. <u>T</u>ypes of libraries
     A. <u>L</u>arge public library
     B. <u>B</u>ookmobile

11. Capitalize the first word in the greeting and closing of a letter.

<u>D</u>ear Marcia,   <u>Y</u>ours truly,

12. Capitalize nationalities, languages, religions, and religious terms.

<u>C</u>hinese   <u>S</u>panish   <u>M</u>exican custom   <u>B</u>uddhism

Practice   Write each sentence. Use capital letters correctly.

1. my favorite book is *the little prince.*
2. "where is the washington monument?" asked pamela.
3. last year, i visited the sistine chapel in rome, italy.
4. have you read the article called "teaching dolphins"?
5. mr. baker moved into the apartment downstairs on tuesday.
6. peg bought the record at the modern music company.
7. angela exclaimed, "wait for me!"
8. we're going to lake wentworth during the fourth of july weekend.

Letter Forms

Friendly Letters A friendly letter has a heading, which gives the writer's address and the date the letter was written. It also includes a greeting, the body of the letter, a closing, and a signature. The style of a friendly letter is casual and informal.

HEADING

215 Evergreen Blvd.
Brookline, MA 02146
April 12, 1983

GREETING

Dear Aunt Emma,

BODY

Thank you so much for the birthday present you sent me. A baseball glove is just what I needed, since I'll be trying out for Little League in a few weeks. This one fits perfectly, and it is just the style I like.

I hope that you'll be able to visit us next month. Maybe you'll get to see me catch a fly ball and win the game!

CLOSING

Love,

SIGNATURE

Yalya

Business Letters   A business letter differs from a friendly letter in several ways. It contains an inside address showing how the envelope will be addressed; a colon is used after the greeting instead of a comma; and the closing is polite and formal, as is the style of the letter.

HEADING

215 Evergreen Blvd.
Brookline, MA 02146
November 23, 1983

INSIDE ADDRESS

Writewell Pen Co.
1945 Main Street
Port Jervis, NY 12771

GREETING

Dear Writewell Pen Co.:

BODY

Two weeks ago I purchased a pen manufactured by the Writewell Pen Co. I was disappointed to find that after a few days the nib broke and the ink reservoir began to leak.

I would like to have the pen repaired or replaced. Should I return it to the store where I bought it, or send it directly to you?

CLOSING

Sincerely yours,

SIGNATURE

Talya Smith

Talya Smith

More Practice

- **Kinds of Sentences**　If the group of words is not a sentence, add words to make it a sentence. If it is already a sentence, rewrite it, adding a period, question mark, or exclamation point. Then label every sentence *declarative, interrogative, imperative,* or *exclamatory.*

  1. what is a peccary
  2. there's no such thing
  3. lives in the area from South America to the southwest United States
  4. they are hoofed forest animals very much like wild hogs
  5. you're kidding me
  6. I've even seen some peccaries
  7. when I visited my aunt and uncle in New Mexico
  8. what do they look like
  9. about 50 centimeters high with a coarse blackish-gray coat
  10. usually peccaries give birth to twins, not single babies
  11. tell me more about them
  12. pigskin items like gloves and jackets are made from peccary hides
  13. because their hides are thin and tough
  14. although they are timid animals, they fight viciously if necessary

- **Finding the Subject and Predicate**　Some of these sentences are in natural order, and some are in inverted order. Find and copy the simple subject and simple predicate of each sentence.

  15. There were two sharp knocks at the door.
  16. Can it be the mail carrier?
  17. Why don't you just open the door?
  18. The piercing sound of the doorbell quickened my steps.
  19. Here I come!
  20. In the doorway stood an old friend of mine.
  21. Come in.
  22. When did you return from Panama?
  23. In his hand was an interesting-looking package.
  24. The beautiful paper on the package looked like gift paper.
  25. Had he brought me a present from Panama?

- **Simple, Compound, and Complex Sentences** Write *simple, compound,* or *complex* to describe each sentence.

26. Certain letters are associated with certain speech sounds.

27. Some languages, like Spanish, have direct and consistent relationships between letters and sounds.

28. When you learn these relationships, you can read aloud almost anything in the language.

29. You may not know the meanings of the words, but you know their pronunciation.

30. The letter *c* in Latin American Spanish is always pronounced like *s* before *e* or *i* but is pronounced like English *k* before *a*, *o*, or *u*.

31. Although the letter *h* alone is always silent, the combination *ch* is always pronounced just as in the English word *child.*

32. In fact, the combination *ch* is considered a single letter in Spanish, and it comes between *c* and *d* in the alphabet.

33. The letters *ll* and *rr* are also considered single letters whenever they appear together.

34. You can read just about any Spanish word after you learn just a very few rules like these.

35. English is quite different, for letters and letter combinations can be pronounced in various ways.

36. Compare *gh* in *ghost, laughing,* and *caught,* or compare *ti* in *tin* and in *action.*

37. Because the letter-sound relationships in English are not always obvious, they may confuse students of the language.

Enrichment

Work with a partner. Read the first sentence below. Your partner will choose a conjunction from the list on the right and will add a clause to complete the sentence. Take turns so that both of you have a chance to add a clause to each sentence.

1. The boy waited on the deck.	until	or
2. My dog greets me excitedly.	whenever	if
3. The party is scheduled for Friday.	and	but
4. The pigs escape from the pen.	unless	after
5. There was a pigeon coop on the roof.	because	while

More Practice

- **Kinds of Nouns** Divide your paper into six columns. Label them *noun, common, proper, concrete, abstract, compound.* List each noun below in the first column. Put a check mark in the *common* or *proper* column and in the *abstract* or *concrete* column. When appropriate, also put a check mark in the *compound* column. Do not repeat nouns.

1. I felt great affection for the little spaniel.
2. In Latin America, Sunday is considered the first day of the week.
3. My friend Muffie Bradshaw has a sister-in-law who works as a ski instructor in the mountains of New Hampshire.
4. For centuries, sailors on the high seas have greeted the sight of a lighthouse with respect and relief.
5. Keepers of the lighthouse led solitary but useful lives.
6. The light warns boats of the danger of rocks or reefs.
7. Ancient Libyans placed burning coal or wood into baskets of metal and hung them from poles on the tops of high towers.
8. Vessels on the Mediterranean Sea received these warnings from the coast of Egypt.
9. In modern times, the operation of these lights has become automatic, and keepers in residence are no longer necessary.
10. The lighthouses frequently use radio beacons that send out signals.
11. Conservationists, historians, and the public have taken an interest in the preservation of old lighthouses as historical monuments.

- **Plural and Possessive Forms of Nouns** Divide your paper into four columns. Label the columns *singular, singular possessive, plural, plural possessive,* in that order. In the first column, copy the singular form of each noun given below. Then, for each noun, write the forms that belong in the other three columns.

12. analysis	**18.** Rachel	**24.** Grady
13. woman	**19.** beauty	**25.** stereo
14. passer-by	**20.** fox	**26.** goose
15. teaspoonful	**21.** hatch	**27.** father-in-law
16. Elias	**22.** torpedo	**28.** calf
17. baby	**23.** flake	**29.** proof

- **Writing with Appositives**   Rewrite each set of sentences as one sentence. Turn the underlined words into an appositive. Add commas where needed.

30. Ouagadougou is the capital city of Upper Volta. Upper Volta is <u>a country in western Africa</u>.

31. The vulture is <u>a fairly large bird</u>. The vulture has no feathers on its head.

32. Dead animals are eaten by the vulture. It is called <u>a bird of prey</u>.

33. A cousin of mine is named <u>Arlette</u>. My cousin is a repairperson for the telephone company.

34. Cicely Tyson spoke at our school last week. She is <u>a well-known and talented actress</u>.

35. The volt is <u>a unit of electrical measurement</u>. The volt is named after Count Alessandro Volta. Volta was <u>the developer of the electric battery</u>.

36. <u>Itzhak Perlman</u> is a violinist. The famous violinist is also an excellent cook.

37. Limpets are <u>small sea animals with protective shells</u>. Limpets live on rocks on seacoasts all over the world.

38. Free mail delivery was established in 49 cities of the United States in 1863. This was <u>an important step linking the country together</u>.

Enrichment

Copy the chart below. Write the noun *stable* down the left side of your paper, putting one letter on each line. Then label five columns as shown—*Food, City,* and so on. Work with a partner to think of nouns that belong in each category and begin with the letter on the left. For example, *soup* is a food beginning with *s,* Sausilito is a city beginning with *s.* If you need help, use a dictionary or an encyclopedia. When you and your partner have finished, you may want to think of another six-letter word and fill in another chart.

	Food	City	Writer	Plaything	Animal
S					
T					
A					
B					
L					
E					

More Practice

- **Main Idea of a Paragraph** Read the following paragraph. Write the numbers of the sentences that do *not* keep to the main idea of the paragraph.

(1) Greece is one of the oldest nations in the world. (2) Over the centuries it has made many contributions to Western civilization. (3) I have always wanted to visit Greece. (4) Democracy, our form of government, is based on a Greek principle. (5) Much of our architecture shows Greek influence, especially in pillars and columns. (6) I don't care much for a lot of modern architecture, do you? (7) The modern Olympic games are a revival of a festival of athletic games first celebrated in ancient Greece. (8) Even our word *alphabet* comes from the Greeks. (9) It is a combination of the Greek letters *alpha* and *beta.* (10) Greek is one of the languages I want to learn someday.

The following group of sentences should be divided into three paragraphs. Decide where each paragraph should begin. Then copy the first sentence of the second paragraph and the first sentence of the third paragraph.

Most scientists agree that the North American spoon weevil is one of the nicest of all insects. This conclusion is based on several facts. In the first place, the spoon weevil never destroys crops or property. Secondly, it never stings or bites people or animals. It never makes too much noise. Finally, the spoon weevil has very good manners. The insects are named after their favorite recreational facility—the spoon. Spoons with drops of water in them are used as swimming pools by hot, young spoon weevils. Teenaged spoon weevils who can afford the equipment like to ski down the inside of the spoon. Older, more determined spoon weevils like to climb to the tops of overturned spoons. Despite its fine temperament and its strong singing voice, the spoon weevil does not make a good pet. In fact, its sesame-seed size prevents it from being any fun at all. For example, a pet spoon weevil will continually slip out of its little leash while being walked. Also, the animal will always refuse to perform its tiny tricks for company.

- **Topic Sentences and Supporting Details**   The following two paragraphs need a topic sentence. Write an interesting sentence to begin each paragraph.

> Early in the morning, while the sky is still grey, birds sing outside the windows of our cabin on the mountain. During the morning, I watch the birds and the butterflies flit in the sun. In the afternoon, chipmunks scurry through the bushes. Rabbits dart across the clearing. At night raccoons scavenge for food from our garbage pails.

> Have you ever seen a bird that has fur and nurses its young? a beaver that lays eggs? a duck that is as venomous as a cobra? The duckbill, or platypus, of eastern Australia and Tasmania is neither a mythical beast nor a practical joke of nature. It is simply an oddity in the animal kingdom. The duckbill's shoulder structure is reptilian. Like both reptiles and birds, it lays eggs. Like some reptiles, it defends itself by injecting poison into its enemies. This strange amphibian defies the old saying that the female of the species is deadlier than the male. Only the male platypus has a poisonous spur on its hind foot. Otherwise, both males and females are defenseless. Once in danger of extinction, the platypus is now protected by strict laws.

Write two topic sentences about each of the following topics. Put a check mark beside the topic sentence you think is the best in each pair.

1. the best meal you ever ate
2. the kind of books or magazines you like to read
3. your favorite sport or game

- **Order in Paragraphs**   Reorder these steps in chronological order. Then use the steps to write a paragraph. Use appropriate order words in some, but not all, of the sentences.

1. Take two eggs, ¼ cup of milk, and beat lightly.
2. Sprinkle cinnamon into the mixture.
3. Place the bread in a hot, greased frying pan.
4. Here's how to make a delicious French toast breakfast for two.
5. When one side is lightly brown, turn, and brown the other side.
6. Serve immediately.
7. Coat four pieces of bread with the egg mixture.

Choose a hobby or interest of yours that involves an activity. Make a list of the steps involved. Put the steps in order, using appropriate order words. Make your wording as clear as possible.

More Practice

- **Kinds of Verbs**   Divide your paper in half. Label one half *Linking Verbs* and the other half *Action Verbs*. Then divide the *Action Verbs* column in half. Label one column *Transitive* and the other *Intransitive*. Find the verb phrase in each sentence, and write it in the appropriate column. Underline the main verb.

  1. The puppy certainly has grown larger since last month.
  2. The water is boiling at last.
  3. Did you boil enough water for several cups?
  4. Pedro should arrange his collection of shells in a more orderly way.
  5. Hasn't Gigi become a fine softball player?
  6. Dr. Beech grows exotic orchids in her elaborate greenhouse.
  7. Bryan ironed his plaid shirt before the party.
  8. Elise doesn't believe the story about the armadillo.
  9. The crowd was roaring its approval of the surprise home run.
  10. The lions roared at us threateningly.
  11. Have you tasted Arnie's special macaroni and cheese?
  12. It must taste either wonderful or terrible.

- **Principal Parts of Verbs**   Some of the verbs listed below are regular, and some are irregular. Write the four principal parts of each verb.

13. chop	16. sing	19. mix	22. grab	25. refer
14. spy	17. do	20. sit	23. hate	26. take
15. grow	18. wear	21. speak	24. miss	27. run

- **Verb Tenses and Forms**   Write *present, past, future, present perfect, past perfect,* or *future perfect* to describe the tense of the verb. If the verb is a progressive form, also write *progressive*.

  28. The chimpanzee is rubbing its stomach.
  29. The elephant had been napping for a while before we arrived.
  30. The hippopotamus in the water seemed asleep.
  31. In a few minutes, we shall have been watching the seals for an hour.
  32. The zoo has grown much larger and will be expanding even more.
  33. Next to the aviary will soon be a new habitat for the goats.

- **Using Tenses Correctly**   Rewrite correctly any sentence that has a needless shift in tense.

   (34) Samantha walked out on stage and sits down at the piano. **(35)** The friendly audience had applauded even before she appeared. **(36)** Although Samantha had been nervous backstage, now she feels calm and confident. **(37)** When she turns fifteen next year, she will have been studying the piano for ten years. **(38)** She is normally a well-rehearsed performer, and her performance that night was certainly no exception. **(39)** She sat tall and straight at the piano and plays with complete assurance. **(40)** The audience shouted its approval after the concert ended. **(41)** If Samantha continues her hard work and dedication, someday she will be a famous pianist.

- **Active and Passive Voice**   Rewrite each active sentence as a passive sentence, and rewrite each passive sentence as an active sentence.

   42. Lorraine caught the ball.
   43. All the acorns were eaten by the squirrels.
   44. Five semi-finalists were chosen by the judges.
   45. Benjamin Richards won the final point of the game.
   46. Ms. Jacobson supplied all of the refreshments.

- **Agreement of Subject and Verb**   Write the correct verb form.

   47. The map and the flashlight (is, are) in the glove compartment.
   48. *The New York Times* (is, are) on the porch.
   49. Where (is, are) my new poultry shears?
   50. Neither the band nor the refreshments (was, were) very good.
   51. Five dollars (is, are) too much for that breakable toy.
   52. Measles (was, were) very common and serious not too many years ago.
   53. The band (is, are) marching in the Thanksgiving Day parade.
   54. Sanchez & Stokes (manufactures, manufacture) fine wood stoves.

Enrichment

   Work with three other students. Write five action verbs on your paper. Then take turns pantomiming the action of the verb and allowing the other students to guess the verb form you pantomime. If any of your verbs are duplicated on someone else's list, that person must think of another action verb.

More Practice

- **Observing Details** From the list below, choose five objects. Pretend you are describing the objects in a letter to a pen-pal in a faraway place. Assume that your pen-pal has never seen or used the object. Make a list of details about each object, using sense words.

  1. an egg beater
  2. a baseball
  3. a stuffed animal
  4. a TV set
  5. a tennis racquet
  6. snow
  7. a potted plant
  8. a hamburger
  9. a toaster
  10. an electric knife

- **Choosing Details** Pick two of the items listed below. Two different points of view are given in parentheses after each one. List five descriptive details that would convey the first point of view about the item. Then list five descriptive details that would convey the second point of view. Make your details as exact and vivid as possible. Remember, you are taking two different points of view toward the *same* item.

  1. a grocery store (new and neat / crowded)
  2. a bicycle (needs cleaning / has just been washed)
  3. a puppy (cute / annoying)
  4. a book (boring / fascinating)
  5. a song (you love it / you dislike it)
  6. a jacket (you would like to have it / you would never buy it)
  7. the view from your window (on a bright summer day / on a rainy winter day)
  8. a hat (you have lost it and want it returned / you are describing why you like it)

- **Using Exact Words** Choose and rewrite three of the following descriptions. Use exact and vivid words in your descriptions. Try to include words that show your point of view. Use at least two comparisons. When you have finished, compare your descriptions with those written by classmates.

1. The lake looked polluted.
2. It was a gloomy night.
3. The child was spoiled. His actions and his mannner of talking showed he was used to getting his own way.
4. The game was an exciting one. Some of the plays were very suspenseful, and the fans really showed that they were enjoying themselves.
5. By the way he was dressed, it was clear that Sam didn't follow the crowd. Even his hair style was unusual.
6. There was something strange about the place. I didn't feel comfortable being there. I wished I was home, but I had no choice.

Complete the following comparisons. Do not use commonly used comparisons; think of your own. Use exact and vivid words.

1. The racing car was as
2. The theater was as quiet as
3. The raindrops on the car's hood shone like
4. The moon rose like
5. In the jungle, tree vines grew as thick as
6. Seen from the plane window, the houses looked like

● **Proofreading**   The following paragraph is from a description of a cat. Read it carefully, looking for errors in spelling, punctuation, and capitalization. If a sentence is punctuated incorrectly, write it correctly on your paper. If a word is misspelled, write it correctly on your paper. You should have one sentence and seven words on your paper.

Somehow, people never said What a sweet kitty!" when they saw Matthew. Those who did allways took it back. That was all right with Matthew. By the time he had gotten the word that cats were suppost to be sweet, it was much too late. Often, the first thing people said was, "Whats wrong with your cat?" What was wrong was that they hadn't said, "Hello, cat," and Matthew was pointing that out in the tone of voice he kept for such ommisions. When Matthew told you something, you had to notice. It wasn't just the tone. He was lean as a panther and so black that he gleemed green and purpel when the sun hit his fur. The blackness made his fangs more outstanding. People looked cautious when Matthew even yawnned.

More Practice

- **Identifying Direct Objects** Copy each direct object. If a sentence has no direct object, write *none*.

    1. I followed the deer into the woods.
    2. Captain Whittaker commands a nuclear submarine.
    3. Despite the warm weather, the plant has not produced buds.
    4. The mixture is cooling on the back porch.
    5. Do the department stores close early tonight?
    6. We heard the sirens through the open window.
    7. Mr. Swenson has been churning the butter.
    8. That story was not amusing.

- **Identifying Indirect Objects** Copy each indirect object. If a sentence has no indirect object, write *none*.

    9. My father has lent me his down jacket for the trip.
    10. I cannot play that difficult new piece for you yet.
    11. Have you given your parents their anniversary gift?
    12. I will give it to them tonight.
    13. Please sing a Portuguese song for my sister and me.
    14. Benjamin owes me fifty cents.
    15. Elizabeth bought herself a new blazer.
    16. She tells the children fascinating, original stories.

- **Identifying Predicate Nouns and Adjectives** Copy each predicate noun or predicate adjective. Label it *PN* or *PA*.

    17. The director is the person responsible for almost everything in the movie.
    18. The caterpillar is becoming a moth inside the cocoon.
    19. Does Bettina appear ill to you?
    20. She has been looking pale and tired lately.
    21. Will Christopher remain a friend forever?
    22. He certainly seems intelligent and charming.
    23. Please don't be stubborn about this situation.
    24. Our fine secretarial staff is the support system of the company.
    25. Is that dog a setter or a terrier?

- **Direct Object or Predicate Noun?** Write the complete verb in each sentence, and decide whether it is an action verb or a linking verb. Then copy the direct object or the predicate noun. Label the object *DO* and the noun *PN*.

26. Do you have a new outfit for graduation?
27. I have mailed the guest list to Ivan.
28. He is preparing formal invitations for all the guests.
29. My aunt is a landscape gardener.
30. She actually designs gardens for people.
31. Lawns and backyards become beautiful settings with her designs.
32. Different kinds of trees grow different kinds of leaves.
33. My aunt can identify trees by their leaves.
34. Leaves have a particular form, design, and color.
35. I have memorized some of these characteristics.
36. Southeast Asia is the original home of the lemon tree.
37. The librarian is ordering some books for our history project.
38. The brothers Grimm collected German folk tales.
39. The painting portrays a busy street scene.
40. That man in the red T-shirt is an old friend of my family's.
41. My dog became a mother this week.
42. Now we have four new golden retriever puppies.

Enrichment

Several lists of words are given below—subjects, linking verbs, action verbs, nouns or pronouns, and adjectives. Combine words from different lists to form different sentences. For example, you might choose the subject *The cat* and the verb *spotted*. Since *spotted* is a transitive verb, you must then choose an appropriate noun or pronoun. You might select *us*. Then your sentence would be *The cat spotted us*. See how many sentences you can make that make sense.

Subjects	Linking Verbs	Action Verbs	Nouns or Pronouns	Adjectives
The cat	appeared	expected	us	restless
My friend	was	cheered	nothing	quiet
The class	became	spotted	a package	comfortable
The crowd	remained	brought	the plan	noisy
Antoinette	seemed	enjoyed	a change	sleepy
The explorers	felt	found	a good actor	curious

More Practice

- **Writing a Good Beginning**   Choose the three beginnings that are weak and rewrite them so that they would catch a reader's attention. Use two or three sentences.

  1. Do you believe in coincidence?
  2. It was one of those really hot days.
  3. I have a great story to tell you.
  4. I knew something was wrong the minute I opened the door.
  5. My cousin told me something disturbing had happened that was bothering her.

- **Writing a Good Ending**   Choose the three endings that are weak, and rewrite them so that they show, rather than tell, what happened. Use two or three sentences.

  1. That was the end of our adventure.
  2. What do you say when a dream comes true?
  3. I was laughing as I walked through that door for the last time.
  4. It turned out in the end that the party was for me after all.
  5. That's all I remember about my first attempt to teach my brother a lesson.

- **Writing Dialogue**   Develop dialogue for one of the following situations. Use at least six sentences.

  1. A conversation between two friends about their plans for the weekend.
  2. A conversation among several students about something that occurred on the play field of the school grounds.

Continue the dialogue begun between the characters in the following paragraphs. Make up at least three direct quotations.

> The sign above the door read, "If you can't rent it from me, I'll buy you a new one." Inside the dusty barn, I asked the cranky owner, "Does your sign really mean what it says?" He sized me up.
> "It does," he said cautiously, "but it isn't that simple. There are some rules you have to follow."

- **Improving Your Sentences** Rewrite the paragraph below, varying the length of the sentences.

Molly felt so alone at camp after her Mom and Dad drove away that she thought she would cry, but she didn't. Soon another girl came over to where she was standing, and she introduced herself and then asked Molly to be her tent mate, so she said "Yes." Suddenly, Molly felt a lot better and decided maybe camp would be fun.

- **Proofreading** Read the following story carefully, looking for errors in spelling, punctuation, and capitalization. If a sentence is punctuated incorrectly, write it correctly. If a word is written incorrectly, write it correctly. You should write two sentences and fourteen words.

I loved the first grade. You could read all the time. I had been trying to do it at home. I drove my mother and sisters crazy by asking them evry singel word in a first-grade book somebody had given me. I must have known thirty words by the time school started.

Mrs. Carper would write *L O O K* on the board. "Who knows what this word is, she would ask. I would wave my hand madly around. "All right, Katy Sue," she would finlly say.

I loved it all. I loved recess. I loved my books. I loved the speshial way mrs. Carper talked to the first-graders.

There was one thing wrong. We had to move to a new school that was being built across the road. I didnt want to go. I wanted everything to stay just the way it was forever.

Then something much worse hapened. Mrs. Carper asked me to stay for a minite at the beginning of reccess.

"Katy Sue, she said, "How would you like to be in the second grade?"

It was unimaginible! The second-graders even went out of our room twice a week to some kind of class. That was another world.

I rushed home to confide my bad experiense to my mother. It seemed that Mrs. Carper had beat me too it. Well, that was good. Now Mama could explain to Mrs. Carper how I felt. I went to bed feeling safe in the first grade.

I had a lot to learn! On the first day in the new school, there I was on the wrong side of the room with the second-graders. There wasn't a thing I could do about it. Mrs. Carper gave me a new orange math book and showed me what page to turn to. Seven puppys were playing around a doghouse. Three of them went inside. How many were left? I had absolutely no idea. Things have never been the same since.

More Practice

- **Personal Pronouns and Their Antecedents**   Write the antecedent of each underlined pronoun. Then write the person (*1, 2, 3*) and number (*singular, plural*) of the pronoun. If it is a third person singular pronoun, also write its gender (*feminine, masculine, neuter*).

  1. Shall we see what is happening in <u>our</u> town this week?
  2. The Bridge School is holding an auction to raise money for <u>its</u> annual sixth-grade trip.
  3. Willie Scott will be doing <u>his</u> magic tricks at the museum.
  4. Many local artisans will be displaying <u>their</u> work at the arts fair.
  5. Mrs. Burke will be exhibiting her handmade stuffed toys to help raise money for <u>her</u> favorite charity.
  6. Do you know Mr. Burke? He does beautiful needlework, and <u>his</u> products will also be for sale.
  7. The members of the recreation department will hold <u>their</u> weekly meeting on Tuesday night.
  8. The high school career center will be opening <u>its</u> doors at last.
  9. Before <u>they</u> can use the service, students must qualify.
  10. Although <u>it</u> is still new, the hospital volunteer service works well.
  11. The Historical Society and the Conservation Commission will be holding <u>their</u> meetings in Ripley Hall.
  12. Since my time is limited, <u>I</u> will attend only one of the meetings.
  13. Have you made up <u>your</u> mind yet?

- **Subject and Object Pronouns**   Write the correct pronoun. Label it subject or object.

  14. The shoes in the window are (they, them).
  15. Both (she, her) and (I, me) have been admiring those shoes.
  16. My friend and (I, me) go by that store every day.
  17. Finally, she asked (I, me) to go into the store with (she, her).
  18. When a salesperson approached (we, us), (we, us) asked (he, him) about the shoes.
  19. Unfortunately, (they, them) were very expensive, and neither my friend nor (I, me) bought (they, them).
  20. The more disappointed one was (she, her), not (I, me).

- **Pronoun Forms** Write the correct form.

21. When (you're, your) concentrating very hard, the expression on (you're, your) face is unmistakable.
22. The tiniest kitten has a white spot over (it's, its) eye.
23. The tables with the reserved signs are (there's, theirs).
24. (They're, Their) all standing by the window with the lovely view.
25. The explorers started out on (they're, their) dangerous expedition into the jungle.
26. (It's, Its) likely that Roberto will win the bike race.
27. (There's, Theirs) no reason to assume that.
28. (Who's, Whose) the man with the red beard?
29. (Who's, Whose) are those shoes under the table?
30. (Who, Whom) shall we ask about the bus schedule?
31. (Who, Whom) plans to accompany us to the station?

- **Indefinite Pronouns** Write the verb and, if there is one, the pronoun that agree with the indefinite pronoun.

32. Most of the passengers (has, have) fastened (its, her, their) seat belts.
33. Everybody in the aisles (is, are) being directed toward a seat.
34. Several of the passengers (is, are) tucking (her or his, their) hand luggage under (her or his, their) seats.
35. Some of the seats (is, are) still in a reclining position and must be straightened.
36. Most of the work (has, have) now been done.
37. Everything (seems, seem) to be ready for takeoff.
38. All of the people in the plane (is, are) ready for (his or her, their) departure.
39. No one (has, have) forgotten (his or her, their) passport, I hope.

Enrichment

Work in groups of four. On each of eight cards or slips of paper, write *subject pronoun, object pronoun, possessive pronoun, interrogative pronoun, demonstrative pronoun, indefinite pronoun, reflexive pronoun,* and *intensive pronoun.* Place the papers in a container, and take turns choosing one. Create a sentence using a pronoun of the kind named on the paper. Try to think of sentences that will tell a continuous story.

More Practice

- **Interviewing** Pretend that you are going to interview a high school gymnast. Rewrite the following yes/no questions so that they encourage the gymnast to give details and explanations.

1. Can you get hurt doing gymnastics?
2. Are some gymnastic exercises more difficult than others?
3. Were you interested in gymnastics when you were in the eighth grade?
4. Is it worthwhile to train long hours when you're very young?

Imagine that you are going to interview one of the following people. Make up a list of ten questions you would prepare in order to get the most out of the interview.

1. the actor or actress who is playing the lead in a play in your town
2. a relative who is studying to be a veterinarian
3. a person who has built his or her own house
4. a friend who has gone rafting with her or his family on the Colorado River
5. a newspaper reporter about his or her job

As a classmate reads you the following interview, take notes on the answers to the questions. Then read the interview aloud to your classmate while he or she does the same thing. Read slowly, but do not stop after each question.

Q. How did you get started cooking?
A. I guess it happened when I was in Denver. I was working there for a year and rooming with another boy. He didn't like to cook and I hated to do dishes, so we compromised. I cooked and he cleaned up, and that's how I got started.
Q. What is the cooking history of your family?
A. There are excellent cooks on both sides. They were mostly women though. You know about Aunt Elizabeth and Aunt Mary.
Q. Do you think you inherited a natural touch for it?
A. I don't know about that. I think the secret of good cooking is a lot of fresh ingredients. Keep it simple.

Q. Do any of the other men in your family cook? Your brothers?

A. Not to my knowledge.

Q. Your father?

A. Not really, but I can't blame Dad, with Mom there to cook.

Q. Well, how does Marilyn feel about it?

A. Oh, she loves it. Usually on weekends I pretty well do the cooking. In fact, it is a ritual here. I have a recipe for scrambled eggs I made up. I guess it varies a little bit every time.

Q. Did you ever take a course in cooking?

A. No. I've always wanted to. A friend of mine is quite a gourmet cook and I've watched him very closely. I do collect cookbooks, though. I have over a hundred.

Q. Do you follow recipes or do you do a lot of creative cooking?

A. Well, the oyster stew is the culmination of a couple of years of experiments. Marilyn and I started out with one recipe, and then took something from another, and later we found a third and took something out of that.

Q. Have you ever thought of making a collection of your own recipes?

A. Mostly things like the oyster stew. People ask for the recipe so I sat down and made a couple of copies.

Q. Maybe this question shouldn't be asked. But who does the cleaning up?

A. It shouldn't be asked!

- **Forming a Working Outline** Imagine that you have interviewed a grocery store owner. Here are some of your notes. Organize them into three sections and make up a heading for each section.

has run store for 42 years
see all kinds of people
some let bills run up
loves talking to people
thinks he's learned more about
    people than he would have anywhere else
works in store alone
has watched kids grow up
used to ask for little boxes of raisins
now buy groceries for families
hard to keep prices down
likes having what his customers want
has 8 grandchildren

More Practice

UNIT II

• **Using the Dictionary**   Use the dictionary entry below to answer the questions that follow it.

> **sat·is·fy** (săt′ĭs-fī′) *v.* **-fied, -fy·ing.** —*tr.v.* **1. a.** To gratify the wish or expectation of; make content. **b.** To supply fully the demands of: *satisfy his appetite.* **2. a.** To free from doubt. **b.** To put an end to; dispel. **3.** To pay off. **4.** To meet or conform to the conditions of. **5.** To make reparation for; redress (a wrong). —*intr.v.* To give satisfaction. —See Syns at **please.** [Middle English *satisfien,* from Old French *satisfier,* from Latin *satisfacere* : *satis,* enough + *facere,* to make.] —**sat′is·fi′er** *n.* —**sat′is·fy′ing·ly** *adv.*

1. From what language did the word *satisfy* originally come?
2. What part of speech is *satisfy*?
3. Does the first syllable of *satisfy* rhyme with *fat* or with *fate*?
4. How many syllables are there in *satisfy*?
5. How many definitions of *satisfy* are there?

• **Using the Library**   Use the card catalog below to answer the questions that follow it.

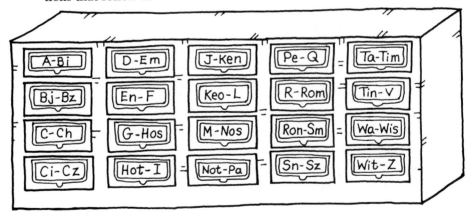

6. In which drawer would you look for information on kangaroos?
7. Which drawer would have an author card for J. R. R. Tolkien?
8. Which drawer would have a title card for *Sounder*?
9. In which drawer would you look for an author card for Laurence Yep?
10. Which drawer would have a subject card for anthropology?

488   **More Practice**

- **Using Reference Aids**   For each question, tell whether you would find the answer in an encyclopedia, an atlas, an almanac, or the *Readers' Guide to Periodical Literature*.

    11. What are the most common kinds of butterflies?
    12. Where can I find an article on home automobile repairs?
    13. How many miles is it from New York City to Montreal.
    14. What is the world's tallest building?

- **The Parts of a Book**   Use this part of a table of contents and index to answer the questions that follow.

    15. What part of the book would refer you to other books and articles on the same subject?
    16. What are the subtopics of Chapter 3?
    17. What does Appendix A contain?
    18. In what chapter are clay tablets discussed?
    19. On what pages is there information on Mayan heiroglyphs?

- **The Parts of a Newspaper**   Study the sample newspaper index below. Write the correct letters and page numbers for the sections or features to which you would turn to answer the questions that follow it.

Arts and Films D36–40	Comics C16	Living B1–8
Business A1–6	Crossword C16	Sports A20–25
Classified C1–15	Editorials A8–10	TV/Radio D41–42

    20. Does the art museum have an exhibit of Picasso's paintings?
    21. Is there a program of country music on the radio tonight?
    22. Are any yard sales being held in my neighborhood?

More Practice

● **Taking Notes** Read the following paragraphs about prehistoric cave paintings. Take notes to answer the question *What can we learn from prehistoric cave paintings?*

The earliest evidence we have of the human ability to create artistic beauty is found in the pictures painted on the walls of the Altamira Caves in Spain. These paintings were made by people who lived more than 20,000 years ago. The paintings show scenes of men hunting wild bulls. The scenes are painted in vivid colors.

Other prehistoric paintings have been found in caves in France and southern Italy. Like the Altamira paintings, they show us that the artists used minerals such as iron oxides to produce colors. They used burnt bones for the black base of their paintings.

No one can know for sure why these beautiful pictures were painted deep inside the dark caves. Like all human beings, the cave-dwellers must have delighted in recreating and celebrating their experiences through art. In addition, these prehistoric people may have believed that their paintings would bring them supernatural assistance in hunting.

● **Making an Outline** The outline that follows is incomplete. Decide where each item in the list below it belongs. Omit any item that does not belong in the outline. Then write the remaining items on your paper with a label to show where they belong, such as I. A. 2. for the item that should go in the first blank.

Basic Steps in Making a Film
  I. The preparation
    A. Script
      1. Choosing the subject
      2.
      3.
    B. Equipment and personnel
      1.
      2. Choosing the crew
      3.

II. The actual filming
  A. Setting the stage for filming
    1. Obtaining permission to film
    2. Getting to the location
    3. Positioning the cameras
  B. Rolling the cameras
    1. Checking the lighting
    2. Exposing the film
    3.
III. The finished film
  A. Putting the film together
    1. Selecting the best shots for editing
    2.
    3. Adding titles and credits
  B. Showing the completed film
    1. Distributing film to theaters
    2. Advertising
    3.

Editing according
  to the script
Destroying old film
Obtaining the equipment
Developing the film

Choosing the actors
Researching the subject
Projecting the film
  onto the screen
Writing the script

Fill in each space in the paragraphs below with an appropriate transition word or phrase. Use the list on page 262 to help you. Do not use any word or phrase more than once.

Many ideas are not well accepted when they first appear. _____ fifteenth-century people laughed at Columbus for saying that the world was round. _____, people of the nineteenth and early twentieth centuries ridiculed scientists who talked about "continental drift." _____ others had done three centuries earlier, these scientists had noticed that the east and west coasts of the Atlantic Ocean fit together like a puzzle. Alfred Wegener, in 1912, suggested other evidence for the drift theory.

Wegener's theory was well argued; _____, it was hotly debated. _____, in the 1950's and early 1960's, two developments added weight to his arguments. Major discoveries about paleomagnetism—the magnetism of ancient rocks—and the structure of the ocean floors occurred. Today we talk casually about ocean ridges and trenches, and continental drift.

More Practice

• **Identifying Adjectives**   List each adjective and the noun or pronoun it modifies. Underline the adjective suffix if there is one. Do not list the articles *a, an, the.*

1. In prehistoric and ancient times, most people thought of lightning as a great natural mystery.
2. To the Romans, it seemed a powerful and deadly weapon of threatening or angry Roman gods.
3. A lightning flash is actually caused by an electrical current.
4. This current can flow in one cloud, between different clouds, or between some clouds and the earth below.
5. A lightning flash is really a huge spark.
6. That spark is similar to the spark in an automobile sparkplug.
7. Lightning seems to have several different forms, but these differences depend on the observation point, not on the lightning itself.
8. Chain lightning looks like brilliant, zigzagging light.
9. Sheet lightning has no special form but is just a bright flash.
10. The famous kite experiment by Benjamin Franklin was an effective but dangerous demonstration of the relationship between electricity and lightning.
11. Franklin, curious and ingenious, constructed a silk kite with a piece of wire near the top.
12. A long string was attached to the kite, with an iron key tied to it.
13. On a dark night, in a heavy thunderstorm, Franklin flew his unique kite and received a brief shock from the metal key.
14. That same year, this inventive man built the first lightning rod.

• **Identifying Adverbs**   List each adverb and the word or words it modifies. Underline each intensifier.

15. Lightning rods conduct lightning charges safely into the ground.
16. Think very clearly when you are caught in a thunderstorm.
17. Always avoid shelter under a tree, and lie down if possible.
18. Indoors, carefully avoid plumbing fixtures and electric appliances.
19. Yesterday, a thunderstorm approached rather suddenly.

20. We were quite surprised, since the sky had been completely clear.
21. Fortunately, our car was nearby.
22. We hastily ran to it and sat safely inside.
23. Luckily, a closed car provides extremely good protection.
24. The storm soon ended, and we happily resumed our walk outdoors.

● **Comparing with Adjectives and Adverbs** Write the correct comparative or superlative form of the modifier in parentheses.

25. That must be the (bad) program in the history of television.
26. Which one of the five begonia plants looks (healthy)?
27. I simply cannot throw the javelin (far) than that.
28. Who of all the players is the (little) likely to fumble?
29. The blue suit seems to be of a (fine) fabric than the gray one.
30. Of all my pets, Fluffy is the (affectionate).
31. The velvet dress is (pretty), but the linen one is (unusual).
32. Who is the (graceful) of the dancers chosen for the show?
33. Nathaniel is a good friend, but he is not my (good) friend.

● **Avoiding Double Negatives** Rewrite each sentence correctly.

34. Please don't interrupt me no more.
35. Hasn't nobody seen my left shoe?
36. I can't hardly feel any heat from that radiator.
37. Haven't you never seen a real cow?
38. Ms. Lincoln can't find her green pen nowhere.
39. We don't expect to sell no more tickets.

Enrichment

The word-search puzzle has eight adjectives and eight adverbs. Can you find all of them? List words usually used as adjectives in one column, and words usually used as adverbs in another.

```
N S O O N E R L I
  I N F A R A B A D
  C U L U E R O S Y
  E G Y P A L A T E
  R E A L L Y O U T
```

More Practice

- **Plot**   Go back and read Bryan's story about Rabbit on pages 316–317, 319, and 320–322. Decide what the basic conflict or problem is, what the climax of the story is, and what the resolution is.

  1. Write two sentences describing the basic problem or conflict.
  2. Write a sentence describing the climax.
  3. Write a sentence describing the resolution.

- **Setting**   Write three sentences describing the setting for the beginning of Bryan's story (see page 319). Use exact words and specific details.

  Choose a setting that you are familiar with, such as your school building, a room in your house, or the street you live on. Then using the same setting, write two descriptions that create sharply different moods. To create these moods, you might want to describe a place when it is night and when it is day, or when it is warm and when it is cold.

- **Character**   Imagine two members of the same family coming to breakfast. Make a list of details for each person. Tell how they look (tired, cheerful, etc.), how they are dressed, what they say, what they eat, and give other details that help set their personalities apart.

  Pick two of the following characters and write five details about each. Choose details that show something about the character of the person as well as trying to give an exact picture of how the person looks.

  1. the captain of a spaceship
  2. a girl who is kidnapped and escapes
  3. a construction worker who finds a treasure hidden in a foundation he or she is digging
  4. a grandmother who does excellent detective work as her secret job
  5. a man who lives alone in a cabin in the woods
  6. a young violinist performing before a large audience
  7. a woman playing in a championship tennis match

- **Point of View**   Think of an adventure that involves two people.

  1. Write four or five sentences about some part of the adventure from the point of view of an all-knowing narrator. Tell something about both of the characters.
  2. Write four or five sentences about the same part of the adventure from the point of view of *one* of the characters. Show that character's own individual point of view. How does the character feel physically? What is the character's mood?

- **Dialogue and Monologue**   Write a brief monologue about the following situation: a six-year-old boy at a circus is about to meet the elephant trainer. In the monologue, try to convey the boy's excitement.

  Write a dialogue based on one of the following situations. Use the dialogue to show what is happening and, if you can, to also show something about characters who are speaking.

  1. Two explorers talk about a mysterious object in the distance.
  2. Two people who have not spoken to each other for a long time discover that their problem was due to a misunderstanding.
  3. Two people are watching something happening on the street in front of them and discussing it.
  4. A mysterious telegram has been received and two people are wondering what it could mean and who could have sent it.

- **Beginnings and Endings**   Use the following instructions to write short beginnings and endings. Your beginnings and endings should be two to four sentences long.

  1. Write two possible beginnings for a story about a girl who survives an apartment building fire. In one, start near the end of the action— when the girl is about to be saved.
  2. Write a story beginning that describes a setting in a way that gets the reader's attention and makes him or her interested or curious.
  3. Write a story beginning that describes a character in a way that will get a reader's attention.
  4. Write a story beginning using dialogue in such a way as to get a reader's attention.
  5. Write a different ending for the story about Rabbit (see page 322). Make sure that your ending shows rather than tells what happens.

More Practice

- **Prepositional Phrases** Copy each prepositional phrase. Underline prepositions once and objects twice.

    1. The establishment of libraries has meant a great deal to the development of humankind.
    2. Libraries rank among the most important service institutions used by people.
    3. Through books and other media, information of all kinds is made available to people in every walk of life.
    4. Because of new developments and changing needs, libraries of today are very different from libraries of the past in their contents, services, and physical setup.

- **Verbals** Divide your paper into three columns, labeled *participle*, *gerund*, and *infinitive*. Find each verbal in the sentences below and list it in the appropriate column.

    5. To learn to read is vital today.
    6. Reading and writing were far less common in other times.
    7. The library has a rotating collection of new books.
    8. What are you interested in reading today?
    9. I am looking for the collected works of George Eliot.
    10. I am going to the library to study.
    11. Irma is attending library school and will soon become a trained librarian.

- **Participial Phrases** Copy each participial phrase. Write the word it modifies.

    12. Designed to meet their patrons' needs, libraries differ drastically in size and services.
    13. Childrens' sections outfitted with low shelves and seats are quite common.
    14. A child wanting a particular book can usually reach it.
    15. Music libraries, equipped with record and tape equipment, are making all types of music available to people.
    16. Following the score closely, Karen listened to a symphony.

- **Gerund Phrases**   Copy each gerund phrase, underlining the gerund. If the sentence does not have a gerund phrase, write *none*.

17. Going to the library today will be especially interesting.
18. One of the librarians is giving a lecture on the filing system.
19. The method of cataloguing books and other materials can vary somewhat in different libraries.
20. Knowing how to use the reference material is important.
21. The hardest part of a report can be finding a certain fact.
22. You can be looking in one place, while the information is actually located in another.
23. I love searching for a piece of information.
24. It is exciting to find it at last.
25. Waiting for the talk to begin, I started looking through a magazine on the training of librarians.

- **Infinitive Phrases**   Copy each infinitive phrase.

26. Larissa plans to finish her report today.
27. To write about the history of libraries was a good idea.
28. She went to the library almost every day to do her research.
29. Because she found the subject interesting to work on, she expects the report to be particularly good.
30. Her objective was to trace the development of public libraries from their beginnings.
31. To her surprise, the desire to establish public libraries goes back to ancient times.

Enrichment

Work with a partner. Make up a sentence using a verbal given below. Then your partner will make up a sentence using the same verbal. Be sure the words are used as verbals, not as verbs.

1. to become
2. whistling
3. known
4. to be
5. shivering
6. insulating
7. sealed
8. bent
9. interested
10. to perform
11. to live
12. writing
13. pointed
14. boiling

More Practice

- **Facts and Opinions**   Identify each of the following as a fact or an opinion. Write *F* for *fact* and *O* for *opinion*.

  1. Retired people need relief from the high cost of living.
  2. The price of swordfish rose 13 percent last year.
  3. France and the United States both have claims in Antarctica.
  4. Natural gas is a better home-heating fuel than oil.
  5. The town should restore the old town hall.

  Below is a list of statements about the shoebill. Under *F* on your paper, write the number of all the statements that are facts. Under *O*, write the number of all the statements that are opinions.

  1. The shoebill is a large bird that is related to the stork.
  2. The shoebill is strange-looking.
  3. It is sometimes called the whale-headed stork.
  4. The bird grows to be about four feet tall.
  5. The bird gets its name from its enormous bill.
  6. When something bothers the shoebill, it snaps its bill open and shut quickly.
  7. The bird's bill makes a rattling sound.
  8. The shoebill stands in water on its long legs and eats fish.
  9. Live fish taste awful.
  10. Shoebills live in pairs.
  11. Shoebills sometimes eat small animals.
  12. Small animals are a nice change from eating fish.
  13. Shoebills build nests on the ground, not in trees.
  14. Shoebills probably don't like to sleep off the ground.
  15. They look funny when they fly.
  16. Shoebills fly with their necks in the shape of an S.

- **Supporting Details and Topic Sentences**   Pick two of the following general topics. List five to ten supporting details for each. Then write a good topic sentence for each.

  1. Write about a product or invention that you wish didn't exist. Write why you wish it didn't exist.

2. Write about a sports contest you have seen. Give your opinion on why the winner played the better game.

3. Write about a place that you think is a good vacation spot.

- **Using Connotations**   Read each sentence below and then write the correct word on your paper.

  1. If you wanted to persuade someone to gain weight, which word would you use to describe that person's thinness?

     skinny   slim   slender   slight

  2. If you wanted someone to choose a more expensive car, which word would you use to describe the less expensive one?

     economical   thrifty   cheap   budget

  3. If you wanted to describe a recent speech of a candidate you support, which of the following words would you *not* use?

     stimulating   exciting   rousing   provoking

  4. Someone has made a rapid decision and you think the decision was wrong. Which of these words would you use to describe it?

     quick   hasty   swift   timely

  5. The mayor is holding a ceremony to celebrate the opening of a new hotel. You think the hotel should not have been built. Which word would you use to describe the ceremony?

     imposing   showy   impressive   moving

- **Openings and Closings**   The sentences below belong to a persuasive paragraph aimed at convincing people to pass laws to protect kangaroos. Write the number of the sentence that you think would make the best opening. Then write the number of the sentence that you think would make the best closing.

  1. Small species of kangaroos which once wandered over a third of Australia are now rare or extinct. The boodie is one such species.
  2. Since kangaroos destroy crops, many farmers feel that they are fair game.
  3. We need strong laws to protect the kangaroo from extinction.
  4. A balance must be found between human and animal rights.
  5. A system that permits controlled hunting of kangaroos is the only possible compromise.

More Practice

- **Subordinate and Independent Clauses** If the group of words is a phrase, write *phrase*. If it is a clause, write *subordinate* or *independent*.

  1. when will the performance end
  2. when the curtain falls
  3. because the dancers' costumes are electric pink
  4. singing is Bernardo's special talent
  5. before this evening is over
  6. before the last skit
  7. before long, Bernardo will sing his show-stopping number
  8. although he has written original lyrics for the song
  9. since many friends and relatives are in the audience
  10. since last week, they have been wondering about the song.
  11. since the day before yesterday
  12. because of all the rehearsals

- **Adjective Clauses** Copy the adjective clause or clauses in each sentence, underlining the relative pronoun. Then label the clause *restrictive* or *nonrestrictive*.

  13. The storm, which was located several hundred miles east of Virginia, was headed toward the Northeast.
  14. People who track weather conditions are called *meteorologists*.
  15. Meteorologists whom you see on television are not the only ones who make predictions about the weather.
  16. Many people of whom you may not be aware also study the weather.
  17. The National Weather Service, which has more than fifty regional offices, employs many such experts.
  18. The task that they have is challenging and important.
  19. People whose job it is to determine things like travel schedules and road-cleaning plans depend on the skill of meteorologists.
  20. There are those whose lives may depend on accurate forecasting—sailors, flyers, people in flood regions and on mountainsides.
  21. Even a mild thunderstorm, which can come up very suddenly, can be dangerous in a place where people are standing outdoors.

- **Adverb Clauses**   Copy each adverb clause, adding a comma where needed. Underline the subordinating conjunction.

22. Weather seems unpredictable because we have not yet learned enough about the forces affecting it.
23. Meteorologists today make use of complex, sensitive new equipment so that they can make accurate observations of the weather.
24. Although they are often correct in their predictions sometimes the weather surprises them.
25. Even though a storm center remains at sea its force and effect can extend hundreds of miles in every direction.
26. Strong winds aloft can take control of a storm unnoticed while other conditions are being carefully measured.

- **Noun Clauses**   Copy each noun clause.

27. Tell whoever is interested to visit the National Meteorological Center.
28. They will learn that there is a continuous flow of weather information in and out of the computers there.
29. Temperature, pressure, humidity, wind, and precipitation information from hundreds of weather stations, as well as satellite images of cloud cover, show that weather factors change constantly.
30. That the computer results must still be interpreted by a human being is what makes weather forecasting really interesting.

- ***Who* and *Whom* in Clauses**   Write *who, whom, whoever,* or *whomever* to complete each sentence correctly.

31. _____ I saw yesterday must remain a secret.
32. Claire will sing for _____ wants to listen.
33. Someone _____ you know well will be surprising us today.
34. I finally met the person _____ will be running for treasurer.

Enrichment

Work in groups of five or six. Take turns thinking of two short, re-lated sentences. Then see who can be first to think of a way to combine the sentences by turning one of them into a subordinate clause. One person should act as secretary and list all the combining words as they are used. See how many different combining words you can make use of in the sentences you create.

INDEX

Numbers in **bold type** indicate pages where item is introduced.
Numbers in *italic* indicate further practice.

Acknowledgments *(continued from page 2)*

"Raymond's Run" (excerpt), from *Tales and Stories for Black Folks,* by Toni Cade Bambara. Copyright © 1971 by Doubleday & Co., Inc. Reprinted by permission of Joan Daves.

"Simile: Willow and Grinkgo," from *It Doesn't Always Have to Rhyme,* by Eve Merriam. Copyright © 1964 by Eve Merriam. Reprinted by permission of the author.

Tell Me How Long the Train's Been Gone (excerpt), by James Baldwin. Copyright © 1968 by James Baldwin. Reprinted by permission of The Dial Press, and Edward J. Acton Inc.

"Thanksgiving Hunter" (excerpt), from *Save Every Lamb* by Jesse Stuart. Copyright © 1964 by Jesse Stuart.

"The Flute," adapted from "Me, Age 11. Mr. Flute—Be All Right" in *Sister,* by Eloise Greenfield. Copyright © 1974 by Eloise Greenfield. Reprinted by permission of Thomas Y. Crowell Company, and Curtis Brown, Ltd.

"The Gulls of Smuttynose Island" (excerpt), from *The Gulls of Smuttynose Island* by Jack Denton Scott. Text copyright © 1977 by Jack Denton Scott. Used by permission of G. P. Putnam's Sons, and Raines & Raines.

"The Medicine Bag" (excerpt), by Virginia Driving Hawk Sneve. Reprinted from *Boys' Life,* published by the Boy Scouts of America. Reprinted by permission of the author.

"The Rolling Scones" (excerpt), by Jane Williams Dugel. Reprinted from *'Teen* magazine.

"The Trophy," from *Year of the Cafeteria* (excerpt), by Mary Alexander Walker. Copyright © 1971 by Mary Alexander Walker. Reprinted by permission of the publisher, The Bobbs-Merrill Company, Inc.

"Song of Greatness," from *Children Sing in the Far West,* by Mary Austin. Copyright 1928 by Mary Austin, © renewed 1956 by Kenneth M. Chapman and Mary C. Wheelwright. Reprinted by permission of Houghton Mifflin Company.

"What Happened to Charles," from *Further Fables for Our Time,* by James Thurber. Copyright © 1956 by James Thurber. Published by Simon & Schuster. Reprinted by permission of Mrs. James Thurber. Reprinted from *Vintage Thurber* by James Thurber, by permission of Hamish Hamilton, Ltd., London, publishers.

Credits

Cover and Title Page Photography by Olmsted Studio

Illustration

Carol Bjork: p. 195.

Pamela Carroll: pp. 374, 387.

Helen CoganCherry: pp. 306, 309, 312, 316, 318, 322, 323.

Laura Cornell: pp. 412–413.

Jon Goodell: pp. 164, 169, 172, 177, 181.

Thomas A. Philbrook: pp. 406, 407.

Blanche L. Sims: pp. 10, 14, 15, 18, 21, 22, 24, 31, 32, 40, 41, 46–47, 51, 52, 53, 57, 62, 67, 69, 70, 73, 75, 100, 104, 106, 111, 112, 113, 117, 120, 122–123, 126, 128, 150, 152, 153, 156, 185, 186, 190, 191, 194, 198, 206, 236, 238, 242, 247, 250, 251, 255, 285, 286, 290, 293, 296, 297, 328, 331, 333, 335, 336, 340, 344, 345, 348, 382, 390, 391, 395, 410, 411, 418, 422.

Robert Gantt Steele: pp. 212, 215, 219, 223, 227, 229, 261, 264, 269, 271, 276, 279.

George Ulrich: pp. 138, 143, 146, 147, 357, 360, 361, 365, 368, 371.

Antowine Warrior: pp. 408–409.

Lane Yerkes: pp. 85, 86, 91, 94, 97.

Handwriting by Cynthia Maciel.

Photography

Rick Friedman/Picture Cube: p. 8; Yoram Lehmann/Peter Arnold: p. 36; Georges Seurat's "Sunday Afternoon on the Island of La Grand Jatte," courtesy of The Art Institute of Chicago, Helen Birch Bartlett Memorial Collection: p. 43; Peter Southwick/Stock, Boston: p. 60; Owen Franken/Stock, Boston: p. 82; Lou Jones: p. 98; Peter Menzel: p. 134; Peter Arnold: p. 136; Craig Aurness/West Light: p. 148; Jonathan Wright/Bruce Coleman: p. 162; Ron and Valorie Taylor/Bruce Coleman: p. 182; Hank Morgan/Rainbow: p. 203; Elizabeth Crews: p. 210; Lou Jawitz/Image Bank: p. 234; Owen Franken/Stock, Boston: p. 256; Stephen Dalton/Animals Animals: p. 258; United Technologies Hamilton Standard: p. 260; Christopher Springmann/Black Star: p. 280; Ed Hof/Picture Cube: p. 304; Rick Friedman/Picture Cube: p. 324; Michal Heron: p. 354; Robert Clark/Photo Researchers: p. 372; Bettmann Archive: p. 378; Brown Brothers: p. 379; Morton Beebe/Image Bank: p. 402; Brian Brake/Photo Researchers: p. 416.